AF134203

THE MESNEVI

BOOK FIRST

JALAL AL-DIN RUMI

Translated by

JAMES W. REDHOUSE

ALICIA EDITIONS

THE MESNEVĪ

(USUALLY KNOWN AS THE MESNEVĪYI SHERĪF, OR HOLY MESNEVĪ) OF MEVLĀNĀ (OUR LORD) JELĀLU-'D-DĪN, MUHAMMED, ER-RŪMĪ.

BOOK THE FIRST.

TOGETHER WITH SOME ACCOUNT OF THE LIFE AND ACTS OF THE AUTHOR, OF HIS ANCESTORS, AND OF HIS DESCENDANTS;

Illustrated by a Selection of Characteristic Anecdotes,

as collected by their historian,

MEVLĀNĀ SHEMSU-'D-DĪN AHMED, EL EFLĀKĪ, EL 'ĀRIFĪ.

translated, and the poetry versified, by

JAMES W. REDHOUSE.

Let the beauty of what you love be what you do.

CONTENTS

THE BOOK OF THE MESNEVĪ

TRANSLATOR'S PREFACE.

The[1] historian El Eflākī was a disciple of Chelebī Emīr 'Ārif, a grandson of the author of the Mesnevī. 'Ārif died in a.d. 1320; but as the dates of 'Ārif's successors are carried down to a.h. 754 (a.d. 1353), when Eflākī's collection of anecdotes was completed, the historian must have outlived this last date. As a disciple of the Emīr 'Ārif, he was a dervish of the order named Mevlevī, as being followers of the rule and practices of Mevlānā Jelālu-'d-Dīn, er-Rūmī, commonly known in English literature as "the dancing dervishes," expressed by Americans: "whirling dervishes." The dervishes of the order do not all dance or "whirl." Some are musicians, and some singers or chanters, who may, however, be occasional dancers also.

Eflākī's work gives a sufficiency of dates to fix the principal events that he commemorates. His dates do not agree exactly with those found in other historians. They are, however, sufficiently near for general purposes not of a chronologically critical nature. They commence with a.h. 605 (a.d. 1208), and thus cover a period of 145 years dated, besides another 30 years of the lifetime of Jelāl's grandfather undated, who was a noble of such high standing and of so great a reputation for learning and sanctity at Balkh, that the king gave him his only daughter in marriage, unsolicited. His mother was also a princess of the same royal house with his wife.

This royal house was the one known in history as that of *Kh'ārezm-shāh* or the Kharezmians. They were overthrown, and Balkh (the ancient Bactra, or Zariaspa), their capital, destroyed, by Jengīz Khān in a.d. 1211. A remnant of their kingdom was continued for twelve years longer by the last of the line, who died, at once a fugitive and an invader, in Azerbāyjān, in a battle fought against the combined forces of Egypt, Syria, and Asia Minor.

Jelāl's family claimed descent from Abū-Bekr, a father-in-law and the first successor of Muhammed, the lawgiver of Islām. One of the descendants of Abū-Bekr was among the conquerors of the ancient Bactria, when it was first brought under Muslim rule, in about a.d. 650, under the Caliph 'Ūthmān; and his children had maintained a prominent position in that country, possessed of great wealth, until the time immediately preceding the irruption of Jengīz.

Jelāl was the youngest of three children, two being sons, born of the princess, his mother, in Balkh. The eldest, a daughter, was already married, and remained behind with her husband, when her father and brothers left their native city some time between a.d. 1208 and 1211, in which latter year they were at Bagdād. There is no further mention of Jelāl's elder brother. Jelāl was five years old when they left Balkh. By way of Bagdād they went to Mekka, thence to Damascus, and next to Erzinjān, in Armenia; thence to Larenda, in Asia Minor. Jelāl's mother was still with the party. He was now eighteen years old; and was married, at Larenda, to a lady named Gevher

(Pearl), daughter of a certain Lala Sherefu-'d-Dīn of Samarqand, in a.d. 1226.[2] She bore him two sons there, 'Alā'u-'d-Dīn (afterwards killed in a tumult at Qonya) and Bahā'u-'d-Dīn Sultān Veled, through whom the succession of the house was continued. She appears to have died rather young; for Jelāl afterwards married another lady of Qonya, who outlived him, and by whom he had two other children, a son and a daughter. (See Anecdotes, Chap, iii., No. 69, for a variant.)

After the birth of Sultān Veled at Larenda, Jelāl's father was invited to Qonya by the Seljūqi king, 'Alā'u-'d-Dīn Kayqubād, where he founded a college, and where he died in a.d. 1231. The king built a marble mausoleum over his grave, with this date inscribed on it. The king himself died, five years later, in a.d. 1236.

At his father's death, Jelāl went to Aleppo and Damascus for several years to study, and then returned to Qonya, where he was appointed professor of four separate colleges. His reputation for learning and sanctity became very great.

But before this journey to Damascus, he appears to have paid a visit to Larenda. For, a former pupil of his father's at Balkh, who had become a great saint and anchoret, came to Qonya to seek Jelāl, and was the cause of his returning from Larenda to the capital.

This was the Sheykh and Seyyid Burhānu-'d-Dīnn, who became Jelāl's spiritual teacher for some time. The dates given do not agree in the various branches of Eflākī's compilation; for he here gives a period of nine years' spiritual study at Qonya under Burhān.

After Burhān's instructions and departure from Qonya to Qaysariyya, where he died, and after Jelāl's studies at Aleppo and Damascus, with his subsequent return to Qonya and appointment to the four colleges, another great saint came to visit Jelāl at this latter city. This was Shemsu-'d-Dīn of Tebrīz, for whom Jelāl conceived a very great friendship. He is mentioned in the Mesnevī several times in very high terms. He appears to have been exceedingly aggressive and domineering in his manner. This roused a fierce animosity against him, which at length broke out in a tumult. Jelāl's eldest son, 'Alā'u-'d-Dīn, was killed or mortally hurt in this disturbance. The local police seized Shemsu-'d-Dīn in consequence, and he was never again seen alive by his friends. Jelāl went himself to Damascus, in hopes that he might have been sent away, or have got away, privately. But the effort was fruitless. Later traditions cause his corpse to have been recovered and buried at Qonya, differing, however, as to the place of interment.

When Jelāl found that he required assistance in conducting all the various duties that fell on him, he selected first for that office his former fellow-student-, Sheykh Salāhu-'d-Dīn Ferīdūn, surnamed Zer-Kūb (the Goldbeater), from his business. He assisted Jelāl for about ten years, and died in a.d. 1258.

Jelāl now took as his assistant his own favourite pupil, Hasan Husāmu-'d-Dīn, surnamed the son of Akhī-Turk, through his being descended from some man of celebrity of the name or designation of Akhī-Turk. There appears to have been a large family of very influential men residing at Qonya and other towns of Asia Minor, all calling themselves Akhī, and distinguished as Akhī Ahmed, Akhī Eshref, &c. The word "Akhī" is Arabic, and signifies "my brother." It may also mean "one related to a brother," as a servant, slave, client, &c., of some prince, &c.; or of some dervish "brother" of some religious order. Indeed, these very numerous individuals named Akhī, may have been each a "brother" of such a fraternity or fraternities, or even of some industrial guild.

Ten years after Husām was taken as his assistant by Jelāl, this latter was called to his rest in December a.d. 1273; and was buried in his father's mausoleum, leaving Husām as his successor. But meanwhile, at Husām's suggestion, and with himself as the first amanuensis thereof, the Mesnevī had been composed, in six volumes, books, or parts, by Jelāl. The second volume was commenced in a.d. 1263. There had been an interval of two years between the completion of the first and this, caused by Husām's grief at the death of his wife. The whole work is stated to contain twenty-six thousand six hundred and sixty couplets. A seventh volume or book has been also attributed to the Mesnevī, to make up the number to that of the "seven planets;" some say it was composed or collected by Sultān Veled. The anecdotes of Eflākī make mention of many hundreds of odes composed also by Jelāl.

He is said to have instituted his peculiar order of dervishes, with their special dress, the Indian garb of mourning, in memory of his murdered friend, Shemsu-'d-Dīn of Tebrīz; and to have adopted the use of instrumental music, the flute, the rebeck, the drum, and the tambourine, with singing or chanting, as an accompaniment to the holy dance, on account of the lethargic nature of the "Romans." As a child is tempted to take a salutary medicine by the exhibition of a little jam or honey, so Jelāl judged that the "Romans" might be tempted to a devotional love for God through the bait of sweet sounds addressed to their outward senses. Dancing or twirling by dervishes was of much older date, as will be recollected in one of the tales of the Arabian Nights.

Husām died in a.d. 1284, just ten years after his teacher Jelāl; whose son, Bahā'u-'d-Dīn, Sultān Veled, succeeded Husām as chief of the order, and died in a.d. 1312. His son, Chelebī Emīr 'Ārif, succeeded him, and passed away in a.d. 1320; two of his half-brothers becoming chiefs of the order after him in succession.

Eflākī informs us that he undertook the compilation of his work at the express desire of his spiritual teacher, Chelebī Emīr 'Ārif. The preface gives the year a.h. 710 (a.d. 1310) as that of its commencement, and the colophon at the end mentions a.h. 754 (a.d. 1353) as the date of its completion. He thus spent forty-three years in his labour of love. The copy used for the present translation was written in a.h. 1027 (a.d. 1617), and belongs to the library of the India Office, being No. 1670. It is a quarto volume of 291 numbered folios of two pages each folio, and twenty-three lines in each page. It is subdivided into a preface, of two folios, and ten chapters of very different lengths, thus:

- 1. Acts of Bahā'u-'d-Dīn Veled, Sultānu-'l-'Ulemā 14 folios.
- 2. Acts of Seyyid Sirr-Dān, Burhānu-'d-Dīn, Termizī 5 "
- 3. Acts of Mevlānā Jelālu-'d-Dīn, Muhammed 155 "
- 4. Acts of Shemsu-'d-Dīn, Tebrīzī 23 "
- 5. Acts of Sheykh Salāhu-'d-Dīn, Zer-Kūb 11 "
- 6. Acts of Husāmu-'d-Dīn, Khalīfa of God 14 "
- 7. Acts of Mevlānā Bahā'u-l'Alcoran-Dīn, Sultān Veled 13 "
- 8. Acts of Chelebī Emīr 'Ārif 45 "
- 9. Acts of Chelebī Emīr 'Ābīd, &c. 6 "
- 10. Genealogical 2 "
- Total 288

The work contains many hundreds of anecdotes, related to Eflākī by trustworthy reporters, whose names are generally given, and a few for which he vouches himself as an eyewitness. Every anecdote is the account of a miracle wrought by the living or the dead; or is the narrative of some strange or striking event. It is, in fact, a species of the Acts of the Apostles of the Mevlevī dervish fathers, and is a rare specimen of what fervid religious enthusiasm can invent or exaggerate, pious credulity can believe, and confiding ignorance accept. In these days of Christian "Spiritualism," let not the reader be overshocked at learning that Muslim "Saints," lovers of their Creator, and beloved by Him in return, hold themselves and are held by their dervish brethren to be the successors and spiritual inheritors of the prophets, from Adam to Muhammed; that, in virtue of this spiritual communion with God, they know all the secrets and mysteries of heaven and earth, and not only suspend or overrule the laws of nature at their will, but also deal out death or disease by their anger, health or prosperity by their blessing; the whole in strict accordance, however, with the eternal will and foreknowledge of Him by whom alone all things are made.

The anecdotes translated are chosen as being characteristic of various points of dervish credence or assertion. Most of them inculcate some moral truth or point of practical wisdom. A few will be found, however, to go far beyond the credible; and one or two, unless totally misunderstood by the translator, are simply and grossly blasphemous. These last are here given as specimens of the exaggerated dervish doctrines which cause the orthodox among the 'Ulemā[3] of Islām to hold all such quasi-religious associations to be more or less heterodox.

The dervishes of Islām appear to be a kind of Gnostics. They style themselves Poor, Impassioned, Adepts, and Perfect. In many respects their doctrines correspond with those of Buddha, Pythagoras, and Plato, making all souls that are destined to salvation to be emanations from the divine Light or Glory of God, in which they will be again congregated; and all those doomed to perdition to have been formed out of the Fire of His wrath, to which also they will eventually be consigned.

It is but too patent to the translator that he is bound to sue for the kind indulgence of a critical public, in offering them the present volume in verse. He has no claim to being a poet himself; and had never practised the art of metrical composition until very lately. Sensible himself to the earnestness of thought and beauty of diction imbedded in the writings of the great poets of Islām, and keenly aware of the condition of dry bones to which literal prose translation almost always reduces a songster's numbers, he has preferred to clothe his author in a presentable garb, though it be but a crumpled wrap, rather than exhibit him to readers of taste as a mangled mass, stripped of all beauty, and in great measure divested even of cognisable form, through the conflict of dictions and diversities of ideas.

He is in the position of the raindrop sung by Sa'dī (see Chap, iii., No. 14, of the Anecdotes), and mentioned of old by Chardin, Addison, and Sir William Jones. May the thoughts in the Mesnevī be the gems that will make his effort acceptable to the British public. At most, he is but the diver who risks extinction in the hope that he may have a chance to offer an acceptable pearl of price to those for whom he has worked:—

"A raindrop, from a cloud distilled,
At sea's expanse with tremor filled,
Mused: 'Where the main rolls, am I aught?
In ocean's presence, sure, I'm naught.'
Itself, thus eyed with scorn profound,
In oyster's bosom nurture found.
Time's wheel wrought changes manifold;
Rich pearl of price the raindrop's told.
Meek modesty its prize received;

By naught's gate ent'ring, worth achieved."

Kilburn Priory, London. 1880.

---

1. For the incidents and dates mentioned in this preface, see the various chapters of the Anecdotes.
2. He must have been born in about a.d. 1204 or 1205, to have been five years old when the family left Balkh. In 1226 he would, therefore, be twenty-one or twenty-two years of age. But see Anecdotes, Chap, i., No. 2, &c.
3. The *"'Ulemā of Islām"* are *the Learned* Doctors of Law and Divinity; their chief is the Lord Chancellor. They are ignorantly spoken of as *"priests"* and *"clergy"* by Europeans. There are no *"priests"* in Islām. The 'Ulemā may be likened to the Jewish Rabbis. They often have followed, and do follow, all kinds of trades.

SELECTED ANECDOTES

FROM THE WORK ENTITLED THE ACTS OF THE ADEPTS (MENĀQIBU 'L 'ĀRIFĪN), BY SHEMSU-'D-DĪN AHMED, EL EFLĀKĪ.

THE ACTS OF THE ADEPTS.[1]

1. There is an allusion in the word 'Arifīn (Adepts) to the name of Eflākī's patron, the Chelebi Emīr 'Arif (well-knowing).

CHAPTER I.

BAHĀ'U-'D-DĪN, VELED, SULTĀNU-'L-'ULEMĀ

(The Beauty of the Religion of Islām, Son, Sultan of the Doctors of the Law).

1.

The king of Khurāsān,[1] 'Alā'u-'d-Dīn Muhammed, Khurrem-Shāh, uncle of Jelālu-'d-Dīn Muhammed Kh'ārezm-Shāh, and the proudest, as he was the most handsome man of his time, gave his daughter, Melika'i-Jihān (Queen of the World), as to the only man worthy of her, to Jelālu-'d-Dīn Huseyn, el Khatībī, of the race of Abū-Bekr.

An ancestor of his was one of the original Muslim conquerors of Khurāsān. He was himself very virtuous and learned, surrounded with numerous disciples. He had not married until then; which gave him many an anxious and self-accusing thought.

He himself, the king, the king's daughter, and the king's Vazīr were all four warned in a dream by the Prince of the Apostles of God (Muhammed) that he should wed the princess; which was done. He was then thirty years old. In due course, nine months afterwards, a son was born to him, and was named Bahā'u-'d-Dīn Muhammed. He is commonly mentioned as Bahā'u-'d-Dīn Veled.

When adolescent, this latter was so extremely learned that the family of his mother wished to raise him to the throne as king; but this he utterly rejected.

By the divine command, as conveyed in the selfsame night, and in an identical dream, to three hundred of the most learned men of the city of Balkh,[2] the capital of the kingdom, where he dwelt, those sage doctors unanimously conferred upon him the honorific title of Sultānu-'l-'Ulemā, and they all became his disciples.

Such are the names and titles by which he is more commonly mentioned; but he is also styled Mevlānāyi Buzurg (the Greater or Elder Master). Many miracles and prodigies were attributed to him; and some men were found who conceived a jealousy at his growing reputation and influence.

2.

In a.h. 605 (a.d. 1208) he, Bahā'u-'d-Dīn Veled, began to preach against the innovations of the king and sundry of his courtiers, declaiming against the philosophers and rationalists, while he pressed all his hearers to study and practise the precepts of Islām. Those courtiers maligned him with the king, calling him an intriguer who had designs on the throne. The king sent and made him an offer of the sovereignty, promising to retire elsewhere himself. Bahā answered that he had no concern with earthly greatness, being a poor recluse; and that he would willingly leave the country, so as to remove from the king's mind all misgivings on his score.

He accordingly quitted Balkh, with a suite of about forty souls, after delivering a public address in the great mosque before the king and people. In this address he foretold the advent of the Moguls to overturn the kingdom, possess the country, destroy Balkh, and drive out the king, who would then flee to the Roman land, and there at length be killed.

So he left Balkh, as the prophet (Muhammed) had fled from Mekka to Medīna. His son Jelālu-'d-Dīn was then five, and the elder brother, 'Alā'u-'d-Dīn, seven years old.

The people everywhere on his road, hearing of his approach or forewarned in dreams of his coming, flocked to meet him and do him honour. Thus he drew near to Bagdād. Here he was met by the great Sheykh Shahābu-'d-Dīn, 'Umer, Suherverdī, the most eminent man of the place, deputed by the Caliph Musta'zim to do him honour. He became the guest of the Sheykh.

The Caliph sent him a present of three thousand sequins, but he declined the gift as being money unlawfully acquired. He also refused to visit the Caliph; but consented to preach in the great mosque after the noon service of worship on the following Friday, the Caliph being present. In his discourse he reproached the Caliph to his face with his evil course of life, and warned him of his approaching slaughter by the Moguls with great cruelty and ignominy. The Caliph again sent him rich presents in money, horses, and valuables, but he refused to accept them.

Before Bahā'u-'d-Dīn quitted Bagdād, intelligence was received there of the siege of Balkh, of its capture, and of its entire destruction, with its twelve thousand mosques, by the Mogul army of five hundred thousand men commanded by Jengīz in person (in a.h. 608, a.d. 1211). Fourteen thousand copies of the Qur'ān were destroyed, fifteen thousand students and professors of the law were slain, and two hundred thousand adult male inhabitants led out and shot to death with arrows.

Bahā'u-'d-Dīn went from Bagdād to Mekka,[3] performed the greater pilgrimage there, proceeding thence to Damascus, and next to Malatia (Melitene, on the Upper Euphrates), where, in a.h. 614 (a.d. 1217), he heard of the death of Jengīz. The Seljūqī Sultan, 'Alā'u-'d-Dīn Keyqubād, was then sovereign of the land of Rome (Rūm, *i.e.*, Asia Minor), and was residing at Sīwās (Sebaste). In a.h. 620 (a.d. 1223) Sultan Jelālu-'d-Dīn, the dispossessed monarch of Kh'ārezm (Chorasmia) was killed in a battle fought by him in Azerbāyjān (Atropatene) against the Sultans of Rome, Syria, and Egypt, when his forces were totally defeated. And thus ended that great dynasty, after ruling about a hundred and forty years.

Bahā'u-'d-Dīn went from Malatia and remained four years near Erzinjān (the ancient Aziris, on the Western Euphrates), in Armenia, at a college built for him by a saintly lady, 'Ismet Khātūn. She was the wife of the local sovereign, Melik Fakhru-'d-Dīn. She and her husband both died, and then Bahā'u-'d-Dīn passed on to Larenda (in Cataonia), in Asia Minor, and remained there about seven years at the head of a college, the princess Melika'i-Jihān, his mother, being still with him.

Here it was that his younger son, Jelālu-'d-Dīn Muhammed, the future author of the Mesnevī, attained to man's estate, being then eighteen years old; when, in a.h. 623 (a.d. 1226), he married a young lady named Gevher Khātūn, daughter of the Lala Sherefu-'d-Dīn, of Samarqand. She gave birth in due course to Jelāl's eldest son, 'Alā'u-'d-Dīn.

The king had now returned to his capital, Qonya (the ancient Iconium). Hearing of Bahā'u-'d-Dīn's great learning and sanctity, the king sent and invited him to the capital, where he installed him in a college, and soon professed himself a disciple. Many miracles are related as having been worked at Qonya by Bahā'u-'d-Dīn, who at length died there on Friday, the 18th of Rebī'u-'l-ākhir, a.h. 628 (February a.d. 1231). The Sultan erected a marble mausoleum over his tomb, on which this date is recorded. Many miracles continued to occur at this sanctuary. The Sultan died also a few years later, in a.h. 634 (a.d. 1236).

(After the death of Bahā'u-'d-Dīn Veled, and the acquisition of still greater fame by his son Jelālu-'d-Dīn, who received the honorific title of Khudāvendgār—*Lord*—the father was distinguished from the son, among the disciples, by the customary title of Mevlānā Buzurg—*the Greater or Elder Master*. The traditions collected by Eflākī, relating to this period, vary considerably from one another on minor points of date and order of succession, though the main facts come out sufficiently clear.)

3.

Jelāl's son, Sultān Veled, related to Eflākī that his father Jelāl used frequently to say, "I and all my disciples will be under the protection of the *Great Master*, my father, on the day of resurrection; and under His guidance we shall enter the divine presence; God will pardon all of us for His sake."

4.

It is related that when the *Great Master* departed this life, his son, Jelālu-'d-Dīn, was fourteen years old. (This is apparently a copyist's error for "twenty-four." Jalāl is said to have been born in a.h. 604—a.d. 1207.) He married when seventeen (or eighteen); and often did he say in the presence of the congregation of his friends, "The *Great Master* will remain with me a few years. I shall be in need of Shemsu-'d-Dīn of Tebrīz (the capital of Azerbāyjān); for every prophet has had an Abū-Bekr, as Jesus had His apostles."

5.

Shortly after the death of the Great Master Bahā'u-'d-Dīn Veled, news was received by the Sultan 'Alā'u-'d-Dīn of Qonya of the arrival of Sultan Jelālu-'d-Dīn Kh'ārezm-Shāh on the borders of Asia Minor. The Sultan went and prayed at the tomb of the deceased saint, and then prepared to meet the Kh'ārezmians, who were in the neighbourhood of Erzenu-'r-Rūm (Erzen of the Romans, the ancient Arzes, now Erzerum). Scouts brought in the intelligence that the Kh'ārezmians were very numerous; and great anxiety prevailed among the Sultan's troops. He resolved to see for himself.

He put on a disguise and set out with a few followers, on fleet horses, for the Kh'ārezmian camp. They gave out that they were nomad Turks of the neighbourhood, their ancestors having come from the Oxus; that latterly the Sultan had withdrawn his favour from them; and that, in consequence, they had for some time past been looking for the Kh'ārezmian advent. This was reported to the king, Jelālu-'d-Dīn, who sent for them and received them kindly, giving them tents and assigning them rations.

During the night King Jelālu-'d-Dīn began to reflect that every one had hitherto spoken well of Sultan 'Alā'u-'d-Dīn, and a doubt arose in his mind in consequence respecting the story of these newcomers, especially as he learned that the Sultan was on his march to meet him.

Consulting with the Prince of Erzenu-'r-Rūm, further perquisition was postponed until the morrow.

But at midnight the deceased saint of Qonya, Bahā-Veled, appeared in a dream to Sultan 'Alā'u-'d-Dīn, and warned him to fly at once. The Sultan awoke, found it was a dream, and went to sleep again. The saint now appeared a second time. The Sultan saw himself seated on his throne, and the saint coming to him, smiting him on the breast with his staff, and angrily saying, "Why sleepest thou? Arise!"

Now the Sultan did arise, quietly called his people, saddled horses, and stole away out of the camp. Towards morning King Jelāl caused guards to be placed round the tents of the strangers to watch them. But afterwards, when orders were given to bring them to the king's presence to be questioned, their tents were found to be empty. Pursuit was attempted, but in vain.

After an interval the two armies came into collision. The Sultan of Qonya was victorious. From that time forward, whenever difficulties threatened, he always betook himself to the shrine of the saint, Bahā Veled, who always answered his prayers.

(As Sultan Jelālu-'d-Dīn Kh'ārezm-Shāh has already been stated to have died in battle in Azerbāyjān in a.d. 1223, whereas the saint of Qonya did not die until a.d. 1231 eight years afterwards, the discrepancy of that date with the present anecdote is irreconcilable.)

6.

The Great Master, Bahā Veled, used to say that while he himself lived no other teacher would be his equal, but that when his son, Jelālu-'d-Dīn, should succeed him at his death, that son of his would equal and even surpass him.

7.

Seyyid Burhānu-'d-Dīn Termīzī[4] is related to have said that one night the door of the mausoleum of Bahā Veled opened of itself, and that a great glory shone forth from it, which gradually filled his house, so that no shadow fell from anything. The glory then gradually filled the city in like manner, spreading thence over the whole face of nature. On beholding this prodigy the Seyyid swooned away.

This vision is a sure indication that the whole human race will one day own themselves the disciples of the descendants of the great saint.

8.

Before he quitted Balkh, Bahā Veled one day saw a man performing his devotions in the great mosque in his shirt sleeves, with his coat upon his back. Bahā reproved him, telling him to put on his coat properly and decently, then to continue his devotions. "And what if I will not?" asked the man in a disdainful tone. "Thy dead-like soul will obey my command, quit thy body, and thou wilt die!" answered Bahā. Instantly the man fell dead; and crowds flocked to become disciples to the saint who spoke with such power and authority.

9.

When Sultan 'Alā'u-'d-Dīn had fortified Qonya, he invited Bahā Veled to mount to the terraced roof of the palace, thence to survey the walls and towers. After his inspection, Bahā remarked to the Sultan, "Against torrents, and against the horsemen of the enemy, thou hast raised a goodly defence. But what protection hast thou built against those unseen arrows, the sighs and moans of the oppressed, which overleap a thousand walls and sweep whole worlds to destruction? Go to, now! strive to acquire the blessings of thy subjects. These are a stronghold, compared to which the walls and turrets of the strongest castles are as nothing."

10.

On one occasion Sultan 'Alā'u-'d-Dīn paid a visit to Bahā Veled. In lieu of his hand the latter offered the tip of his staff to be kissed by the Sultan, who thought within himself: "The proud scholar!" Bahā read the Sultan's thoughts as a seer, and remarked in reply thereto: "Mendicant students are bound to be humble and lowly. Not so a Sultan of the Faith who has attained to the utmost circumference of the orbit thereof, and revolves therein."

11.

A certain Sheykh Hajjāj, a disciple of Bahā Veled and one of God's elect not known to the herd of mankind, quitted the college after the decease of his teacher, and betook himself to his former trade of a weaver, therewith to gain an honest livelihood. He used to buy the coarsest brown bread of unsifted flour, mash this up with water, and break his fast with this sop alone. All the rest of his earnings he saved up until they would reach to two or three hundred piastres. This sum he would then carry to the college, and place it in the shoes of his teacher's son,

Jelālu-'d-Dīn, the new rector. This practice he continued so long as he lived.

At his death a professional washer was appointed to perform the last ablution for Sheykh Hajjāj. In the execution of his office the washer was about to touch the privities of the deceased, when the defunct seized his hand with so strong a grip as to make him scream with pain and fright. The friends came to rescue him, but they were unable to release the imprisoned hand. They therefore sent word to Jelālu-'d-Dīn of what had occurred. He came and saw, knew the reason, and whispered into the ear of the deceased man: "The poor simpleton has been unaware of the high station of thy sanctity. Pardon his unintentional transgression for my sake." Immediately the poor washer's hand was released; but three days afterwards he was himself washed and borne lifeless to his grave.

12.

The Sultan had a governor of his childhood still living, the Emīr Bedru-'d-Dīn Guhertāsh, commonly known as the Dizdār (Castellan), whom he held in great esteem. One day, as Bahā Veled was lecturing in the mosque, in presence of the Sultan and his court, he suddenly called upon the Dizdār to recite any ten verses of the Qur'ān, saying he would then expound them to the congregation. The Dizdār had been admiring the eloquence of the preacher's expositions. Upon this sudden call, without the slightest hesitation and without ever having committed them to memory, he recited the first ten verses of chapter xxiii., "The believers have attained to prosperity," &c., which Bahā forthwith explained in such a manner as to draw down the plaudits of the assembly. The Dizdār, with the Sultan's permission, went to the foot of the pulpit and declared himself a disciple to Bahā. "Then," said the preacher, "as a thank-offering for this happy event, do thou build and endow a college where my descendants shall teach their disciples after me." The Dizdār did so, and richly endowed it. This is the college where Jelālu-'d-Dīn afterwards lived. When the Dizdār died he left all his possessions to enrich the foundation. (See chap. iii. No. 69.)

13.

The Sultan had a dream (something like one of Nebuchadnezzar's). He saw himself with a head of gold, a breast of silver, a belly of brass, thighs of lead, and shanks of tin. Bahā Veled explained the dream as follows:—"All will go well in the kingdom during thy lifetime. It will be as silver in the days of thy son; as brass in the next generation, when the rabble will get the upper hand. Troubles will thicken during the next reign; and after that the kingdom of Rome will go to ruin, the house of Seljūq will come to an end, and unknown upstarts will seize the reins of government."

---

1. Eastern Persia.
2. The ancient *Bactra*, sometimes called *Zariaspa*, the capital of Bactria.
3. Incorrectly written Mecca by Europeans.
4. Of Termīz (Tirmez), on the north bank of the Oxus, near to Balkh.

CHAPTER II.

SEYYID BURHĀNU-'D-DĪN, SIRR-DĀN, EL MUHAQQIQ, EL HUSEYNĪ, OF THE POSTERITY OF YĀ-SĪN (MUHAMMED).

(He[1] is called Seyyid, the "Syud" of our East India authorities, for the reason that he was a descendant of the prophet, of whom Yā-Sīn is one of the titles, as it is also the name of the thirty-sixth chapter of the Qur'ān, at the head of which the two letters stand which form the name. Burhānu-'d-Dīn means The Proof of the Religion; Sirr-Dān signifies The Confidant, one who possesses a knowledge of a secret or secrets, a mystery or mysteries. Muhaqqiq is one who verifies, who probes the truth; and Huseynī indicates that the Seyyid was of the branch of Huseyn, the younger of the two sons of Fātima, Muhammed's only child that left posterity.)

1.

Seyyid Burhānu-'d-Dīn was popularly known by the name of Sirr-Dān at Balkh, Bukhārā (Alexandria Oxiana?), and Termīz. His discourse was continually running upon the subjects of spiritual and mental phenomena, of the mysteries of earth and of heaven.

When Bahā Veled quitted Balkh, the Seyyid went to Termīz, and there secluded himself as a hermit. After a while again he began to lecture in public on the significations of knowledge. Suddenly, one morning, that of Friday the 18th of Rebī'u-'l-ākhir, a.h. 628 (February, 1231 a.d.), he cried out most bitterly, in a flood of tears, "Alas! my master has passed away from this tabernacle of dust to the abode of sincerity!" His words and the date were noted down, and, on inquiry, after his arrival in Qonya, were found to correspond exactly with the moment of Bahā Veled's decease.

2.

For forty days the disciples at Termīz mourned for the death of the great teacher. At the end of that period the Seyyid said: "The son of my master, his successor, Jelālu-'d-Dīn Muhammed, is left alone and is wishing to see me. I must go to the land of Rome and place myself at his service, delivering over to him the trust which my teacher confided to my safe-keeping."

3.

When the Seyyid reached Qonya, Bahā Veled had been dead about a year, and Jelāl had gone to Larenda. The Seyyid applied himself for several months to devotional seclusion in one of the mosques of Qonya; after which he sent off a letter to Jelāl by the hands of two mendicants, saying: "Come and meet this stranger to thee at the resting-place of thy father, for Larenda is not a place of permanency for thee. From that hill (on which Bahā's mausoleum was built) a fire will shower down on the city of Qonya."

After reading this epistle Jelāl returned to Qonya with all possible despatch. There he went at once to visit the Seyyid, who came forth from the mosque to receive him. They embraced. They now entered into conversation on various subjects. So delighted was the Seyyid with the expositions set forth by Jelāl that he kissed the soles of his feet, and exclaimed:

"A hundredfold hast thou surpassed thy father in all knowledge of the humanities; but thy father was versed also in the mysteries of mute reality and ecstasy. From this day forward my desire is that thou shouldest also acquire that knowledge,—the knowledge possessed by the prophets and the saints, which is entitled *The Science of Divine Intuition*—the science spoken of by God (in Qur'ān xviii. 64): 'We have taught him a science from within us.' This knowledge did I acquire from my teacher; do thou receive it from me, so that thou mayest be the heir to thy father in spiritual matters as well as in things temporal. Thou wilt then be his second self."

Jelāl complied with all the Seyyid pressed upon him. He took the Seyyid to his college, and for nine years received instruction from him. Some accounts make it appear that Jelāl first became the Seyyid's disciple at this time; but others go to show that Bahā Veled gave Jelāl as a pupil to the Seyyid at Balkh, and that the Seyyid used now and then to carry Jelāl about on his shoulders, like as is practised by the nursing-tutors—*lala*—of children. (Compare chap. iii., Nos. 6 and 8.)

4.

Husāmu-'d-Dīn told us that Jelāl had informed him of the following occurrence:—

The Seyyid once arrived at a certain city in Khurāsān named Sāmānek. The chief people went forth to meet him and show him honour, all excepting the Sheykhu-'l-Islām of the place (the local vice-chancellor). Nevertheless the Seyyid went to pay his respects to the legal functionary. The latter went barefoot to the door of the house to meet the Seyyid, whose hand he kissed, and to whom he offered excuses for his seeming lack of courtesy.

In reply, the Seyyid said to him:

"I am come to inform you that, on the 10th day of next month, Ramazān, you will have occasion to go forth to a hot-bath. On your way thither you will be assassinated by the emissaries of the *Old Man of the Mountain*. This I communicate to thee, that thou mayest set thy affairs in order, and repent thee of thy sins."

The Sheykhu-'l-Islām fell at the Seyyid's feet, wailing; but the latter remarked: "This is of no avail. Events are in God's hands, and He has so ordered it. Still, as thou showest so much contrition, I may add, for thy consolation, that thou wilt die in the faith, and shalt not be cut off from the divine mercy and grace."

And so it happened as thus predicted. The assassins took his life on the very day foretold by the Seyyid.

(The stronghold, Alamūt, of the *Old Man of the Mountain*, was stormed by forces sent against it by Helagū, grandson of Jengīz, in about the year a.h. 654 (a.d. 1256). The last prince of the dynasty was sent to China, and there put to death by the emperor; and thus these detestable scourges of humanity were at length suppressed.)

5.

After a certain time the Seyyid asked permission of Jelāl to go for a while to Qaysariyya (Cæsarea), but Jelāl could not spare him. So he remained at Qonya still.

Somewhat later a party of friends took the Seyyid out for a ride among the vineyards. The thought occurred to him that, without saying anything to anybody, he might now easily abscond and get away to Qaysariyya. Scarcely had he conceived this vagabond idea than his beast reared with him, threw him, and broke his leg. His friends raised him, set him again on his horse, and conducted him to a neighbouring country-house to which Jelāl had also come.

On seeing Jelāl the Seyyid exclaimed to him, "Is this the proper way to reward your teacher—to break his leg?" Jelāl at once ordered the Seyyid's boot to be removed, and saw that his foot and toes were crushed. He now passed his hands along the injured limb and blew on it. The limb was at once restored whole. Jelāl now granted permission, and the Seyyid forthwith proceeded to Qaysariyya.

6.

When the time was come that the Seyyid should die, he told his servant to prepare for him an ewer of warm water, and to go. The water was made ready, placed in the Seyyid's room, and the servant went forth. The Seyyid called after him: "Go and proclaim that the stranger Seyyid has departed to the other world." He then bolted the door, that none should enter to him.

The servant, however, had his curiosity excited by those words, and went back to the door, to listen and to see what might happen. Through a chink he saw his master perform an ablution, arrange his dress, lie down on his couch, and cry out: "All ye angels, saints, and heavens, who have at any time intrusted to me a secret, come to me now and receive back your charges. Ye are here all present."

He then recited the following hymn:—

> *"God, my beloved, darling God, adored, to me incline;*
> *My soul receive; intoxicate, release poor me distraught.*
> *In Thee alone my heart finds peace; it fire with love divine;*
> *Take it unto Thyself; to it both worlds are naught."*

These were the Seyyid's last words, ere he yielded up his spirit. The servant carried the news to the Seyyid's friends, who gathered together, carried him forth, and buried him.

A mausoleum was raised over his grave by a rich and powerful disciple. The departed saint would not allow a cupola to stand. Twice the dome was shaken down by earthquakes, and in a dream the Seyyid himself forbade its third edification.

After the usual forty days of mourning, a letter was sent to Jelāl, who at once journeyed from Qonya to Qaysariyya, and prayed at the tomb of his deceased teacher, returning home again afterwards.

---

1. The two letters Yā and Sīn heading the thirty-sixth chapter of the Qur'ān are said to stand for the words, Yā insān, *O man!* as Muhammed is there addressed.

CHAPTER III.

MEVLĀNĀ JELĀLU-'D-DĪN MUHAMMED, THE REVERED MYSTERY OF GOD UPON EARTH.

1.

Jelālu-'d-Dīn[1] is related to have been born at Balkh on the 6th of Rebī'u-'l-evvel, a.h. 604 (29th September 1207).

When five years old, he used at times to become extremely uneasy and restless, so much so that his attendants used to take him into the midst of themselves.

The cause of these perturbations was that spiritual forms and shapes of the absent (invisible world) would arise before his sight, that is, angelic messengers, righteous genii, and saintly men—the concealed ones of the bowers of the True One (spiritual spouses of God), used to appear to him in bodily shape, exactly as the cherubim and seraphim used to show themselves to the holy apostle of God, Muhammed, in the earlier days, before his call to the prophetic office; as Gabriel appeared to Mary, and as the four angels were seen by Abraham and Lot; as well as others to other prophets.

His father, Bahā'u-'d-Dīn Veled, the Sultānu-'l-'Ulemā, used on these occasions to coax and soothe him by saying: "These are the Occult Existences. They come to present themselves before you, to offer unto you gifts and presents from the invisible world."

These ecstasies and transports of his began to be publicly known and talked about; and the affectionately honorific title of Khudāvendgār, by which he is so often mentioned, was conferred upon him at this time by his father, who used to address him and speak of him by this title, as "My Lord."

2.

His son, Sultan Veled, related that there was a paper in the handwriting of his father, Bahā Veled, which set forth that at Balkh, when Jelāl was six years old, he was taking the air one Friday, on the terraced roof of the house, and reciting the Qur'ān, when some other children of good families came in and joined him there.

After a time, one of these children proposed that they should try and jump from thence on to a neighbouring terrace, and should lay wagers on the result.

Jelāl smiled at this childish proposal, and remarked: "My brethren, to jump from terrace to terrace is an act well adapted for cats, dogs, and the like, to perform; but is it not degrading to man, whose station is so superior? Come now, if you feel disposed, let us spring up to the firmament, and visit the regions of God's realm." As he yet spake, he vanished from their sight.

Frightened at Jelāl's sudden disappearance, the other children raised a shout of dismay, that some one should come to their assistance; when lo, in an instant, there he was again in their midst; but with an altered expression of countenance and blanched cheeks. They all uncovered before him, fell to the earth in humility, and all declared themselves his disciples.

He now told them that, as he was yet speaking to them, a company of visible forms, clad in green raiment, had led him away from them, and had conducted him about the various concentric orbs of the spheres, and through the signs of the Zodiac, showing him the wonders of the world of spirits, and bringing him back to them so soon as their cries had reached his ears.

At that age, he was used not to break his fast more often than once in three or four, and sometimes even seven, days.

3.

A different witness, a disciple of Jelāl's father, related that Bahā Veled frequently affirmed publicly that his Lord, Jelāl, was of exalted descent, being of the lineage of a king, and also of an hereditary saint.

His maternal grandmother was a daughter of the great Imām Es-Sarakhsī[2] (died at Damascus a.h. 571, a.d. 1175), who was of the lineage of the Prophet. The mother of Es-Sarakhsī was descended from the Caliph 'Alī; and Jelāl's paternal grandmother was a daughter of the King of Kh'ārezm, who resided at Balkh.

Jelāl's paternal great-great-grandmother, also, the mother of Ahmed, El-Khatībī, grandfather of Jelāl's father, was a daughter of a king of Balkh. These particulars establish that Jelāl was well descended on both sides, in a mundane and in a spiritual sense. The well-known proverb—

"Hereditary disposition ever insinuates itself,"

proved fully true in his most illustrious case.

4.

When Jelāl was seven years old, he used every morning to recite the very short chapter, cviii., of the Qur'ān—

"Verily we have given unto thee the abounding good. Therefore, do thou perform thy devotions unto thy Lord, and slaughter victims. Verily, he who evil entreateth thee is one who shall leave no issue after him."

He used to weep as he recited these inspired words.

Suddenly, God one day vouchsafed to appear to him visibly. On this he fainted away. Regaining consciousness, he heard a voice from heaven, that said—"O Jelālu-'d-Dīn! By the majesty (jelāl) of Our glory, do thou henceforward cease to combat with thyself; for We have exalted thee to the station of ocular vision."

Jelāl vowed, therefore, out of gratitude for this mark of grace, to serve the Lord to the end of his days, to the utmost of his power; in the firm hope that they who followed him would also attain to that high grade of favour and excellence.

5.

Two years after the death of his father, Jelāl went from Qonya to Haleb (Aleppo) to study. (This account is altogether subversive, as to time and date, of that already given in chap. ii. No. 3.)

As he was known to be a son of Bahā'u-'d-Dīn Veled, and was also an apt scholar, his professor showed him every attention.

Others were offended, and evinced their jealousy at the preference thus accorded to him. They complained to the governor of the city that Jelāl was immoral, as he was in the habit, each night, of quitting his cell at midnight for some unknown purpose. The governor resolved to see and judge for himself. He therefore hid himself in the porter's room.

At midnight, Jelāl came forth from his room, and went straight to the locked gate of the college, watched by the governor. The gate flew open; and Jelāl, followed at a distance by the governor, went through the streets to the locked city gate. This, too, opened of itself; and again both passed forth.

They went on and came to the tomb of Abraham (at Hebron, about 350 miles distant), the "Friend of the All-Merciful." There a domed edifice was seen, filled with a large company of forms in green raiment, who came forth to meet Jelāl, and conducted him into the building.

The governor hereupon lost his senses through fright, and did not recover until after the sun had risen.

Now, he could see nothing of a domed edifice, nor one single human being. He wandered about on a trackless plain for three days and three nights, hungry, thirsty, and footsore. At length he sank under his sufferings.

Meanwhile, the porter of the college had given intelligence of the governor's pursuit after Jelāl. When his officers found that he did not return, they sent a numerous party of guards to seek him. These, on the second day, met Jelāl. He told them where they would find their master. The next day, late, they came up with him, found him to be nearly dead, and brought him home.

The governor became a sincere convert, and a disciple to Jelāl for ever after.

(A parallel tale is told of Jelāl's fetching water from the Tigris for his father by night when he was a little child at Bagdad. There, too, all the gates opened to him of themselves.)

6.

It is related that the Seyyid Burhānu-'d-Dīn was often heard to narrate that, when Jelāl was a child, the Seyyid was his governor and tutor. He had often taken Jelāl up on his shoulder, and so carried him to the empyrean. "But now," he would add, "Jelāl has attained to such eminence of station that he carries me up." These sayings of the Seyyid were repeated to Jelāl, who confirmed them with the remark: "It is quite true; and a hundredfold more also; the services rendered to me by that man are infinite."

7.

When Jelāl went to Damascus to study, he passed by Sīs in Upper Cilicia. There, in a cave, dwelt forty Christian monks, who had a great reputation for sanctity, but in reality were mere jugglers.

On the approach of Jelāl's caravan to the cave, the monks caused a little boy to ascend into the air, and there remain standing between heaven and earth.

Jelāl noticed this exhibition, and fell into a reverie. Hereupon, the child began to weep and wail, saying that the man in the reverie was frightening him. The monks told him not to be afraid, but to come down. "Oh!" cried the child, "I am as though nailed here, unable to move hand or foot."

The monks became alarmed. They flocked around Jelāl, and begged him to release the child. After a time, he seemed to hear and understand them. His answer was: "Only through the acceptance of Islām by yourselves, all of you, as well as by the child, can he be saved."

In the end they all embraced Islām, and wished to follow Jelāl as his disciples. He recommended them, however, to remain in their cave, as before, to cease from practising jugglery, and to serve God in the spirit and in truth. So he proceeded on his journey.

8.

Jelāl remained seven years, or four years, at Damascus; and there he first saw his great friend Shemsu-'d-Dīn of Tebrīz, clothed in his noted black felt and peculiar cap. Shems addressed him; but he turned away, and mixed in the crowd. Soon afterwards, he returned to Qonya by way of Qaysariyya. At this latter place, under the guiding supervision of his spiritual teacher, the Seyyid Burhānu-'d-Dīn, Jelāl fasted three consecutive periods of forty days each,[3] with only a pot of water and two or three loaves of barley bread. He showed no signs of suffering. Burhān now pronounced him perfect in all science, patent and occult, human and spiritual. (Compare chap. ii. No. 3.)

9.

In the year a.h. 642 (a.d. 1244), Shemsu-'d-Dīn of Tebrīz came to Qonya.

This great man, after acquiring a reputation of superior sanctity at Tebrīz, as the disciple of a certain holy man, a basket-maker by trade, had travelled about much in various lands, in search of the best spiritual teachers, thus gaining the nickname of Perenda (the *Flier*, *Bird*, &c.).

He prayed to God that it might be revealed to him who was the most occult of the favourites of the divine will, so that he might go to him and learn still more of the mysteries of divine love.

The son of Bahā'u-'d-Dīn Veled, of Balkh, was designated to him as the man most in favour with God. Shems went, accordingly, to Qonya; arriving there on Saturday, the 26th of Jemādà-'l-ākhir, a.h. 642 (December a.d. 1244). He engaged a lodging at an inn, and pretended to be a great merchant. In his room, however, there was nothing but a broken water-pot, an old mat, and a bolster of unbaked clay. He broke his fast once in every ten or twelve days, with a damper soaked in broth of sheep's trotters.

One day, as he was seated at the gate of the inn, Jelāl came by, riding on a mule, in the midst of a crowd of students and disciples on foot.

Shemsu-'d-Dīn arose, advanced, and took hold of the mule's bridle, addressing Jelāl in these words: "Exchanger of the current coins of recondite significations, who knowest the names of the Lord! Tell me: Was Muhammed the greater servant of God, or Bāyezīd of Bestām?"

Jelāl answered him: "Muhammed was incomparably the greater—the greatest of all prophets and all saints."

"Then," rejoined Shemsu-'d-Dīn, "how is it that Muhammed said: 'We have not known Thee, O God, as Thou rightly shouldest be known,' whereas Bāyezīd said: 'Glory unto me! How very great is my glory'?"

On hearing this question, Jelāl fainted away. On recovering his consciousness, he took his new acquaintance home with him. They were closeted together for weeks or months in holy communications.

Jelāl's disciples at length became impatient, raising a fearful and threatening tumult; so that, on Thursday, the 21st of Shewwāl, a.h. 643 (March a.d. 1246), Shemsu-'d-Dīn mysteriously disappeared; and Jelāl adopted, as a sign of mourning for his loss, the drab hat and wide cloak since worn by the dervishes of his order.

It was about this time, also, that he first instituted the musical services observed by that order, as they perform their peculiar waltzing. All men took to music and dancing in consequence. Fanatics objected, out of envy. They said Jelāl was gone mad, even as the chiefs of Mekka had said of old of the Prophet. His supposed malady was attributed to the malefic influence of Shemsu-'d-Dīn of Tebrīz.

10.

The widow of Jelāl, Kirā (*or* Girā) Khātūn, a model of virtue, the Mary of her age, is related to have seen, through a chink in the door of the room where he and Shems were closeted in spiritual communion, that the wall suddenly opened, and six men of majestic mien entered by the cleft.

These strangers, who were of the occult saints, saluted, bowed, and laid a nosegay at the feet of Jelāl, although it was then in the depth of the midwinter season. They remained until near the hour of dawn worship, when they motioned to Shemsu-'d-Dīn to act as leader on the occasion of the service. He excused himself, and Jelāl performed the office. The service of worship over, the six strangers took leave, and passed out by the same cleft in the wall.

Jelāl now came forth from the chamber, bringing the nosegay in his hand. Seeing his wife in the passage, he gave her the nosegay, saying that the strangers had brought it as an offering to her.

The next day, she sent her servant, with a few leaves from her nosegay, to the perfumers' mart of the city, to inquire what might be the flowers composing it, as she had never seen their like before. The merchants were all equally astonished; no one had ever seen such leaves.

At length, however, a spice merchant from India, who was then sojourning in Qonya, saw those leaves, and knew them to be the petals of a flower that grows in the south of India, in the neighbourhood of Ceylon.

The wonder now was: How did these Indian flowers get to Qonya; and in the depth of winter, too?

The servant carried the leaves back, and reported to his lady what he had learnt. This increased her astonishment a hundredfold. Just then Jelāl made his appearance, and enjoined on her to take the greatest care of the nosegay, as it had been sent to her by the florists of the lost earthly paradise, through those Indian saints, as a special offering.

It is related that she preserved them as long as she lived, merely giving a few leaves, with Jelāl's express permission, to the Georgian wife of the king. If any one suffered with any disease of the eyes, one leaf from that nosegay, applied to the ailing part, was an instant cure. The flowers never lost their fragrance or freshness. What is musk compared with such?

11.

To prove that man lives through God's will alone, and not by blood, Jelāl one day, in the presence of a crowd of physicians and philosophers, had the veins of both his arms opened, and allowed them to bleed until they ceased to flow. He then ordered incisions to be made in various parts of his body; but not one drop of moisture was anywhere obtainable. He now went to a hot bath, washed, performed an ablution, and then commenced the exercise of the sacred dance.

12.

One of Jelāl's disciples died, and there was a consultation among his friends as to whether he should be buried in a coffin or without one.

Another disciple, after Jelāl had been consulted, and had told them to do as they pleased, made the observation that it would be better to bury their relative without a coffin. On being asked why, he answered: "A mother can better nurse her child, than can her child's brother. The earth is the mother of the human race, and the wood of a coffin is also the earth's child; therefore, the coffin is the man's brother. Man's corpse should be committed, then, not to a coffin, but to mother earth, his loving, affectionate parent."

Jelāl expressed his admiration for this apposite and sublime doctrine, which, he said, was not to be found written in any then extant book.

The name of the disciple who made this beautiful remark was Kerīmu-'d-Dīn, son of Begh-Tīmūr.

13.

Many of the chief disciples of Jelāl have related that he himself explained to them, as his reasons for instituting the musical service of his order, with their dancing, the following reflections:—

"God has a great regard for the Roman people. In answer to a prayer of the first Caliph, Abū-Bekr, God made the Romans a chief receptacle of His mercy; and the land of the Romans (Asia Minor) is the most beautiful on the face of the earth. But the people of the land were utterly void of all idea of the riches of a love towards God, and of the remotest shade of a taste for the delights of the inner, spiritual life. The great Causer of all causes caused a source of affection to arise, and out of the wilderness of causelessness raised a means by which I was attracted away from the land of Khurāsān to the country of the Romans. That country He made a home for my children and posterity, in order that, with the elixir of His grace, the copper of their existences might be transmuted into gold and into philosopher-stone, they themselves being received into the communion of saints. When I perceived that they had no inclination for the practice of religious austerities, and no knowledge of the divine mysteries, I imagined to arrange metrical exhortations and musical services, as being captivating for men's minds, and more especially so for the Romans, who are naturally of a lively disposition, and fond of incisive expositions. Even as a sick child is coaxed into taking a salutary, though nauseous medicine, so, in like manner, were the Romans led by art to acquire a taste for spiritual truth."

14.

As an instance of the great value attached to the poetry of Jelāl, the following anecdote is related:—

Shemsu-'d-Dīn Hindī, (Prince of Shīrāz in the province of Fars, Southern Persia), wrote a flattering letter to the renowned poet, Sheykh Sa'dī, of Shīrāz (who lived a.h. 571-691, a.d. 1175-1291, and was consequently a contemporary of Jelāl's), begging him to select the best ode, with the most sublime thoughts, that he knew of as existing in Persian, and to send it to him, for presentation to the great Khān of the Moguls (who then ruled over nearly all Asia).

It so happened that the ode by Jelāl had just become known at Shīrāz, which commences:—

> *"Divine love's voice each instant left and right is*
> *heard to sound,*
> *We're bound for heaven. To witness our*
> *departure who'll be found?"*

This ode had captivated the minds of all the men of culture in the city; and this ode Sa'dī selected, wrote it out, and sent it to the prince, with the remark: "A monarch, of auspicious advent, has sprung up in the land of Rome, from whose privacy these are some of the breathings. Never have more beautiful words been uttered, and never will be. Would that I could go to Rome, and rub my face in the dust under his feet!"

The prince thanked Sa'dī exceedingly, and sent him valuable presents in return. Eventually, Sa'dī did go to "Rome," arrived in Qonya, and had the gratification to kiss the hand of Jelāl. He was well received in that city by the dervish circle.

The prince was himself a disciple of Sheykh ... 'd-Dīn, of Bakharz (in Khurāsān, about midway between Tūrshīz and Herāt), to whom he sent a copy of the ode, to learn what the Sheykh would think of it. All the learned men of Bakharz assembled round the Sheykh. He read the ode attentively, and then burst out into exclamations of the wildest delight and most fervid admiration, rending his garments, and acting as though mad. At length he calmed down and said: "O wonderful man! O thou champion of the Faith! Thou pole of the heavens and of the earth! Verily, thou art a wonderful Sultan, who hast appeared on earth! In good sooth, all the Sheykhs of bygone ages who were seers, have been frustrated in not having seen this man! They would have supplicated the Lord of Truth to allow them to meet him! But it was not to be; and this mercy will last until the end of time, as has been sung:—

"A fortune, by the men of ancient times in
dreams long sought,
Has been vouchsafed to modern men; without
their efforts caught."

"One ought to put on ironed shoes, and take in hand an ironed staff, to set out at once and visit this great light. I make it a legacy to all my friends to do so without the least delay, if they have the means and the strength, so as to achieve the happiness and secure the honour of making the acquaintance of this prince, so obtaining the grace and favour of hearing him. His father, Bahā Veled, and his ancestors, were great Sheykhs and most illustrious; their great progenitor having been the first Caliph, Abū-Bekr, the glorious Confirmer of the truth spoken by the Apostle of God. I am myself old and infirm, unequal to the fatigues of travel. Otherwise, I would have walked, not on the soles of my feet, but on the tips of my great toes, to visit that eminent man."

The Sheykh's eldest son, Muzahhiru-'d-Dīn, was there present. To him the Sheykh addressed himself, saying: "My son, I do hope that thy eyes will behold this sacred visage; and, if God so will, convey to him my salutation and my respects."

After the death of the old man, his son went to Rome, had the felicity to see Jelāl, and presented his father's message. He returned to Bakharz; but it is said that a son of his lies buried at Qonya.

15.

Kirā Khātūn, the widow of Jelāl, is reported to have related to a friend that there was in their household a candlestick of the height of a man, before which Jelāl used to stand on foot the night through, until daydawn, studying the writings of his father.

One night, a company of the genii, dwellers in the college where Jelāl and his wife lived, appeared to her in a body, to complain of the great inconvenience and suffering to which they were subjected by this practice of Jelāl's, and saying: "We can put up with it no longer. Take care, lest we do a mischief to some one in the college."

The lady reported this complaint of the genii to her husband. He merely smiled, and took no further notice of the matter for several days.

At the end of that time, however, he spoke of it, and told his wife to trouble herself no more about the threat of the genii, as he had converted them all. They had become disciples of his, and would certainly do no harm to any friend or dependent of their teacher.

16.

It was related by one of the chief of Jelāl's disciples, a butcher by trade, a trainer of dogs for the chase, and a purveyor of horses of the best kind, which he used to sell to princes and grandees at high prices, that, at a certain time, Jelāl was much exercised by visions from the spiritual world, so that for forty days he was as though beside himself, passing through the streets with his head bare, and his turban twisted round his neck.

After that, he came suddenly one day, bathed in perspiration, to the butcher, and said he wanted a certain unbroken horse to be saddled for him immediately. The butcher, with the help of three stable-men, managed with the utmost difficulty to saddle the horse and bring him out. Jelāl mounted him without opposition, and set off in a southerly direction. The butcher asked whether he should accompany him, and Jelāl replied: "Give me your prayers and holy good wishes."

In the evening Jelāl returned covered with dust. The poor horse, though of gigantic frame, was reduced to mere skin and bone, being nearly broken-backed with fatigue.

The next day he came again, and asked for another horse, better than the one of yesterday, mounted it, and rode off. He returned at the hour of sunset devotions, and this horse also was reduced to a pitiable condition. The butcher dared not offer a word of remonstrance.

On the third day he came again, mounted a third horse, and returned as before, at sunset. He sat down now in the most composed manner possible, and called out cheerily: "Good news! Glad tidings, O ye of the Faith! That dog of hell has gone back to his pit of fire!"

The butcher was too much astonished at his manner to feel any inclination to inquire what these words might mean; but a certain number of days afterwards, a large caravan came into Qonya from Syria, and brought news that the Mogul army had besieged Damascus, and had reduced it to straits.

Helaw Khan (Holagu, Helagu) had taken Bagdad in a.h. 655 (a.d. 1257-58). Two years later, a.h. 657 (a.d. 1259-60), he advanced against Aleppo and Syria, sending his general, Ketbuga, against Damascus with a numerous army. He laid siege to the city. But the inhabitants witnessed, with their very own eyes, that Jelāl came and joined himself there to the forces of Islām. He inflicted defeat on the Mogul forces, who were compelled to retreat, totally frustrated.

The butcher was overjoyed at this welcome intelligence, and went forthwith to communicate the news to Jelāl. The latter smilingly replied: "Yes, yes! Jelālu-'d-Dīn was the horseman who obtained a victory over the enemy, and showed himself a Sultan in the eyes of the people of Islām." On hearing this, his disciples rent the air with their shouts of joy and triumph, and the townspeople of Qonya decked out and illuminated the city, holding public rejoicings.

This miracle of power became noised abroad, and everywhere Jelāl's friends and adherents were transported with ecstasy at its occurrence.

17.

On one occasion a rich merchant of Tebrīz came to Qonya. He inquired of his agents there who was the most eminent man of learning and piety in the city, as he wished to go and pay his respects to him. He remarked to them: "It is not merely for the sake of making money that I travel about in every country on earth; I desire also to make the acquaintance of every man of eminence I can find in each city."

His correspondents told him that the Sheykhu-'l-Islām of the capital had a great reputation for learning and piety, and that they would be proud to present him to that celebrated luminary. Accordingly, he selected a number of rarities from among his store, to the value of thirty sequins; and the party set out to visit the great lawyer.

The merchant found the dignitary lodged in a great palace, with guards at the gate, crowds of servants and attendants in the courtyard, and eunuchs, pages, grooms, ushers, chamberlains, and the like, in the halls.

Turning to his conductors, he expressed some doubt as to whether they had not, by mistake, brought him to the king's palace. They quieted his fears, and led him into the presence of the great fountain of legal erudition. He felt a very great dislike for all he saw; and he remarked to his friends: "A great lawyer is never anything the worse for possessing a clear conscience. A physician may himself indulge in sweetmeats; but he does not prescribe them to a patient suffering with fever."

He now offered his presents; and then inquired of the great lawyer whether he could solve a doubt under which he was then labouring. This he stated as follows: —"Of late, I have been sustaining a series of losses. Can you indicate a way by which I may escape from that unfortunate position? I give, every year, the fortieth part of my liable possessions to the poor; and I distribute alms besides, to the extent of my power. I cannot conceive, therefore, why I am unfortunate."

Other remarks he made also to the same effect. They appeared to be lost on the great luminary, who affected to be otherwise preoccupied. At length the merchant took leave without obtaining a solution to his difficulty.

The day following he inquired of his friends whether there did not chance to be, in the great city, some poor mendicant of exemplary piety, to whom he might offer his respects, and from whom he might, haply, learn what he longed to know, together with advice that would be of service to him. They answered: "Just such a man as thou describest is our Lord, Jelālu-'d-Dīn. He has forsaken all pleasures, save only his love towards God. Not only has he given up all concern for worldly matters, he has also renounced all care as to a future state. He passes his nights, as well as his days, in the worship of God; and he is a very ocean of knowledge in all temporal and spiritual subjects."

The Tebrīz merchant was enchanted with this information. He begged to see that holy man, the bare mention of whose virtues had filled him with delight. They accordingly conducted him to the college of Jelāl, the merchant having privately furnished himself with a rouleau of fifty sequins in gold as his offering to the saint.

When they reached the college, Jelāl was sitting alone in the lecture-hall, immersed in the study of some books. The party made their obeisances, and the merchant felt himself completely overpowered at the aspect of the venerable teacher; so that he burst into tears, and could not utter a word. Jelāl addressed him, therefore, as follows:—

"The fifty sequins thou hast provided as thy offering are accepted. But better for thee than these are the two hundred sequins thou hast lost. God, whose glory be exalted, had determined to visit thee with a sore judgment and a heavy trial; but, through this thy visit here, He hath pardoned thee, and the trial is averted from thee. Be not dismayed. From this day forth thou shalt not suffer loss; and that which thou hast already suffered shall be made up to thee."

The merchant was equally astonished and delighted at these words; more so, however, when Jelāl proceeded with his discourse: "The cause and reason of thy bygone losses and misfortunes was, that, on a certain day thou wast in the west of Firengistān (Europe), where thou wentest into a certain ward of a certain city, and there sawest a poor Firengī (European) man, one of the greatest of God's cherished saints, who was lying stretched out at the corner of a market-place. As thou didst pass by him, thou spattest on him, evincing aversion from him. His heart was grieved by thy act and demeanour. Hence the visitations that have afflicted thee. Go thou, then, and make thy peace with him, asking his forgiveness, and offering him our salutations."

The merchant was petrified at this announcement. Jelāl then asked him: "Wilt thou that we this instant show him to thee?" So saying, he placed his hand on the wall of the apartment, and told the merchant to behold. Instantly, a doorway opened in the wall, and the merchant thence perceived that man in Firengistān, lying down in a market-place. At this sight he bowed down his head and rent his garments, coming away from the saintly presence in a state of stupor. He remembered all these incidents as facts.

Immediately commencing his preparations, he set out without delay, and reached the city in question. He inquired for the ward he wished to visit, and for the man whom he had offended. Him he discovered lying down, stretched out as Jelāl had shown him. The merchant dismounted from his beast, and made his obeisance to the prostrate Firengī dervish, who at once addressed him thus: "What wilt thou that I do? Our Lord Jelāl suffereth me not; or otherwise, I had a desire to make thee see the power of God, and what I am. But now, draw near."

The Firengī dervish then clasped the merchant to his bosom, kissed him repeatedly on both cheeks, and then added: "Look now, that thou mayest see my Lord and Teacher, my spiritual Master, and that thou mayest witness a marvel." The merchant looked. He saw the Lord Jelāl immersed in a holy dance, chanting this hymn, and entranced with sacred music: —

"His kingdom's vast and pure; each sort its
fitting place finds there;
Cornelian, ruby, clod, or pebble be thou on His
hill.
Believe, He seeks thee; disbelieve, He'll haply
cleanse thee fair;
Be here a faithful Abū-Bekr; Firengī there; at
will."

When the merchant happily reached Qonya on his return, he gave the salutations of the Firengī saint, and his respects, to Jelāl; and distributed much substance among the disciples. He settled at Qonya, and became a member of the fraternity of the Pure Lovers of God.

18.

Jelāl was one day passing by a street, where two men were quarrelling. He stood on one side. One of the men called out to the other: "Say what thou will; thou shalt hear from me a thousandfold for every word thou mayest utter."

Hereupon Jelāl stepped forward and addressed this speaker, saying: "No, no! Whatsoever thou have to say,

say it to me; and for every thousand thou mayest say to me, thou shalt hear from me one word."

On hearing this rebuke, the adversaries were abashed, and made their peace with one another.

19.

One day, a very learned professor brought all his pupils to pay their respects to Jelāl.

On their way to him, the young men agreed together to put some questions to Jelāl on certain points of Arabic grammar, with the design of comparing his knowledge in that science with that of their professor, whom they looked upon as unequalled.

When they were seated, Jelāl addressed them on various fitting subjects for a while, and thereby paved the way for the following anecdote:—

"An ingenuous jurist was once travelling with an Arabic grammarian, and they chanced to come to a ruinous well.

"The jurist hereupon began to recite the text (of Qur'ān xxii. 44): 'And of a ruined well.'

"The Arabic word for 'well' he pronounced 'bīr,' with the vowel long. To this the grammarian instantly objected, telling the jurist to pronounce that word with a short vowel and hiatus—bi'r, so as to be in accord with the requirements of classical purity.

"A dispute now arose between the two on the point. It lasted all the rest of the day, and well on into a pitchy dark night; every author being ransacked by them, page by page, each sustaining his own theory of the word. No conclusion was arrived at, and each disputant remained of his own opinion still.

"It so happened in the dark, that the grammarian slipped into the well, and fell to the bottom. There he set up a wail of entreaty: 'O my most courteous fellow-traveller, lend thy help to extricate me from this most darksome pit.'

"The jurist at once expressed his most pleasurable willingness to lend him that help, with only one trifling condition—that he should confess himself in error, and consent to suppress the hiatus in the word 'bi'r.' The grammarian's answer was 'Never.' So in the well he remained."

"Now," said Jelāl, "to apply this to yourselves. Unless you will consent to cast out from your hearts the '*hiatus*' of indecision and of self-love, you can never hope to escape from the noisome pit of self-worship,—the well of man's nature and of fleshly lusts. The dungeon of 'Joseph's well' in the human breast is this very 'self-worship;' and from it you will not escape, nor will you ever attain to those heavenly regions—'the spacious land of God'" (Qur'ān iv. 99, xxix. 56, xxxix. 13).

On hearing these pregnant words, the whole assembly of undergraduates uncovered their heads, and with fervent zeal professed themselves his spiritual disciples.

20.

There was a great and good governor (apparently) of Qonya, of the name of Mu'īnu-'d-Dīn, whose title was the Perwāna (moth or fly-wheel, viz., of the far-distant Mogul Emperor, resident at the court of the king). He was a great friend to the dervishes, to the learned, and to Jelāl, whose loving disciple he was.

One day, a company of the dervishes and learned men united in extolling the Perwāna to the skies, in Jelāl's presence. He assented to all they advanced in that respect, and added: "The Perwāna merits a hundredfold all your eulogiums. But there is another side to the question, which may be exemplified by the following anecdote:—

"A company of pilgrims were once proceeding towards Mekka, when the camel of one of the party fell down in the desert, totally exhausted. The camel could not be got to rise again. Its load was, therefore, transferred to another beast, the fallen brute was abandoned to its fate, and the caravan resumed its journey.

"Ere long the fallen camel was surrounded by a circle of ravenous wild beasts,—wolves, jackals, &c. But none of these ventured to attack him. The members of the caravan became aware of this singularity, and one of them went back to investigate the matter. He found that an amulet had been left suspended on the animal's neck; and this he removed. When he had retreated to a short distance, the hungry brutes fell upon the poor camel, and soon tore him piecemeal."

"Now," said Jelāl, "this world is in an exactly similar category with that poor camel. The learned of the world are the company of pilgrims, and our (Jelāl's) existence among them is the amulet suspended round the neck of the camel—the world. So long as we remain so suspended, the world will go on, the caravan will proceed. But so soon as the divine mandate shall be spoken: 'O thou submissive spirit, come thou back to thy Lord, content and approved' (Qur'ān lxxxix. 27-8), and we be removed from the neck of the world-camel, people will see how it shall fare with the world,—how its inhabitants shall be driven,—what shall become of its sultans, its doctors, its scribes."

It is said that these words were spoken a short time before Jelāl's death. When he departed this life, not much time elapsed ere the Sultan, with many of his great men of learning and nobles, followed him to the grave, while troubles of all kinds overwhelmed the land for a season, until God again vouchsafed it peace.

21.

During one of his expositions, Jelāl said: "Thou seest naught, save that thou seest God therein."

A dervish came forward and raised the objection that the term "therein" indicated a receptacle, whereas it could not be predicated of God that He is comprehensible by any receptacle, as this would imply a contradiction in terms. Jelāl answered him as follows:—

"Had not that unimpeachable proposition been true, we had not proffered it. There is therein, forsooth, a contradiction in terms; but it is a contradiction in time, so that the receptacle and the recepted may differ,—may be two distinct things; even as the universe of God's qualities is the receptacle of the universe of God's essence. But, these two universes are really one. The first of them is not He; the second of them is not other than He. Those, apparently, two things are in truth one and the same. How, then, is a contradiction in terms implied? God comprises the exterior and the interior. If we cannot say He is the interior, He will not include the interior. But He comprises all, and in Him all things have their being. He is, then, the receptacle also, comprising all existences, as the Qur'ān (xli. 54) says: 'He comprises all things.'"

The dervish was convinced, bowed, and declared himself a disciple.

22.

Jelāl was one day seated in the shop of his great disciple the Goldbeater, Salāhu-'d-Dīn; and was surrounded by a circle of other disciples, listening to his discourse; when an old man came rushing in, beating his breast, and uttering loud lamentations. He entreated Jelāl to help him in his endeavours to recover his little son, a child seven years old, lost for several days past, in spite of every effort made to find him.

Jelāl expressed his disapprobation at the extreme importance the old man appeared to attach to his loss; and said:

"Mankind in general have lost their God. Still, one does not hear that they go about in quest of Him, beating their breasts and making a great noise. What, then, has happened to thee so very particular, that thou makest all this fuss, and degradest thyself, an elder, by these symptoms of grief for the loss of a little child? Why seekest thou not for a time the Lord of the whole world, begging assistance of Him, that peradventure thy lost Joseph may be found, and thou be comforted, as was Jacob on the recovery of his child?"

The old man at once followed Jelāl's advice, and begged forgiveness of God. Just then, news was brought him there that his son had been found. Many who were witnesses of these circumstances became devoted followers of Jelāl.

23.

Jelāl was one day lecturing, when a young man of distinction came in, pushed his way, and took a seat higher up than an old man, one of the audience.

Jelāl at once remarked: "In days of yore it was the command of God, that, if any young man should take precedence of an elder, the earth should at once swallow him up; such being the divine punishment for that offence. Now, however, I see that young men, barely out of leading-strings, show no respect for age, but trample over those in years. They have no dread of the earth's swallowing them up, nor any fear of being transformed into apes.[4] It happened, however, that one morning the Victorious Lion of God, 'Alī, son of Abū-Tālib, was hasting from his house to perform his devotions at dawn in the mosque of the Prophet. On his way, he overtook an old man, a Jew, who was going in the same direction. The future Caliph, out of innate nobility and politeness of nature, had respect for the Jew's age, and would not pass him, though the Jew's pace was slow. When 'Alī reached the mosque, the Prophet was already bowed down in his devotions, and was about to chant the '*Gloria;*' but, by God's command, Gabriel came down, laid his hand on the Prophet's shoulder, and stopped him, lest 'Alī should lose the merit attaching to his being present at the opening of the dawn service; for it is more meritorious to perform that early service once, than to fulfil the devotions of a hundred years at other hours of the day. The Prophet has said: 'The first act of reverence at dawn worship is of more value than the world and all that is therein.'

"When the Apostle of God had concluded his *worship*, offered up his *customary prayers*, and recited his usual *lessons* from the Qur'ān, he turned, and asked of Gabriel the occult cause of his interruption at that time. Gabriel replied that God had not seen fit that 'Alī should be deprived of the merit attaching to the performance of the first portion of the dawn worship, through the respect he had shown to the old Jew he had overtaken, but whom he would not pass.

"Now," remarked Jelāl, "when a saint like 'Alī showed so much respect for a poor old misbelieving Jew, and when God viewed his respectful consideration in so highly favourable a manner, you may all infer how He will view any honour and veneration shown to an elderly saint of approved piety, whose beard has grown grey in the service of God, and whose companions are the elect of their Maker, whose chosen servant he is; and what reward He will mete out in consequence. For, in truth, glory and power belong to God, to the Apostle, and to the believers, as God hath Himself declared (Qur'ān lxiii. 8): 'Unto God belongeth the power, and to the apostle, and to the believers.'

"If then," added he, "ye wish to be prosperous in your affairs, take fast hold on the skirts of your spiritual elders. For, without the blessing of his pious elders, a young man will never live to be old, and will never attain the station of a spiritual elder."

24.

One day Jelāl took as his text the following words (Qur'ān xxxi. 18):—

"Verily, the most discordant of all sounds is the voice of the asses." He then put the question: "Do my friends know what this signifies?"

The congregation all bowed, and entreated him to expound it to them. Jelāl therefore proceeded:—

"All other brutes have a *cry*, a *lesson*, and a *doxology*, with which they commemorate their Maker and Provider. Such are, the *yearning cry* of the camel, the *roar* of the lion, the *bleat* of the gazelle, the *buzz* of the fly, the *hum* of the bee, &c.

"The angels in heaven, and the genii, have their doxologies also, even as man has his doxology—his *Magnificat*, and various forms of worship for his heart (or mind) and for his body.

"The poor ass, however, has nothing but his *bray*. He sounds this bray on two occasions only: when he desires his female, and when he feels hunger. He is the slave of his lust and of his gullet.

"In like manner, if man have not in his heart a doxology for God, a cry, and a love, together with a secret and a care in his mind, he is less than an ass in God's esteem; for He has said (Qur'ān vii. 178): 'They are like the camels; nay, they are yet more erring.'" He then related the following anecdote:—

"In bygone days there was a monarch, who, by way of trial, requested another sovereign to send him three things, the worst of their several kinds that he could procure; namely, the worst article of food, the worst dispositioned thing, and the worst animal.

"The sovereign so applied to sent him some *cheese*, as the worst food; an Armenian slave, as the worst-dispositioned thing; and an ass, as the worst of animals. In the superscription to the epistle sent with these offerings, the sovereign quoted the verse of Scripture pointed out above."

25.

On a certain day, the Lord Jelālu-'d-Dīn went forth to the country residence of the saint Husāmu-'d-Dīn, riding on an ass. He remarked: "This is the saddle-beast of the righteous. Several of the prophets have ridden on asses: as Seth, Ezra, Jesus, and Muhammed."

It so chanced that one of his disciples was also mounted on an ass. The creature suddenly began to bray; and the rider, annoyed at the occurrence, struck the ass on the head several times.

Jelāl remonstrated: "Why strike the poor brute? Strikest thou him because he bears thy burden? Returnest thou not thanks for that thou art the rider, and he the vehicle? Suppose now, which God forbid, that the reverse were the case. What wouldst thou have done? His cry arises from one or the other of two causes, his gullet or his lust. In this respect, he shares the common lot of all creatures. They are all continually thus actuated. All, then, would have to be scolded and beaten over the head."

The disciple was abashed. He dismounted, kissed the hoof of his ass, and caressed him.

26.

On a certain occasion, one of his disciples complained to Jelāl of the scantiness of his means and the extent of his needs. Jelāl answered: "Out upon thee! Get thee gone! Henceforward, count me not a friend of thine; and so, peradventure, wealth may come to thee." He then related the following anecdote:—

"It happened, once, that a certain disciple of the Prophet said to him: 'I love thee!' The Prophet answered: 'Why tarriest thou, then? Haste to put on a breastplate of steel, and set thy face to encounter misfortunes. Prepare thyself, also, to endure straitness, the special gift of the friends and lovers (of God and His Apostle)!'"

Another anecdote, also, he thus narrated:

"A Gnostic adept once asked of a rich man which he loved best, riches or sin. The latter answered that he loved riches best. The other replied: 'Thou sayest not the truth. Thou better lovest sin and calamity. Seest thou not that thou leavest thy riches behind, whilst thou carriest thy sin and thy calamity about with thee, making thyself reprehensible in the sight of God! Be a man! Exert thyself to carry thy riches with thee, and sin not; since thou lovest thy riches. What thou hast to do is this: Send thy riches to God ere thou goest before Him thyself; peradventure, they may work thee some advantage; even as God hath said (Qur'ān lxxiii. 20): 'And that which ye send before, for your souls, of good works, shall ye find with God. He is the best and the greatest in rewarding."

27.

It is related that one day the Perwāna, Mu'īnu-'d-Dīn, held a great assembly in his palace. To this meeting were collected together all the Doctors of the Law, the Sheykhs, the men of piety, the recluses, and the strangers who had congregated from various lands.

The chiefs of the law had taken their places in the highest seats. The Perwāna had had a great desire that Jelāl should honour the assembly with his presence. He had a son-in-law, Mejdu-'d-Dīn, governor to the young princes, the sons of the king. This son-in-law of his was a disciple of Jelāl's, and a man of very eminent qualities, with great faith in his teacher. He offered to go and invite Jelāl to the meeting.

Hereupon, the arch-sower of doubts and animosities in the human breast spread among the chiefs of the law, there present, the suspicion that, if Jelāl should come, the question of precedence would arise: "Where should he be seated?" They all agreed that they were themselves in their proper places, and that Jelāl must find a seat where he could.

Mejdu-'d-Dīn delivered the Perwāna's courteous message to his teacher. Jelāl, inviting Husāmu-'d-Dīn and others of his disciples to accompany him, set out for the Perwāna's palace. The disciples went on a little ahead, and Jelāl brought up the procession.

When Husām entered the apartment of the Perwāna, all present rose to receive him, making room for him in the upper seats. Lastly, Jelāl made his appearance.

The Perwāna and other courtiers crowded forward to receive Jelāl with honour, and kissed His Lordship's blessed hands with reverence, expressing regret that he had been put to inconvenience by his condescension. He returned compliment for compliment, and was shown upstairs.

On reaching the assembly room, he saw that the grandees had occupied the whole of the sofa, from end to end. He saluted them, and prayed for God's grace to be showered upon them; seating himself then in the middle of the floor. Husāmu-'d-Dīn immediately rose from his seat, descended from the sofa, and took a place by the side of Jelāl.

The grandees of the assembly now arose also, excepting those who, in spite and pride, had formed the confederacy mentioned above. These kept their seats. Some of them were of the greatest eminence in learning; and one, especially, was not only very learned, but also eloquent, witty, and bold.

He, seeing what had taken place, and that all the men of rank had quitted the sofa, to seat themselves on the floor, asked in a jocose manner: "Where, according to the rules of the Order, is the chief seat in an assembly?"

Some one answered him: "In an assembly of the learned, the chief seat is in the middle of the sofa, where the professor always sits." Another added: "With recluses, the cell of solitude is the chief seat." A third said: "In the convents of dervish brethren, the chief seat is the lower end of the sofa, where, in reality, people put off their shoes."

After these remarks, some one present, as an experiment, asked Jelāl, saying:

"In your rule and opinion, where is the chief seat?" His answer was: "The chief seat is that where one's beloved is found." The interrogator now asked: "And where is your beloved?" Jelāl replied: "Thou must be blind, not to see."

Jelāl then arose, and began to sing. Many joined; and the singing became so enthusiastic, that the nobles rent their garments.

It so happened that, after Jelāl's death, this interlocutor of his went to Damascus, and there became blind. Friends flocked to visit him, and to condole with him. He wept bitterly, and cried aloud: "Alas, alas! what have I not suffered? That very moment, when Jelāl gave me that fatal answer, a black veil seemed to fall down over my eyes, so that I could not distinguish objects clearly, or their colours. But I have hope and faith in him, that, out of his sublime generosity, he will yet take pity on me, and pardon my presumption. The goodness of the saints is infinite; and Jelāl himself hath said: 'Despair not because of one sin; for the ocean of divine mercy accepteth penitence.'"

The foregoing incident is also related with the following variation:—

Shemsu-'d-Dīn of Tebrīz had just then returned to Qonya, and was among those who accompanied Jelāl to the Perwāna's palace, sitting down near him on the floor. When the question was put: "Where is your beloved?" Jelāl arose, and cast himself on the breast of Shems. That occurrence it was that made Shems, from that time forward, a man of mark in all Qonya.

28.

There was in Qonya a great physician, of eminence and ability, who used occasionally to visit Jelāl.

On one of those days, Jelāl requested him to prepare seventeen purgative draughts by a certain time, propitious for taking medicine, as that number of his friends required them.

When the specified time came, Jelāl went to the physician's house, and received the seventeen draughts. He immediately began, and, in the physician's presence, drank off the whole seventeen in succession, thence returning home.

The physician followed him there, to render the assistance he felt sure would be wanted. He found Jelāl seated as usual, in perfect health, and lecturing to his disciples. On inquiring how he felt, Jelāl answered, in the words so often repeated in the Qur'ān (ii. 23, &c.): "Beneath which rivers flow." The physician recommended Jelāl to abstain from water. Jelāl instantly ordered ice to be brought and broken up small. Of this he swallowed an inordinate quantity, while the physician looked on.

Jelāl then went to a hot-bath. After bathing, he began to sing and dance; continuing in those exercises three whole days and nights, without intermission.

The physician declared this to be the greatest miracle ever wrought by prophet or by saint. With his whole family, and with many of the greatest in the medical profession, he joined himself to the multitude of Jelāl's disciples of the most sincere.

29.

The Perwāna is related to have said publicly, in his own palace, that Jelāl was a matchless monarch, no sovereign having ever appeared in any age like unto him; but that his disciples were a very disreputable set.

These words were reported to them, and the company of disciples were greatly scandalised at the imputation. Jelāl sent a note to the Perwāna, of which the following is the substance:—

"Had my disciples been good men, I had been their disciple. Inasmuch as they were bad, I accepted them as my disciples, that they might reform and become good,—of the company of the righteous. By the soul of my father, they were not accepted as disciples, until God had made Himself responsible that they would attain to mercy and grace, admitted among those accepted of Him. Until that assurance was given, they were not received by me, nor had they any place in the hearts of the servants of God. 'The sons of grace are saved; the children of wrath are sick; for the sake of Thy mercy, we, a people of wrath, have come to Thee.'"

When the Perwāna had read and considered these words, he became still more attached to Jelāl; arose, came to him, asked pardon, and prayed for forgiveness of God, distributing largely of his bounty among the disciples.

30.

Another great and good man once observed: "Jelāl is a great saint and a sovereign; but he must be dragged forth from among his disciples." This was reported to Jelāl, who smiled, and said: "If he can!"

Soon afterwards he added: "Why, then, is it that my followers are looked upon with spite by the men of the world? It is because they are beloved of God, and favourably regarded by Him. I have sifted all mankind; and all have fallen through my sieve, excepting these friends of mine. They have remained. My existence is the life of my friends, and the existence of my friends is the life of the men of the world, whether they know this, or whether they ignore it."

31.

There was a young merchant, whose house was near Jelāl's college, and who had professed himself a sincere and ardent disciple.

He conceived a desire and intention to make a voyage to Egypt; but his friends tried to dissuade him. His intention was reported to Jelāl, who strictly and rigorously prohibited his undertaking the voyage.

The young man could not divest himself of his desire, and had no peace of mind; so one night he clandestinely stole away, and went off to Syria. Arrived at Antioch, he embarked in a ship, and set sail. As God had willed, his ship was taken by Firengī pirates. He was made prisoner, and was confined in a deep dungeon, where he had a daily portion of food doled out to him, barely sufficient to keep his body and soul together.

He was thus kept imprisoned forty days, during which he wept bitterly, and reproached himself for having been disobedient to the injunction of Jelāl; saying: "This is the reward of my crime. I have disobeyed the command of my sovereign, following after my own evil propensity."

Precisely on the night of the fortieth day, he saw Jelāl in a dream, who addressed him, and said: "To-morrow, to whatever questions these misbelievers may ask thee, do thou return the answer: 'I know.' By that means shalt thou be released." He awoke bewildered, returned thanks to Heaven, and sat down in holy meditation, awaiting the solution of the dream.

Shortly, he saw a company of Firengī people come to him, with whom was an interpreter. They asked him: "Knowest thou aught of philosophy, and canst thou practise therapeutics? Our prince is sick." His answer was: "I know."

They immediately took him out of the pit, led him to a bath, and dressed him in a handsome vestment of honour. They then conducted him to the residence of the sick man.

The young merchant, inspired of God, ordered them to bring him seven fruits. These he prepared with a little scammony, and made the whole into a draught, which he administered to the patient.

By the grace of God, and the intercession of the saints, his treatment was crowned with success, after two or three visits. The Firengī prince recovered; and by reason that the favour of Jelāl was upon that young merchant, though he was utterly illiterate, he became a philosopher. Jelāl assisted him.

When the Firengī prince had entirely recovered his health, and had arisen from his sick-bed, he told the young merchant to ask of him whatsoever he might wish. He asked for his freedom, and for leave to return home, that he might rejoin his teacher. He then related all that had befallen him;—his disobedience, his vision, and the assistance of Jelāl. The whole audience of Firengīs, without sight of Jelāl, became believers in him, and wooers of him.

They set the young merchant free, and allowed him to depart, bestowing on him rich presents and a bountiful outfit.

On his arrival at the metropolis, before going to his own house, he hastened to pay his respects to Jelāl. On beholding the sacred features from afar, he threw himself on the earth, embraced Jelāl's two feet, kissed them, rubbed his face upon them, and wept. Jelāl raised him, kissed both his cheeks, and said: "It was a narrow escape through thy curing the Firengī prince. Thou didst abscond; but henceforward, do thou remain at home, and occupy thyself in earning what is lawful. Take contentment as thy exemplar. The sufferings of the sea, the commotion of the ship, the calamity of captivity, and the darkness of the dungeon, are so many evils. Contentment is a very blessing from God."

32.

Jelāl one day was going from his college into the town, when by chance he met a Christian monk, who made him an obeisance. Jelāl asked him which was the elder, himself or his beard. The monk replied: "I am twenty years older than my beard. It came forth that number of years later." Jelāl answered him:

"Then I pity thee. Thy young beard has attained to maturity, whereas thou hast remained immature, as thou wast. Thou art as black, and as weak, and as untutored as ever. Alas for thee, if thou change not, and ripen not!"

The poor monk at once renounced his rope girdle, threw it away, professed the faith of Islām, and became a believer.

33.

A company of black-habited ones (Christian priests or monks) chanced to meet Jelāl one day, as they came from a distant place. When his disciples espied them afar off, they expressed their aversion from them by exclaiming: "O the dark-looking, disagreeable things!"

Jelāl remarked: "In the whole world, none are more generous than they are. They have given over to us, in this life, the faith of Islām, purity, cleanliness, and the various modes of worshipping God; while, in the world to come, they have left to us the everlasting abodes of paradise, the large-eyed damsels, and the pavilions, as well as the sight of God, of which they will enjoy no share; for God hath said (Qur'ān vii. 48): 'Verily God hath made both of them forbidden things to the misbelievers!' They walk in darkness and misbelief, willingly incurring the torments of hell. But, let only the sun of righteousness rise upon them suddenly, and they will become believers."

Being now come near enough, they all made their obeisances to Jelāl, entered into conversation with him, and professed themselves true Muslims. Jelāl now turned to his disciples, and added: "God swallows up the darkness in the light, and the light in the darkness. He also makes in the darkness a place for the light." The disciples bowed, and rejoiced.

34.

A certain well-known disciple related that, on one occasion, Jelāl and his friends went forth to the country-seat of Husām, and there held a grand festival of holy music and dancing until near daybreak. Jelāl then left off, to give his followers a little rest.

They dispersed about the grounds; and the narrator took a seat in a spot from whence he could see and observe Jelāl. The others all fell asleep; but he occupied himself with reflections on the miracles performed by various of the prophets and of the saints. He thought to himself: "I wonder whether this holy man works miracles. Of course he does; only, he keeps the fact quiet, to avoid the inconveniences of notoriety."

Hardly had the thought crossed his mind, when Jelāl called him by name. On his approaching Jelāl, the latter stooped, picked up a pebble from the earth, placed it on the back of his own hand, and said to him: "Here, take this; it is thy portion; and be thou one of the thankful" (Qur'ān vii. 141).

The disciple examined the pebble by the light of the moon, and saw that it was a large ruby, exceedingly clear and brilliant, not to be found in the treasuries of kings.

Utterly astounded, he shrieked out, and swooned away; awaking the whole company with his shout; for he was a very loud-voiced man. On recovery, he told the others what had occurred. He also expressed to Jelāl his contrition for the temerity of his reflections.

Jelāl told him to carry the stone to the queen, and to mention how he had become possessed of it. The queen accepted it, had it valued, and gave to him a hundred and eighty thousand pieces of silver in return, besides rich gifts. She also distributed presents to all the members of the fraternity.

35.

A certain sheykh, son of a sheykh, and a man of great reputation for learning, came to Qonya, and was respectfully visited by all the people of eminence residing there.

It so happened that Jelāl and his friends were gone that day to a mosque in the country; and the new-comer, offended at Jelāl's not hasting to visit him, made the remark in public: "Has Jelāl never heard the adage: 'The newly-arrived one is visited'?"

One of Jelāl's disciples chanced to be present, and heard this remark. On the other hand, Jelāl was expounding sublime truths in the mosque to his disciples, when suddenly he exclaimed, "My dear brother! I am the newly-arrived one, not thou. Thou and those like thee are bound to visit me, and so gain honour to yourselves."

All his audience were surprised at this apostrophe; wondering to whom it was addressed. Jelāl then spake a parable: "One man came from Bagdād, and another went forth out of his house and ward; which of the two ought to pay the first visit to the other?"

All agreed in opinion that the man from Bagdād ought to be visited by the other. Then Jelāl explained, thus: "In reality, I am returned from the Bagdād of *nulliquity,* whereas this dearly beloved son of a sheykh, who has come here, has gone forth from a ward of this world. I am better entitled, therefore, to be visited than is he. I have been hymning in the Bagdād of the world of spirits the heavenly canticle: 'I am the Truth,' since a time anterior to the commencement of the present war, ere the truth obtained its victory." The disciples expressed their concurrence, and rejoiced exceedingly.

By and by, the sheykh's son was informed of this wonder. He at once arose, went on foot to visit Jelāl, uncovered his head, and owned that Jelāl was right. He further declared himself Jelāl's disciple, and said:

"My father enjoined me to put on ironed sandals, taking an iron-shod staff in my hand, and go forth in quest of Jelālu-'d-Dīn, since it is a duty of all to visit and reverence him who has spoken the truth and reposes on the truth. But the majesty of Jelāl is a hundredfold greater than what my father explained to me."

36.

Jelāl once commanded one of his attendants to go and arrange a certain matter. The attendant answered: "God willing."

Upon this, Jelāl was wroth, and shouted to him: "Stupid, garrulous fool!" The attendant fainted and foamed at the mouth.

The disciples interceded. Jelāl expressed his forgiveness; and the attendant recovered.

37.

On the occasion of a grand religious commemoration at the house of the Perwāna, in the presence of the Sultan Ruknu-'d-Dīn, this monarch was taken unwell, and the exercises were suspended, only, one of the disciples continued to sing and shout.

The Sultan remarked: "How ill-behaved is that man! Does he pretend to be more ecstatic than his teacher Jelālu-'d-Dīn?"

Jelāl heard this, and answered the king: "Thou art unable to withstand an attack of fever. How then canst thou expect a man devoured with an enthusiasm that threatens to swallow up even heaven itself, to calm down on a sudden?"

When the disciples heard this, they set up a shout; and the Sultan, after himself witnessing one or two of the mighty signs wrought by Jelāl, made his obeisance to him, and became a disciple.

38.

It has been related by some that the final overthrow of the rule of the Seljūqī dynasty in Asia Minor (in a.h. 700, a.d. 1300), was in this manner:—

The Sultan Ruknu-'d-Dīn had adopted Jelāl as his (spiritual) father. After a while, he held a great dervish festival in the palace. But, about that period, a certain Sheykh Bāba had created for himself a great name in Qonya, and certain intriguers had led the king to visit him.

It was shortly after that visit that the king held the revival in honour of Bāba in the Hall of the Bowls.

The sheykh was met and introduced in state by the court officials, and was then installed on the throne, with the Sultan seated on a chair by his side. Jelāl now made his appearance, saluted, and took his seat in a corner of the hall. Portions of the Qur'ān were recited, and exhortations were delivered, with hymns.

The Sultan then turned to Jelāl, and spoke: "Be it known to the Lord Jelāl, to the Doctors of the Law, and to the grandees, that I have adopted the Sheykh Bāba as my (spiritual) father, who has accepted me as his dutiful and affectionate son."

All present shouted their approval, and prayed for a blessing on the arrangement. But Jelāl, burning with divine jealousy, instantly exclaimed (in words traditionally related of the prophet, Muhammed): "Verily, Sa'd is a jealous man; but I am more jealous than Sa'd; and God is still more jealous than I am." To this he further added: "Since the Sultan has made the sheykh his father, we will make some other our son." So saying, he gave his usual religious shout of ecstasy, and stalked out from the assembly.

Husāmu-'d-Dīn related that he saw the Sultan, when Jelāl thus quitted the presence, turn pale, as though shot with an arrow.

The grandees ran to stop Jelāl; but he would not return.

A few days afterwards, the officers of state adopted the resolution to invite the Sultan to go to another city, that they might take measures to get rid of Sheykh Bāba. The Sultan now went to consult Jelāl, and ask for his blessing before setting out. Jelāl advised him not to go. The matter had, however, been officially promulgated, and there was no possibility to alter arrangements.

On arriving at the other town, the Sultan was conducted to a private apartment, and forthwith strangled with a bowstring. Ere his breath failed, he invoked the name of Jelāl.

At that moment Jelāl was at his college, lost to consciousness in the enthusiasm of a musical service. Suddenly, he put his two forefingers into his two ears, and ordered the trumpets and chorus to join in. He then shouted vociferously, and recited aloud two of his own odes, of which one commences thus:

"My words were: 'Go not; I'm thy friend; the
world is rife
With threats of dire destruction; I'm the Fount
of Life.'"

~

When the service was over, the disciples requested Jelāl's son, Sultan Veled, to inquire of his father what all this might signify. In reply, he merely put off his cloak, and said aloud: "Let us perform the service for the burial of the dead."

He acted as Precentor in the service, and all present joined in. Then, without waiting for his son to put any question, he addressed the assembly, saying: "Yea, Bahā'u-'d-Dīn and my friends! They have strangled the poor Sultan Ruknu-'d-Dīn. In his agony, he called on me, and shrieked. God had so ordained. I did not wish his voice to ring in my ears, and interrupt my devotions. He will fare better in the other world."

(There is a serious anachronism in the foregoing account. Sultan Ruknu-'d-Dīn, whose name was Suleyman son of Key-Khusrew, was put to death by order of the Mogul emperor Abaqa Khān, in a.h. 664 (a.d. 1265), thirty-six years before the final extinction of the dynasty by order of Qāzān Khān, between Abaqa and whom no less than four emperors reigned. Besides this, Jelāl himself died in a.h. 672 (a.d. 1273), twenty-seven years before the last of the Seljūqī sovereigns, Key-Qubād son of Ferā murz son of Key-Kāwus, was slaughtered, together with all living members of the race. Historians differ much respecting the names and order of succession of the last sovereigns of the dynasty; and the present anecdote shows how confused had become on the spot the legend of these puppets. Ruknu-'d-Dīn caused his own brother to be poisoned, as he had become jealous of the favour shown to that brother by the Mogul emperor. His own death was the reward of that act.)

39.

One day, in lecturing on self-abasement and humility, Jelāl spake a parable from the trees of the field, and said: "Every tree that yields no fruit, as the pine, the cypress, the box, &c., grows tall and straight, lifting up its head on high, and sending all its branches upwards; whereas all the fruit-bearing trees droop their heads, and trail their branches. In like manner, the Apostle of God was the most humble of men. Though he carried within himself all the virtues and excellencies of the ancients and of the moderns, he, like a fruitful tree, was more humble, and more of a dervish, than any other prophet. He is related to have said: 'I am commanded to show consideration to all men, to be kind to them; and yet, no prophet was ever so ill-treated by men as I have been.' We know that he had his head broken, and his teeth knocked out. Still he prayed: 'O our Lord God, guide Thou my people aright; for they know not what they do.' Other prophets have launched denunciations against the people to whom they were sent; and certainly, none have had greater cause to do so, than Muhammed."

"Old Adam's form was moulded first of clay
from nature's face;
Who's not, as mire, low-minded's not true son of
Adam's race."

In like manner, Jelāl also had the commendable habit to show himself humble and considerate to all, even the lowest; especially so to children, and to old women. He used to bless them; and always bowed to those who bowed to him, even though these were not Muslims.

One day he met an Armenian butcher, who bowed to him seven times. Jelāl bowed to him in return. At another time he chanced upon a number of children who were playing, and who left their game, ran to him, and bowed. Jelāl bowed to them also; so much so, that one little fellow called out from afar: "Wait for me until I come." Jelāl moved not away, until the child had come, bowed, and been bowed to.

At that time, people were speaking and writing against him. Legal opinions were obtained and circulated, to the effect that music, singing, and dancing, are unlawful. Out of his kindly disposition, and love of peace, Jelāl made no reply; and after a while all his detractors were silenced, and their writings clean forgotten, as though they had never been written; whereas, his family and followers will endure to the end of time, and will go on increasing continually.

40.

Jelāl once wrote a note to the Perwāna, interceding for a disciple who had been involved in an act of homicide, and had taken refuge in the house of another.

The Perwāna demurred; saying it was a very grave matter, a question of blood. Jelāl thereupon facetiously replied: "A homicide is popularly termed 'a son of 'Azrā'īl (the angel of death).' Being such, what on earth is he to do, unless he kill some one?"

This repartee so pleased the Perwāna, that he pardoned the culprit, and paid himself to the heirs of the slain man the price of his blood.

41.

Jelāl one day went forth and preached in the market. Crowds collected round him. But he continued until night fell around him; so he was at length left alone.

The dogs of the market-place now collected in a circle about him, wagging their tails and whining.

Seeing this, Jelāl exclaimed: "By the Lord, the Highest, the Strongest, the All-Compelling One, besides whom none is high, or strong, or powerful! These dogs comprehend my discourse, and the truths I expound. Men call them dogs; but henceforward let them not be so termed. They are of the family of the '*Seven Sleepers*.'"[5]

42.

The Perwāna much wished Jelāl to give him private instruction at his palace; and requested Jelāl's son, Sultan Veled, to intercede for him in the matter; which he did.

Jelāl replied to his son: "Bahā'u-'d-Dīn! He cannot bear that burden." This was thrice repeated. Jelāl then remarked to his son: "Bahā'u-'d-Dīn! A bucket, the water of which is enough for forty, cannot be drained by one."

Bahā made the reflection: "Had I not pressed the matter, I had never heard this wonderful saying."

43.

At another time, the Perwāna, through Bahā'u-'d-Dīn, requested Jelāl to give a public lecture to all the men of science of the city, who were desirous to hear him.

His answer was: "A tree laden with fruit, had its branches bowed down to the earth therewith. At the time, doubts and gainsayings prevented the gardeners from gathering and enjoying the fruit. The tree has now raised its head to the skies, and beyond. Can they hope, then, to pluck and eat of its fruit?"

44.

Again, the Perwāna requested Jelāl himself to instruct him and give him counsel.

After a little reflection, Jelāl said:

"I have heard that thou hast committed the Qur'ān to memory. Is it so?" "I have." "I have heard that thou hast studied, under a great teacher, the Jāmi'u-'l-Usūl, that mighty work on the 'Elements of Jurisprudence.' Is it so?" "It is."

"Then," answered Jelāl, "thou knowest the Word of God, and thou knowest all the words and acts reported of His Apostle. But thou settest them at naught, and actest not up to their precepts. How, then, canst thou expect that words of mine will profit thee?"

The Perwāna was abashed, and burst into tears. He went his way; but from that day he began to execute justice, so as to become a rival of the great Chosroes. He made himself the phœnix of the age, and Jelāl accepted him as a disciple.

45.

A company of pilgrims arrived one year at Qonya from Mekka, on their way home elsewhere. They were taken in succession to visit all the chief men of rank and learning in the capital, and were received with every demonstration of respect.

At last they were conducted to Jelāl also, in his college. On seeing him seated there, they all screamed out and fainted away.

When they were recovered, Jelāl began to offer excuses, saying to them: "I fear you have been deceived, either by an impostor, or by some person resembling me in feature. There are men who strongly resemble one another."

The pilgrims one and all objected:

"Why talks he thus? Why strive to make us doubt our eyes? By the God of heaven and earth, he was with us in person, habited in the very dress he now wears, when we all assumed the pilgrim garb at Mekka. He performed with us all the ceremonies of the pilgrimage, there and at 'Arafāt.[6] He visited with us the tomb of the Prophet at Medīna; though he never once ate or drank with us. Now he pretends that he does not know us or we know him."

On hearing this declaration, Jelāl's disciples were transported with joy, a musical festival ensued, and all those pilgrims became disciples.

46.

A certain rich merchant of Qonya, a disciple, as was his wife, of Jelāl's, went to Mekka one year for the pilgrimage.

On the day when the victims are slaughtered, the lady had a dish of sweetmeat prepared, and sent some of it in a china bowl to Jelāl, to be eaten at dinner. She made the request that, when he partook of the food, he would favour her absent husband with his remembrance, his prayers, and his blessing.

Jelāl invited his disciples to the feast; and all ate of the lady's sweetmeat to repletion. But the bowl still remained full.

Jelāl then said: "Oh, he too must partake of it." He took the bowl, ascended to the terraced roof of the college with it, returning immediately empty-handed. His friends asked him what he had done with the bowl and the food. "I have handed them," said Jelāl, "to her husband, whose property they are." The company remained bewildered.

In due course of time, the pilgrims from Qonya returned home from Mekka; and out of the baggage of the merchant, the china bowl was produced, and sent in to the lady, who was much astonished at sight of it. She inquired of her husband how he had become possessed of that identical dish. He replied: "Ah! I also am at a loss to know how it happened. But, on the eve of the slaughter of the victims, I was seated in my tent, at 'Arafāt, with a company of other pilgrims, when an arm projected into the tent, and placed this dish before me, filled with sweetmeat. I sent out servants to see who had brought it to me; but no one was found." The lady at once inferred the truth, and guessed what had happened. Her husband was more and more astonished at such miraculous power.

Next day, husband and wife went to Jelāl, stood bareheaded before him, wept for joy, and related what had occurred. He answered:

"The whole thing is the effect of your trust and belief. God has merely made use of my hand as the instrument wherewith to make manifest His power."

47.

Jelāl was accustomed to go every year for about six weeks to a place near Qonya, called *"The Hot Waters,"* where there is a lake or marsh inhabited by a large colony of frogs.

A religious musical festival was arranged one day near the lake, and Jelāl delivered a discourse. The frogs were vociferous, and made his words inaudible. He therefore addressed himself to them, with a loud shout, saying: "What is all this noise about? Either do you pronounce a discourse, or allow me to speak." Complete silence immediately ensued; nor was a frog ever once heard to croak again, so long as Jelāl remained there.

Before leaving, he went to the marsh, and gave them his permission to croak again now as much as they pleased. The chorus instantly began. Numbers of people, who were witnesses of this miraculous power over the frogs, became believers in Jelāl, and professed themselves his disciples.

48.

A party of butchers had purchased a heifer, and were leading her away to be slaughtered, when she broke loose from them, and ran away, a crowd following and shouting after her, so that she became furious, and none could pass near her.

By chance Jelāl met her, his followers being at some distance behind. On beholding him, the heifer became calm and quiet, came gently towards him, and then stood still, as though communing with him mutely, heart to heart, as is the wont with saints; and as though pleading for her life. Jelāl patted and caressed her.

The butchers now came up. Jelāl begged of them the animal's life, as having placed herself under his protection. They gave their consent, and let her go free.

Jelāl's disciples now joined the party, and he improved the occasion by the following remarks:—"If a brute beast, on being led away to slaughter, break loose and take refuge with me, so that God grants it immunity for my sake, how much more so would the case be, when a human being turns unto God with all his heart and soul, devoutly seeking Him. God will certainly save such a man from the tormenting demons of hell-fire, and lead him to heaven, there to dwell eternally."

Those words caused such joy and gladness among the disciples that a musical festival, with dancing, at once commenced, and was carried on into the night. Alms and clothing were distributed to the poor singers of the chorus.

It is related that the heifer was never seen again in the meadows of Qonya.

49.

A meeting was held at the Perwāna's palace, each guest bringing his own waxlight of about four or five pounds' weight. Jelāl came to the assembly with a small wax-taper.

The grandees smiled at the taper. Jelāl, however, told them that their imposing candles depended on his taper for their light. Their looks expressed their incredulity at this. Jelāl, therefore, blew out his taper, and all the candles were at once extinguished; the company being left in darkness.

After a short interval, Jelāl fetched a sigh. His taper took fire therefrom, and the candles all burnt brightly as before. Numerous were the conversions resulting from this miraculous display.

50.

One day, the poet-laureate, Qāni'ī, came to visit Jelāl at his college. He was the very Khāqānī[7] of the age, and was accompanied by a crowd of noble admirers.

After much conversation, Qāni'ī remarked that he did not like the writings of the poet Sanā'ī,[8] and Jelāl inquired the reason. The poet-laureate replied: "Sanā'ī was not a Muslim." Again Jelāl asked why he had formed that opinion; and Qāni'ī replied: "He has quoted passages from the Qur'ān in his poetry, and has even used them as his rhymes."

Jelāl hereupon rebuked him most severely, as follows:—

"Do hold thy peace. What sort of a Muslim art thou? Could a Muslim perceive the grandeur of that poet, his hair would stand on end, and his turban would fall from his head. That Muslim, and thousands such as he,—such as thee,—out of this lower world, and out of the land of spirits, would become real Muslims. His poetry, which is an exposition of the mysteries of the Qur'ān, is so beautifully embellished, that one may apply to it the adage: 'We have drawn from the ocean, and we have poured out again into the ocean.' Thou hast not understood his philosophy; thou hast not studied it; for thou art a Qāni'ī (Follower of one who is satisfied). The vicars of God have a technology, of which the rhetoricians have no knowledge. Hence these truths appear to be imperfect, because men of crude minds are prevented from comprehending them. Though thou hast no part in the lot of the recondite mysteries of the saints, it does not thence follow that thou shouldest deny their position, and so place thyself in a position where destruction may be brought down upon thee. On the contrary, shouldest thou fix thy faith upon them, and act with true sincerity, thou shalt find in the day of judgment no heavy burden on thy shoulders. In lieu thereof, a burden-bearer will be present at thy side,—a refuge, who will prove thy most earnest intercessor."

Struck with these words, the poet-laureate arose, uncovered, begged forgiveness, confessed contrition for his disrespect, and became one of Jelāl's disciples.

51.

A disciple of Husāmu-'d-Dīn wished to make a vow never to do an act not expressly authorised by the Canon Law of Islām. For the purpose of administering the oath to him, instead of the Qur'ān, a copy of the Ilāhī-nāma (Divine Hymns) of the philosopher Sanā'ī was placed on a lectern, covered over with a cloth, and tendered as "the Book" on which he was to swear.

Just then, Jelāl came into the room, and asked what was going on. Husām replied: "One of my disciples is going to make a vow against backsliding. We shrank from swearing him on the Qur'ān, and have therefore prepared a copy of the Ilāhī-nāma for the occasion."

Jelāl observed: "Indeed! Why, the Ilāhī-nāma would draw down on a forswearer a more severe chastisement than the Qur'ān itself. The Word of God is but milk, of which the Ilāhī-nāma is the cream and the butter!"

52.

When Adam was created, God commanded Gabriel to take the three most precious pearls of the divine treasury, and offer them in a golden salver to Adam, to choose for himself one of the three.

The three pearls were: *wisdom*, *faith*, and *modesty*.

Adam chose the pearl of *wisdom*.

Gabriel then proceeded to remove the salver with the remaining two pearls, in order to replace them in the divine treasury. With all his mighty power, he found he could not lift the salver.

The two pearls said to him: "We will not separate from our beloved wisdom. We could not be happy and quiet away from it. From all eternity, we three have been the three compeers of God's glory, the pearls of His power. We cannot be separated."

A voice was now heard to proceed from the divine presence, saying: "Gabriel! leave them, and come away."

From that time, wisdom has taken its seat on the summit of the brain of Adam; faith took up its abode in his heart; modesty established itself in his countenance. Those three pearls have remained as the heirlooms of the chosen children of Adam. For, whoever, of all his descendants, is not embellished and enriched with those three jewels, is lacking of the sentiment and lustre of his divine origin.

So runs the narrative reported by Husām, Jelāl's successor, as having been imparted to him by the latter.

53.

A certain flute-player named Hamza, much beloved by Jelāl, happened to die. Jelāl sent some of his disciples to array the defunct in his grave-clothes. He himself followed them to the house of the deceased.

On entering the room, Jelāl addresses the dead body: "My dear friend Hamza, arise!" Instantly, the deceased arose, saying: "Lo, here I am!" He then took his flute, and for three whole days and nights a religious festival was kept up in his house.

Above a hundred Roman misbelievers were thereby converted to the faith of Islām. When Jelāl left the house, life departed from the corpse also.

54.

Among the disciples there was a hunchback, a devout man, and a player on the tambourine, whom Jelāl loved.

On the occasion of a festival, this poor man beat his tambourine and shouted in ecstasy to an unusual degree. Jelāl was also greatly moved in the spirit with the holy dance.

Approaching the hunchback, he said to him: "Why erectest thou not thyself like the rest?" The infirmity of the hunch was pleaded. Jelāl then patted him on the back, and stroked him down. The poor man immediately arose, erect and graceful as a cypress.

When he went home, his wife refused him admittance, denying that he was her husband. His companions came, and bare witness to her of what had happened. Then she was convinced, let him in, and the couple lived together for many years afterwards.

55.

It was once remarked to Jelāl, with respect to the burial service for the dead, that, from the earliest times, it had been usual for certain prayers and Qur'ānic recitations to be said at the grave and round the corpse; but, that people could not understand why he had introduced into the ceremony the practice of singing hymns during the procession towards the place of burial, which canonists had pronounced to be a mischievous innovation.

Jelāl replied: "The ordinary reciters, by their services, bear witness that the deceased lived a Muslim. My singers, however, testify that he was a Muslim, a believer and a lover of God."

He added also:

"Besides that; when the human spirit, after years of imprisonment in the cage and dungeon of the body, is at length set free, and wings its flight to the source whence it came, is not this an occasion for rejoicings, thanks, and dancings? The soul, in ecstasy, soars to the presence of the Eternal; and stirs up others to make proof of courage and self-sacrifice. If a prisoner be released from a dungeon and be clothed with honour, who would doubt that rejoicings are proper? So, too, the death of a saint is an exactly parallel case."

56.

One of Jelāl's chief disciples related that, when he first began to study under that teacher, a company of pilgrims from Mekka came to Qonya, and among them was a very handsome young man of this latter city, son to one of the chief professors there.

This young man brought rich presents to Jelāl, and gifts for the disciples, relating to the latter the following adventure:—

"We were travelling in the desert of Arabia, and I chanced to fall asleep. The caravan went on without me. When I awoke, I found myself alone in the trackless sands. I knew not which way to turn. I wept and lamented for a considerable time, took a direction at hazard, and walked until I was thoroughly exhausted.

"To my surprise and joy I espied a large tent at a distance, with a great smoke rising by it. I made for the tent, and there encountered a most formidable-looking personage, to whom I related my misadventure. He bid me welcome, asked me in, and invited me to rest myself. Within the tent I observed a large kettle, full of fresh-cooked sweetmeat of the finest kind, and a plentiful supply of cool clear water.

"My wonder was great. I asked my host what these preparations might mean, and he answered: 'I am a disciple of the great Jelālu-'d-Dīn of Qonya, son of Bahā'u-'d-Dīn of Balkh. He is used to pass by here every day. I have therefore pitched this tent for him, and I prepare this food. Perchance, he may honour and bless me with his presence, partaking of hospitality here.'

"As he yet spake, in walked Jelāl. We saluted; and he was begged to partake of the food. He took a little morsel, no larger than a filbert, giving me some also. I fell at his feet, and told him I was from Qonya on pilgrimage, and had missed the caravan by falling asleep. 'Well,' answered he, 'as we are fellow-townsmen, be of good cheer.' He then bade me close my eyes. I did so; and on opening them again I found myself in the midst of my companions of the caravan. I am now come here, on my return home in safety, to offer my thanks for that miraculous kindness, and to profess myself a disciple of the holy man."

57.

A man of great learning came once to visit Jelāl. By way of a test, he asked Jelāl two questions: "Is it correct to speak of God as *'a living soul*?' since God hath said (Qur'ān iii. 182): 'Every living soul shall taste death!'" and: "If one ought not to call God 'a living soul,' what did Jesus mean when he said (Qur'ān v. 116): 'Thou knowest what is in my soul, but I know not what is in Thy soul'?" The second question was: "Can God properly be called 'a thing'? If He can be so called, what is the signification of His word (Qur'ān xxviii. 88): 'Every thing shall perish, save His cause'?"

Jelāl immediately replied: "'But I know not what is in Thy soul' means *in Thy knowledge, in Thy absentness,* or, as we seers say, *in Thy secrecy.* Thus the passage would be paraphrased: *Thou knowest what is in my secrecy; but I know not what is in the secret of Thy secrecy;* or, as '*the people of heart*' would put it: *Thou knowest what issues from me in the world; but I know not the secret of what issues from Thee in the world to come.* It is quite proper to speak of God as 'a thing;' for He hath said (Qur'ān vi. 19): 'What thing is greatest in testimony? Say thou: "God;"' *i.e.,* God is the greatest thing in testimony; 'God will be a witness between me and you in the day of the resurrection.' The signification of the passage 'Every thing shall perish' is: *every created thing shall perish;* not the Creator, *i.e.,* 'save He.' The thing excepted from the general category is 'He.' But God knows best."

The man of learning instantly professed himself a disciple, and composed a panegyric on Jelāl.

58.

The legend goes that Jelāl made a practice of seeing the new moon of the Arabian new year, and always uttered the following prayer on seeing it:—"O our Lord God! Thou art the Past-eternal One, the Future-eternal One, the Ancient One! This is a new year. I beg of Thee therein steadfastness to withstand the lapidated Satan,[9] and assistance against the rebellious spirit (within me); also, occupation in what will approximate me to Thee, and an avoidance of what might elongate me from Thee. O God! O the All-merciful One, the All-compassionate One! Through Thy mercy, O Most-compassionate of the merciful ones! O thou Lord of majesty and of honour!"

59.

It is related that Jelāl cured one of his disciples of an intermittent fever by writing down the following invocation on paper, washing off the ink in water, and giving this to the patient to drink; who was, under God's favour, immediately relieved from the malady:—"O Mother of the sleek one (a nickname of the tertian ague)! If thou hast believed in God, the Most Great, make not the head to ache; vitiate not the swallow; eat not the flesh; drink not the blood; and depart thou out of So-and-So, betaking thyself to some one who attributes to God partners of other false gods. And I bear witness that there is not any god save God, and I testify that Muhammed is His servant and apostle."

60.

One day Jelāl paid a visit to a great Sheykh. He was received with the utmost respect, and seated with the Sheykh on the same carpet, both together falling into ecstatic heart-communion with the world of spirits.

A certain dervish was there present also, who had repeatedly performed the pilgrimage at Mekka. The dervish addressed Jelāl, and inquired: "What is poverty?" Jelāl returned no answer; and the question was thrice repeated.

When Jelāl took his leave, the great Sheykh accompanied him to the street door. On his return to his room, he reprimanded the dervish severely for his insolent intrusion on the guest; "especially," said the Sheykh, "as he fully answered thy question the first time thou puttest it." The dervish, surprised, asked what the answer had been. "The poor man," said the Sheykh, "when he hath known

God, hath his tongue tied. That is being a real dervish; who, when in the presence of saints, speaks not; neither with the tongue, nor with the heart. This is what is signified by (Qur'ān xlvi. 28): 'Hold ye your peace.' But now, prepare thyself for thy end. Thou art struck by a shaft from heaven."

Three days later, the dervish was met by a gang of reprobates, who attacked and killed him, carrying off every thing he had about him. *Salve fac nos, Domine!*

61.

In the days of Jelāl there was in Qonya a lady-saint, named Fakhru-'n-Nisā (the Glory of Women). She was known to all the holy men of the time, who were all aware of her sanctity. Miracles were wrought by her in countless numbers. She constantly attended the meetings at Jelāl's home, and he occasionally paid her a visit at her house.

Her friends suggested to her that she ought to go and perform the pilgrimage at Mekka; but she would not undertake this duty unless she should first consult with Jelāl about it. Accordingly she went to see him. As she entered his presence, before she spoke, he called out to her:

"Oh, most happy idea! May thy journey be prosperous! God willing, we shall be together." She bowed, but said nothing. The disciples present were puzzled.

That night she remained a guest at Jelāl's house, conversing with him till past midnight. At that hour he went up to the terraced roof of the college to perform the divine service of the vigil. When he had completed that service of worship, he fell into an ecstasy, shouting and exclaiming. Then he lifted the skylight of the room below, where the lady was, and invited her to come up on to the roof also.

When she was come, he told her to look upwards, saying that her wish was come to pass. On looking up, she beheld the Cubical House of Mekka in the air, circumambulating round Jelāl's head above him, and spinning round like a dervish in his waltz, plainly and distinctly, so as to leave no room for doubt or uncertainty. She screamed out with astonishment and fright, swooning away. On coming to herself, she felt the conviction that the journey to Mekka was not one for her to perform; so she totally relinquished the idea.

62.

Jelāl was once standing at the edge of the moat round the city of Qonya, when a company of students, undergraduates of one of the colleges in the neighbourhood, seeing him, agreed to try him by asking the question: "Of what colour was the dog of the Seven Sleepers?"

Jelāl's immediate, unpremeditated answer was: "Yellow. A lover is always yellow (sallow); as am I; and that dog was a lover." The students bowed to him, and all became disciples.

63.

The Superior of the monks of the monastery of Plato was an old man, and was held in the very highest esteem for his learning in all Constantinople and Firengistān, in Sīs, Jānik, and other lands. (Sīs was capital of the kingdom of Lower Armenia, and Jānik was the secondary "Roman Empire" of Trebizond.) From all those lands did disciples flock to learn wisdom from him.

This Superior related the following anecdote:—

"One day, Jelāl came to the monastery of Plato, situated at the foot of a hill, with a cavern therein, from whence issued a stream of cold water. Jelāl entered the cavern, and proceeded to its farther extremity. The Superior remained at the cavern's mouth, watching for what might happen. For seven whole days and nights Jelāl remained there, seated in the midst of the cold water. At the end of that period he came forth from the cavern, and walked away, singing a hymn. Not the slightest change was apparent in his features, nor in his eyes."

The Superior made oath that all he had read about the person and qualities of the Messiah, as also in the books of Abraham and Moses, were found in the person of Jelāl, as well as the grandeur and mien of the prophets, as set forth in books of ancient history, and far more besides.

64.

Shemsu-'d-Dīn of Tebrīz once asserted, in Jelāl's college, that whosoever wished to see again the prophets, had only to look on Jelāl, who possessed all their qualifications; more especially of those to whom revelations were made, whether by angelic communications, or whether in visions; the chief of such qualities being serenity of mind with perfect inward confidence and consciousness of being one of God's elect. "Now," said he, "to possess Jelāl's approbation is heaven; while hell is to incur his displeasure. Jelāl is the key of heaven. Go then, and look upon Jelāl, if thou wish to comprehend the signification of that saying *'the learned are the heirs of the prophets,'* together with something beyond that, which I will not here specify. He has more learning in every science than any one else upon earth. He explains better, with greater tact and taste, as also more exhaustively, than all others. Were

I, with my mere intellect, to study for a hundred years, I could not acquire a tenth part of what he knows. He has intuitively thought out that knowledge, without being aware of it, in my presence, by his own subtlety."

65.

One of the greatest teachers of Qonya was one day giving a lecture on a terraced roof, when suddenly he heard the sound of a lute. He exclaimed: "These lutes are an innovation on the prophetic usages. They must be interdicted."

Forthwith, the form of Jelāl appeared before him, and answered: "That must not be." On this the teacher fainted away.

When he regained his consciousness, he sought to make his peace with Jelāl, by sending an apology and a recantation to him, through the medium of Jelāl's son, Sultan Veled; but Jelāl would not accept them. He answered: "It would be easier to convert seventy Roman bishops to Islām, than to clear away from the mind of that teacher the stains of hate, and so set him on the right road. His soul is as foul as the paper on which children practise their writing exercises."

At length, however, he allowed himself to be appeased by his son; so that he permitted the teacher, with his pupils, to constitute themselves his disciples.

66.

Jelāl one day addressed his son, saying:

"Bahā'u-'d-Dīn, dost thou wish to love thy enemy, and to be loved of him? Speak well of him, and extol his virtues.

He will then be thy friend; and for this reason: In like manner as there is a road open between the heart and the tongue, so also is there a way from the tongue to the heart. The love of God may be found by hearing His *comely names*. God hath said: 'O My servants, take ye heed that ye often commemorate Me, so that sincerity may abound.' The more that sincerity prevails, the more do the rays of the light of truth shine into the heart. The hotter a baker's oven is, the more bread will it bake; if cool, it will not bake at all."

67.

Sultan Veled, Bahā'u-'d-Dīn, is said to have recounted of his father, Jelāl, this saying: "A true disciple is he who holds his teacher to be superior to all others. So much so, that, for instance, a disciple of Bāyezīd of Bestām was once asked whether Bāyezīd or Abū-Hanīfa was the greater, and he replied that his teacher, Bāyezīd, was the greater. 'Then,' said the questioner, 'is Bāyezīd the greater, or is Abū-Bekr?' 'My teacher is the greater.' 'Bāyezīd or Muhammed?' 'Bāyezīd.' 'Bāyezīd or God?' 'I only know my teacher; I know no other than him; and I know that he is greater than all others.'

"Another was asked the last question, and his reply was: 'There is no difference between the two.' A third was asked it also, and he replied: 'It would require a greater one than either of the two to determine which of them is the greater.'

"As God does not walk in this world of sensible objects, the prophets are the substitutes of God. No, no! I am wrong! For if thou suppose that those substitutes and their principal are two different things, thou hast judged erroneously, not rightly."

68.

Sultan Veled is reported to have said:

"My grandfather, the Great Master, used to recommend to his disciples to honour his son Jelāl exceedingly, as one of noble extraction and exalted pedigree, of an eternal descent in the past; since the mother of his mother was the daughter of the Imām Sarakhsī, a descendant from Huseyn, son of 'Alī, and grandson of the Prophet."

69.

Sultan Veled is also reported to have said: "My father told his disciples that I was seven, and my brother 'Alā'u-'d-Dīn eight years old, when the Dizdār Bedru-'d-Dīn Guhertāsh had us circumcised at Qara-Hisār." (See chap. i., No. 12.)

He is also reported to have declared: "When the Sultan invited my grandfather to Qonya, a year passed, and then the Emīr Mūsa invited my grandfather to Larenda, and took my father to be his own son-in-law; so that I was born in that town." (See chap. i., No. 2. The account now given here is at variance with that mentioned in the preface, which makes 'Alā'u-'d-Dīn and Bahā'u-'d-Dīn to have been born at Larenda before Jelāl and his father went to Qonya. Moreover, their mother, Gevher Khātūn, is there said to have been the daughter of Lala Sherefu-'d-Dīn of Samarqand. Is that an alias of the Emīr Mūsa of the present anecdote; or did Jelāl marry two ladies of Larenda at different times? There are several difficulties here. Sultan Veled puts only one year as the difference of age between himself and his elder brother. If the daughter of the Emīr Mūsa was the mother of both these brothers, Jelāl's stay at Larenda must have been of about two years at least. If they were by different mothers, and born, the one before, the other after Bahā Veled's settling at Qonya, there must have been a greater difference in their ages. Jelāl's age at his marriage is also variously stated. These discrepancies show that the anecdotes were collected from traditions of various sources, long after the events recorded.)

70.

Sultan Veled is said to have related that one day, two Turks, law-students, brought to Jelāl an offering of a few lentils, excusing the paucity of the gift, as the result of their poverty. Jelāl thereupon narrated the following anecdote:—

"God revealed to Mustafa (Muhammed) that the believers should contribute of their possessions, for the service of God, as much as they could spare. Some brought the half, some the third part; Abū-Bekr brought the whole of what he possessed. Thus a large treasure was collected, of money, beasts, and arms, for God's service.

"A poor woman, too, brought three dates and a cake of bread—all she had on earth.

"The disciples smiled. Mustafa perceived their action, and said that God had showed him a vision, which he desired to tell to them. They all begged he would favour them with the recital. He therefore thus proceeded:

"'God hath removed the veils from before me. And lo, I saw that the angels had placed in one scale of a balance the whole of your very liberal offerings together, and in the other scale the three dates and one cake of this poor woman. The latter scale was preponderant; its contents outweighed all the rest.'

"The disciples bowed, thanked the prophet, and inquired the hidden explanation of this mystery. He answered: 'This poor woman has parted with her all, whereas my disciples have kept back a part of their possessions. Proverbs say: "The generous one is generous out of what he possesses," and, "A little, in the eyes of the Most Great, is much." You put into the earth a single date-stone, intrusting it to God. He makes that stone become a tree, which yields fruits without number; because the stone was confided to Him. Therefore, let your alms be given to the poor, and to God's servants, as a trust committed unto God. For it is said: "Alms fall first into God's hand, before reaching the hands of the poor;" and again: "Alms for the poor and the destitute."'

"The poor of Mekka and Medīna, refugees and auxiliaries, shouted their admiration as they heard these words."

When the two Turkish students heard this anecdote related, they professed themselves disciples of Jelāl.

71.

When Jelāl was quite young, he was one day preaching on the subject of Moses and Elias (Qur'ān xviii. 59-81). One of his disciples noticed a stranger seated in a corner, paying great attention, and every now and then saying: "Good! Quite true! Quite correct! He might have been the third one with us two!" The disciple surmised that the stranger might be Elias. (Elias is believed by Muslims to be always visible somewhere, but that people know him not. Did they recognise him, they could obtain from him a knowledge of the secret of eternal life, which he possesses.) He therefore seized hold of the stranger's skirt, and asked for his spiritual aid. "Oh," said the stranger, "rather seek assistance from Jelāl, as we all do. Every occult saint of God is the loving and admiring friend of him." So saying, he managed to disengage his skirt from the disciple's hold, and instantly disappeared. The disciple went to pay his respects to Jelāl, who at once addressed him, saying: "Elias, and Moses, and the prophets, are all friends of mine." The disciple understood the allusion, and became more and more devoted at heart to Jelāl than he even was before.

72.

It is related that when the burial service was about to be performed over the corpse of Jelāl, the precentor gave a shriek, and swooned away. After a while, he recovered, and then performed his office, weeping bitterly.

On being asked the cause of his emotion, he answered:

"As I stood forward to perform my office, I perceived a row of the most noble of spiritual saints of the spiritual world, as being present, and as being engaged in reciting the prayers for the dead over the departed one. Those angels of heaven wore robes of blue (the mourning of some sects of Muslims), and wept."

For forty days, that precentor and others daily visited Jelāl's grave.

73.

At Damascus, when a young student, Jelāl was frequently seen by others to walk several arrow-flights' distance in the air, tranquilly returning to the terraced roof on which they were standing.

Those fellow-pupils were among his earliest believers and disciples.

74.

A friend of Jelāl's once took leave of him at Qonya, and went to Damascus. On his arrival there, he found Jelāl seated in a corner of his room. Asking for an explanation of this surprising phenomenon, Jelāl replied: "The men of God are like fishes in the ocean; they pop up into view on the surface here and there and everywhere, as they please."

75.

Jelāl once met a Turk in Qonya, who was selling fox-skins in the market, and crying them: "Dilku! Dilku!" (Fox! Fox! in Turkish.)

Jelāl immediately began to parody his cry, calling out in Persian: "Dil kū! Dil kū!" (Heart, where art thou?) At the same time he broke out into one of his holy waltzes of ecstasy.

76.

In the time of Sultan Veled (a.d. 1284-1312), a young man, of the descendants of the Prophet, and son of the guardian of the holy tomb of Muhammed at Medīna, came to Qonya with a company of his fellow-descendants, belonging to that city. He was presented to Sultan Veled, and became his disciple.

He wore a most singular head-dress. One end of his turban hung down in front to below his navel; while the other end was formed into the *sheker-āvīz*[10] of the Mevlevī dervishes.

When they had become somewhat intimate, Sultan Veled asked him how it happened that he wore the *sheker-āvīz* of the Mevlevis, when nobody else but those dervishes wear it, in imitation of their founder, Jelāl.

The young man explained that his family were descended from the Prophet. That the Prophet, on the night of his ascension to heaven, after seeing God and many mysteries, had returned a certain distance, and, as is well known, then went back to intercede with God for his people. He now perceived, on the pinnacle of God's throne, the ideal portrait of a form, so beautiful, that he had not hitherto witnessed anything so charming among the angels and inhabitants of heaven.

After contemplating the lovely vision, in amazement, for some time, Muhammed was able to notice that the ideal form wore on its head a *sheker-āvīz*. He asked Gabriel what that ideal portrait might portend, which was so attractive in its beauty as to surpass all the wonders he had witnessed in all the nine heavens. "Is it the portrait of an angel, a prophet, or a saint?" Gabriel replied:

"It is the portrait of a personage of the descendants of Abū-Bekr, who will appear in the latter days among the people of thy Church, and will fill the whole world with the effulgence of the knowledge of thy mysteries. To him will God vouchsafe a precedency, and a pen, and a breath, such that kings and princes will profess themselves his disciples; and he will be a most pure upholder of thy religion, being, in every respect, the counterpart of thyself in aspect and in morals. His name will be Muhammed, as is thine; and his surname will be Jelālu-'d-Dīn. His words will explain thy sayings, and will expound thy Qur'ān."

On his return home, the Prophet adopted the form of turban he had seen worn in that ideal portrait, making one end hang down a span in front, and binding the other end behind into a *sheker-āvīz*.

"From that day to this," said the young man, "the fathers of our family have followed that fashion, so adopted by the Prophet; and we continue to do so too."

It is said that when Abū-Bekr heard this narrative from the Prophet, respecting his great descendant that was thus foretold, he gave the whole of his possessions to the Prophet, to be expended in God's cause.

When Muhammed died, Abū-Bekr wept long and bitterly. But the Prophet appeared to him, and consoled him by saying: "One day I will reappear among my people from out of the collar of one of thy race."

The young man continued: "From that time onwards, our family were on the outlook for the manifestation of the holy personage whose ideal portrait the Prophet so saw. Thank God that I have witnessed the realisation of their hope."

The Qonya pilgrims published this communication to all the disciples there present.

77.

In the days of Sultan Veled, a great merchant came to Qonya to visit the tomb of Jelāl. He offered many rich gifts to Sultan Veled, making presents also to the disciples. He related to them many anecdotes of adventures encountered by him in his travels, such as the following: —

He once went to Kīsh and Bahreyn in quest of pearls and rubies. "An inhabitant told me," said he, "that I should find some in the hands of a certain fisherman. I went to him, and the fisher showed me a chest, containing pearls of inestimable value, such as impressed me with astonishment. I asked him how he had collected them; and he told me, calling God to witness, that he, his three brothers, and his father, were formerly poor fishermen. One day they hooked something that gave them immense trouble before they could bring it to land.

"They now found they had captured a 'Lord of the Waters,' also named a 'Marvel of the Sea,' as is commonly known.[11]

"We wondered," said he, "what we could do with the beast. We wept for the ill fortune that had brought us such a disappointment. The creature looked at us as we spoke. Suddenly my father cried out: 'I have it! I will put him on a cart, and exhibit him all over the country at a penny a head!'

"Through the miraculous power of Him who has endowed man with speech and His creatures with life, the beast broke forth and exclaimed: 'Make me not a staring-block in the world, and I will do anything you may wish of me, so as to suffice for you and your children for many years to come!'

"Our father answered: 'How should I set thee free, when thou art so strange and unparalleled a creature?' The beast replied: 'I will make an oath.' Our father said: 'Speak! Let us hear thy oath.'

"The beast now said: 'We are of the faith of Muhammed, and disciples of the holy Mevlānā. By the soul of the Mevlānā, the holy Jelālu-'d-Dīn of Rome, I will go, and I will return.'

"Our father fainted away with astonishment. I, therefore, now asked: 'How hast thou any knowledge of him?' The beast replied: 'We are a nation of twelve thousand individuals. We have believed in him, and he frequently showed himself to us at the bottom of the sea, lecturing and sermonising to us on the divine mysteries of the truth. He brought us to a knowledge of the true faith; so that we continually practise what he taught us.'

"Our father instantly told him he was free. He went back, therefore, into the water, and was lost to sight. But two days later he returned, and brought with him innumerable pearls and precious stones. He asked whether he had been true and faithful to his promise; and on our expressing our satisfaction on that score, he took an affectionate farewell from us.

"We were thus raised from the depths of poverty to the pinnacle of wealth. We became merchant princes, and our slaves are the great merchants of the earth. Every dealer who wishes for pearls and rubies comes to us. We are known as the *Sons of the Fisherman*. Our father went to Qonya, and paid his respects to the Mevlānā.

"Through his narrative, I formed the design, now carried into effect, to visit the son of that great saint."

This wonderful narrative has been handed down ever since in the mouths of the merchants of Qonya.

78.

(The following appears to be an account of one of the first visits of the Perwāna to Jelāl, to whom he subsequently became so devotedly attached.)

One of the most eminent among the men of learning in Qonya was visited by the Perwāna. The learned man held forth eloquently on several exalted themes, and then informed the Perwāna that he had, the night before, been taken up into the highest heaven, and had there learnt many mysteries. He said that he there saw Jelāl hold a higher station of proximity to God than any other saint, as he stood on a level with God's throne.

A day or two later, the Perwāna, filled with reverence for Jelāl's unequalled sanctity, went and paid him a visit with the utmost deference. Before the Perwāna could broach any subject of conversation, Jelāl said to him: "Mu'īnu-'d-Dīn! the vision related to you by your learned friend is quite true in the main facts, though I never saw him there at any time." He then extemporised the following ode:—

"Fellow-visitant wert thou? Then say what thou
sawest there last night.
'Twixt my heart and inspiring loved darling
what passed in thy sight?
And if thou, in thy dream, with thy eyes sawest
my beautiful love,
Tell us then, in the earrings he wore there what
jewels were wove.
If with me thou be fellow in coat, as in thoughts
and in creeds,
Let us hear the details of that ragged old
mendicant's weeds.
If thou poverty's son be, and unspoken mysteries
hear,
Thou'lt recount all the words that were thought
by my silent compeer,
If thou'st learnt whence the source of mankind
and of souls did proceed.
Since the source was but one, what then means
all this search, all this greed?
And if thou hast not seen any place of his form
and face free,
Say then what, in the thoughts of his lovers, that
face and form be.
And if I head the lists of those lovers, as thou
seemest to say,

Tell us, What are those lists? What his messages,
words, answers? Pray!"

A musical service was then got up, this ode being chanted during its performance. The Perwāna was so utterly bewildered by this incident, that he could say nothing. He therefore rose, bowed, and took his leave.

79.

One day, it is said, the Prophet (Muhammed) recited to 'Alī in private the secrets and mysteries of the "Brethren of Sincerity" (who appear to be the "Freemasons" of the Muslim dervish world), enjoining on him not to divulge them to any of the uninitiated, so that they should not be betrayed; also, to yield obedience to the rule of implicit submission.

For forty days, 'Alī kept the secret in his own sole breast, and bore therewith until he was sick at heart. Like a pregnant woman, his abdomen became swollen with the burden, so that he could no longer breathe freely.

He therefore fled to the open wilderness, and there chanced upon a well. He stooped, reached his head as far down into the well as he was able; and then, one by one, he confided those mysteries to the bowels of the earth. From the excess of his excitement, his mouth filled with froth and foam. These he spat out into the water of the well, until he had freed himself of the whole, and he felt relieved.

After a certain number of days, a single reed was observed to be growing in that well. It waxed and shot up, until at length a youth, whose heart was miraculously enlightened on the point, became aware of this growing plant, cut it down, drilled holes in it, and began to play upon it airs, similar to those performed by the dervish lovers of God, as he pastured his sheep in the neighbourhood.

By degrees, the various tribes of Arabs of the desert heard of this flute-playing of the shepherd, and its fame spread abroad. The camels and the sheep of the whole region would gather around him as he piped, ceasing to pasture that they might listen. From all directions, north and south, the nomads flocked to hear his strains, going into ecstasies with delight, weeping for joy and pleasure, breaking forth in transports of gratification.

The rumour at length reached the ears of the Prophet, who gave orders for the piper to be brought before him. When he began to play in the sacred presence, all the holy disciples of God's messenger were moved to tears and transports, bursting forth with shouts and exclamations of pure bliss, and losing all consciousness. The Prophet declared that the notes of the shepherd's flute were the interpretation of the holy mysteries he had confided in private to 'Alī's charge.[12]

Thus it is that, until a man acquire the sincere devotion of the linnet-voiced flute-reed, he cannot hear the mysteries of the Brethren of Sincerity in its dulcet notes, or realise the delights thereof; for "faith is altogether a yearning of the heart, and a gratification of the spiritual sense."

"To whom, alas, the pangs my love for thee
excites, to breathe?
My sighs, like 'Alī, I'll to some deep well's recess
bequeathe.
Perchance some reeds may spring therefrom, its
brink to overgrow;
Those reeds may moaning flutes become, and so
betray my woe.

Who hear will say: 'Be silent, flutes! We're not love's confidants;
To that sweet tyrant make excuse for us and for those plants!'"

80.

One of Jelāl's disciples possessed a slave girl of Roman origin, whom Jelāl had named Siddīqa (after Muhammed's virgin wife 'Ā'isha). Occasionally she had miraculous visions. She used to see aureolas of heavenly light, green, red, and *black*. Various of the angels used to visit her, and souls of the departed.

Her master was vexed at her being so favoured above himself. Once he was visited by Jelāl, and expressed his chagrin to him on the subject. Jelāl replied: "True! There is a heavenly light resides in the pupils of some eyes. These occasionally mislead a few with visions of beauteous form, with which they fall in love. Others they preserve in chastity, and lead them to their adored Maker. Others, again, they may lead to take delight in exterior objects, so as to cast their eyes on every pretty face they see, while the wife at home is curtained away from her husband. Thus, whenever God opens a way to any one, appearing to him, and showing him glimpses of the hidden world, he is apt to become entranced therewith, and to lose all power of further progress, saying to himself: 'How greatly in favour am I!' Others, in short, use every endeavour; but nothing is vouchsafed to them in visions, until they be favoured with a special sight of God Himself, and they be admitted to a near approach unto Him."

The girl's master was comforted, and bowed to his teacher, whose disciples then broke out into a holy service of psalmody and dancing.

81.

There was once a wise monk in the monastery of Plato, who was on very friendly terms with Jelāl's grandson 'Ārif. He was very aged, and used to be visited by the dervishes of his neighbourhood, to whom he was very polite, and towards whom he exhibited great confidence; so much so that, one day, some of them inquired of him how he had found Jelāl, and what he had thought of him.

The monk replied to them: "What do you know of him, as to who or what he was? I have seen signs and miracles without number worked by him. I became his devoted servant. I had read in the gospel and in the prophets the lives and the works of the saints of old, and I saw that he compassed them all. I therefore had faith in the truth of his reality.

"One day he came here, conferring on me the honour of a visit. For forty days he shut himself up in ecstatic seclusion. When at length he came forth from his privacy, I laid hold of his skirt, and said to him: 'God, in His holy scripture hath said (Qur'ān xix. 72): "And there is none of you but shall come to it (hell-fire)." Now, since it is incontestable that all shall come to the fire of hell, what preference is there in Islām over our faith?'

"For a little time he made no answer. At length, however, he made a sign towards the city, and went away in that direction. I followed after him leisurely. Near the city, we came to a bakehouse, the oven of which was being heated. He now took my black cassock, wrapped it in his own cloak, and threw the bundle into the oven. He then withdrew for a time into a corner, sunk in meditation.

"I saw a great smoke come out of the oven, such that no one had the power of utterance. After that, he said to me: 'Behold!' The baker withdrew the bundle from the oven, and assisted the saint to put on his cloak, which had become exquisitely clean; whereas my cassock was, as it were, branded and scorched, so as to fall in pieces. Then he said: 'Thus shall we enter therein, and thus shall you enter!'

"That selfsame moment I made my bow to him and became his disciple."

82.

The reason why the Mesnevī was written is related to have been the following:—

Husāmu-'d-Dīn learnt that several of the followers of Jelāl were fond of studying the Ilāhī-nāma of Sanā'ī, the Hakīm, and the Mantiqu-'t-Tayr of 'Attār, as also the Nasīb-nāma of the latter.

He therefore sought and found an opportunity to propose that Jelāl should indite something in the style of the Ilāhī-nāma, but in the metre of the Mantiqu-'t-Tayr; saying that the circle of friends would then willingly give up all other poetry, and study that alone.

Jelāl immediately produced a portion of the Mesnevī, saying that God had forewarned him of the wishes of the brethren, in consequence of which he had already begun to compose the work. That fragment consisted of the first eighteen couplets of the introductory verses:—

"From reed-flute hear what tale it tells,

What plaint it makes of absence' ills," &c.

It is of the metre *Remel*, hexameter contracted:

- ⏑ - - | - ⏑ - - | - ⏑ - ‖ - ⏑ - - | - ⏑ - - | - ⏑ - ‖

Jelāl frequently mentions Husām as the cause of the work's having been begun and continued. In the fourth book he addresses him in the opening couplet:—

"Of Truth, the light; of Faith, the sword; Husāmu-'d-Dīn aye be;

Above the lunar orb has clomb my Mesnevī, through thee."

And again the sixth book has for its opening verse the following apostrophe:—

"O thou, Husāmu-'d-Dīn, my heart's true life!
Zeal, for thy sake,
I feel springs up in me sixth book hereby to
undertake."

Often they spent whole nights at the task, Jelāl inditing, and Husām writing down his inspirations, chanting it aloud, as he wrote it, with his beautiful voice. Just as the first book was completed, Husām's wife died, and an interval ensued.

Two years thus passed without progress. Husām married again; and in that year, a.h. 662 (a.d. 1263), the second book was commenced. No other interval occurred until the work was brought to a conclusion. The third couplet of the second book mentions Husām in these terms—

"When thou, of Truth the light, Husāmu-'d-
Dīn, thy courser's rein
Didst turn, descending earthward from the
zenith's starry plain."

The third, fifth, and seventh books have similar addresses to Husām in their opening verses. His name is also mentioned cursorily in the third tale of the first book.

83.

On the death of Jelāl, a party of zealots went in a body to the Perwāna, explaining to him that the new practices of music and dancing, introduced by Jelāl, were innovations altogether contrary to the canonical institutes, and begging him to use his utmost endeavours to suppress them.

The Perwāna called on the learned Mufti of Qonya, Sheykh Sadru-'d-Dīn, and consulted him on the subject. The Mufti's answer was: "Do nothing of the kind. Listen not to such biased suggestions. There is an apostolical saying to this effect: 'A laudable innovation, introduced by a perfect follower of the prophets, is of the same nature with the customary practices of the prophets themselves.'" The Perwāna resolved, therefore, to do nothing towards suppressing Jelāl's institutions.

84.

A certain great man, who esteemed Jelāl, was nevertheless shocked that he should, with all his learning and piety, sanction the use of music and dancing.

He had occasion to visit Jelāl, who at once addressed him as follows:—"It is an axiom in the sacred canons that a Muslim, if hard pressed, and in danger of death, may eat of carrion and other forbidden food, so that the life of a man be not sacrificed. This rule is admitted and approved by all the authorities of the law. Now, we *men of God* are exactly in that position of extreme danger to our lives; and from that danger there is no escape, save by song, by music, and by the dance. Otherwise, through the awful majesty of the divine manifestations, the bodies of the saints would melt away as wax, and disappear like snow under the beams of a July sun."

The personage thus addressed was so struck with the earnestness of Jelāl's manner, and the cogency of his reasoning, that he became convinced, and thenceforward was a defender and upholder of Jelāl's institutions, so that these formed, as it were, the very nourishment of his heart. Many of the learned followed his example, and joined themselves to Jelāl's followers and disciples.

85.

Kālūmān and 'Aynu-'d-Devla were two Roman painters. They were unrivalled in their art of painting portraits and pictures. Both were disciples of Jelāl.

Kālūmān one day narrated that in Constantinople, on a certain tablet, the portraits of the Lady Meryem and of Jesus were painted, in such style as to be matchless. From all parts of the world artists came and tried their best; but none could produce the equal of those two portraits.

'Aynu-'d-Devla undertook, therefore, to journey to Constantinople, and see this picture. He made himself an inmate of the great church of Constantinople for a whole year, and served the priests thereof in various ways.

One night, then, he spied his opportunity, took the tablet under his arm, and absconded with it.

On reaching Qonya, he paid his respects to Jelāl, who inquired of him where he had been. He narrated to Jelāl all that had occurred with the tablet, which he exhibited.

Jelāl found the picture exceedingly beautiful, and gazed on it long with the utmost pleasure. He then spake as follows:—

"These two beautiful portraits complain of you, saying that you are not a faithful admirer of theirs, but are an untrue lover." The artist asked: "How?" Jelāl replied: "They say they are not supplied with food and rest. On the contrary, they are kept sleepless every night, and fasting every day. They complain: 'Aynu-'d-Devla leaves us, sleeps himself all night, and takes his meals by day, never remaining with us to do as we do!'"

The artist remarked: "Food and sleep are to them impossibilities. Neither have they speech, with which to say anything. They are mere lifeless effigies."

Jelāl now replied: "Thou art a living effigy. Thou hast acquired a knowledge of various arts. Thou art the handiwork of a limner whose hand has framed the universe, the human race, and all things on earth and in heaven. Is it right that thou forsake Him, and enamour thyself of an insignificant lifeless effigy? What profit is there in these portraits? What advantage can accrue to thee from them?"

Touched by these reproaches, the artist vowed repentance of his sin, and professed himself a Muslim.

86.

When the time of Jelāl's death drew near, he cautioned his disciples to have no fear or anxiety on that account; "for," said he, "as the spirit of Mansūr[13] appeared, a hundred and fifty years after his death, to the Sheykh Ferīdu-'d-Dīn 'Attār, and became the Sheykh's spiritual guide and teacher, so, too, do you always be with me, whatever may happen, and remember me, so that I may show myself to you, in whatever form that may be;—that I may always belong to you, and ever be shedding in your breasts the light of heavenly inspiration. I will simply remind you now that our dear Lord, Muhammed, the Apostle of God, said to his disciples: 'My life is a blessing unto you, and my death will be a blessing unto you. In my life I have guided you, and after my death I will send blessings on you.'"

Jelāl's friends shed tears all, and broke out into sighs and lamentations; but bowed their heads in reverence.

It is said that he gave directions to get ready his grave-clothes, and that his wife, Kirā Khātūn, began to wail, tearing her clothes, and exclaiming: "O thou light of the world, life of the human race; unto whom wilt thou commit us? Whither wilt thou go?"

He answered her: "Whither will I go? Verily, I shall not quit your circle." She then asked: "Will there be another like unto thee, our Lord? Will another become manifest?" He replied: "If there be, he will be I." After a while he added:

"While in the body, I have two attachments; one, to you; the other, to the flesh. When, by the grace of the unique Spirit, I become disembodied,—when the world of unbodied spirits, unity, and singleness, shall appear, my attachment to the flesh will become attachment to you, and I shall then have but one sole attachment."

87.

With his last breath Jelāl recommended to Husāmu-'d-Dīn to lay him in the upper part of his tomb, so that he might be the first to rise at the last day.

As he lay in his extreme sickness, there were earthquakes for seven days and nights, very severe, so that walls and houses were overthrown. On the seventh occasion, all his disciples were alarmed. He, however, calmly remarked: "Poor earth! it is eager for a fat morsel! It shall have one!"

He then gave his last instructions to his disciples, as follows:—"I recommend unto you the fear of God, in public and in private; abstemiousness in eating and in sleeping, as also in speaking; the avoidance of rebelliousness and of sin; constancy in fasting, continuous worship, and perpetual abstinence from fleshly lusts; long-suffering under the ill-treatment of all mankind; to shun the companionship of the light-minded and of the common herd; to associate with the righteous and with men of worth. For verily *'the best of mankind is he who benefiteth men,'*[14] and *'the best of speech is that which is short and to the purpose.'"*[15]

88.

The following is a prayer taught by Jelāl, on his deathbed, to one of his friends, to be used whenever affliction or care might weigh upon him:—

"O our Lord God, I breathe but for Thee, and I stretch forth my spirit towards Thee, that I may recite Thy doxologies abundantly, commemorating Thee frequently. O our Lord God, lay not on me an ailment that may make me forgetful to commemorate Thee, or lessen my yearning towards Thee, or cut off the delight I experience in reciting the litanies of Thy praise. Grant me not a health that may engender or increase in me presumptuous or thankless insolence. For Thy mercy's sake, O Thou Most-Merciful of the compassionate. Amen."

89.

A friend was seated by Jelāl's pillow, and Jelāl leaned on that friend's bosom. Suddenly a most handsome youth appeared at the door of the room, to the utmost astonishment of the friend.

Jelāl arose and advanced to receive the stranger. But the friend was quicker, and quietly asked his business. The stranger answered: "I am 'Azrā'īl, the angel of departure and separation. I am come, by the divine command, to inquire what commission the Master may have to intrust to me."

Blessed are the eyes that can perceive such sights!

The friend was near fainting at this answer. But he heard Jelāl call out: "Come in, come in, thou messenger of my King. Do that which thou art bidden; and, God willing, thou shalt find me one of the patient."

He now told his attendants to bring a vessel of water, placed his two feet therein, and occasionally sprinkled a little on his breast and forehead, saying: "My beloved (God) has proffered me a cup of poison (bitterness). From his hand I drink that poison with delight."

The singers and musicians now came in, and executed a hymn, while the whole company of friends wept, and sobbed loudly.

Jelāl observed:

"It is as my friends say. But, were they even to pull down the house, what use? See my panting heart; look at my delight. The sun sheds a grateful light on the moth. My friends invite me one way; my teacher Shemsu-'d-Dīn beckons me the other way. Comply ye with the summoner of the Lord, and have faith in Him. Departure is inevitable. All being came out of nothing, and again it will be shut up in the prison of nullity. Such is God's decree from all eternity; and, to decree belongeth unto God, the Most High, the All-Great!"

His son Sultan Veled had been unremitting in his attentions. He wept and sobbed. He was reduced to a shadow. Jelāl therefore said to him: "Bahā'u-'d-Dīn, my son, I am better. Go and lie down a little. Rest thyself, and sleep awhile!"

When he was gone, Jelāl indited his last ode; thus:—

"Go! head on pillow lay; alone, in peace, me leave,
Loved tyrant, plague by night, while all around thee grieve.
That peerless beauty (God) has no need kind care to show;
But, sallow lovers, ye must patient faith still know.
Perplexity is ours to bear; 'tis his to own hard heart;
Shed he our blood; what sin? He'll not pay murder's smart.
To die's hard, after all; but remedy there's none;
How, then, to crave a remedy? The evil's done.
Last night, in dream, a warder, from my love's abode,
Made sign to me, and said: 'This way! Hold thou my lode.'"

90.

It is related that, after his death, when laid on his bier, and while he was being washed by the hands of a loving and beloved disciple, while others poured the water for the ablution of Jelāl's body, not one drop was allowed to fall to the earth. All was caught by the fond ones around, as had been the case with the Prophet at his death. Every drop was drunk by them as the holiest and purest of waters.

As the washer folded Jelāl's arms over his breast, a tremor appeared to pass over the corpse, and the washer fell with his face on the lifeless breast, weeping. He felt his ear pulled by the dead saint's hand, as an admonition.

On this, he fainted away, and in his swoon he heard a cry from heaven, which said to him:

"Ho there! Verily the saints of the Lord have nothing to fear, neither shall they sorrow. Believers die not; they merely depart from one habitation to another abode!"

91.

When the corpse was brought forth, all the men, women, and children, who flocked to the funeral procession, smote their breasts, rent their garments, and uttered loud lamentations. These mourners were of all creeds, and of various nations; Jews and Christians, Turks, Romans, and Arabians were among them. Each recited sacred passages, according to their several usages, from the Law, the Psalms, or the Gospel.

The Muslims strove to drive away these strangers, with blows of fist, or staff, or sword. They would not be repelled. A great tumult was the result. The Sultan, the Heir-Apparent, and the Perwāna all flew to appease the strife, together with the chief Rabbis, the Bishops, Abbots, &c.

It was asked of these latter why they mixed themselves up with the funeral of an eminent Muslim sage and saint. They replied that they had learnt from him more of the mysteries shrouded in their scriptures, than they had ever known before; and had found in him all the signs and qualities of a prophet and saint, as set forth in those writings. They further declared: "If you Muslims hold him to have been the Muhammed of his age, we esteem him as the Moses, the David, the Jesus of our time; and we are his disciples, his adherents."

The Muslim leaders could make no answer. And so, in all honour, with every possible demonstration of love and respect, was he borne along, and at length laid in his grave.

He had died as the sun went down, on Sunday, the fifth of the month Jumāda-l-ākhir, a.h. 672 (16th December a.d. 1273); being thus sixty-eight (lunar) years (sixty-six solar years) of age.

92.

Sultan Veled is reported to have related that, shortly after the death of his father, Jelāl, he was sitting with his step-mother, Jelāl's widow, Kirā Khātūn, and Husāmu-'d-Dīn, when his step-mother saw the spirit of the departed saint, winged as a seraph, poised over his, Sultan Veled's, head, to watch over him.

93.

Jelāl had a female disciple, a saint, named Nizāma Khātūn, an intimate friend of his wife's.

Nizāma formed the design to give a spiritual party to Jelāl, with an entertainment for his disciples. She possessed nothing but a Thevr (*or* Sevr)[16] veil, which she had destined to be her own winding-sheet.

She now ordered her servants to sell this veil, and so procure the necessaries for the projected feast. But, that same morning, Jelāl came to her house with his disciples, and, addressing her, said: "Nizāma Khātūn, sell not thy veil; to thee it is a piece of necessary furniture. Lo! we are come to thy entertainment."

He and his disciples remained with her, engaged in spiritual exercises, three whole days and nights.

94.

After Jelāl's death, Kīgātū Khān, a Mogul general, came up against Qonya, intending to sack the city and massacre the inhabitants. (He was emperor from a.h. 690 to 696, a.d. 1290-1294.)

That night, in a dream, he saw Jelāl, who seized him by the throat, and nearly choked him, saying to him: "Qonya is mine. What seekest thou from its people?"

On awaking from his dream, he fell on his knees and prayed for mercy, seeking also for information as to what that portent might signify. He sent in an ambassador to beg permission for him to enter the city as a friendly guest.

When he arrived at the palace, the nobles of Qonya flocked to his court with rich offerings. All being seated in solemn conclave, Kīgātū was suddenly seized with a violent tremor, and asked one of the princes of the city, who was seated on a sofa by himself: "Who may the personage be that is sitting at your side on your sofa?" The prince looked about, right and left; but saw no one. He replied accordingly. Kīgātū answered: "What? How sayest thou? I see by thy side, seated, a tall man with a grisly beard and a sallow complexion, a grey turban, and an Indian plaid over his chest, who looks at me most pryingly."

The prince sagaciously suspected forthwith that Jelāl's shade was there present by his side, and made answer: "The sacred eyes of majesty alone are privileged to witness that vision. It is the son of Bahā'u-'d-Dīn of Balkh, our Lord Jelālu-'d-Dīn, who is entombed in this land."

The Khān replied: "Last night I saw him in my dream. He went nigh choking me, and told me Qonya is his possession. Now, prince, thee I call my adoptive father; and I entirely forego my intention to devastate this city. Tell me; has that holy man any son or descendant alive here?"

The prince told him of Bahā Veled, now Sheykh of the city, and the peerless saint of God. Kīgātū expressed the wish to go and visit the Sheykh. The prince conducted him and his suite of nobles to Sultan Veled. They all declared themselves his disciples, and assumed the dervish turban. Bahā recounted to the Khān the history of his grandfather's expulsion from Balkh, and of all that followed. The Khān offered him royal presents, and accompanied him on a visit of reverence to the shrine of the deceased saint.

---

1. The truly eminent author of the Mesnevī.
2. From the city of Sarakhs in Khurāsān.
3. Had Dr. Tanner, the forty days' faster at New York, heard of these performances?
4. As related of certain Sabbath-breaking Jews, in Qur'ān ii. 61
5. Qur'ān xviii. 8, &c.
6. The mount where the victims are slaughtered by the pilgrims.
7. The great Persian poet Khāqānī, born at Shirwān, died and was buried at Tebrīz a.h. 582 (a.d. 1186).
8. Sanā'ī, of Gazna in Afgānistān, surnamed "the Wise," or "the Philosopher," died and was buried at the place of his birth, a.h. 576 (a.d. 1180).
9. "*Satan, the Lapidated One,*" is the chief title of the accursed one. Muslims believe that the "shooting stars" are missiles cast by angels at demons who attempt to approach heaven for eavesdropping purposes.
10. I have not met with an explanation of this word in any Persian dictionary. Literally it signifies *sugar-hanging*. In the Bahāri-'Ajem alone is it mentioned, with a distich from Hāfiz; but it is left unexplained.
11. Apparently a "*merman*" is intended.
12. This is a much more poetical account of the origin of the reed-flute than the pagan Greek myths of Orpheus and his lyre, Pan and his pipe, for which no reasons are assigned.
13. Mansūr, son of 'Ammār, thus mentioned by D'Herbelot: "Scheikh des plus considérés parmi les Musulmans. On le cite au sujet d'un passage du chapitre Enfathar de l'Alcoran (lxxxii.), où Dieu est in-

troduit faisant ce reproche aux hommes: *Qu'est-ce qui vous rend si orgueilleux contre votre maître qui vous fait tant de biens?* (v. 6). Ce Scheikh disait: Quand Dieu me fera ce reproche, je lui repondrai: *Le sont ces biens et ces graces mêmes que vous me faites, qui me rendent si superbe."* As Sheykh 'Attār lived about a.h. 600, Mansūr must have died about a.h. 400 (a.d. 1020). He is mentioned in No. 51, p. 68, of the *Nafahātu-'l-Uns.*

14. Khayru 'n nāsi, men yenfa'u 'n nāsa.—*Arabic Proverb.*
15. Khayru 'l kelāmi, qasīruhu 'l mufīdu.—*Arabic Proverb.*
16. *Thevr* is the name of a tribe of Arabians, and of two hills, one at Mekka, the other at Medīna; but the explanation of the term *"a Thevr* or *Sevr veil"* I have not met with.

CHAPTER IV.

SHEMSU-'D-DĪN TEBRĪZĪ, MUHAMMED SON OF 'ALĪ SON OF MELIK-DĀD.

1.

Shemsu-'d-Dīn of Tebrīz was surnamed the Sultan of Mendicants, the Mystery of God upon earth, the Perfect in word and deed. Some had styled him the Flier, because he travelled about so much; and others spoke of him as the Perfect One of Tebrīz.

He went about seeking for instruction, human and spiritual. He had visited many of the chief spiritual teachers of the world; but he had found none equal to himself. The teachers of all lands became, therefore, pupils and disciples to him.

He was always in quest of the beloved object of the soul (God). His corporeal frame he habited in coarsest felt, shrouding his eminent greatness from all eyes in what are really the jewelled robes of spirituality.

At Damascus it was, where he was then studying, that he first saw Jelālu-'d-Dīn by chance in a crowded market-place; but Jelāl, who was at that time a student also, avoided him.

Ultimately, he was led to Qonya in Jelāl's traces, and first arrived there at dawn, on Saturday, the twenty-sixth of Jumāda-'l-ākhir, a.h. 642 (28th November, a.d. 1244), Jelāl being then professor at four colleges there. They met as is related in a former chapter (chap. iii. Nos. 8, 9).

At the end of three months' seclusion together, passed in religious, scientific, and spiritual disquisitions and investigations, Shemsu-'d-Dīn became satisfied that he had never met Jelāl's equal.

2.

When Shemsu-'d-Dīn was quite worn out by a series of divine manifestations and the consequent ecstasies, he used to break away, hide himself, and work as a day-labourer at the water-wheels of the Damascus gardens, until his equanimity would be restored. Then he would return to his studies and meditations.

In his supplications to God, he was constantly inquiring whether there was not in either world, corporeal and spiritual, one other saint who could bear him company. In answer thereto, there came at length from the unseen world the answer, that the one holy man of the whole universe who could bear him company was the Lord Jelālu-'d-Dīn of Rome.

On receiving this answer, he set out at once from Damascus, and went in quest of his object to the land of Rome (Asia Minor).

3.

Chelebī Emīr 'Ārif related that his father, Sultan Veled, told him that one day, as a trial and test, Shemsu-'d-Dīn requested Jelāl to make him a present of a slave. Jelāl instantly went and fetched his own wife, Kirā Khātūn, who was as extremely beautiful as virtuous and saintlike, offering her to him.

To this act of renunciation Shemsu-'d-Dīn replied: "She is my most esteemed sister. What I want is a youth to wait on me." Jelāl thereupon produced his own son, Sultan Veled, who, he said, would be proud to carry the shoes of Shems, placing them before him for use when required for a walk abroad. Again Shems objected:

"He is as my son. But, perhaps, you will supply me with some wine. I am accustomed to drink it, and am not comfortable without it."

Jelāl now took a pitcher, went himself to the Jews' ward of the city, and returned with it full of wine, which he set before Shems.

"I now saw," continued Sultan Veled in his recital, "that Shemsu-'d-Dīn, uttering an intense cry, rent his garment, bowed down to Jelāl's feet, lost in wondering admiration at this implicit compliance with the behests of a teacher, and then said: 'By the truth of the First, who had no beginning, the Last, who will have no end, there never has been, from the commencement of creation, and there never, until the end of time, will be, in the universe of substance, a lord and master, heart-captivating and Muhammed-like, as thou art.'"

He now bowed down again, declared himself a disciple to Jelāl, and added: "I have tested and tried to the utmost the patient long-suffering of our Lord; and I have found his greatness of heart to be totally unlimited by any bounds."

4.

Jelāl is reported to have said: "When Shemsu-'d-Dīn first came, and I felt a mighty spark of love for him lighted up in my heart, he took upon himself to command me in the most despotic and peremptory manner.

"'Study,' said he, 'the writings of thy father.' For a while I studied nothing else. 'Keep silent, and speak to no one.' I ceased from all intercourse with my fellows.

"My words were, however, the food of my disciples; my thoughts were the nectar of my pupils. They hungered and thirsted. Thence, ill feelings were engendered amongst them, and a blight fell upon my teacher.

"He came to me another day as I was, by his command, studying the writings of my father. Thrice he called out to me: 'Study them not.' From his sacred features the effulgence of spiritual wisdom streamed. I laid down the book, and never since have I opened it."

5.

Jelāl is said to have related that Shemsu-'d-Dīn forbade him to study any more the writings of his father, Bahā Veled, and that he punctually obeyed the injunction.

But one night he dreamt that he was in company with a number of friends, who were all studying and discussing with him those very writings of Bahā Veled.

As he woke from his dream, Shems was entering the room with a severe look. Addressing Jelāl, he asked: "How hast thou dared to study that book again?" Jelāl protested that, since his prohibition, he had never once opened his father's works.

"Yes," retorted Shems, "there is a study by reading, and there is also a study by contemplating. Dreams are but the shadows of our waking thoughts. Hadst thou not occupied thy thoughts with those writings, thou wouldst not have dreamt about them."

"From that time forward," remarked Jelāl, "I never again busied myself with my father's writings, so long as Shemsu-'d-Dīn remained alive."

6.

Jelāl is related to have informed his disciples that Shemsu-'d-Dīn was a scholar in every science known to man, and also a great alchemist; but that he had renounced them all, to devote himself to the study and contemplation of the mysteries of divine love.

7.

Shemsu-'d-Dīn was one day sitting with his disciples, when the public executioner passed by. Shems remarked to those around him: "There goes one of God's saints."

The disciples knew the man, and told Shems that he was the common headsman. Shems replied:

"True! In the exercise of his calling, he put to death a man of God, whose soul he thus released from the bondage of the body. As a recompense for this kind act of his, the saint bequeathed to him his own saintship."

On the following day the executioner relinquished his office, vowed repentance, came to Shemsu-'d-Dīn, made his bow, and professed himself a disciple.

8.

Sheykh Husāmu-'d-Dīn was originally a young man who showed great respect and humility towards Shemsu-'d-Dīn, to whom he rendered services of every kind.

One day Shems said to him: "Husām, this is not the way. Religion is a question of money. Give me some coin, and offer your services to the Lord; so, peradventure, thou mayest rise in our order."

Husām at once went forth to his own house, collected all his own valuables and money, with his wife's jewels, and all the provisions of the house, brought them to Shems, and laid them at his feet. He furthermore sold a vineyard and country-seat he possessed, bringing their price also to his teacher, and thanking him for having taught him a duty, as also for having deigned to accept so insignificant a trifle from his hand.

"Yes, Husām," said Shems, "it is to be hoped that, with God's grace, and the prayers of the saints, thou wilt henceforth attain to such a station, as to be the envy of the most perfect men of God, and be bowed down to by the *Brethren of Sincerity*. It is true that God's saints are not in want of anything, being independent of both worlds. But, at the outset, there is no other way to test the sincerity of one we love, and the affection of a friend, than to call upon him to sacrifice his worldly possessions. The next step is, to summon him to give up all that is not his God. No disciple who wishes to rise, has ever made progress by following his own devices. Advancement is earned by rendering service, and by spending in God's cause. Every pupil who sacrifices possessions at the call of his teacher, would also lay down his life, if needs were. No lover of God can retain both mammon and religion."

Shems then restored to Husām the whole of his goods, keeping back only one piece of silver. Nine times as much more did he bestow upon Husām from first to last; and, as the results of all things are in God's hands, so did Husām at length become the ruler of God's saints, and Jelāl made him the keeper of God's treasury. He it was who wrote down the twenty-four thousand six hundred and sixty couplets contained in the six books of the Mesnevī.

9.

Shemsu-'d-Dīn left Qonya, at the end of his first visit, on Thursday, the twenty-first day of the month of Shawwal, a.h. 643 (14th March, a.d. 1246), after a stay of about sixteen months.

He returned to Damascus; and his departure left Jelāl in a state of great uneasiness and excitement. (Compare a conflicting date given in No. 13, further on.)

10.

Shemsu-'d-Dīn was one day at Bagdād, and entered one of the palaces there. A eunuch who saw him enter, without being himself visible, made a sign to a slave to go and drive away the mendicant.

The slave drew his sword, and raised it to strike; but his arm withered, and fell palsied.

The eunuch then motioned to another slave to execute the commission; and he, too, became similarly incapacitated.

Shems then went away of himself, and none dared to pursue him. Two days later, the eunuch died also.

11.

Jelāl's father, Bahā Veled, had a disciple, who, for some reason, gave offence to Shemsu-'d-Dīn; the latter, in punishment, inflicted a deafness on both the disciple's ears.

After a time, Shems pardoned the offender, and restored his hearing. But the man bore him a grudge in his heart, nevertheless. One day, Shems said to him: "Friend, I have pardoned thee; wherefore art thou still cast down? Be comforted." Notwithstanding this, his rancour remained.

One day, however, he met Shems in the midst of a market. Suddenly, he felt a new faith glow within him, and he shouted out: "There is no god save God; Shemsu-'d-Dīn is the apostle of God."

The market-people, on this, raised a great hubbub, and wished to kill him. One of them came forward to cut him down; but Shems uttered so terrific a shout, that the man at once fell down dead. The rest of the market-people bowed, and submitted.

Shems now took the disciple by the hand, and led him away, remarking to him: "My good friend, my name is Muhammed. Thou shouldest have shouted: 'Muhammed is the apostle of God.' The rabble will not take gold that is not coined."

12.

One beautiful moonlight night, Jelāl and Shems were together on the terraced roof of the college, and all the inhabitants of Qonya were sleeping on their housetops.

Shems remarked: "See all these poor creatures! They are dead to every sense of their Creator on this beautiful night of God's decree. Wilt thou not, Jelāl, of thy infinite compassion, wake them up, and let them gain a share in the shower of blessings of this night?"

Thus appealed to, Jelāl faced toward Mekka, and offered up this prayer to God: "O Thou Lord of heaven, and of earth, for the love of Thy servant Shemsu-'d-Dīn, vouchsafe wakefulness to this people."

Immediately a black cloud gathered from the unseen world. Thunders and lightnings burst forth; and so heavy a rain fell, that all the sleepers, catching up what clothing they could find, quickly took refuge in their houses below. Shems smiled at the saintly joke, and was greatly amused.

When daylight dawned, the disciples gathered round, numerous as the raindrops of that shower; and Shems related to them the story, with the following remarks:—

"Hitherto, all the prophets and saints have ever sought to hide from vulgar eyes the miraculous powers they have possessed, so that none should be aware of the fact. But now, our Lord and Master, Jelāl, has been so successful in secretly following up the path of mystic love, that his miraculous powers have hitherto escaped the searching eyes of even the chiefest of God's elect, even as it hath been said: 'Verily, God hath saints of whom no man knoweth.'"

13.

Kimiyā Khātūn, the wife of Shemsu-'d-Dīn, was a very beautiful, and also a very virtuous, woman. One day, however, it so happened that, without his permission or knowledge, the grandmother of Sultan Veled, and her attendant ladies, took Kimiyā with them for an outing to the vineyards of the city.

As chance would have it, Shems came home while she was still away. He asked for her, and was informed where she had gone, and with whom. He was exceedingly annoyed at her absence.

Kimiyā had scarcely returned home, ere she began to feel unwell. Her limbs stiffened like dry firewood, and became motionless. She continued screaming and moaning for three days, and then gave up the ghost, in the month of Sha'bān, a.h. 644. (December, a.d. 1246. But compare a conflicting date given in No. 9, further back.)

14.

It is related that, a second time, Shems and Jelāl shut themselves up for a whole six months in Jelāl's room at the college, without partaking of meat or drink, and with out the entrance of a single individual to interrupt them, or either of them coming forth, Sultan Veled and one other disciple alone excepted.

15.

Shemsu-'d-Dīn was extremely bitter in his preachings and lectures to the learned auditory who used to gather around him in Qonya. He likened them to oxen and asses. He reproached them with being further than ever astray from the path of living love, and taxed them with the presumption of supposing themselves the equals of Bāyezīd of Bestām.

He once went to Erzen-of-Rome (Erzrūm), the prince of which city had a son so extremely stupid, though very handsome, that he could be taught nothing, or next thereto.

Shems let no one know who or what he was; but opened a school for children. Inquiries were made by the prince, and Shems undertook to instruct the child, and enable him, in one month, to recite the whole Qur'ān by heart.

He kept his promise. The young prince acquired, further, during the same period, a beautiful handwriting, and sundry other accomplishments.

It began to be suspected, now, that he was a saint in disguise. He therefore quietly slipped away from that city.

16.

There is a tradition that Jelāl one day called his son Sultan Veled, gave him a large sum of money, and bade him go, with a suite of the disciples, to Damascus, and request Shems to return to Qonya.

Jelāl told his son that he would find Shems in a certain inn, playing at backgammon with a young Firengī (European, Frank), also one of God's saints. Sultan Veled went, found Shems exactly so occupied, and brought him back to Qonya, the Firengī youth returning to his own country, there to preach Jelāl's doctrines, as his vicar.

Sultan Veled walked the whole way from Damascus to Qonya, at the stirrup-side of Shems, as a groom walks by the side of a prince's charger. The whole city went forth to receive them. Jelāl and Shems embraced each other. Jelāl became more than ever devoted to his friend; and his disciples resented his neglect of them, as they had done before. Not long afterwards, the dolorous event occurred that terminated the life of Shemsu-'d-Dīn.

17.

The Vazīr of Qonya had built a college. On its completion, he gave a great entertainment, in the college, of religious music and dancing, all the learned men of the city being present.

The Qur'ān was first recited in its entirety; after which, the holy waltzing began. The Vazīr and Shemsu-'d-Dīn both joined in the dance. Several times they came into collision; or, the Vazīr's skirt swept against Shems's person, as he observed no caution in his gyrations.

Jelāl expressed great indignation at this want of courtesy and reverence for his guest and friend. He took Shems by the hand, to lead him away. The grandees present essayed to appease him, but their entreaties were of no avail. The police of the Sultan were therefore sent for; and when they arrived, they instantly seized Shems, led him forth a prisoner with every mark of indignity, and put him to death without further inquiry or formality.

18.

Chelebī Emīr 'Ārif related, as informed by his mother, Fātima Khātūn, that when Shemsu-'d-Dīn was thus made a martyr, his executioners threw his corpse down a well.

Sultan Veled saw Shems in a dream, and was informed by him where the body would be found. Sultan Veled went therefore at midnight with some friends, recovered the corpse, washed it, and privately buried it in the college grounds, by the side of the founder.

19.

Forty days after the disappearance of Shemsu-'d-Dīn, Jelāl, wishing to appease his own sorrow, and quell the mutinous spirit that had broken out among the disciples, appointed Husāmu-'d-Dīn his local deputy, and set out to seek Shems at Damascus for the third time. All the learned men of Syria became his disciples, and he was absent about a year, more or less.

The Sultan and the nobles grew impatient at this long absence, and wrote him an urgent petition, begging him to return to Qonya. With this request he complied.

Naturally, he had failed to find Shemsu-'d-Dīn in the flesh at Damascus; but he had found within himself what was still greater. He went to the lodging of Shems, and wrote on the door, with red ink: "This is the station of the beloved one of Elias, on whom be peace!"

It is said that the body of Shemsu-'d-Dīn disappeared, and that he was buried by the side of Jelāl's father, Sultan Bahā Veled the Elder.

CHAPTER V.

SHEYKH SALĀHU-'D-DĪN FERĪDŪN, SURNAMED ZER-KŪB (GOLDBEATER).

1.

Sheykh Salāhu-'d-Dīn[1] was originally a fellow-disciple with Jelāl, as pupils to Seyyid Burhānu-'d-Dīn. He afterwards became a goldbeater, as his parents were poor.

After a while, when Jelāl's reputation became great, Salāh went and paid him his respects. Jelāl knew how highly Burhān had esteemed Salāh, when his pupil. He therefore received him in a very friendly manner, and their intercourse became warmly renewed.

One day, after the murder of Shemsu-'d-Dīn, and the return of Jelāl from Damascus, he sent for Salāh, and appointed him his own assistant in the government and instruction of the disciples, presenting him also to the king in that capacity.

2.

Jelāl's first royal protector, 'Alā'u-'d-Dīn Keyqubād, was now dead, and his son, Gayāsu-'d-Dīn Key-Khusrev, reigned in his stead.

The monarch one day made a feast in the vineyards, and went forth into the fields for a walk, alone. He picked up a young snake, carried it indoors, placed it in a gold box, sealed this up, and then rejoined his courtiers.

To those attendants the king exhibited the sealed packet, as having just then been privately received from the Qaysar[2] of Constantinople with a message to this effect: "If your religion of Islām be the true faith, some one of your wise men will be able to see into this packet without breaking its seals, and to tell what it contains."

The king then called upon his ministers to prove their loyalty to him, and their faithfulness to their religion, by solving this riddle. None of them was able.

The packet was now sent round in succession to all the eminent teachers and theologians of the city; but none could unravel the enigma.

At last it was brought to Jelāl, as Sheykh Ferīdūn and he were sitting together. Jelāl invited Ferīdūn to tell them the contents of the packet; and he immediately replied: "It is not a dignified act in the king to imprison a young snake in a gold box, sealing this up as a packet, and then tempting his courtiers, ministers, and learned men with a false pretence. A saint, however, knows not only the solution of so paltry a trick as this, but is also aware of every thought in the king's heart, and every secret of earth and heaven."

When this answer was reported to the king, he came to the college, and professed himself a disciple, remarking:

"If the disciples of Shemsu-'d-Dīn possess such power, and work such miracles, how great must have been the sanctity of the murdered martyr."

Ferīdūn acted for ten years as assistant to Jelāl.

3.

Fātima, the daughter of Sheykh Salāhu-'d-Dīn Ferīdūn, was married to Sultan Veled, Jelāl's son. Jelāl used to teach her to read the Qur'ān and other books.

Jelāl used to call Fātima his *right eye*; her sister Hediyya, his *left eye*; and their mother, Latīfa Khātūn, *the personification of God's grace.*

When Fātima's marriage was solemnised, all the angels of heaven were present, and wished the young couple all happiness.

She was a saint, and continually worked miracles. She fasted by day and watched by night, tasting food only once in three days. She was very charitable to the poor, the orphans, and the widows, distributing to them food and raiment.

Sheykh Ferīdūn died on New Year's Day, a.h. 657 (28th December, a.d. 1258).

---

1. Saladin of European writings. The words mean: *the Fitness of the Religion* (of Islām).
2. The Muslim world knows but one *Qaysar* (Cæsar), the Emperor of Rome (Old or New), which title is now borne by the Emperor of Austria.

CHAPTER VI.

CHELEBĪ HUSĀMU-'L-HAQQI-WA-'D-DĪN, HASAN, SON OF MUHAMMED, SON OF HASAN, SON OF AKHĪ-TURK, RELATED TO ESH-SHEYKHU-'L-MUKERREM.

1.

On the death of Sheykh Ferīdūn[1], Chelebī Husāmu-'d-Dīn was appointed by Jelāl his assistant in place of the deceased saint. For another ten years these two spiritual friends worked together in perfect unity as Superior and Assistant. Husām was surnamed "the Juneyd and the Bāyezīd[2] of the age," "the Key of the Treasuries of God's throne," "the Trustee of the Treasures on earth," and "God's next Friend in the World."

2.

Husām once made his obeisance to Jelāl, and related to him that, when the disciples recited the poetry of the Mesnevī, and became entranced, he had himself seen a company of invisible ones, armed with clubs and scimitars, keeping guard over them. If any one did not listen to those sacred words with reverence and believing, the clubs and swords were brought into play, and he was hurled into the pit of hell-fire. Jelāl confirmed, as being a fact, all Husām had related.

3.

Husāmu-'d-Dīn was very eloquent, pious, and God-fearing. He would never use the water, even, of the college, for drink or for ablutions; but always brought his water from his own home for those purposes. He distributed, to the very last farthing, the whole of the revenues of the college among the disciples.

4.

Sultan Veled and his friends went one day to Husām's garden. Some of the disciples felt a desire to eat of some honey, but had said nothing on the subject. Husām read their thoughts. He therefore ordered his gardener to bring some new honeycomb from a certain hive. More, and more, and still more comb was brought, until all were satisfied; still, the hive was yet full. When they left his garden, Husām sent the hive with them; and for a long time it supplied all their wants.

5.

A severe drought afflicted Qonya and its environs. Prayers for rain were publicly offered without avail.

Recourse was now had to Husāmu-'d-Dīn, who was begged to intercede for the people, and to pray for rain.

He first went to Jelāl's tomb, there performed his devotions to God, and then put up the prayer for rain, his disciples weeping as they chanted "Amen."

Clouds now began to collect and lower; shortly after which an abundance of rain was vouchsafed.

6.

Not only were all the revenues of the college, arising from its endowments, committed by Jelāl to the sole administration of Husām, but, whatever gifts and contributions were offered by princes and friends, in money or in kind, they were all consigned to his care, to augment the resources of the general fund. Jelāl's family, and also his son, though often pinched, fared as the disciples.

7.

The disciples were both surprised and scandalised, at one time, by Husām's publicly speaking very much in praise of certain individuals who bore an extremely bad character, while he disparaged certain others who were noted for their pious lives.

They complained to Jelāl; but he confirmed what Husām had said, and remarked to them: "God looks only to man's heart. Those seemingly lewd fellows are really God-loving saints, while those outwardly pious livers are merely inward hypocrites."

8.

One day Husām was lecturing. Suddenly he beckoned to one of the disciples, and told him to go with all speed to the royal palace, ask to see the queen, give her his greeting, and say to her: "Instantly quit this apartment thou art in, if thou wouldest avoid impending destruction, the result of God's decree."

The queen believed his word, and at once removed to another part of the palace. The apartment was speedily stripped of its furniture; and scarcely had the last loads been removed, when, with a loud crash, the building fell in. Her faith in his miraculous power was thenceforward increased a hundredfold.

9.

A certain Sheykh died at Qonya, who was rector of two different colleges. The prince who was the trustee of both, elected to nominate Husāmu-'d-Dīn as rector of one of them; and a great entertainment was prepared by the prince for the occasion.

Jelāl was informed of the arrangement, and he expressed the intention to bear himself Husām's carpet to his new college, and himself spreading it for Husām in his new seat.

A certain brawler, a kinsman of Husām's, Akhī Ahmed by name, was of the company; and he had felt nettled at Husām's appointment. He came forward, snatched away Husām's carpet, gave it to one of his companions to cast out of the building, and exclaimed: "We will not suffer this fellow to be installed here as Sheykh."

Great confusion ensued. Several nobles of the Akhī clan, who were present, drew their swords and knives, a scene of blood appearing to be about to commence.

Jelāl now addressed the crowd, reproaching them for such behaviour. He told them that their family and college would not prosper, but that the Mevlevī order, founded by himself, and his lineal posterity would go on ever steadily increasing. He then related the following anecdote:—

"A certain Sheykh from Samarqand, Abū-'l-Lays by name, went on his travels for about twenty years, with a view to study, partly at Mekka. At length he set out on his return home, whither his reputation, as well as numerous disciples, had preceded him.

"Arrived at the outskirts of his native place, he went to the riverside to perform an ablution. There he found a number of women, occupied with laundry work. From among these, one old woman advanced, looked at him attentively, and then exclaimed: 'Why, if here isn't our little Abū-'l-Lays come back again! Go quickly, girls, and carry the news to our family.'

"The Sheykh returned forthwith to his party of fellow-travellers, and gave orders for their beasts to be at once reloaded for an immediate return to Damascus. On being questioned as to his reason for this sudden change of intention he answered: 'My people still think of me as *"little Abū-l-Lays,"* and will treat me with familiar indignity accordingly, esteeming me of small account, and thereby committing a grievous sin; for it is an incumbent duty on all to honour the learned and the wise. To respect them is to show reverence to the apostle of God, and to revere him is to serve the Creator.'

"Now, the truth was that, when a child, his father had always called him 'little Abū-'l-Lays.' But strangers would not so understand that term of endearment; they would think it one of too free and easy familiarity, and as likely to draw down on the city and its inhabitants the divine displeasure. It was not consistent with true affection to allow the possibility of such a visitation to occur."

Having delivered himself of this constructive reprimand, Jelāl left the college barefoot, and in high dudgeon. The chief people came after him to intercede, but he would not be pacified. Their intervention was declined, and he refused to be reconciled with the broiler, Akhī Ahmed. He would not consent to go near that offender, who died soon afterwards; though most of his sons, relatives, and even his fellow-revellers, became disciples of Jelāl's.

The Sultan would have caused him to be put to death at once; but Jelāl would not permit that.

Akhī Ahmed was never again allowed to show himself at any public reception, and was shunned by all, like the wandering Jew.

Eventually, Husāmu-'d-Dīn was appointed rector of both the colleges in question; and Ahmed's son, Akhī 'Alī, was a disciple of Sultan Veled.

10.

Jelālu-'d-Dīn was of the school of Abū-Hanīfa; but Husām belonged to that of Shāfi'ī.[3] He thought of joining the Hanefī school, out of deference to his teacher. Jelāl, however, recommended him to remain what he had always been, and to strive to inculcate to all the doctrine of divine love, as set forth by Jelāl.

11.

After Jelāl's death, his widow, Kirā Khātūn, suggested to her stepson, Sultan Veled Bahā'u-'d-Dīn, that he ought to have succeeded his father as Rector of the fraternity, and not Husām.

Sultan Veled answered that it had been his father's bequest that Husām should succeed, that he himself had sworn the oath of fealty to Husām, and that Husām was now become a kind of spiritual beehive, through the incessant and multitudinous visitations of angelic ministers sent to him with messages from on high.

12.

Husāmu-'d-Dīn had a gardener, whose name was Sheykh Muhammed. About four years after Jelāl's death, Husām had reason to reprimand the gardener, who took offence at this, and went away to another garden, resolved never to return to Husām's service.

As he sat reflecting, he fell asleep. In his dreams he saw Jelāl coming towards him, with an executioner by his side, who held up an axe. Jelāl ordered the executioner to cut off Muhammed's head, as the punishment for his having offended Husām.

This was done; and Muhammed saw his own head fall off, and his own blood flow. He knew that he was dead.

After a while he saw Jelāl return, pick up Muhammed's decapitated head, place it in proper junction with the neck of the corpse, and utter the exclamation: "In the name of God, with God, from God, and to God." Muhammed saw himself instantly alive again, felt very penitent, threw himself at Jelāl's feet, and cried out piteously.

He now awoke and arose. No one was in sight. All traces of blood had vanished, and no sign of a wound was discernible on his neck. In all speed he returned to Husām's garden, and resumed his work with alacrity.

But now he saw Husām approaching, who said to him:

"Well, Sheykh Muhammed! Until Jelālu-'d-Dīn chastised thee, thou wert no Muslim, and wert given over to stiff-neckedness. Had not I interceded for thee, thou hadst been dead to all eternity, shut out from every hope of heaven."

Muhammed protested his sincere repentance, became a dervish, and professed himself a disciple.

13.

When Husāmu-'d-Dīn had faithfully executed for ten years, as a just and wise steward, all his duties as successor to Jelālu-'d-Dīn, he one day went, with his companions and disciples, to visit the shrine of his predecessor.

As he drew near to the mausoleum, information was brought to him that the gilt crescent surmounting the cupola had fallen down.

On the moment, Husām felt himself to be stricken. He asked for an examination of dates to be made, and found that ten years previously Jelāl had departed this life. He therefore said to those around him: "Lead me back home. The time for my dissolution is at hand."

He was conducted to his chamber, where, a few days later, on Thursday, the twenty-second of Sha'bān, in the year a.h. 683 (4th November, a.d. 1284), he breathed his last exactly at the time when the gilt crescent was replaced over Jelāl's tomb, and the works brought to a close.

14.

Shortly after the death of Husāmu-'d-Dīn, the widow of Jelāl, Kirā Khātūn, too, departed this life, and was buried by the side of her husband.

As her corpse was being borne towards its last resting-place, the procession passed through one of the gates of the town. Here, the bearers found themselves arrested by some unseen power, so that they could not move, hand or foot. This singular effect lasted for about half an hour.

Her stepson, Sultan Veled, with the other mourners, struck up a hymn, and commenced a holy dance. Soon after this, the bearers recovered the use of their limbs, and found themselves able to proceed. All now went well, and the interment was completed.

That same night, a holy man of the fraternity saw Kirā Khātūn in heaven near to her husband.[4] He inquired of her concerning the arrestation of the funeral. She informed him thus: "The day previous, a man and a woman had been stoned to death at that gate for the sin of adultery. I took compassion on them, interceded for their forgiveness, and obtained for them admittance to paradise. My preoccupation in their cause was the reason of the delay met with by the funeral procession."

15.

One day, while Jelāl was yet living, Satan appeared in person to Husāmu-'d-Dīn, and complained bitterly of the torments inflicted on him by the continuous pious exercises of Jelāl. He said that such was his deep reverence for Jelāl and his followers, that he dared not attempt to seduce one of them; and that, had he known that, of the seed of Adam, so holy a race of men were to spring, he never would have tempted the father of mankind. He further added: "I entertain a hope that the kindness of heart of his sons will lead them to intercede with Jelāl for me, and so obtain my eventual release and salvation."

Husām related this occurrence to Jelāl, who smiled, and said: "There is reason to hope that he need not despair. God forbid that he should despair!"

16.

Whenever the grandees of Qonya entertained a desire to have an audience of the Sheykh Shemsu-'d-Dīn of Tebrīz, during his lifetime, they used to request Husām to beg Jelāl to intercede for them with Shems, and so obtain for them the desired interview.

Jelāl and Husām used to tax those nobles for this favour, according to their means and circumstances.

On one occasion the Grand Vazīr solicited an audience, and was taxed at forty thousand pieces of silver; which, after much chaffering, was reduced to thirty thousand.

At his audience with Shems, the Vazīr was so charmed with the mysteries revealed to him, that, on his return therefrom, he voluntarily sent the ten thousand pieces of silver to Husām, which had been abated from the sum originally fixed.

These monies were always expended by Husām, as he saw fit, in relieving the necessities of the holy community, and the families of Jelāl, the Goldbeater, and their various dependants.

---

1. *The Honoured Elder*; by which Abū-Bekr is probably intended; but see a note to the Preface of the Mesnevī.

2. Juneyd and Bāyezīd of Bestām were two great doctors of mysticism; the latter died in a.h. 234 or 261 (a.d. 848 or 874), and the former in a.h. 297-8 (a.d. 909-10).
3. These are two of the four orthodox schools of Islām; they differ in certain details. There are reputed to be seventy-two schismatic or heretical sects.
4. This anecdote directly contradicts the foolish idea, so common in Europe, that, in the religious system of Islām, women are held to have no souls, and no hope of paradise.

CHAPTER VII.

THE SULTAN OF THEM WHO ATTAIN TO THE TRUTH, IN WHOM ARE MANIFESTED THE MYSTERIES OF POSITIVE KNOWLEDGE, BAHĀ'U-'L-HAQQI-WA-'D-DĪN, EL VELED.

1.

While Sultan Veled,[1] was yet a child, his father, Jelālu-'d-Dīn, was once discoursing on the miracle of the rod of Moses, which swallowed up the rods and other engines of Pharaoh's magicians, related to have been in such quantities as to form seventy camel-loads, and yet that staff became no thicker or longer than before.

Turning to Sultan Veled, his father asked how this could be, and to what it could be likened for the sake of illustration.

The child at once replied: "In a very dark night, if a lighted taper be brought into a large room or hall, it instantly devours all the darkness, and yet remains a little taper."

Jelāl jumped up from his seat, ran to his son, took the child to his bosom, kissed him with effusion, and then said: "May God bless thee, my child! Verily, thou hast strung a pearl of the very first water on the string of illustration."

2.

Sultan Veled's elder brother, 'Alā'u-'d-Dīn, was killed in the tumult for which the police authorities of Qonya put to death the Sheykh Shemsu-'d-Dīn of Tebrīz. Sultan Veled ruled the dervish community, in room of his father (after the death of Husāmu-'d-Dīn), for many years (from a.h. 683 to 712, being twenty-nine lunar years). He composed three volumes of poetry in couplets, like the Mesnevī (hence styled *Mesneviyāt,* Mesnevian Poems), and a volume (*Dīwān*) of odes in the Arabian style, arranged in the alphabetical order of their rhymes.

3.

It is related that when Husāmu-'d-Dīn was in his last illness, Sultan Veled came to visit him. Finding the sickness was unto death, he began to wail and lament, asking what would become of himself after the removal of so dear a friend and so able a director.

Husām collected himself, and, leaning on Sultan Veled, sat up. He then addressed the latter thus: "Be of good cheer, and let not thy heart be dismayed through my departure in the body. In another form, I will ever be near thee still. Thou shalt never be in need of counsel from another. In all difficulties and troubles that may beset thee, I will always be present, and in the visions of the night will I solve every doubt, and direct thee in each matter, whether it relate to the spirit and religion, or whether it pertain to the flesh and mundane affairs. Whenever thou shalt receive counsel in this manner, know of a surety that it is I who suggest it to thee—it will be none other than I myself. I will show myself to thee in thy visions; and I will be thy counsel and thy guide."

Sultan Veled was the first who narrated his dreams in his poems. Seek them there; there shalt thou find them consigned.

4.

One day a great man asked Sultan Veled whether God ever speaks to His servant—man.

This inquirer had frequently had the idea to send an offering to Sultan Veled; but had hesitated between a gift of money and one of Indian muslins.

Sultan Veled answered his inquiry thus: "God does certainly speak to His servants. And as to the method by which He addresses them, I will relate to thee an anecdote."

"There was in Balkh a preacher, who was also one of God's most precious saints. He had many disciples, who loved him dearly. I heard him once say, during one of his discourses: 'Long hath God spoken to you in words; but you will not hearken to Him. This conduct is strangely improper on the part of obsequious servants. In God's name, therefore, I warn you that you ought to hearken to God's words, and yield obedience to His commands.'

"Just then, a dervish in the congregation stood up, and begged that some one would bestow on him a handkerchief.

"A merchant, who was seated in a corner of the mosque, thrice conceived the resolve to give the dervish a handkerchief; but thrice he failed to carry that design into effect.

"That merchant now rose, and, addressing the preacher, said: 'Sir, how does God speak to His servants? Pray explain this, that the method may be known unto us.'

"The preacher answered: 'For one handkerchief, God does not speak more than three times!'

"The merchant was petrified. He cried aloud, and cast himself at the feet of the preacher. What he had thrice resolved to do, and had not performed, he now carried out, giving a handkerchief to the dervish, and professing himself a disciple to the preacher."

"Now," added Sultan Veled, "I say unto thee, O grandee, do thou also hearken unto the words of God. Give the Indian handkerchiefs, and distribute also the money. When thou shalt have hearkened to the words of God, He will listen also to that which thou mayest say unto Him. All thou mayest ask of Him, God will give thee; and whatsoever thou seekest of Him, thou shalt find."

Forthwith that grandee became a sincere convert and disciple. Similar miraculous works of Sultan Veled are beyond all count.

5.

Sultan Veled died on Saturday, the tenth day of Rejeb, a.h. 712 (11th November, a.d. 1312). He had as many as a dozen children by his wife Fātima, daughter of the Sheykh Salāhu-'d-Dīn Ferīdūn, the Goldbeater; but they all died in infancy, immediately after birth, or ere they were six months old. At length, on a Monday, the eighth day of the month of Zū-'l-Qa'da, a.h. 670 (6th May, a.d. 1272), his son and successor, Chelebī Emīr 'Ārif, was born.

Soon after his birth, or when only a few months old, the Emīr 'Ārif, at the invitation of his grandfather, Jelālu-'d-Dīn, and in the hearing of a numerous circle of assembled friends, thrice pronounced, audibly and distinctly, God's great name. His grandfather prophesied thence that he would be a very great saint, and would sit in the seat of his own successorship, after his father Sultān Veled. The Emīr 'Ārif lived about fifty years, surviving his father, however, but the short term of eight or nine summers.

---

1. The Beauty of the Truth and of the Religion (of Islām).

CHAPTER VIII.

CHELEBĪ EMĪR 'ĀRIF, JELĀLU-'D-DĪN.

(Ninety pages of the volume by Eflākī give more than two hundred anecdotes of the acts and miracles, of various kinds, of this illustrious grandson of Jelālu-'d-Dīn, the teacher and friend of the author, who vouches as an eyewitness for the truth and correctness of some of the narratives.
The Emīr 'Ārif passed the far greater portion of his life in travelling about to various cities in central and eastern Asia Minor, and north-western Persia, countries then subject to the great Khāns, descendants of Jengīz. He appears to have been of a more energetic or bellicose character than his father, and to have ruled with vigour during his short Rectorship.)

1.

On the last day but one of the period of the greater pilgrimage at Mekka, the eve of the Festival of Sacrifices, the ninth of the month of Zū-'l-Hijja, a.h. 717 (11th February, a.d. 1318), the Emīr 'Ārif, and the historian Eflākī, his disciple, were together at Sultāniyya, in the north of Persia, the new capital of the great western Mogul empire.

They were visiting at the convent of a certain Mevlevī dervish, named Sheykh Suhrāb,[1] with sundry of the friends and saints, all of whom were engaged in the study of different books, at about the hour of midday, excepting 'Ārif, who was enjoying a *siesta*.

Suddenly, 'Ārif raised his head, and gave one of his loud, awe-inspiring shouts, which caused all present to tremble. Without a word, however, he again composed himself to sleep.

When he at length fully roused himself, and finally woke up from his sleep, Sheykh Eflākī ventured to inquire what it was that had disturbed him.

He answered: "I had gone in the spirit to pay a visit to the tomb of my great-grandfather, when there I saw the two Mevlevī dervishes, Nāsiru-'d-Dīn and Shujā'u-'d-Dīn Chanāqī, who had seized each other by the collar, and were engaged in a violent dispute and struggle. I called out to them to desist; and two men, with one pious woman, being there present, saw me."

Eflākī at once made a note of this narrative, putting down the date and hour of the occurrence.

Some time afterwards, 'Ārif returned to the land of Rome, and went to the town of Lādik (*Laodicæa Combusta*, not far from Qonya); and there they met the above-named Nāsiru-'d-Dīn. In the presence of all the friends, 'Ārif asked Nāsir to relate to them the circumstances of his quarrel with Shujā'.

Nāsir replied: "On the eve of the Festival of Sacrifices, I was standing at the upper end of the mausoleum, when Shujā' came there, and committed an unseemly act, for which I reprehended him. He immediately collared me, and I him; when suddenly, from the direction of the feet of the holy Bahā Veled, the voice of 'Ārif was heard shouting to us, and made us tremble. In awe thereat, we immediately embraced each other, and bowed in reverence. That is all I know of the matter."

'Ārif then addressed Eflākī, and said: "Pray relate to our friends what thou knowest thereof, that they may be edified."

Eflākī now produced his memorandum-book, and showed the entry he had made, with the date. The friends marvelled at this, and rejoiced exceedingly, their spirits being refreshed with an influence from the invisible world.

'Ārif then said: "By the soul of my ancestor, I dislike exceedingly to make a display of any miraculous power. But, now and then, for the edification of my disciples, such scenes will slip out. Then Eflākī takes note thereof."

Such miracles are known by the names of "manifestations," and "ekstasis of the spirit."

When Qonya was reached, three friends, one a lady, bore testimony to having seen 'Ārif at the tomb on that day, and to their having heard him shout.

2.

'Ārif's last journey was from Lārenda to Aq-Serāy (on the road to Qonya). In the latter place he remained about ten days; when, one night, he laid his head on his pillow, and wept bitterly, continuously moaning and sobbing in his sleep.

In the morning his friends inquired the cause. He said he had seen a strange dream. He was seated in a vaulted chamber, with windows looking on to a garden as beau-

His sickness lasted about five and twenty days. On the twenty-second of Zū-'l-Hijja there was a violent shock of earthquake.

There was then in Qonya a certain saint, commonly known as "*the Student*," a successor of the legist Ahmed. In his youth he had made himself a great reputation for learning, in all its branches. But, for forty years, he had been paralysed, and had never risen from his seat, summer or winter. He was well versed in all mysteries, and now began to say: "They are taking away the lamp of Qonya! Alas, the world will go to utter confusion! I, too, will follow after that holy man!"

Shocks followed after shocks of the earthquake; and 'Ārif exclaimed: "The hour of departure is at hand! See, the earth yawns for the mouthful it will make of my body. It shows signs of impatience for its food!"

He then asked: "Look! what birds are these that are come here?" His eyes remained fixed for a time on the angelic visions which he now saw. From time to time he would start, as though about to fly. The assembled disciples, men and women, wept bitterly. But he again spoke, and said—

"Sheykhs, be not troubled! Even as my descent into this world was for the regulation of the affairs of your community, so is my existence of equal advantage to you, and I will at all times be with you, never absent from you. Even in the other world will I be with you. Here below, separation is a thing unavoidable. In the other world there is union without disrupture, and junction without a parting. Let me go without a pang. To outward appearance, I shall be absent; but in truth, I shall not be away from you. So long as a sword is in its sheath, it cuts not; but, when it shall be drawn, you shall see its effects. From this day forward, I dash my fist through the curtain that veils the invisible world; and my disciples shall hear the clash of the blows."

As he spake these words, his eldest son, Shāh-Zāda, and his own half-brother, Chelebī 'Ābid, entered the room. Sheykh Eflākī asked him what commands he had to give for them. 'Ārif replied: "They belong to the Lord, and have no longer a relation to me; He will take care of them."

Eflākī now asked: "And what are your wishes with respect to me, your most humble servant?" The answer was: "Do thou remain in the service of the mausoleum. Forsake it not. Go not elsewhere. That which I have commanded thee to do, as to collecting in writing all the memoirs of my ancestors and family, that do thou in all diligence until its completion. So mayest thou be approved of the Lord, and blessed by His saints."

All wept.

'Ārif now recited some verses; pronounced thrice the holy name of God, with a sigh; recited some more verses; and then, between the noon and afternoon hours of worship, having recited two short chapters of the Qur'ān, he departed, in peace and rejoicing, to the centre of his existence, on Tuesday, the twenty-fourth day of Zū-'l-Hijja, a.h. 719 (5th February, a.d. 1320). Unto God be all glory, now and for ever!

He was buried on the 25th, where he had himself indicated, by the side of his grandfather. His half-brother 'Ābid succeeded him.

---

1. Europeanised Armenians have made this into *Zohrab*, as their own family name.

CHAPTER IX.

GENEALOGY OF JELĀLU-'D-DĪN, RŪMĪ.

On his father's side, the remote ancestor of Jelālu-'d-Dīn, during Islāmic times, was Abū-Bekr, the dearest and most faithful friend of Muhammed the Arabian lawgiver, and his successor in the government of the community of Islām, as the first of the long line of Caliphs.

Like Muhammed himself, Abū-Bekr was of the tribe of Quraysh, which claims descent, through Ishmael, from Abraham, the chosen Friend of God, and Father of the faithful. The stem of Abū-Bekr's branch of the tribe unites with that of Muhammed in Murra, ancestor to Muhammed in the seventh degree, and to Abū-Bekr in the sixth.

Abū-Bekr was, furthermore, one of Muhammed's fathers-in-law, as his daughter 'Ā'isha was the Prophet's only virgin bride.

A son or grandson of Abū-Bekr is said to have been among the Arabian conquerors of Khurāsān during the caliphate of 'Uthmān (Osmān), about a.h. 25 (a.d. 647), and to have settled at Balkh (the capital of the ancient Bactria), where his family flourished until after the birth of Jelālu-'d-Dīn.[1]

At an uncertain period subsequent to a.h. 491 (a.d. 1097), a daughter of one of the Kh'ārezmian kings of Central Asia was given in marriage to Jelālu-'d-Dīn's great-great-grandfather, whose name is either not mentioned by Eflākī, or I have missed it. She gave birth to Jelāl's great-grandfather, Ahmed, surnamed El-Khatībī (as being, apparently, a son or descendant, or a client, of a public preacher, Khatīb).

Nothing more is mentioned of Ahmed by Eflākī, than that he had a son Huseyn, surnamed Jelālu-'d-Dīn, who married a daughter of a certain Khurrem-Shāh, King of Khurāsān, and became grandfather, by her, to the author of the Mesnevī. His son, Muhammed, surnamed Bahā'u-'d-Dīn, styled Sultānu-'l-'Ulemā, and commonly known as Bahā'u-'d-Dīn Veled, or shorter as Bahā Veled, appears also to have married a lady, by whom he had three children, a daughter and two sons.

Bahā Veled's eldest child, his daughter, was married off, and remained at Balkh, when Bahā Veled, his mother, and two sons left it, a year or so before it was taken and devastated by Jengīz Khān in a.h. 608 (a.d. 1211). His elder son is not again mentioned by Eflākī after their departure from Balkh. Neither is the mother of his children once mentioned. But his own mother, the princess, was alive, and was still with him in about a.d. 1230; after which, she too is not again mentioned.

Bahā Veled's youngest child, his most celebrated son Muhammed, surnamed Jelālu-'d-Dīn, Mevlānā, Khudāvendgār, and Rūmī, the principal personage of these memoirs, the founder of the order of the Mevlevī dervishes, and author of the Mesnevī, had four children, three boys and a girl, by two wives. His eldest son was killed in the broil that caused the murder of his father's friend Shemsu-'d-Dīn of Tebrīz. His youngest son is not taken further notice of; but his daughter was married off to a local prince, and left Qonya.

His second son, and eventually his successor as Principal or Abbot of his order, was named Muhammed, and surnamed Bahā'u-'d-Dīn. He is commonly known as Sultan Veled.

Sultan Veled had six children, a boy and two girls by his wife Fātima, daughter of Sheykh Ferīdūn the Goldbeater, and three boys, of whom two were twins, by two slave women. The daughters married well, and all his sons, or three of them, succeeded him as Abbot, one after the other. The eldest was Mīr 'Ārif (Chelebī Emīr 'Ārif), the second was named 'Ābid, the third Zāhid, and the fourth Wāhid.

Chelebī Emīr 'Ārif, the eldest, and Eflākī's patron, had two sons and a daughter. His eldest son, Emīr 'Ālim, surnamed Shāh-zāda, succeeded eventually to the primacy after his uncles. With him, Eflākī's memoir is brought to a close.

Such was the natural line of this dynasty of eminent men. But Eflākī has also given the links of a spiritual series, through whom the mysteries of the dervish doctrines were handed down to and in the line of Jelālu-'d-Dīn.

In the anecdote No. 79, of chapter iii., the account is given of the manner in which the prophet Muhammed confided those mysteries to his cousin, son-in-law, and afterwards his fourth successor, as Caliph, 'Ālī son of Abū-Tālib, the "Victorious Lion of God."

'Ālī communicated the mysteries to the Imām Hasan of Basra, who died in a.h. 110 (a.d. 728); Hasan taught them to Habīb the Persian,[2] who confided them to Dāwūd of the tribe of Tayyi',—Et-Tā'ī (mentioned by D'Herbelot, without a date, as Davud Al Thai; he died a.h. 165, a.d. 781).

Dāwūd transmitted them to Ma'rūf of Kerkh (who died a.h. 200, a.d. 815); he to Sirrī the merchant of damaged goods (Es-Saqatī?; died a.h. 253, a.d. 867); and he to the great Juneyd (who died in about a.h. 297—a.d. 909). Juneyd's spiritual pupil was Shiblī (died a.h. 334, a.d. 945); who taught Abū-'Amr Muhammed, son of Ibrāhīm Zajjāj (the Glazier), of Nīshāpūr (who died in a.h. 348—a.d. 959); and his pupil was Abū-Bekr, son of 'Abdu-'llāh, of Tūs, the Weaver, who taught Abū-Ahmed (Muhammed son of Muhammed, El-Gazālī (who died a.h. 504—a.d. 1110)), and he committed those mysteries to Ahmed el-Khatībī, Jelāl's great-grandfather, who consigned them to the Imām Sarakhsī (who died in a.h. 571—a.d. 1175).

Sarakhsī was the spiritual teacher of Jelāl's father Bahā Veled, who taught the Seyyid Burhānu-'d-Dīn Termīzī, the instructor of Jelāl. He again passed on the tradition to Shemsu-'d-Dīn of Tebrīz, the teacher of Jelāl's son, Sultan Veled, who himself taught the Emīr 'Ārif.

At the same time that the mysteries were thus being gradually transmitted to Jelālu-'d-Dīn and his successors by these links, they were also being diffused in thousands of other channels, and are at this day widely diffused over the world of Islām, which daily boasts of its living saints and their miracles. These latter are perhaps not less veracious than those continually blazoned forth by the Church of Rome, and by its Eastern sisters. We, too, have our spiritualists. Credulity will never forsake mankind and prodigies will never be lacking for the credulous to place faith in. There is much that is human in man, all the world over.

---

1. A genealogy is given in the Turkish preface to my copy of the Mesnevī, which traces the descent of Jelālu-'d-Dīn Muhammed from Abū-Bekr in ten degrees, as follows:—"Jelālu-'d-Dīn, son of Bahā'u-'d-Dīn, son of Huseyn, son of Ahmed, son of Mevdūd, son of Sābit (Thābit), son of Museyyeb, son of Mutahhar, son of Hammād, son of 'Abdu-'r-Rahmān, son of 'Abū-Bekr." Now, Abdu-'r-Rahmān, the eldest of all the sons of Abū-Bekr, died and was buried at Mekka in a.h. 53 (a.d. 672), and Jelālu-'d-Dīn was born at Balkh in a.h. 604 (a.d. 1207). Between these two there are nine degrees of descent given, for a period of 535 years, or 66 years for each life after the birth of the next link. This alone suffices to show that the genealogy is not to be depended on. Supposing the names given to be true, many other links must be missing; as many, probably, as those given.
2. Habīb the Persian, a wealthy man, converted to Islām by one word from Hasan of Basra, whose devoted disciple he became. He died a.h. 106 (a.d. 724).

THE BOOK OF THE MESNEVĪ

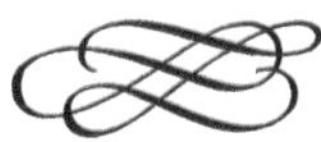

THE BOOK OF THE MESNEVĪ OF MEVLĀNĀ JELĀLU-'d-DĪN, MUHAMMED, ER-RŪMĪ, OF QONYA.

IN THE NAME OF GOD,
THE ALL-MERCIFUL, THE VERY-COMPASSIONATE.

PREFACE.

This is the book of the Rhymed Couplets (Mathnawī, Mesnevī). It contains the roots of the roots of the roots of the (one true) Religion (of Islām); and treats of the discovery of the mysteries of reunion and sure knowledge. It is the Grand Jurisprudence of God, the most glorious Law of the Deity, the most manifest Evidence of the Divine Being. The refulgence thereof "is like that of a lantern in which is a lamp"[1] that scatters beams more bright than the morn. It is the paradise of the heart, with springs and foliage. One of those springs is "the fount named Salsabīl"[2] by the brethren of this religious order (of mystical devotees known as the *Mevlevī* or *Dancing Dervishes*); but, by saints and the miraculously endowed, it is called "the Good Station"[3] and "the Best Resting-place."[4] The just shall eat and drink therein, and the righteous shall rejoice and be glad thereof. Like the Egyptian Nile, it is a beverage for the patient, but a delusion to the people of Pharaoh and to blasphemers; even as God, whose name be glorified, hath said: "He misleads therewith many, and He guides therewith many; but He misleads not therewith (any), save the wicked."[5]

It is a comfort to men's breasts, an expeller of cares. It is an exposition of the Qur'ān, an amplification of spiritual aliments, and a dulcifier of the disposition; written "by the hands of honorable scribes,"[6] who inscribe thereon the prohibition: "Let none touch it save the purified."[7] It is (a revelation) "sent down (from on high) by the Lord of (all) the worlds,[8] which vanity approacheth not from before, nor from behind,"[9] which God watches over and observes, He being "the best as a Preserver,"[10] and "the Most Compassionate of the merciful ones,"[11] unto whom pertain (many) titles, His utmost title being God, whose name be exalted.

We have been brief in (stating) this little; for a little is an index to much, and a mouthful may point out a pond, as a handful may serve as a sample for a whole threshing-floor, however large.

Thus saith the feeble servant, in need of the mercy of God, whose name be extolled, Muhammed son of Muhammed son of Huseyn, of (the city of) Balkh,[12] of whom may God accept it: "I have exerted myself to enlarge this book of poetry in rhyming couplets, which contains strange and rare narratives, beautiful sayings, and recondite indications, a path for the devout, and a garden for the pious, short in its expressions, numerous in their applications. This have I done at the instance of my lord and master, my trust, and as the soul in my body, the moral store of my to-day and my morrow, the Sheykh Hasan son of Muhammed son of Hasan, commonly known by the appellation of Akhī-Turk (my brother Turk), a chief of the knowing ones (Gnostics?), a leader of right direction and sure knowledge, a helper of the human race, a confidant of men's hearts and minds, a charge of God among His creatures, His pure one among

His reasoning servants, (a compendium of) His commandments to His Prophet, of His mysteries with His chosen one, a key to the treasures of the throne, a custodian of the riches of the extended earth, a man of excellencies, a sharp sword for the severance of truth and religion (from falsehood and blasphemy),[13] the Bāyezīd[14] of the age, the Juneyd[15] of the period, the true friend son of a true friend son of a true friend, may God be pleased with him and with them, originally from the town of Urmiyya,[16] and related to the venerated Sheykh,[17] as he himself expressed it: 'I was a Kurd one evening, and was an Arabian in the morning.'[18] May God sanctify his spirit, and the spirits of his successors! Blessed is such a predecessor; blessed are such successors! He was descended from a line on which the sun had cast its lustrous mantle, and personal nobility such that the stars shed their lights around it. May their courtyard ever be a centre to which the sons of saints will turn, and a temple of hopes about which embassies of spotless men will circulate. May it not cease to be thus while a constellation rises and a sparkling orb appears above the horizon in the east; so that it may be a thing held to by those who are possessed of insight, the godly, the spiritual, the heavenly, the celestial, the men of light, who keep silence and observe, who are absent though present, who are kings clothed in rags, the nobles of nations, endowed with virtues, the lights of guidances. Amen, O Lord of (all) the worlds. And this is a prayer not to be rejected; for it is a prayer joined in by all the good. And glory be to God in His unity. And may God pronounce blessings on our lord, Muhammed, and on his family and kin, the good, the clean!"

---

1. Qur'ān xxiv. 35.
2. Qur'ān lxxvi. 18.
3. Qur'ān xix. 74.

4. Qur'ān xxv. 26.
5. Qur'ān ii. 24.
6. Qur'ān lxxx. 15.
7. Qur'ān lvi. 78.
8. Qur'ān lvi. 79.
9. Qur'ān xli. 42.
10. Qur'ān xii. 64.
11. Qur'ān vii. 150.
12. Balkh, to the south of the west part of the Upper Oxus, is in latitude 36°, 48′ N., longitude 67°, 4′ E. from Greenwich. It represents the ancient *Bactra,* otherwise called *Zariaspa.*
13. Husāmu-'l-Haqqi-wa-'d-Dīn, his full title of honour. (See Anecdotes, chap. vi.)
14. Bāyezīd or Abū-Yazīd, of Bestām, in Khurāsān, Persia, latitude 36°, 25′ N., longitude 55°, 0′ E., a celebrated teacher and saint among the mystics of Islām, died a.h. 261, a.d. 874 (though a.h. 234, a.d. 848, has also been mentioned by some). His name was Tayfūr, son of 'Isà, son of Ādam, son of Surūshān, a Zoroastrian who embraced Islām.
15. Juneyd, surname of Abū-'l-Qāsim Sa'īd son of 'Ubayd, entitled Sultan of the Sūfī Community, a saint who died at Bagdad in a.h. 287 (a.d. 900).
16. Urmiyya, on the lake of that name, south-west from Tebrīz, the capital city of Azerbāyjān, the north-west province of Persia.
17. The expression of: "*The venerated Sheykh,*" might, perhaps, at first, be thought to indicate the Caliph Abū-Bekr, the Sheykh *par excellence,* as he and his successor 'Umer (Omar) were designated "*the two Sheykhs,*" from each being a father-in-law to Muhammed, whereas the third and fourth caliphs, 'Uthmān (Osmān) and 'Alī, were his sons-in-law. If this supposition were correct, Jelāl and Husām would have been descended from the same remote ancestor. The commentators, however, I am informed, name a certain "Seyyid Abū-'l-Wefā, the Kurd," as being intended. Particulars as to his individuality and history have not, unfortunately, reached me.
18. I have not met with an explanation of this expression, which is again introduced in Tale xiv., distich 40.

BOOK I

PROEM. THE REED-FLUTE.

From reed-flute[1] hear what tale it tells;
What plaint it makes of absence' ills:
"From jungle-bed since me they tore,
Men's, women's, eyes have wept right sore.
My breast I tear and rend in twain,
To give, through sighs, vent to my pain.
Who's from his home snatched far away,
Longs to return some future day.
I sob and sigh in each retreat,
Be't joy or grief for which men meet.
They fancy they can read my heart;
Grief's secrets I to none impart.

My throes and moans form but one chain,
Men's eyes and ears catch not their train.
Though soul and body be as one,
Sight of his soul hath no man won.
A flame's the flute's wail; not a breath,
That flame who feels not, doom him death.
The flame of love, 'tis, prompts the flute,
Wine's ferment, love; its tongue not mute.
The absent lover's flute's no toy;
Its trills proclaim his grief, his joy.
Or bane, or cure, the flute is still;
Content, complaining, as you will.
It tells its tale of burning grief;
Recounts how love is mad, in brief.
The lover lover's pangs best knows;
As ear receives tongue's plaint of woes.
Through grief, his day is but a dawn;
Each day of sorrow, torment's pawn.
My days are waste; take thou no heed,
Thou still are left; my joy, indeed.
Whole seas a fish will never drown;
A poor man's day seems all one frown.

What boot from counsel to a fool?
Waste not thy words; thy wrath let cool.
Cast off lust's bonds; stand free from all.
Slave not for pelf; be not greed's thrall.
Pour rivers into one small gill,
It can but hold its little fill.
The eye's a vase that's ne'er content;
The oyster's filled ere pearl is sent.[2]
The heart that's bleeding from love's dart,
From vice of greed is kept apart.
Then hie thee, love, a welcome guest;—
Physician thou to soothe my breast.
Thou cure of pride and shame in me;
Old Galen's skill was nought to thee!
Through love, this earthly frame ascends
To heaven; a hill, to skip pretends.
In trance of love, Mount Sinai shakes,
At God's descent; 'and Moses quakes.'[3]
Found I the friend on whom I dote,
I'd emulate flute's dulcet note.
But from my love, while torn away,
Unmeaning words alone I say.

The spring is o'er; the rose is gone;
The song of Philomel is done.
His love was all; himself, a note.
His love, alive; himself, dead mote.
Who feels not love's all-quick'ning flame,
Is like the bird whose wing is lame.
Can I be quiet, easy, glad,
When my delight's away? No! Sad.
Love bids my plaint all bonds to burst.
My heart would break, with silence curst.
A mirror best portrays when bright;
Begrimed with rust, its gleam grows slight.
Then wipe such foul alloy away;
Bright shall it, so, reflect each ray."
Thou'st heard what tale the flute can tell;
Such is my case; sung all too well.

---

1. The *reed-flute* is the sacred musical instrument of the Mevlevī dervishes, commonly known as the *Dancing Dervishes,* from their peculiar religious waltz to the sound of the reed-flute, &c., with outstretched arms and inclined head, in their special public services of commemoration. They love the reed-flute as the symbol of a sighing absent lover.
2. There is a poetical Eastern notion that pearls are formed in the oysters by dewdrops or raindrops falling into them at a certain season.
3. Qur'ān vii. 139, where the words are: "*And Moses fell down, swooning.*"

I. THE PRINCE AND THE HANDMAID.

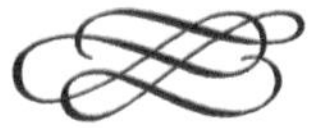

A prince there was, long since in time it is.
Of Church and State the power and wealth were his.
The chase on horse one day to follow, bent;
With pompous courtier-train afield he went.
A handmaid[1] fair was wand'ring near a grove.
Her he espied, and straightway fell in love.
His heart was snared; her form its cage, its stall.
He lavished gold; and made her thus his thrall.
But now, behold the wayward spite of fate!
The maid fell sick, this prince's joy to bate.
An ass had Hodge; no saddle to the fore.
A saddle bought; a wolf straight Jacky tore.

A jug had Dick; the well, alas, was dry.
The well then filled; the jug was broke hard by.
Now leeches called the prince, from left, from right.
"Two lives," quoth he, "depend upon your might.
My health is naught; she's life of life to me.
I'm sad at heart; my sov'reign balm is she.
Who finds a remedy to save her life,
Much gold, with jewels, his; and thanks more rife."
All promised marvels; each, to use his skill;
To search the case; to ease the maiden's ill.
"Each one of us has Jesu's[2] healing power.
Of all their ills we cure men every hour."
Through pride, "God willing" said they not, I trow.[3]
Man's nothingness, in them the Lord would show.
That is to say—to leave out this good word
Is sin; said by mere rote, it will not please the Lord,
How many shrink from tonguing it aloud,
Whose hearts each action with "God willing" shroud.
The doctors now prescribe full many a drug.
In vain they ponder, vain their shoulders shrug.
The maid a very skeleton became;
The prince's tears their want of skill did blame.

Their trains one column formed from mingling bands;
Their hearts united, fettered not their hands.
The prince: "Would thou'dst my soul enslaved; not she!
But here below effect a cause must see.
Be my Muhammed! I thy 'Umar stand,
With girded loins awaiting thy command."
Pray God to grant thee ever meek respect;
The puffed-up fool's remote from Heaven's elect.
A shameless monarch to himself's a curse,
A firebrand to his realm; nay, even worse.
Food in the wilderness by God was sent;
Food without toil, food gratis, without stint.
Some graceless scoffers out of Moses' host
Dared to demand the onions, lentils lost.[5]
Such toilless food then ceased to fall from Heaven;
To dig, to sow, to reap, in lieu is given.
Fresh suit, much later, Jesus made; God willed;
Again food rife became; men's dishes filled.
That food's a gift from Heaven is clearly said,
In Jesu's prayer: "Give us our daily bread."[6]
Men's bold presumption Heaven again incensed,
When basketsful to beggars were dispensed.

Jesus proclaimed the miracle would last;—
That food would never lack as in the past.
Men doubted, asked for more to store away;
They trusted not God's word for bread each day.
Importunate those suitors, full of greed;
Heaven's gate of mercy closed against their breed.
Withheld is rain when alms have ceased to flow;
Where fornication reigns, black death will grow.
Whatever grief and sorrow's on us sent,
Of wickedness and guilt's a punishment.
The hardened sinner, who his God offends,
A ruthless robber is; he spoils his friends.
He who is shameless in his words and deeds,
Despair from disappointment is his meed.
Yon orbs of heaven obey their Maker's word;
The holy angels meekly serve the Lord.
The sun's eclipse is but a check to pride;
E'en Satan's fall presumption caused to tide.
Return we now the sequel to attest,
Of what befell our prince with his new guest.
His circling arms the welcome form embraced,

And, lover-like, with joy his neck enlaced.
Kisses bestowed he on his hand and brow;
Hoped kindly he'd fared well from home till now.
His health and welfare asking, led him in.
"Its own reward is patience," thought he then.
Patience at first is bitter; but at length
Its fruit is sweet. It gives us heart's content.
Then he aloud: "A gift from God thou'rt come,
The proverb's pith: 'By patience overcome.'
This meeting's the reward of all my prayer;
Thou'lt solve the riddle of my dark despair.
Th' expounder, thou, of all my soul's desires,
Thou'lt extricate me from despond's deep mires.
Be welcome, then; a very friend in need;
Hadst thou delayed, my case were sad indeed.
Prince of physicians! Who'd not welcome thee,
Deserves rejection. Do his eyes not see?"
Urbanity's requirements thus bested,
Our prince the stranger to a chamber led.
The maiden's tale and case he there unfolds.
The patient, next, unveiled, the guest beholds.
Complexion, pulse, *egesta,* all are seen;

Disposing causes, symptoms, sought, I ween.
Then he: "The remedies till now adduced,
Have detrimental been, no good produced.
The case has been from first misunderstood.
Protect us, Heaven! A blundering brotherhood!"
He saw her trouble; thence divined her ill.
Her secret kept he; hidden held it still.
The sickness was not caused by bile or spleen.
The scent of perfume's better smelt than seen.
He traced her suffering to a mind oppressed;
Her body sound, her soul a wish suppressed.
Her hesitations made him guess her love;
The symptoms plain,—her heart was sick, poor dove!
A lover's smart is not from fleshly pine;
A probe is love; it sounds hearts' depths, divine.
Let love proceed from this or other cause,
It matters not; heavenward it mortals draws.
However well we strive love to portray,
We blush thereat, when love our hearts doth sway.
Words make most matters plain and manifest;
But love unspoken speaks whole volumes best.
When pen took up from zeal the writing trade,

In love's description, oh! such blots it made!
Our wits in love's affairs stand sore perplexed;
Love only can elucidate love's text.
The sun alone can well explain the sun.
Wilt see't expounded? Turn to him alone.
A shade, 'tis true, of him gives some small hint;
The shining sun surpasses all comment.
A shade, like evening chitchat, sends to sleep,
From sun's effulgence does full knowledge leap.
That day-orb, still, each eve sets, here below;
The soul-sun, God, shines in eternal glow.
'Mong things extern that orb has not a peer;
But mock suns we can make, our nights to cheer.
On heart unless the soul-sun cast a ray,
No thought, no picture can its sheen portray.
Can mind His glorious essence comprehend?
His presence, then, to image who'll pretend?
Of poet's verse when God's the holy theme,
Its minished head the sun may hide, 'twould seem.
At mention of His name each breast must find,
A duty 'tis His grace to call to mind.
The breath of life He to this body gave,

With Him to reunite, should mercy save.
These years I've conversed with Him. Life serene!
One repetition more! O blissful scene!
How pleasant heaven and earth their smiling hold!
He offers soul, mind, eye, a hundredfold!
Beyond my strength, O try me not these days!
My reason 'd fail to falter forth Thy praise.
The song of man, when uninspired by Thee,
Mere fulsome, flattering trash is seen to be.
Bid me describe, whose every nerve is seared,
A lover's woe, whom mistress never cheered.
His lonesomeness, the anguish of his breast,
Not here I'll paint; elsewhere it may be best.
He cries: "O succour me; I faint, I pant;
And quickly; lest delay the dagger plant!"
The Mystic[7] true relieves each moment's need;
"To-morrow" 's not a point in his pure creed.
Art not persuaded so? The proverb scan:
"Delay's the thief of time;" say: "bane of man."
Love's sweetest favours are conferred by stealth;
Its darksome hints are treasured mines of wealth.
The tale's most pleasant to a lover's ears,

That tells of joys he's tasted, ills he fears.
Speak, meddler, then, in plain, unvarnished guise;
No subterfuge employ; deal not in lies.
The veil tear off, dissimulation lost:
"When unadorned, beauty's adorned the most."
Should my sweet love unveil'd her charms display,
Thy smirks and smiles would all be borne away.
Thy suit prefer; use moderation still:
A blade of grass ne'er overturns a hill.
The sun that lights and warms this nether world,
If brought too near, had all to ruin hurled.
Seek not to sow dissension in the earth;
Vaunt not the Sun of Tebrīz'[8] holy birth.
Contention's never-ending. Better far,
Commit to memory this wordy war.
The guest, convinced that love had caused her ill,
Proceeded next the prince's mind to still.
"These chambers clear of every mortal soul;
Leave me alone the patient to control.
No prying ear may linger in the hall;
I've things to ask may not be heard by all."

The place was cleared; no soul remained within,
Save leech and patient; other, none was seen.
In gentlest tones he asked: "Where was thy home?
For each town's folk a different cure must come.
What friends, what family hast left behind,—
Companions, playmates, who to thee were kind?"
On pulse his finger. He then, one by one,
Inquired anew each point, omitting none.
So he whose foot is wounded with a thorn,
Upon his knee doth take the limb that's torn.
With needle's point he seeks the intrusive dart;
Not finding it, from lip he soothes the smart.
If thorn in foot is thus a task to find,
Judge what must be a rankling pang of mind.
Could every chance observer spy those ills,
Where'd be the cankering care, the grief that kills?
Boys place a thorn beneath an ass's tail;
The cure Ned knows not; jumping's no avail.
Whisking's still worse; it deeper drives the dart.
'Tis reason's task to ease the burning smart.
The ass, if sharper grow the throbs and pains,
Kicks, plunges, rolls, his hide with gore bestains.

Our doctor's mind, by art full well prepared,
With gentle measures sought the ill he feared.
Once more, with tact, he bids fresh memories come,
And leads the maid again to talk of home.
The spring once tapped, the stream began to flow;
She told th' inquirer much he wished to know.
He lends his ear as she each scene displays;
His finger notes her pulse, as on she strays;
To learn if any name should raise a start,
And thus betray the secret of her heart.
Anew he mentions every friend, each place;
Repeated such as gave of hope a trace.
He asked: "On quitting, thou, thy native town,
Where first was it thy guardians set thee down?"
A place she named, and on to others passed;
Nor blush, nor pulse gave sign, or notice massed.
Of lords and citizens she gave report,
Of festivals, and seats of gay resort.
Town after town, house after house, by name,
She spoke about; no blush, no throb still came.
Her pulse retained its normal ebb and flow.
Till Samarqand's name made her cheeks to glow,

Her pulse beat high, her colour went and came;
Of goldsmith youth she there had been the flame.
This point drawn forth,—this secret once confessed,
More easily our leech the sequel guessed.
"O maiden, let me know this youth's abode."
"At Holywell, near Bridge-end's public road."
"I knew," said he, "at once, thy case was such.
Now trust me. Thee to serve I will do much.
Make thyself happy. Cast away all care,
As showers cheer meadows, thee I'll greatly spare.
I'll prove thy guardian angel; never fear;
Thy father's place I'll take;—thy burden bear.
Tell not this secret unto mortal soul,
However much the prince may thee cajole.
Keep safe this knowledge in thy own heart's core;
So mayest thou, lass, thy lover see once more.
Our holy Prophet's sacred maxim 'twas:
'Who keeps his secret, speedy success has.'
The seed to earth committed sure must be,
Ere field or garden's pride men may it see.
If gold and silver were not hard to find,
How could they grow?[9] They soon would be out-mined."

The good physician's soothing words perceived,
Our maiden's mind from carking care's relieved.
Some promises are truly meant, sincere;
Others are merely made to cheat the ear.
A good man's promise is a gem of price;
Rely not on the words of sons of vice.
Our doctor, now, with subtle speech and wiles,
The maiden's grief had turn'd to sunny smiles.
He leaves her then; seeks out the prince; and tells
The news he'd learnt, the source of all her ills.
"What's now to do?" the prince's care inquired;
"Delay is dangerous; patience may grow tired."
The doctor then: "Send for him; come he must,
From his far home to fill some post of trust.
Invite him here; a dress of honour give;
On him shower gold; new life 'twill make him live."
The prince assented; took the doctor's plan;
Thought it was sound and wise from such a man.
Two trusty messengers he quickly sent,
Sedate, fair-spoken, loved where'er they went.
To Samarqand they journeyed, prompt and sure.
The goldsmith found; the prince's message bore.

"Great man of art, the marvels of thy skill,
Are viewed with rapture, or with envy still.
Our prince has need of thee, his mint to guide;
For none like thee is heard of, far and wide.
This dress of honour, yonder gold he sends;
Requests thou'lt come, and be his best of friends."
The gold and dress of honour won his heart;
Good-bye to home he said, with them to start.
He travels joyous; thinks his luck is great;
And never dreams of what's to be his fate.
An Arab charger proudly bore him on;
He recked not at what price all this was won.
O fatuous fool! Thou hastest to thy doom.
The post thou dream'st of, soon will be thy tomb.
His fancy webs of power and fame did weave;
Death's angel thundered: "Come, and all this leave!"
Arrived betimes at his long journey's end,
The doctor led him to the prince, his friend.
Most nobly was he there received in turn.
One trims the lampwick, still, to make it burn.
The prince addressed him; bade him welcome there;
Mint-master nam'd him, treasurer, and mayor.

Our doctor once again his counsel gave:
"The damsel to this youth for service leave.
United to him, she'll her health regain;
Love's fever will subside with absence' pain."
The prince bestows the sick one on her mate.
United were the two in solemn state.
Six months they feasted on love's joys so sweet;
The handmaid's health from day to day more meet.
The doctor, now, a potion mixed for him.
His health declines; he every day grows slim.
The coin that passes much from hand to hand
Soon loses currency, has no demand.
So he, when beauty no more graced his cheek,
Began to lack worth with the handmaid sleek.
All love that's built on outer skin-deep charms,
Is not true love. At length shame 'tis that warms.
Would it were shame alone that pricks him now!
He'd not been victimised and brought thus low.
His eyes pour forth two streams of bitter tears;
His altered features the worst foe he fears.
The peacock's enemy his plumage call.

The monarch bleeds whose splendours neighbours gall.
The musk-deer for the musk-pod still is slain;
His blood for that alone the ground will stain.
The marten for its fur is trapped, surprised,
And strangled. Kings its pelt have prized.
The elephant, sagacious creature, dies,
For iv'ry pierced with weapons as he flies.
"He who slays me for what I leave behind,
Reflects not: 'Blood that's spilt demands its kind.'
To-day 'tis I; to-morrow 'twill be thou;
Who'll be most loser? 'Tis not I, all know.
The shadow of a wall, 'tis true, is wide;
The sun revolves; the shadow's turn'd aside.
The world's a mountain; all our works, a voice;
Our voice goes forth; its echo has no choice."
Reflecting thus, the goldsmith breath'd his last;
The handmaid's love and grief behind her cast.
A dead mate's love can never more be shown;
A dead mate's voice will never more be known;
Love for the living, in the heart and eyes,
Will ever spring; the dead no more can rise.
One Living is there, death that never knows;

Love Him! The life from Him alone still flows.
Love Him, whom saints and prophets all have loved;
Through whom alone we all have lived and moved.
Say not thou canst not to His throne approach;
He's gracious. His rich grace bears no reproach!
The goldsmith's death through lethal drugs, be sure,
Was not from hope, or fear, or baser lure.
The doctor kill'd him, not to please our prince;
Him some divine suggestion did convince.
The story of the child by angel slain[10]
Cannot be fully grasped by minds too plain.
A saint that acts on Heaven's high behest,
Can never do amiss; 'tis always best.
He who can pardon, he may also doom;
He's God's vicegerent; acts in Heaven's room.
As Ishmaël beneath his father's knife,[11]
Do thou for such a prince lay down thy life;
Thus may thy soul, in future blessed abode,
Muhammed-like, in peace be with thy God.
His lovers joyful are, most, when they slay
Their worldly joys with their own hands, as play.
Our prince took not the goldsmith's life through lust.

Chase such suspicion from thy mind thou must.
Imagine not he'd stoop to mortal sin.
Can holy saint have tainted heart within?
The trial of the fire, and of the flame,
Is but to cleanse pure gold from every blame.
So too, temptation on us all is sent,
To part the good from those of bad intent.
Had he not acted thus by God's command,
No prince, a wolf he'd been, rav'ning the land.
From lust, greed, foul caprice, his soul was free;
So did God will, whate'er the cause may be.
Elias sank his ship in full design;[12]
That wreck to future blessings was the sign.
Moses was shock'd thereat, with all his skill
And inspiration. Thou must needs judge ill.
A blood-red rose call not by murder's name;
Just retribution see thou do not blame.
Had righteous blood been shed by him as naught,
Blasphemer were I to extol him aught.
Praise of the wicked God with horror views;
The good contemn all flatterers of sin's crews.
Our prince was kind and virtuous, wise and just,

A man God-fearing, and in God's full trust.

A victim put to death by such a friend,

Is slain in error, or for some wise end.

215

Did not our God mean mercy in His wrath,

How could the Lord of Mercies thunder forth?

A child may tremble at the lancet's smart;

His mother knows there's healing in the dart.

It may half kill him, but restores sound life;

So God's great mercies far surpass our strife.

Men judge of what they see by what they think.

From judging justice, men of sense will shrink.

219

---

1. In Islām a free person cannot legally be bought and sold.
2. By way of hyperbole, a clever physician is always compared to Jesus, in his miraculous healing powers, by Muslims.
3. Qur'ān xviii. 23, teaches: "Say not, 'I will do so and so,' unless (thou add): 'God willing.'"
4. Divine service in Islām is entirely worship and praise. It is erroneous to talk of Muslims saying their prayers. Praise, laud, and glory is what they are bound to offer. Prayer is voluntary; and is prohibited, unless in some duly authorised form as a *collect*.
5. Qur'ān ii. 58.
6. Qur'ān ii. 114.
7. The word "sūfī," used in the original, is probably the Greek σοφόι, but is explained as meaning, literally, "*clad in woollen*," from "sūf," *wool*. Metaphorically, in common use, it means: *a pious man*.
8. The holy Sheykh Shemsu-'d-Dīn, of Tebrīz, is meant; who was a friend of the author for many years, visiting Qonya at intervals, where he was put to death (in a.d. 1262?). See the "Anecdotes," Chap. iv.; especially No. 17.
9. It was generally believed in bygone days that gems and metals grew and ripened in their mines.

10. The story is in Qur'ān xviii. 73. The angel was disguised as a servant to Moses. The passage says: "And they two proceeded until they met a boy; and he slew him."
11. With Muslims, Ishmaël was to have been sacrificed; not Isaac. The Qur'ān xxxvii. 98-111, relates the story, but gives no name to the "boy." Commentators supply it, by tradition.
12. A continuation of the story from Qur'ān xviii. 70. Some commentators make Elias the servant of Moses on the occasion. There is a tale in one of the essayists of last century,—the "Spectator," if I rightly remember,—that gives these two adventures and others; the angel at last explaining to his companion the secret causes of all his actions.

II. THE OILMAN AND THE PARROT.

An oilman there was, who a parrot possessed,
Soft-voiced, and green-coated; could talk with the best.
The oilshop her charge when the man was away;
The customers coaxed she the whole live-long day.
Her speech was quite human, her words full of sense,
In all parrot-tricks she was void of offence.
One day the man popped out, on bus'ness intent;
The parrot, as usual, had charge while he went.
A cat, as it chanced, of a mouse in full chase
Bounced into the shop. This poor Poll could not face.
From perch away flew she; took refuge on shelf;
Some jars she knocked over; the oil spread itself.

The master returning, first sat himself down,
As lord of the manor; the shop was his own.
The oil-pools he spied, and then Polly's wet coat;
A blow on the head made her feathers drop out.
In silence some days Polly brooded, from grief;
The oilman's bereft of his wits, to be brief.
He plucked at his beard; he heaved a deep sigh;
"Alas!" then, he shrieked out, "day's darkened on high
My hand, would it withered had, ere I'd struck Poll;
I've silenced her prattle that always was droll!"
His alms now he showers on each passing scamp,
In hopes Poll her chatter 'd get back by some tramp.
Three days and three nights in this guise did he pass,
Despair at his heart, like a lorn lovesick lass;
Incessantly sobbing and sighing, his word
Was: "Pray now, will speech e'er return to my bird?"
A bare-headed mendicant happened to pass;
Whose scalp was close shaved, smooth and shining as glass.
At once our Poll-parrot her silence forswore,
Screamed after the mendicant: "Poor head! Sore! Sore!
Old bald-pate! old bald-pate! What is it thou'st done?

Upset some one's oil jar? The oil is't all gone?"
The passers-by smiled all at Polly's mistake,
'Tween bald-head and bare-head no diff'rence to make.
So thou, my dear friend, think thyself not a saint;
A quean to a queen bears resemblance, but faint.
Mankind on this point in great error still stands;
Th' elect of the Lord are ignored on all hands.
The equals of prophets acknowledged they be;
Of saints they're the brethren, as all men agree.
Fools say: "The elect are but human, you see;
To eat and to sleep they're constrained, just as we."
Through blindness they miss the real point of the strife,
The diff'rence between them's immense all through life.
The wasp and the bee eat and drink from the fields;
The one stings, the other sweet honey still yields.
The deer of both sorts browse the same mountain's side;
The one gives rich musk; dung the other; go, hide.
The canes of two species in one land may grow;
Quite empty that one; from this, sugar will flow.
By thousands, examples of pairs thus are known,
Which differ as much as does cheese from the moon.
Our bread, in one case, turns to dirt in our meat;

Another produces the mind, God's own seat.
His food the one man swells with envy and greed;
By like means another gains virtue indeed.
One soil is productive; one barren and salt;
One angel's in heaven; the other's at fault.
In form, many pairs may appear as though one,
Clear water is sometimes as hard as a stone.
Excepting the taster by practice, who knows
The wholesome from unwholesome water that flows?
Supposing saints' miracles tricks, magic-wrought,
They fancy them both the result of deep thought.
Magicians, at bidding of Pharaoh, did cast
Their wands down, to Moses' rod as a repast.
From his rod to their wands a chasm there must be;
From his act to theirs we an interval see.
God's curse on their witchcraft and devilish art!
His blessing on Moses, who chose the best part!
To me, like as apes are man's miscreants all;[1]
To speak of them causes me, straight, sick to fall!
Whatever men practise, apes will copy still;
Our actions they mimic; of thought they know *nil*.
They cunningly do what they've seen that man did;

The reason they seek not; from them that is hid.
A man acts from reason; an ape from mere whim.
Perdition may seize all such actors, and him!
The hypocrite[2] worships[3] as aping the saint,
For form's sake, or worse. His religion's mere feint.
In pilgrimage, worship, and fasting, and alms,[4]
Believers and hypocrites vie, as in psalms.
Believers shall win in the last judgment day;
The hypocrites then shall receive their due pay.
The two are contending one great game of deeds,
As factions of Mervites and Rāzites[5] with creeds.
They each shall go there, where their party shall stand;
And each shall be classed as their actions demand.[6]
Just style these "Believers" their hearts fill with glee;
But dub them all "Hypocrites," rage then thou'lt see.
The first one's ashamed of the last one's true self;
This last-named's a plague to the first, like an elf.
No virtue in mere words or letters is found;
"Believer"'s a word in itself but a sound.
If "Hypocrite!" cast in their teeth be at last,
As scorpion's sting to their souls it clings fast.
If "Hypocrite"'s name be not product of hell,

So bitter at all times why does its sound tell?
This name's great repulsion is not in its form;
The bitter it smacks of is not from a corm.
The word's but a vase; 'tis its sense is the wine;
The sense of a book in the title may shine.
Sweet lakes and salt seas do we find here on earth;
The barrier between them: "Thus far; go not forth!"
They both, in their origin, flow from one source;
Look not at their severance; it's matter of course.
The touchstone's the test by the which thou must try
If gold be quite pure, or debased with alloy.
The touchstone of conscience, where planted by God,
What's certain, what's doubtful, makes plain without nod.
A fishbone that sticks in the throat of a man
No ease ever gives till it's coughed out again.
In ten thousand mouthfuls should one bone be found,
As soon as perceived, it's spit out on the ground.
Perception of things mundane guides here below;
Religion's keen sense leads where God's glories glow.
The health of his senses man asks of the leech;
Religion's sound sense from the Lord we beseech.[7]

For healthy perceptions, our frame must be sound;
Religion's enjoyments through suff'rings are found.
The health of the soul's through a waste of the flesh,
But after much searching it builds up afresh.
How blest is the soul that, for love of its God,[8]
Has flung away wealth, health, e'en life, as a sod!
Has pulled down its house a hid treasure to find,
And built it again from that treasure refined!
Who cuts off the streamlet to clear out its bed;
Then turns on the water with which it is fed!
Who gashes his skin to extract the spear-head!
(The skin may now heal, for the irritant's fled.)
Who wrecks a strong castle to drive out the foe,
Then rears it still stronger, to hold evermo'!
The will of Almighty God who shall control?
These sentences written are parables all.
Sometimes in one way, in another sometimes,
Religion confuses before it sublimes.
Not terror, bewilderment, loathing, dismay;
But ecstacy, rapture, love, come into play.
In trance of love fixed, one contemplates the Lord,

Another, self losing, unites with his God.
Observe the rapt features of that one, of this;
Perchance by such watching thy soul may gain bliss.
Too numerous demons in human form walk;
Beware, then, with whom thou engagest in talk.
The fowler his whistle may ply in the field,
To lure the poor birds, saying: "Come and be killed."
Each songster conceives 'tis the voice of its mate,
Descends from the air, and meets with its fate.
The sinner, in pious cant, uses a wile,
To trap the unwary who ponders no guile.
The upright deal faithfully, truly, in trust;
The wicked imagine but fraud and distrust.
A lion of wool is a beggar's device;[9]
Musaylama's named Muhammed in a trice.[10]
Musaylama liar, deceiver we know,
Muhammed was faithful in weal and in woe.
The wine of God's love was the food of his soul.
The wine that inebriates dash from thy bowl.

---

1. In its true sense, the word "miscreant" signifies *one who holds an erroneous belief*. We corruptly say now: *an infidel*.
2. "Hypocrites," in Islām, form a faction. They profess the faith openly, but inwardly they hate or despise it.

3. The Muslims "worship" God in their appointed devotions. If they "pray" also, subsequently, this is a voluntary act.
4. "Worship, fasting, alms, and pilgrimage" are the four acts by which a Muslim outwardly attests his faith. "Worship," five times daily; "fasting," one month yearly; "pilgrimage," at Mekka, once, as a duty, in a lifetime; "alms," whenever property of a certain amount is possessed.
5. "Mervites and Rāzites," citizens of Merv and Rey (Rhages), two great Persian cities in former days, now in ruins. Merv is at present a Turkman camping-ground, aimed at by Russia as a halting place on the road to Herāt and India. Rey, the Rhages of the book of Tobit, not far from Tihrān, the Shāh's present capital of Persia. The two parties were like Ireland's Orangemen and Ribbonmen of our time.
6. Heaven and Hell; the "sheep" and the "goats."
7. The original has "the Darling;" the highest title given to Muhammed by Muslims is *God's Darling*; which is not found in the Qur'ān.
8. The original has "its dear one;" God is *the dear one* of mystics.
9. A *woollen lion* is a toy made and sold or exhibited by mendicants.
10. Musaylama was a prince of Naja, who gave himself out as a prophet, and wrote to Muhammed, proposing that they should divide Arabia between them. His epistle began: "Musaylama, the Apostle of God, to Muhammed, the Apostle of God." Muhammed's answer commenced with: "Muhammed, the Apostle of God, to Musaylama the liar." He was eventually defeated and slain in battle, in the eleventh year of the Hijra after Muhammed's decease; when all Arabia submitted to Islām. He was killed by Wahshi, the Ethiopian slave who, in the battle of 'Uhud, had formerly driven the selfsame javelin through the body of Hamza, Muhammed's uncle. Wahshi lived long after these events, in Syria. He used to say that, as a pagan, he had slain one of the best of men, and, as a Muslim, one of the worst. When Mekka was taken, he was proscribed; but he got away safely. Not long afterwards, he made his submission, and Muhammed forgave him, as he did others in analogous circumstances.

III. THE JEWISH KING, PERSECUTOR OF THE CHRISTIANS.

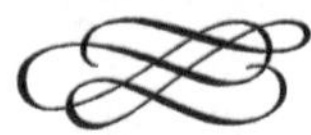

A certain Jewish King[1], in savage, brutal scenes,
From hate of Jesus, persecuted Nazarenes.
'Twas Jesu's age, when he the Gospel first did teach;
In Jesus, Moses, and in Moses, Jesus preach.
That King God made squint-eyed; things straight he could not see.
A King and squint-eyed? Ah! that one the two should be!
A master once a squint-eyed slave commanded so:
"Come here; that bottle from its shelf, go, fetch me; go."
The squint-eye straightway asked: "Which, master, of the two?[2]
The case explain; clear up the doubt, and truly show."
His master answered: "Two there's not; there is but one;

Put off thy strabism; with stupidity have done."
"Good master," quoth he, "chide me not; 'tis nature's fault."
The master quick rejoined: "Look now; break one; halt! halt!"
As soon as one was broken, both were gone from sight.
Poor squint-eye nearly lost his wits in childish fright.
There was but one; his eyes were cause that he saw two.
The one away, the other consequently was gone too.
Desire or rage, at times, makes people double see.
The mind's distortion brings the eyes perverse to be.
From passion's mists our reason ever blinded lies.
The heart its clouds sends up; the mind's eye's vision flies.
The judge to taking bribes who basely bends himself,
Can never well discern the right and wrong, from pelf.
Our King through Israelitish rancour grew so blind,
As nothing to distinguish in his rage of mind.
By thousands, faithful seekers of God's will he slew.
"Vouchsafe us help, O God of Moses, Jesus too!"
He had a Vazīr, brigandlike for craft and force.
In knavish stratagems he had no peer; of course.
He whispered to the King: "These Christians, as in hives,

All keep their faith a mystery, to save their lives.
To kill them thus is profitless. Give breathing-time,
Religion can't be smelt out just like musk or thyme.
A secret 'tis, well wrapped in many folds of guile.
In outward show, as friends, perfidiously they smile."
The King, with grimace fierce: "What have we then to do?
What remedy proposest thou to make them rue?
I will not leave alive one Christian in the land,
Whose faith is shown to all, or in his bosom banned."
The Vazīr to him: "King, my hands and ears cut off;
My nose and lips the same. Give orders; let them scoff.
Unto the gallows send me; I'll of all be seen.
Then let an intercessor plead,—some prince,—your queen.
Let all this happen where some spacious public place
May let all see, that all may know of my disgrace.
Then drive me forth; away from thee in exile sent;
And they'll receive me, under feint of sorrow bent.
'In secret,' I'll pretend, 'a Christian I'm at heart;
Call God to witness how my faith has worked my hurt.
The King a knowledge gained of zeal in me that burned;
Its flame to put out quite, his anger on me turned.

I strove to hide my faith, my leaning to keep hid;
Affected still to be, think, act, just as he bid.
Suspicion crossed his mind; my secret he espied;
All I could plead for nothing went; he said I lied.
"Thy specious words," quoth he, "are needles in a loaf;[3]
My eye, as through a glass, sees all thy thoughts; thou oaf!
No curtain of thy trickeries can veil thy faith from me;
I'm proof against thy knaveries; thy cunning I can see."
Were not the faith of Jesus the refuge of my heart,
He'd not have mutilated me in this sad sort.
For love of Jesus, head and life I will lay down;
All persecution suffer to gain a martyr's crown.
My life I will not grudge to lose for Jesus' sake.
His faith I hold from point to point without mistake.
I dread his doctrine's fall to uninstructed guides.
The truth from their bad teaching still to ruin glides.
Thanks be to God, to Jesus thanks, who me have made
A teacher perfect of the faith so free from shade.
The Jew and Judaism I have forsworn in sooth;
About my loins the sacred cord[4] I wear; 'tis truth.
This age the age of Jesus is; O men, give ear!

His doctrine take to heart; nought else have you to fear.'"
The Vazīr having laid this plot before the King,
All shame and scruple vanished; 'twas a perfect thing.
In presence of the public, nose, ears were cut off.
The rabble wondered greatly; now's the time to scoff.
He fled unto the Christians; begged them him to hear;
And straightway set up preaching; saintlike was he there.
The Christians soon with one accord accepted him,
In multitudes they round him flocked, all meek and prim.
The Gospel's holy words, the prayer, the cord, he'd preach;
The mysteries of all of these to them he'd teach.
To outward view a guide to sanctity was he;
In very truth, a trap and fowler's whistle; see.
Of such effect his wiles, disciples were deceived;
From Jesu's teaching fell, and in this cheat believed.
It is so. Often does the flesh, for selfish end,
Intrude itself across the soul's most fervent trend.
Meek virtue was not what they sought to gain the most;
Of him they learned to ferret out new sins, and boast.
Hair-splitting casuists, point by point they sin dissect;
They grow too wise; 'twixt rose and garlic links detect.

By night the monarch knows no state, no pomp retains;
The merchant counts no more, in sleep, his gains and loss;
The prince and peasant, equal, on their couches toss.
The Gnostic[8] is so e'en by day, when wide awake;
For God hath said: "Let quietude care of him take."[9]
Asleep to all the things of earth by night, by day,
As pen in writer's hand he doth his guide obey.
Whoever sees not in the lines the writer's hand,
May fancy 'tis the pen alone has all command.
Of this, the Gnostic's privilege, a trace 'd suffice
To rob of sleep and reason vulgar souls of ice.
His spirit wanders in the groves of th' absolute.
His soul is easy; body, still, calm, quiet, mute.
The two absolved from greed, lust, sense, care, fear also;
Each, like a bird uncaged, is free; roams to and fro.[10]
Should he, birdlike, be whistled back to trap of sense,
Again he sinks, the slave of every vile pretence.
When light of dawn paints bright the blushing sky with red,
Ere orb of day comes forth as bridegroom from his bed,
Shrill chanticleer, as though it were last judgment's trump,
Calls back to consciousness the sleepers. Up they jump.

The souls return their bodies to inhabit, then;
Each body fraught with thoughts, and words, and deeds again.
The soul turned loose, without the body's cares or ken,
Attests the truth: "Sleep is death's brother,"[11] to all men.
But lest it should escape, and not come back at call,
A tether to it's bound; it's not quite free withal.
It must come back by day from roaming where it wills,
The cares of life to bear;—a burthen that soon kills.
O! Would, O God, Thou'd keep my soul in Thy own hand,
As Sleepers in the Grotto;[12] Noah's ark once to land!
Then had I 'scaped the tempest waking thoughts aye raise;
My mind, eyes, ears, had rested; all my task Thy praise!
Sev'n Sleepers?—Many are there of them in this world,
Before, behind me, right and left; they're round me hurl'd!
My "Cave"[13] art Thou; my "Mate" art Thou; O God, my friend!
Men's eyes and ears are sealed; they know not where they wend.
A Caliph asked of Laylà: "Art thou really she
For whom poor Majnūn went distracted? For I see,

Than other beauties thou art not so passing fair."
Said she: "Be silent! Thou'rt not Majnūn; nor his pair."
A man awake is sound asleep; more, he can't be.
His watchfulness is worse than sleep; how should he see?
Our souls, if not awake to God's most holy truth,
Are not awake. We're slaves to them. The greater ruth!
The soul all day is buffeted by fancy's whims;
Of loss or profit, life or death, as frenzy swims.
No peace enjoyed; no dignity remains in hand;
No vigour to attempt a flight to heaven's strand.
Asleep is he who's slave to every sordid wish;
Who begs of fancy; parleys with it, even. Pish!
A demon in his sleep he sees; an angel deems.[14]
Through lust he swoons with sensual pleasure as he dreams.
His seed he sows in sandy, salt, and desert land;
And wakes to find no harvest's ripened to his hand.
A headache, with a beating heart, is all he feels;
"Alas!" he sobs, "that treach'rous gnome! My whole frame reels!"
A bird flies in the air; its shadow flits on earth;
A second bird it seems to be, though nothing worth.
Some simpleton runs after it; to catch it tries;

Himself tires out; meanwhile the creature safely flies.
The fool still knows not 'tis a shadow he pursues,
Its substance where to seek he has no power to muse.
He shoots his arrows at the fleeting, mocking shade;
His quiver emptied, he returns; no booty made.
Our life's our quiver. When our years are vainly spent
In chasing phantoms, grief will one day have its vent.
Let God's protection mercifully on us rest,
All fancies and all phantoms stand at once confest.
God's servants are His shadows here below on earth;
To this world dead, but living in a second birth.
To their skirts cling; from them thy soul's nutrition seek.
So may'st thou 'scape the perils of this scene's last week.
The holy text of: "How He stretcheth forth the shade!"[15]
Of saints gives notice. Them his glory doth pervade.
Without their guidance venture not to thread this maze;
Like Ab'ram answer: "Fading things do not me please!"[16]
In days of trouble, consolation's sun seek out.
The skirts of "Tebrīz' Sun" will wipe out care, no doubt.[17]
Know'st not the road to that good man, and grief survene?
Inquire of his and my friend, great Husāmu-'d-Dīn.[18]

While on thy way, should envy seize thee by the throat,
Know, Satan's sin was envy; malice made him gloat.
He envied Adam's rise to such sublime estate.
He wars with all who're good, through envy and through hate.
No mountain-pass as this life's progress is so steep;
Let envy not increase thy load; thou canst but creep.
The flesh a hot-bed is of envy and of strife.
These soil the soul; for envy's bane of mortal life.
Should envy seek thy soul to kill, invoke the Lord,
The God of mercy thee can save, with His true Word.
"Make clean My house, ye two," did Ab'ram's God once say.[19]
His house our frame; a house of glory, though of clay.
Should envy fill thy breast 'gainst one that envies not,
Foul stains ensue; thy heart's impure; all good's forgot.
Prostrate thyself, then, at the feet of holy men;
Cast dust upon thy head, God's pardon to attain.
The Vazīr of our Jewish king was envy's self;
His nose and ears he sacrificed, as 'twere but pelf,
In hopes the sting of envy 'd find an easy way,
To pour the selfsame wounds he 'd open lay.
His nose, from envy, in the air, who carries high,

His ears and nose to envy 'd give without a sigh.
The nose the organ is by which we trace a scent;
The scent then guides to where the odour finds its vent.
Who has no sense of smell is truly *minus* nose,
Its odour we should trace to where religion blows.
To scent religion's fragrance, not returning thanks,
Ingratitude is. Nose to lose merit such pranks.
Be grateful, thou; and venerate all grateful men;
Abase thyself; a champion be of theirs. Amen.
Be not a cut-throat, like that Vazīr, of men's faith;
Seek not to turn believing souls from what God saith.
That Vazīr seemed a pastor of the truth, in sham;
As one who bitter aloes mixed in sweet plum jam.
Some men of sense discernment used, his ways to scan,
His honied phrases smacked to them of knavish plan.
Refined truisms, double-meaning, he'd deal out,
Like syrup into which some mortal poison's put.
Be thou not caught with knavery's fairly-spoken word;
A hidden meaning it may have. Be on thy guard.
Of evil-minded men the speech is never good;
Their hearts are dead and putrid; life cannot there brood.

A man's an offset from a man, by nature's law,
As sure as cake of bread is bread, and not mere straw.
God's Lion,[20] 'Ali, saith: "All words in folly made,
As weeds on dunghills, crowd apace; as quickly fade."[21]
He who would rashly, thoughtlessly, repose thereon,
Begrimed will be, befouled, befooled, and spat upon.
He that gives vent to wind, mere wind, is bound to wash;
His worship else is vain; pollution doth it quash.[22]
The Vazīr's talk was all: "Be diligent in pray'r."
His acts proclaimed aloud: "Of duty never care."
In surface silver's white and glittering to the eye;
With friction, hands and purse it soils, though e'er so dry.
A fire is jocund to the view; its flame may please.
But venture not too near it; black is its surcease.
The lightning flashes brightly, shining as it flies;
But oft, alas, it strikes man blind, or dead he lies.
Be wise betimes; for "he that's void of common sense,
Is like the ox with yoke on neck." So 'Alī,—Hence!
For six years was the Vazīr absent from the king;
Disciple seemed of Jesu's faith; bad news to bring.
Their hearts and faith the people all pinned on to him;

At his command they every one would change each whim.
His purpose all the time was fraud and gross deceit;
He pondered naught but wiles, to compass their defeat.
By secret message, with the king he held converse.
The king to him fair gratulations sent, diverse.
A missive came to him at length: "My faithful son,
'Tis time my heart was set at rest. What hast thou done?"
His answer was: "The thing's prepared; have patience yet;
The Christian folk to puzzle soon, we'll not forget."
The Christians portioned were, for purposes of war,
In legions twelve; to each, a captain void of fear.
The men of every legion to their captain bound
By ties of trust and confidence, in each heart found.
These legions and those captains twelve, to that bad man
Had yielded up their every thought;—as mankind can.
Should he command to die, not one of them would fail
To give his life right joyfully,—without one wail.
A volume he prepared in name of each of them;
The matter of these registers not all the same.
The style of every one was in a different guise;
From end to end each book's contents were forgeries.

In one, the pangs of hunger mortified the flesh;
With penitence, with fasting made, and prayer, to clash.
A second taught that fasting did no good at all;
That charity, beneficence, was all in all.
A third explained: "Thy fasting,—charity itself,—
Syntheism[23] is. With God, thou deifiest thyself.
To trust with resignation's all religion's plan.
In weal and woe are springs to trap the soul of man."
A fourth declared: "Faith without works is truly dead.
Alone is service valued; faith's a sin to dread."
A fifth laid down: "The Law's commands and warnings all
Are not for practice; they're mere symbols of man's fall.
By showing us man's weakness, God is made more strong;
The decalogue this purpose serves; the rest's all wrong."
The sixth, again: "For man to talk of weakness here,
Ingratitude is, simply; God's grace is so clear;
Think, now, how wonderful is man; how great; how wise;
'Tis God has made him thus; to thank Him in us lies."
A seventh suggests: "Leave power and weakness unto Me;
They're idols, both, as also are all things ye see."

An eighth contends: "Put not thy light behind a shade.
Let all men see thy light; to glad their eyes 'twas made.
Removed from sight if 'tis, an evil thence will loom.
Thou, too, wilt be removed at midnight from the groom."
A ninth expounds: "Put out the light; thou'lt have more joy.
The sense of sight is one: joy's feelings, many; boy.
Put out the light. The sense of touch thou may'st then use.
The bride is timid; in the dark she'll not refuse.
Renunciation of the world's a very farce.
Renounce. The world, and more, thou'lt dream of in thy trance."
A tenth assures: "That which the Lord hath given to man,
God hath made pleasant to the eyes. Deny, who can.
Take what is thine. Avert thee not; 'tis folly still
To take to groaning, moaning, when all's at thy will."
Another yet: "Forsake all things thou hast possessed.
Retention of them by thee baseness is, confessed.
How many roads diverse traced for their feet men deem;
Each one to one sole "church" the only road doth seem.
If way there were secure, for hitting out the truth,
The Jews and Magi surely 'd not missed it, forsooth."

Again another: "Moral food makes heart to live.
We see this clearly; every hour a proof doth give.
Enjoyments sensuous, fleshly, when to fade they haste,
Leave no result behind; they're desert mirage, waste.
Regret's their only issue, grief for loss of time;
A bankrupt's stock; their commerce gives no gain, no prime.
Pursuit of them has never ended in success;
Dire failure still must be the fruit of recklessness.
Distinguish thou betimes the foolish from the wise;
The end of each scan well; 'tis there the difference lies."
And still one more: "True wisdom strive thou to find out.
True wisdom's not the fruit of noble birth. Poor lout!
Each 'church' has had in view to gain a happy end.
But one and all have failed and could but fail. God send!
To palm off jugglers' tricks is not true wisdom's part,
Or man had never seen so many faiths take start."
And one again: "True wisdom thou hast surely found.
Thou knowest men of wisdom;—wisdom's safest ground.
Be manful. Let not men by fraud make mock of thee.
Thy own path choose; turn not from it for aught thou see."
To one he said: "Thy unity is all in all;

Besides thee, aught existence never had, nor shall."
One volume taught: "The universe is unity.
Who teaches two exist, is but a squint-eye, he."
The last gave out: "A hundred really are but one."
Unless a madman, whom could have such doctrines won?
In them these paradoxes fitly found their place,
In words and sense his doctrines lacked all claim to grace.
Each volume was the antithesis of the next;
If one was honey, poison was the other's text.
Wouldst thou escape his honey and his poison too,
Forsake thou not the holy word of scripture true.
Twelve volumes thus were writ with fraudulent research,
By that Vazīr, the hidden foe of Jesu's church.
Jesu's one-mindedness for him had no perfume;
The wine of Jesu's jar no *bouquet* to his grume.
A many-coloured garment washed in that pure wine,
As snowy white comes out, and clear as is sunshine.
Not faded or plain-coloured, such as gives offence;
But clear as crystal water, in which fishes glance.
Dry land, chameleon-like, gay-coloured scenes displays;
But fishes dry land shun; they love clear water's sprays.

What is the fish, and what the water, in my tale,
That they should symbolise God's kingdom on small scale?
Whole shoals of fishes, great and small, the water's realm,
In adoration mute, with praise to God o'erwhelm.
What showers of bounty from God's outstretched hand
Have made the seas with pearls of price to deck the strand!
What brilliant suns of brightest goodness must have shone,
Ere clouds and sea could have produced the matchless stone![24]
What rays of wisdom poured on water and on land
Ere earth could nourish seed, yield corn to our demand!
The earth, a faithful trustee, gives back what we sow,
No fraud, embezzlement, in its trust do we know.
This faithfulness to trust arises, with time's run,
From generous warmth infused by glow of justice' sun.
Whene'er God's symbol quickening summer back doth bring,
The mysteries of the earth straight from her bosom spring.
Th' All-Bountiful, who gave to senseless earth, of grace,
This faithfulness, trustworthiness, in every place,

In mercy plans forth inorganic matter's course.

In wrathful wisdom's counsel blinds man to its source.

Our hearts and souls have not the grace to understand.

To whom address me? Not one ear's at my command!

Who lends his ear, shall also quickly find an eye.

Whose ear's, like stone, to counsel deaf, shall surely die.

Of wond'rous power is God possessed. What's magic's skill!

Miraculous works He enacts. Where's witchery's spell!

To sing His praise in me a want of feeling shows.

It proves I breathe. To breathe, to live, breaks true love's laws.

205

In His existence let my being sink, quite lost.

To be, is to be blind and blear-eyed at the most.

If blind I were not, swooned, unconscious should I be.

The Sun of Glory's might and power then could I see.

Were not my sight grown blear, through weeping in my dreams,

Had I stood, ice-like, frozen, 'neath His mercy's beams?

Just like his king, this Vazīr was shortsighted seen.

The Ancient, 'twas, of Days, he wrestled 'gainst, I ween.

Th' Almighty One, who with one breath, one word, did bring

Ten thousand worlds from naught to join in being's ring.

Ten thousand worlds, besides, disclose themselves to sight,
If thou direct thy vision towards the God of Light.
In man's esteem the world is vast, without an end;
With Power Infinite compared, a grain of sand.
The world's around the soul a dismal prison-den.
Arise! Escape! Regain the fields at large! Be men!
The world is finite; He is infinite. Confide!
Earth's forms and qualities God's essence from us hide.
The million spears of Pharaoh, vaunting in his might,
By Moses' wand were broken in th' appointed night.
And many sons of skill, for healing science famed,
By Jesu's curing halt, lame, blind, deaf, mad, were shamed.
How many poets, orators, great men of note,
By word of the Illiterate One[25] were shown to dote.
For love of our Almighty God, the Lord of all,
Who would not die, a stock, a block, we needs must call.
Dead heart of stone if He but touch with love's live coal,
A magnet straight becomes, no longer quits the pole.[26]
Plume not thyself as one endowed with cunning guile;
The meek more surely draw rich gifts from Heaven's smile.

How many treasure-hiders, treasure-seekers, here,
Have been derided, laughed to scorn, by that All-Seer!
What art thou, man? Canst thou in thought with Him compare?
What's the whole earth? A blade of grass, His might to dare?
A woman, once, through foul adultery's sin estranged,
By God, in punishment, to Venus' star was changed.[27]
From woman into Venus? Sure, that change was sad.
To dust and ashes turn. Less shame in this. Art mad?
Thy soul it is must lift thee to heaven's highest home;
The flesh can but consign thee deep to hell's dark dome.
Thyself it is that dooms thee to that woful fate;
The angels' envy art thou, here, in man's estate.
Consider, then, this doom; revolve it in thy mind;
That woman's change, compared with this, was joy, thou'lt find.
To push ambition's course beyond the stars thou'st sought?
Refused hast thou first Adam to adore, as naught?[28]
But seed of Adam art thou, O degenerate man!
Why wilt thou then as glory count dark shame's foul ban?

Why proudly vaunt thou'lt conquer all this teeming earth?
Why fondly fancy rumor 'll sound thy passing worth?
Should winter's snow in heaps encumber all earth's soil,
One gleam of summer's sun the frigid cloak will foil.
So, too, that Vazīr's scheme of fraud, nor his alone,
Reduced to nothing was by one word from God's throne.
Such crafty wiles as these He changes into weal;
As poisons by His power receive the gift to heal.
What doubtful was, becomes confest, at His decree;
True love springs up, where hatred plotted was to be.
He safely carries through the fire His chosen friend;[29]
The fear of death He maketh peace of mind to lend.
Through Him are treasures hid beneath the ruin's waste;
Thorns roses yield; our bodies joys of soul foretaste.
By workings of the pang of love for Him I burn;
Though sophistlike I rave, 'tis unto Him I turn.
Another stratagem the Vazīr next conceived;
From public life withdrew, and solitude achieved.
Admiring followers all were fain to mourn his loss;
For forty days, and more, in cell he bore his cross.
Their yearning for him grew more fierce from day to day;

They missed his good example, words, and zeal to pray.
They grieved that he in solitude should vex his flesh;
Their sympathies clung round him every day afresh.
"Without our teacher we're a pastorless poor flock;
Blind beggars without staff to guide us to our nook.
For mercy's sake, for love of God, have pity now;
No longer us deprive of consolation's show.
We're infants all, and thou our feeder, tutor thou,
Protection shed around; forsake us not just now."
His answer was: "My spirit's present with you, friends.
But issue from this hermitage my power transcends."
The captains twelve, of legions, intercession made;
His grieved disciples raised a wail, a serenade:
"Great evil's lighted on us! Ah! Beloved One!
We're orphans made; our parent, thou, away art gone!
Raise not such pretext; push us not to our wit's end.
We sob and sigh; we beat our breasts. Do comfort send!
Thou'st pampered, spoilt us with thy wondrous eloquence;
With doctrine from thy lips our souls cannot dispense.
Torment us not, for God's sake! Pity on us take!
Be kind! This day, 'To-morrow' say not; to us wake!

Our hearts are rapt in thee; no heart in us remains.
Heartless and spiritless are we, poor bankrupt swains!
Like fishes out of water, so we writhe and gasp.
The dam break down; let flow the stream; avert death's grasp!
Thou art the very paragon, the phœnix of the age.
Heaven's mercy, save us; or, we perish, we enrage!"
To them he thus: "O men of little sense, take heed;
You foolishly are seeking elsewhere what you need.
Your ears stop up with wool; list not to speech of man;
The mote that blinds your eyes cast out. Then, see you can.
With cotton in your outward ears, you'll plainly hear
The still small voice of conscience, drowned now by your fear.
All outward sense discard; all thought, reflection flee;
And straight you'll hear, within, God's voice: 'Come unto Me.'
So long as with chitchat you keep yourselves awake,
Communion with the angels you in sleep forsake.
Our words and acts make up our outward habitudes;
Our inward man's our converse with infinitudes.
Our senses barren are; they come of barren soil;

Our soul, like Jesus, walks the sea without turmoil.

Our outer man's a barren wilderness, I ween;

The inner man, 'tis, sounds the depths of the Unseen.

If all our life be spent in chase of mundane things,

Our paths must lead o'er wastes, o'er hills, o'er ocean springs.

The Fount of Life,[30] where shall we find in such a course?

Death's billows how avoid, and how escape remorse?

The desert's moving sandhills are our schemes and plans.

Life-rills are abnegation, self-denial, man's."

Him answered his disciples: "Master, grieve us not.

Fresh sorrow, through pretences, add not to our lot.

Such heavy burden to endure we've not the power.

Poor suffering weaklings we, in sad affliction's hour.

The heavens appear to raise themselves all vastly high;

But true sublimity's God's attribute. We sigh.

The food of every bird He gives in providence;

He says whose figs devoured shall be these ten days hence.

Who 'd give, in lieu of mother's milk, to infants, bread,

Would kill them with improper food before them spread.

But when their teeth are grown, and deck their little mouths,

Themselves will ask for bread; milk suits not then their growths.

The unfledged chick is yet for flight all unprepared;

Attempting it, he falls a prey to puss, poor bird!

His wings well pinioned, he soars high in breezy air;

Needs no encouragement; his instinct leads him there.

Each howling imp is stilled at sound of thy sole voice;

And words from thee are utmost joy to all our race.

Our ears are gladdened as they catch thy tongue's converse,

Each desert grows a garden, when thou'rt freshness' source.

With thee amongst us, earth a foretaste gives of heaven,

Thou'rt our delight, from morn to eve our longed-for leaven.

Without thee, day's refulgence we cannot employ,

If thou art present, every care is turned to joy.

High station, true, may be attained by charlatan;

But moral worth alone gives eminence to man."

To them, now, he replied: "Your prayer 's of no avail.

My counsel take and ponder. Naught else shall prevail.

If I'm a trusted man, my word is not a lie,

E'en though I'd say that black is white, or earth is sky.

If I'm perfection, who the perfect's word denies?
If I am otherwise, why all this fuss and noise?
Forth from my solitude to come I'm not designed.
I'm communing with God; to His will I'm resigned."
They still insisted: "Vazīr, that we'll not deny,
But our remonstrance is a truly piteous cry.
We weep our eyes out through our grief thee not to see,
With sighs our hearts burst, vainly looking out for thee.
An infant quarrels not with its attentive nurse;
And yet it weeps, through knowing not what's good from worse.
We are thy harps. The plectrum's stroke is from thy hand.
'Tis thus we moan; smit by thy cunning harpist wand.
Like flutes of reed, our utterances are through thee found;
Or mountain vale, our echo's but child of thy sound.
Or as chess-players, striving in their dubious game;
Our 'check' and 'mate' are from thee, man of mighty name.
What are we,—can we be? 'Tis thou'rt our life of life,
So long as thou'rt among us. If not, all is strife.
We're naught;—we're nothings. All our being is in thee.
Existence' very self by thy frail form we see.
We're lions, true; but stand on vanes of weathercocks,

Our twists and twirls, our starts, our jumps, are from wind's shocks.

These lions' movements are in sight; the winds unseen.

The Great Unseen, th' Almighty One, 's behind the screen.

Our moving wind, our very being from thee springs.

Existence, else, were vain, not sheltered 'neath thy wings.

'Tis thou hast taught us, nothings, valued life to prize;

'Twas thou that made us, erring, lovers of th' Allwise.

Take not from us the savour sweet of thy good gifts,

Thy cup, thy wine, thy relish, absence from us lifts.

But shouldst thou still refuse, who to repine 'd have heart?

Can pictures of the painter's hand complain, and art?

No notice of us take; from us avert thy face;

But ne'er deride the claims of thy prevailing grace.

We were not; prayers from us arose not to thy ear;

Thy grace alone 'twas sought us out; thou drewest near.

Before the artist and his brush, the picture's null;

Like unborn babe in mother's womb, till time be full.

Before almighty power creation stands in wait,

As canvas 'fore the needle 'broiderer's hand may mate.

A demon here, an angel there, or man, is bid

To be; now joy, now sorrow, rises up amid.

We have no hand to move; defend ourselves we can't.

We have no breath, no speech to pray for aid in want."

The Qur'ān ponder this my verse to understand.[31]

There God hath said: "Thou threwst not, when thou threwst" the sand.[32]

Although we shoot an arrow swiftly to its mark,

The bow, the arrow, we ourselves, are from God's ark.

There's no compulsion here, though God can all compel.

'Tis not complaint, if I of God's compulsion tell.

All our complaints of our felt needs are indices.

If shame we feel, of our freewill a sign it is.

Without choice were we, there 'd be no pretext for shame.

Why blush and hang the head, cast down the eyes so tame?

What doth a master in disciple always chide?

Why teacheth he in Providence still to confide?

Shouldst thou assert God carelessly makes us to act,—

That sun of verity He hides in mists of fact,—

An answer I will give,—just lend thy ear to me;

Forsake all blasphemy,—of God's faith ever be:

"The longings, the regrets, that every sick man feels,

Awakings are of conscience. Sickness this reveals.
The moment man is ailing,—prisoner to bed sent,
He counts his sins, he asks for grace, vows to repent.
He sees the wickedness of all he's said and done;
He promises, in future, errant ways to shun.
'If but I'm spared,' he says, 'I never will sin more;
I'll righteousness ensue, all trespasses abjure.'
By this thou seest that sickness is not all an ill.
'Tis but a time for waking conscience good to will.
Know then the aphorism, O seeker after truth,—
Whoe'er thou be, to whom scent of it may give ruth:
'The man that's most awake, with most of pain will reel;
The more his conscience pricks, more sorely sad he'll feel!'
If thou wert really conscious God 'tis thee compels.
What need to feel ashamed;—to utter frightful yells?
Thou art not so; thou feelest not a captive's chain;
Thou know'st thou'rt free to act, or from each act abstain.
Whoever saw a captive sporting in his bonds?
Whoever heard of prisoners acting vagabonds?
Hast thou had fetters fastened on to both thy feet?
Hast e'er beheld kings' guardsmen resting in thy seat?

Then be not thou to others hard as jailer man.

Obduracy befits not him a king may ban.

Compulsion since thou feel'st not, make it not pretext.

Say'st that thou feel'st it? Where's the proof? Show us it next.

In every act to which thou inclination hast,

Thou know'st thyself free agent: what thou willst, thou dost.

If any case arise thy will, thy wish, to brave,

Straightway compulsionist thou art: 'God so would have.'"

The prophets were compulsionists to this world's string.

Miscreants are compulsionists towards heaven's King.

The prophets chose the better part, futurity;

The foolish choose the worse, the world's fatuity.

Each bird will flock with birds of its own feather still;

The cock well knows his mate, and follows where she will.

Miscreants are the brood of hell, to which they go;

The goods of worldly life they choose. Then be it so.

The prophets are of race from heaven deriving birth;

To heaven they tend with heart and soul while here on earth.

'Twould never end the branches of this theme to count.

So let us sip again from our old story's fount.

Within his cell ensconced, the Vazīr answer gave:
"Disciples mine, my firm resolve from me receive.
To me a very strict commandment Jesus spake:
'From friends and kin of every class seclusion seek.
Thy face set tow'rds a wall; sit in some cell apart,
Forsake thyself; forgetfulness cast o'er thy heart.'
Permission's thus denied with men to hold discourse.
I've naught to say; with mortals more I'll not converse.
Good-bye, my friends! Adieu! You'll never see me more,
My journey's unto heaven; there I've laid my store.
Th' empyrean beneath, so long as I have strayed,
Like firewood in a furnace have I wept; still prayed.
Henceforward I shall sit on Jesu's own right hand,
In highest heaven enthroned, blest Paradise's strand."
The legion-captains now he called to him apart;
But one by one, in secret, counsels to impart.
To ev'ry one he said: "Successor thee I name,
The faith of Jesus to uphold and keep from shame.
All other captains thy commands will have to hear;
'Tis Jesus thus appoints thee others' loads to bear.
Should any one against thee neck rebellious raise,

Him kill, imprison, or in exile end his days.
But while I live divulge not what to thee I've told,
Keep secret till my death this charge thou hast to hold.
Let no one know till then 'tis thou art chosen out,
Proclaim not thou thyself a king or prince devout.
Behold this scroll; take, study it; thyself instruct,
'Tis Jesu's doctrine pure; from this His Church construct."
Thus one by one their minds prepared were to be chief:
"'Tis thou'rt the chosen one; all else would be a thief."
He named them each successor; made them so to feel.
Whate'er he told to one, to each did he reveal.
He gave to each a volume, writ from end to end;
No two alike; each different, and hard to blend.[33]
Their doctrines various, of every changing hue;
Diverse in sense, as objects' forms exposed to view.
Their precepts and commands a very maze of guile,
Their sentiments impossible to reconcile.
The Vazīr now delayed another forty days;
Then slew himself,—set free his soul from earth's affrays.
The people, hearing of his death, were sorely grieved;
Around his corpse collected; eyes, ears, scarce believed.
With many bitter moans to sorrow they gave vent;

Their breasts they beat, their hair they tore, their clothing rent.

To count their multitudes is in God's power alone;

Turks, Arabs, Kurds, and Romans,[34] men of every zone.

They scattered o'er their heads the dust from his last home;

To mourn for him was balm, all ills to overcome.

They wept. Their bitter, briny tears they shed in floods;

His grave a pool; those tears, as streamlets from the woods.

To lose him was a grief unspeakable that fell

On rich and poor, on high and low, too sad to tell.

A month of mourning past, the people sought to know

Whom he'd appointed in his place their way to show.

Whom must we recognise successor to our saint?

Into whose hands commit the task of our restraint?

He was a sun of light; his fire hath turned to fume,

A candle now we need our darkness to illume.

Our friend is gone,—is lost to our inquiring eyes.

A substitute we seek,—memorial we may prize.

Our rose is withered;—rosebush leaves all blown away,

Which vase holds now the rose-scent in its perfumed clay?"

God is invisible to weakly mortal sight,
His prophets are a need, to guide His Church aright.
No! That's not right! That phrase is sadly incorrect.
A prophet's one with God; not two. Think well! Reflect!
They are not two; they're one. Thou blind materialist!
With God they're one; their forms but make Him manifest.
Thou seest the form alone; thy two eyes are at fault.
Look with thy soul; thou'lt see as God from heaven's vault.
Thy two sights will united be straightway in one,
When thou behold'st the Light of God's eternal throne.
Set up ten burning candles in one selfsame place,
A separate body, each, diffuses light and grace.
Their powers combine in one, to brighten that retreat;
Distinction now there's none; one light alone we meet.
Count out a hundred apples, quinces, pears, or plums;
When mashed together, all their juice, their pulp, their scums.
Things spiritual division, number, parts, know not,
They split not into fractions, form no separate lot.
'Tis sweet when friends with friends together come and meet.

Trust then the spirit. "'Tis the letter kills"—repeat.
Thy body mortify; thy flesh consume with pains.
Behind it hid thou'lt find God's unity—thy gains.
If thou the body vex not,—bring not low betimes,
The flesh will thee destroy, my friend, in fiery flames.
The flesh it is that shows itself to human heart;
The flesh it is demands asceticism's sharp smart.
We simple were; one essence was the source of all.
Nor head, nor foot had we; one pristine lot did fall.
One substance held us; we were clear as is the sun;
No knots or gnurs within us, free as water's run.
On taking fleshly form, that simple essence, then,
Became divided, split, like shadows in each glen.
Make low the hills and hillocks, level make the plain;
No shadow's left; the whole becomes one scene again.
With pleasure I'd this matter clearer put, and joy.
But tender consciences I seek not to annoy.
Abstruser points there are, as keen as sword in fight.
If reason's shield thou hast not, refuge take in flight.
My arguments contest not, unless well prepared.
Sharp blade will cut; it pities not; no life is spared.
I sheathe my sword of argument,—will not make assault.

Lest muddlers read me wrong, and say 'tis I'm at fault.

We come now back again, to follow up our tale,

To keep our faith with readers, feminine and male;

And say again, the people rose up as one man,

Demanding who should work out our dead Vazīr's plan.

One legion-captain forward came, out of the twelve,

That grieving people's furrowed field anew to delve.

Said he: "Behold! successor am I to the saint.

In Jesu's stead I'm regent, by his own constraint.

You see this scroll. 'Tis evidence of what I say:

The dead Vazīr's successorship is mine to-day!"[35]

A second captain started up, as from ambush;

Contested all those words; his own claim then did push.

Forth from his bosom he another scroll produced,

And then the people's wrath flamed high; not soon reduced.

The other captains, too,—each his own train at back,—

Unsheathed their swords, and threatened both their skulls to crack.

Then each one of the twelve, his sword and scroll in hand,

Upon the others set, like baited bull on brand.

The slain were strewn in heaps of many hundred men,

Their heads were piled in pyramids, by thousands ten.

Their blood was shed in torrents, flowing on the plain.

The dust arose in clouds through this commotion vain.

The seeds of discord sown by that knave's treacherous hand,

Had now produced their harvest, fatal to the land.

The nuts he cracked were skulls; their kernels, human brains.

The bodies slain through him held precious souls in chains.

Be killed, or die, as in thy lot may be decreed.

So with pomegranates, apples, when sliced up at need.

The sweet and sound are prized, and straightway put to use;

The sour and rotten cast away, worthless refuse.

A word with sense and meaning's ever eloquent;

Bald nonsense is laughed down in scorn or merriment.

Thou fool, materialist! Think closer: look to sense.[36]

The spirit 'tis gives value; words are mere pretence.

Prefer the company of those who spirit seek.

So mayst thou grace attain,—"God's servant be,"[37] and meek.

A life without a soul or spirit in our frame,

Like wooden sword in sheath, were but a senseless name.

Within its sheath while kept, of value it may seem;
When drawn, 'tis only fit for matchwood, men will deem,
Arm not thyself with wooden sword in battle's day.
Examine well thy weapon, if thou 'd have fair play.
Shouldst find thy sword of wood, another seek forthwith;
If adamant it prove to be, then join thy kith.
The truest swords are found in th' arm'ry of the saints.
Their converse is to thee a balm for all complaints.
The wise have ever said, with uniform accord:
"Most truly wise was he, 'the Mercy of the Lord.'"[38]
Dost buy a pomegranate? A burst fruit still elect.
The crack reveals its grains; thou seest they've no defect.
E'en so, good friend, blest be the man whose mouth reveals
The heart-thought pearls their casket, his pure soul, conceals.
But inauspicious is the opening tulip's crack;
This patent makes to all that its heartcore is black.
The burst pomegranate is a sunny orchard's pride.
So speech of worthy men may waft thee to truth's side.
Society with saints no doubt's of great avail;
To piety it leads; "God's fear shall never fail."[39]
Thou wast a very rock, a worthless pebble stone;

By saints' communion fined, a pearl of price thou'st shone.

Then love the saints. Their love plant deeply in thy heart.

The pure of mind alone deserve a pure love's part.

Court not despair; hope ever springs in human breast.

Seek not the dark; the Sun of Light shines full confest.

The spirit ever leads to haunts of holy men;

The flesh would cast thee in the pit of sin again.

Beware! Feed thou thy soul with love from holy ground.

Make haste! Seek means of grace from one who grace has found.

Petition make! Seize hold upon the skirts of saints.

Through them thou'lt learn how God his favour grants.

The Gospel names the name of Ahmed;[40] he the last,

As chief of prophets;—purity's bright ocean, vast.

His lineaments, his virtues, ways of matchless good;

With notice of his wars, his fasts, and eke his food,

Some Christian folks, on mention of that sacred name,

And this recital of his qualities and fame,

A merit to acquire, were wont to kiss the book,

To bow with reverence deep, humility in look.

That folk in all the troubles we've related now

Were safe; nor bloodshed, nor foul faction did them know.

Secured were they from scrolls, sword, captains, and Vazīr,

In name of Ahmed Mustafà they'd trust, not fear.

Descendants, numerous in race, they left behind;

Their faith in Ahmed they a tower of strength did find.

But other Christian folks to him refused to bow.

The blessed name of Mustafà they deemed too low.

Requital brought them punishment for this offence;

A prey they fell unmourned to that Vazīr's pretence.

Their false creed, with their tribes, was quickly brought to end,

Through those twelve lying volumes his deceit had penn'd.

The name of Ahmed, thus, a friend is proved, of might;

Of light by day a pillar, shelt'ring cloud by night.

A castle inexpugnable, a stronghold safe,

As he himself was Trusty,[41] though his foes might chafe.

How fatal the disasters pictured here above,

The fruit of foul duplicity's pretended love.

---

1. Who are intended by this Jewish squint-eyed king, and his self-sacrificing, treacherous Vazīr?
2. It is a common belief in the East that squint-eyed people see double.

3. Needles, or pins, are hidden in bread that is given to a dog or other beast in order to destroy it.
4. The rope worn by monks, like the Brahmin's sacred thread, is supposed by Muslims to be worn by all Christians.
5. Muhammed.
6. In time of immediate danger during war the "Service of Fear" is enjoined instead of the usual form of worship.
7. In visions.
8. The original word, *conversant,* like our "Adept" and "*Illuminato,*" is applied by the mystics to themselves. It is a trace of the old Gnosticism.
9. Being given in Persian, I cannot quote chapter and verse for the original Arabic.
10. Like lunatics, they are supposed to be heedless of all things around them.
11. *Sleep is Death's brother* is an ancient Arabian proverb.
12. The Seven Sleepers; mentioned in Qur'ān xviii. 8-25.
13. Muhammed's "Cave-Mate" was Abū-Bekr, who was his sole companion on quitting Mekka at the Emigration or "Flight." They concealed themselves in a cave; and Muhammed remarked: "God is the third in our little party." Hence the title of "Cave-Mate," applied to Abū-Bekr.
14. A species of nightmare in the form of a lascivious dream.
15. Qur'ān xxv. 47.
16. Qur'ān vi. 76.
17. See "Anecdotes," Chap. iv.
18. See his name as an honorific title in a note to the author's preface; and in the "Anecdotes," Chap. vi.
19. Qur'ān ii. 119.
20. "*The Lion of God,*" so called from his courage and strength. Shīr-Ali, Hayder-Ali, are among the forms of the title.
21. One of the sayings attributed to him and become proverbial.
22. In Persian, empty promises and boastings are also called "wind." Hence, the poet suggests ablution to cleanse from such;—mental ablution.
23. "*Syntheism*" is the correct rendering of the "*shirk*" of Islām. "*Polytheism*" is very incorrect. Dualists (Magians) and Trinitarians (Christians) are *Syntheists,* but they are not polytheists in a correct sense.
24. An allusion to the idea that a pearl is a raindrop caught and nourished by an oyster.
25. "The Illiterate Prophet," or, rather, "the Gentile Prophet," reputed barbarous and illiterate by the Jews and Christians, is one of Muhammed's highest titles.
26. The original here uses the simile of a certain "*cunning bird,*" known also as the "*Truth-calling bird,*" that hangs by a claw and calls all night: *haqq! haqq!* (Truth! Truth!).

27. Such is an eastern myth. Poets call the planet Venus the *"Harpist of the Spheres."*
28. In Qur'ān ii. 32, God commands the angels to fall down in adoration to Adam, when first created. Iblīs, Satan, alone refused, through pride and envy.
29. In Qur'ān iv. 124, Abraham is called the *Chosen Friend* of God; and in xxi. 69, the story is mentioned of his being saved from the fire into which he was cast by Nimrod.
30. *The Fountain of Life,* or *Water of Life,* is imagined to take its rise in a land of darkness beyond the limits of the inhabited earth.
31. In the original I have not found it possible to feel sure where the break should be made from the remonstrance to the poet's reflections. Much of what precedes seems addressed to God; but Eastern hyperbole is wide.
32. Qur'ān viii. 17. Muhammed cast sand at the foe in two battles, Badr and Hunayn.
33. This account of the Vazīr's various forged books is an allusion to the various Gospels and Epistles, canonical and spurious, that sprang up in the early Christian Church.
34. The Roman conquest of Greece, Asia Minor, and Syria completely effaced from the Eastern mind all recollection of previous actors on those scenes. Even "Alexander the Great" is to them *"Alexander the Roman,"* like our Jelālu-'d-Dīn, *"Er-Rūmī."*
35. An allusion to the contests of the bishops of Rome, Constantinople, Alexandria, Antioch, Jerusalem, &c., &c.
36. The mystics of Islām call God and the spirit *the sense,* of which material existences are the outward expression; as we say: *"The letter and the spirit."* The constant play of the original on these words is lost in the version.
37. An allusion to Qur'ān xviii. 12; not a verbal quotation.
38. A grammatical variant of Qur'ān xxi. 107. Muhammed is meant.
39. An allusion to Qur'ān xlix. 3; not a quotation.
40. In Qur'ān lxi. 6, is the assertion that Jesus, in the Gospel, foretold the advent of Muhammed by the name of Ahmed. This is generally explained as a translation of περικλιτός, misread for παράκλητος in John xiv. 26. The two words have very much the same meaning: *much-praised, most laudable, laudatissimus.* Muhammed is mentioned by many names, forty, fifty, sixty; some say a thousand.
41. Muhammed gained the name of Trusty, El-Emīn (Al-Amīn), long before he declared himself commissioned to call his countrymen to acknowledge the unity of God, the resurrection, judgment, and future life.

IV. ANOTHER JEWISH KING, PERSECUTOR OF CHRISTIANS.

A second Jewish king, descendant of the first,
To persecute the Christians showed hate's fiercest thirst.
If information's sought about this wicked king,
That chapter of the Qur'ān read: "Heaven's Girdle-Ring."[1]
A sorry rite it was the first had introduced;
With cruel zeal this wicked rite the last abused.
The introducer of a rule that tends to ill,
Draws on his head deep curses, morn and even, still.
The good decease; their bright example serves as guide;
The wicked soon decay; their name all men deride.
The children of those sinners, till the trump of doom,

Are cursed as soon as born; no lot more full of gloom.
How many springs burst forth, one salt, the other sweet;
Their savour changes, while the days and nights compete.
The good are promised their inheritance aloft,
Of waters sweet;[2] in Scripture mentioned oft and oft.[3]
The seeker's wish, if rightly we consider it,
A scintillation is of flame from holy writ.
No flame exists apart from body whence it burns;
Where'er the burning body hies, the flame, too, turns.
A window-light will wander all around a room;
Because the rising sun to sunset tends, and gloom.
That which to any constellation's stars pertains,
Must move with it, rise, set, south, as its place ordains.
The man who under Venus' influence was born
Is joyous, amorous, ambitious, with greed torn.
If Mars his planet be, his temper's bellicose;
War, scandal, litigation,—these he most does choose.
But other stars there are, the planets, seven, beside;
And unto men from them nor good, nor ills betide.
Revolving in another firmament than they,
Above the spheres that bear the orbs of night and day.

Bright through the moral splendour lent them by the Lord;
Not bound together quite, nor yet in disaccord.
The man whose soul is influenced by one of those,
Like meteors, still shall drive away the spirit's foes.
His disposition feeleth not the rage of Mars;
He temporises;—meekly acts in prosperous wars.
His light's triumphant;—darkness it shall never know.
Between two fingers holdeth he the truth, I trow.
The truth doth shed a shining light on human souls,
Received by heaven's favourites, in special ghostly strolls.
Illumined with that light, as spangles deck a bride,
They turn their souls to God, contemning all beside.
Who feels not keenly love's great soul-compelling might,
Is portionless of spangles from truth's flashing light.
All *parts* must ever share the nature of their *whole*,
As nightingale pours out unto one rose its soul.
Whatever *property* may qualify a *thing*
Externally, man's qualities are mind's offspring.
From purity, rich colours rise, good qualities;
Stains,—moral, or as dyes,—from gross impurities.
"God's Baptism" is the name of all that's good in man;

"The curse of God," of all that's evil in our plan.[4]
In which of these two seas our streamlets may subside,
They but return into the source from whence their tide.
From mountain-tops, swift torrents rushing down apace.
From men's frames, love-inspired souls, anon the race.
The counsel hear, that now, this Jewish dog did take.
Beside a fire a hideous idol he did make,
And proclamation ran: "Whoever 'd save his soul,
This idol worships; or in fire he's burnt to coal."[5]
Thus having made his hate an idol to himself,
A second idol straightway he invents, this elf.
The mother of all idols is our fleshly pride.
They're dragons; this, the egg of cockatrice's bride.
The flesh is flint and steel; our pride is but its spark.
That pride pervades the flesh as fecundation's mark.
Can moisture quench the latent spark in flint and steel?
Can man be safe while flesh and pride he lives to feel;
In flint and steel we know that fire is still alive.
No water's of avail that fire from them to drive.
With water we put out a fire when burning bright;
The spark in flint and steel is safe from water's might.
From flint and steel of flesh what burnings still ensue!

Their sparks, the blasphemies of Christian and of Jew!
If water in the jug and pitcher come to end,
On wellspring we must draw, a fresh supply to send.
Our idol is the muddy dregs left in our jug;
The flesh the sewer from whence it filters, spite of plug.
The graven idol (fed from blackest sewer tide
In flesh, its graver), was as fountain by wayside.
The inward idol, pride, the filthy jug's black slush;
The prurient flesh, the source from which it had its gush.
A hundred potters' pitchers one small stone can break;
And spill the cooling water drawn our thirst to slake.
To smash an idol, too, quite easy may appear;
Not easy to root out the flesh; too hard, I fear.
Would see the picture of the flesh, inquiring youths?
Description read of hell, with seven yawning mouths.[6]
From each soul's flesh comes forth a special mode of guile.
Each guile, a whirlpool ready Pharaoh's hosts to spoil.
In Moses, and in Moses' God, seek refuge then.
Abandon not God's faith for Pharaohs and their men.
The one true God adore; in Ahmed's faith believe.
Thy soul and body save,—from Abū-Jahl retrieve.[7]

The Jew a Christian mother to that idol brought.

An infant in her arms; the fire with blazes fraught.

"Fall down and worship;" cried he, "senseless stock adore;

The fire shall then not harm thee, now, nor evermore."

That mother was a woman firm in true belief;

And thence disdained prostration, though 't should give relief.

They snatched her infant; next, they dashed it in the flame.

The mother's spirit quailed to see this deed of shame.

Though not herself, to save her infant, she'd bow down.

But lo! a miracle! The babe cried: "Let alone!

Uninjured am I here. Come in. Be not dismayed.

'Tis cool and pleasant. Cease to feel of fire afraid;—

Mere blinding bandage to the eyes;—naught but a veil.

God's mercy's here revealed,—made manifest. All hail!

Come in, my mother, dear. The truth thou shalt record.

Thou'lt here perceive how saints hold converse with the Lord.

Come in; and witness water blazing high, as fire.

This is a world where flame like water is;—not dire.

Come. Look on miracles for blessed Abr'am wrought;[8]

Whose furnace changed to gardens, out of firewood brought.

Death then I underwent, when I was born of thee.

The fear of death swept o'er me, ere my eyes could see.

With birth I 'scaped from prison, narrow, dark, and drear;

Emerging to a world, vast, radiant, bright, and clear.

Alas! that world, you see, is but a second womb.

Joy, comfort, happiness, are found beyond the tomb.

Within this fire a realm of wonders lies around;

Each atom's here a Jesus;—balm to heal each wound.

This world I'm in's reality;—not merely form.

The scene I've left's all vanity;—food for the worm.

Come in, my mother; quick! Seize this auspicious hour.

Come in! Let opportunity not 'scape thy pow'r.

Come in; come in; in name of parent's tenderness.

Come in! This fire has no devouring ruthlessness.

Come in! Thou'st witnessed all that Jewish dog can move.

Come in! The grace and power of God Almighty prove.

'Tis from my love for thee I thus so much insist;

From pleasure felt by me, for thee I've fear dismissed.

Come in; come in! And others call, to follow thee.

The Great King here His bounteous table's spread for me.

Come in; come in! All of you, saints of God, elect!

Resigned ones![9] Faith's cup of martyrdom select!

Come in! Flock in; in crowds; as moths around a light!

This year has tens of thousands springs; but not one night."

Thus loudly cried the infant from its bed of flame.

Th' assembled crowds all heard it. All were seized with shame.

A sudden holy impulse urged them to obey.

In crowds those men and women cast their lives away.

No force was needed;—no compulsion;—all was love;

For bitterness is sweet to all whom love doth move.

To such a point it came that guards and soldiers, all,

Were fain to cry: "Withhold! The fire is more than full!"

The Jewish king at sight of all this love and zeal,

Was shamed,—was thunderstruck; his wicked heart did reel.

He saw that faith can give the lover's ardent flame.

Self-sacrifice is naught in true devotion's name.

Thank God! Beelzebub was conquered in that Jew.

Thank God! 'Twas Satan's self these darksome deeds did rue.

The shame he sought to bring upon the cheeks of some,

A hundredfold was heaped on his own head at home.
He thought from others' shame the veiling leaf to tear;
He saw them safe, his own foul nakedness laid bare.
A ribald fellow once, by lewdest mob sustained,
Called railing out on Ahmed. Wry his mouth remained.
He then came begging pity, in the Prophet's trace:
"Forgive, Muhammed, who'rt endued with wisdom's grace.
For want of knowing better, insolent I was.
'Tis I that merit scorn and mockery. Alas!"
When God decides to humble any sinner, proud,
A demon stirs this last t' insult some man of God.
And he whom God elects to cloak where 'tis he halts,
Has grace bestowed on him to cover others' faults.
Should favour from the Lord in mercy reach a man,
Humility is given him; to pray 's part of his plan.
How blessed are the eyes that smart with sorrow's brine!
How blessed is the heart inflamed with love divine!
Contrition's tears are ever hallowed by heaven's smile.
The latter end of all things man should scan awhile.
Wherever water flows, the fields are fresh and green.
Tears followed are by grace;—as all the prophets ween.

Then imitate the water-wheel, that groans and weeps.[10]
By prayers, and moans, and tears, a man his heart pure keeps.
Wouldst thou shed tears? Feel pity, when thou meetest woe.
Wouldst mercy find? Show mercy, when men bow them low.
The Jewish king reproached the fire: "O raging thing!
Thy all-destructive might, where is it? Where's thy sting?
If thou wilt not consume, what quality hast thou?
Or has my fortune veered; and with it, thy dread glow?
Thou sparest not thy worshippers, the Magian race.
Whence comes it; these who spurn thee, Christians, meet with grace?
Thou never wast, O fire, for patience noted here.
Why burn'st thou not? What is there? Hast thou lost thy power?
Is this eye-binding?[11] Is it, rather, reason's blind?
How is't thy flames consume not all their hated kind?
Bewitched thee have they? Or is't magic natural?
Or is't my fortune wills that thou turn prodigal?"
To him the fire: "O miscreant! I'm still the same.
Come in and try, thou, how thou'lt find my smallest flame.

My nature, as my substance, has not suffered change.
Outside my nature's limit I've no power to range.
At door of Turkman's tent the savage household dogs
Do wag their tails before a guest, and crouch like logs.
But should a stranger pass by, near the guarded tent,
Him then those dogs assail, with lion-like intent.
Less than a dog I'm not, in service to my Lord.
Than Turkman less, there's none, in rights, upon earth's sward."
When fire thy body injures, and inflicts some harm;
Remember, its consuming power can also warm.
And when a fire thus serves thee, acts some needful part,
Reflect! Those qualities thou seest did God impart.
Art injured, 'haps? Fall down; entreat the Lord with prayer.
The hurtful power was given by Him in gracious care.
Should He so will, each injury a blessing is.
Chained captives find their freedom by a word of His.
Fire, air, earth, water, all are servants of their God.
I, thou, them lifeless deem. He knows they live and plod.
In presence of the great Creator fire must still
Its service do; and, lover-like, work out His will.
Thou strikest flint on steel; fire instantly leaps forth.

'Tis by commandment of the Lord it thus takes birth.

Strike not together, thou, the flint and steel of lust.

For, male and female like, they'll generate; they must.

The flint and steel are means. Far higher raise thy look.

With reason thou'rt endowed. Go; read the holy book.

One means comes from another means; and cause from cause.

Without a means or cause, no means from self e'er rose.

The means by which all prophets' miracles are wrought,

Of higher order are than earthly means; no doubt.

Man's mind can compass how these latter act, and when;

The former hidden are from all but prophet's ken.

These former 'tis that give the latter power to act;

And rarely, that, their normal action, counteract.

A means a rope is, by the help of which we reach;

And in this worldly pit by means each reaches each.

Around its coiling cylinder the well-rope's wound.

To shut our eyes to this would blind indeed be found.

The ropes by means of which results are seen to steer,

In this our world, deem not they're moved by star or sphere;

Lest thou become confused and giddy like a wheel;—

Take fire, consume, like tinder, sparks of shame to feel.

The air becomes a fire at times by God's decree.
Both air and fire run wild with joy, His means to be.
The streams of mercy, the consuming fires of wrath,
Thou'lt see, my son, are both from God. Look well, forsooth.
Were not the wind aware of God's almighty power,
How had it ever blown the blast of 'Ād's[12] last hour?
Around his Muslims Hūd a saving circle drew.
The wind within that mystic circuit softly blew.
While all that were beyond were dashed to pieces soon.
Like chaff before the breeze, their limbs around were strewn.
Shaybān the shepherd, too, a circle round his fold
Was used to draw; whate'er the season, hot or cold;
On Fridays, when, at midday's sacred hour of praise,
He to a congregation hied; lest wolf should seize.
No wolf was ever known to break the holy spell;
Nor sheep to stray beyond; each knew the limit well.
To wind, to wolf, to sheep, and lusts of every one,
The circle traced by saint a barrier was, like stone.
To Gnostic, so likewise, the harmless gale of death
Blows mild and gentle, summer-breezes-like on heath.
And fire was fangless; could not Abraham offend.

How should it hurt him? Was he not God's "Chosen Friend"?
The pious man burns not in fire of fleshly lust.
But sinners still consumed are upon earth's crust.
The Red Sea waves, all raging by divine command,
The host of Israel knew; but Pharaoh's armies drown'd.
The earth, again, wide gaping at Jehovah's word,
Did Korah and his wealth devour; but Moses spared.[13]
In Jesu's hand, warmed with his breath, the fictile clay
As living birds arose, spread wing, and flew away.[14]
Thy lauds and praises, too, breath from thy frame account.
Sincerity them vivifies; to heaven they mount.
The rock of Sion danced at sight of Moses' God[15]
As perfect cenobite; its faults were all removed.
What wonder if a hill should dance and saint become?
Was not great Moses' self a clod of clay and loam?
The Jewish king now manifested great surprise.
These things, he said, were mockeries, mere patent lies.
His councillors conjured him more sedate to be;
And not to push his hardihood to rash degree.
These councillors he fettered, into prison cast;
Injustice to injustice adding, first and last.

A shout was heard from heaven when matters reached that point:
"Jew dog! Prepare for vengeance from on high! Aroynt!"
The fire then blazed amain; its flames lapped all around.
It slew and burnt the mob of Jews from off the ground.
Their origin was hell, from whence their souls had come;
Their goal was also hell; to it they now went home.
The Jewish race is hellish; many proofs are shown.
Parts are they of a whole accursed; as is well known.
Their nature hellish; all their joy God's saints to burn.
Their fire recoiled upon themselves. 'Twas justice' turn.
For them, who were, by nature, children born of wrath,
The lowest depths of hell were fittest cells, forsooth.
A mother ever yearneth after her own child;
A dam is ever followed by her offspring wild.
Though true that water may enclosed be in a tank,
The air will it absorb. 'Twas thence to earth it sank.
Air sets it free; direct, restores it to its source,
By little and by little. None perceive its course.
So, too, our breath, in manner like, steals soul away,
By little and by little, from this house of clay,
In words of praise, ascending to God's holy throne,

From us to where He reigns;—as known to Him alone.
Our breathings rise on wings of true sincerity,
The offerings of our hearts to all eternity.
We then receive rewards for those poor words of praise,
In tenfold showers of mercy from th' Ancient of Days.
And we are still constrained to utter songs of thanks,
That man should so be raised above th' angelic ranks.
This rising and descending alternates for aye.
The Lord forbid that I should fail therein one day!
We're drawn, we are attracted, so to love the Lord;
As we were first instructed, firm to trust His word.
Each man will turn his eyes in hope towards the place,
Where he has tasted joy some former day of grace.
The pleasures of each kind are most with their own kin;
As part must share with whole its qualities, its sin.
Things needs must be assigned unto a common class,
If aught they have in common; two will form a race.
Thus bread and water are not human at the first;
But human they become, through hunger and through thirst.
In form they have no tie with us of human kind;
But through a special link they kindred with us find.

If pleasure, then, we find in what's not of our race,

Be sure there's some connection through which this takes place.

If that connection but resemblance be in shape,

It will not last; it's for a time; it must escape.

'Tis true that birds find pleasure in a whistle's note;

But then they fancy 'tis their mate's, on whom they dote.

And if a thirsty man take pleasure in his wine,

He tastes the lees, and loathes. To water he'll incline.

A pauper may amused be with counterfeited coin;

But take this to the mint; defaced 'twill be, in fine.

Then be not thou misled with gilded counterfeit;

Delusion will thee plunge headlong into hell's pit.

---

1. Qur'ān, chap. lxxxv., the name of which literally means "*the Towers,*" but is also applied to the *Signs of the Zodiac*. These Christians were the people of Nejrān in south-western Arabia; their persecutor Dhū-Nuwās, a Jew, king of Yaman, some time before Muhammed.
2. "Gardens beneath which rivers flow" is a frequently recurring expression in the Qur'ān. Some have special names.
3. See Qur'ān xxxv. 29: "Then we caused" thee "to inherit the Scripture."
4. In Qur'ān ii. 132, Islām is termed "*God's Baptism*."In ii. 156, and again in vii. 42, and xi. 21, "God's curse" is invoked on sinners.
5. This is the story alluded to in Qur'ān lxxxv., quoted above. In traditions, Dhū-Nuwās was the name of the Jewish king of Yaman, who burnt the Christians of Nejrān in a fiery trench on their refusing to forsake their faith. The idol is imaginary; from Nebuchadnezzar.

6. Qur'ān xvi. 41; xxxvii. 72; xl. 76; speaks of the "Gates of Hell;" and a commentary to the last says they are held to be seven.
7. Abū-Jahl was a surname given by Muhammed to one of his most inveterate enemies of the Quraysh, killed at Badr. The word means: *"Father of Ignorance,"* and here indicates *fleshly pride*. He had formerly borne the surname of Abū-'l-Hakem, which means: *Father of the Arbitrator*.
8. In Qur'ān xxi. 69, is related the miracle by which Abraham was saved from the fire into which he was cast by Nimrod for his refusal to worship an image.
9. The word *"Muslim,"* whence the corruption *Moslem*, means, in Arabic, *"one who acquiesces in the truth and will of God."* As such, Muslims have existed under every dispensation.
10. The creaking, leaky water-wheel, the Persian wheel, is well known in the East.
11. *"Eye-binding"* is a name for sorcery. The spectator is supposed to have his sight *spell-bound*, so as not to see what is really done.
12. 'Ād, a pre-Semitic, perhaps Turanian, people in south-eastern Arabia, often mentioned in the Qur'ān. They refused to believe the prophet Hūd (supposed to be *Heber*), and were destroyed, lxix. 6-7, by an eight days' tempest.
13. Qur'ān xxiii. 76, &c.
14. Qur'ān iii. 43.
15. Qur'ān vii. 139.

V. THE LION AND THE BEASTS.

Kalīl' and Dimna's book relates a charming tale,[1]
From which males may a moral draw;—and eke, female.
Within a shelter'd vale, four-footed game in droves,
Were kept in tremor by a lion from its groves.
So frequently had he borne victims off from thence,
The vale a prison had become in every sense.
A consultation held, they fair proposals state,
To satisfy the lion's hunger by a rate;
But on condition that he rapine lay aside,
And not prolong disquiet in that valley wide.
The lion gave consent, if they'd perform their part;
Remarking: "I've a victim been to wily art.

Man persecutes me with his deadly stratagems;
The snake and scorpion sting me;—rancour's true emblems.
But worse than any man, in venom and in spleen,
The fleshly lust within me traitor's always been.
But I've grown wary. Has not Ahmed said: 'Rely!
Believers are not twice caught by the selfsame lie?'"[2]
Their answer was: "O most sagacious, knowing guide,
Thy caution pray dismiss; decree of God abide.
Suspicion, caution, ever is corroding ill.
Put trust in Providence; and God thy maw will fill.
Strive not with Providence, however strong thou be;
Lest Providence should take offence, and war with thee."
He answered them: "Sure! Sure! Trust Providence we must.
His prophets in the Lord have always placed their trust.
To trust in God, and yet put forth our utmost skill,
The surest method is, to work His holy will.
The Prophet plainly said to his disciple train:
'Put trust in God, and bind thy camel's shank amain.'[3]
Remember the old saw: 'The friend of God must work.'[4]
Through trust in God, neglect not ways and means, O clerk."

Abashed they were not; answer thus they promptly made:

"To gain aught from the poor is fraud; a trick of trade.

There is no gain so good as trust placed in the Lord.

What more praiseworthy than to build upon His word?

How many flee *this* danger, falling into *that*!

From fryingpan leaps one, to light in fire right pat.[5]

Man plans a stratagem; in it is caught himself.

That which he took for health, he finds is death itself.

He locks his door when treason's lurking in his house.

So Pharaoh deemed he'd danger shun ere it should rouse.

How many thousand infants did he doom to death;

While Moses, whom he feared, his own roof was beneath.

Our eyes afflicted are with various kinds of ills.

Then go and make them blind, by seeing God 'tis wills.

God's sight of providence is keener than men's eyes.

By seeing with His sight, thou'lt find all thou wilt prize.

An infant, that can neither grasp nor walk as yet,

Takes seat upon his father's neck, and runs. Sweet pet.

Some seasons past, he scarcely gains some strength of limb;

When sorrow fastens on him;—sharp, and ghastly grim.

The hearts of men, before they gain or power or wealth,

Decline away from duty, pleasures seek by stealth.
And since by God's decree from paradise they're rent,
They prisoners become to rage, lust, discontent.
We are the household of that Householder, whose word
Thus spake: 'Creation's all as children of the Lord.'[6]
He that doth send the fattening rain upon the earth,
In mercy, too, can feed His creatures from their birth."
The lion thus replied: "'Tis true. But still, the Lord
A ladder sets before our feet to be explor'd.
Step after step we have to mount unto the roof.
Th' idea of compulsion's quite devoid of proof.
Two feet thou hast. Then why thyself hold to be lame?
Two hands also. Why maimed account thyself in name?
Whene'er a master puts a spade in hand of slave,
He has no need to speak; the act expression gave.
Our hands just so are given; spades they are to us.
Think out this problem well; it needs not any fuss.
When thou hast laid this unction to thy soul amain,
In duty's path to lay down life thou'lt count as gain.
Those symbols indices are, whence are secrets known.
Responsibility's from thee withdrawn; work shown.
Thou'rt surely burdened. Borne also most truly art.

Recipient; hence accepted;—fully on His part.
Recipient be of God's command; content thou'lt be.
Seek unto Him; and to Him joined thyself thou'lt see.
To strive to give thanks power provides this to perform.
Allege compulsion. Gratitude's ground thou'lt deform.
Thanks for thy powers the power of thanks tenfold expands.
Take favour for compulsion. Power will leave thy hands.
Compulsion dost affirm? That's sleeping by the way.
Go not to sleep until thou'st fairly won the day.
Sleep not, Compulsionist! Thou man, with folly rife!
Until thou reach the goal, the fruitful Tree of Life.
The cool breeze there will rustle through its leaves profuse,
Each moment scattering fruits for food and future use.
Compulsion's creed is sleep among the highwaymen;
Unseasonable bird is mercilessly slain.[7]
If thou at God's signs carp and peck, so finding fault,
Though man thou count thyself, 'tis womanlike assault.
The little sense thou hadst has really taken flight;
A head that has no brains is tail turn'd round to sight.
Ungrateful men are ever cursed of God on earth;
And after death are flung to hell-fire's vengeful hearth.

If thou repose thy trust in God's almighty pow'r,

Sow first thy seed; and then, await the harvest hour."

The beasts a clamour raised; they would not be repressed:

"They who on means depend, are urged by greed confessed.

The millions upon millions, man and womankind,

Are pinched by want; they suffer need; they food scarce find.

By millions and by millions, since creation's day,—

Insatiate dragons,—they their gaping jaws display.

A crowd of would-be wise men stratagems invent,

Enough to upset mountains, could they give them vent.

So God himself described in His most holy book

Their arts: 'By which they'd tear away the hills.'[8]

Just look.

Except the lot decreed by Providence of yore,

By hunting or by toiling none can swell his store.

Device of man, his plans, shall all be brought to naught.

God's dispensations sole will stand, with wisdom fraught.

Strive not then, man of sense; except good name to leave.

Exertion's a delusion. Out! Thou sottish knave!"

A simpleton one morning rushing came in haste,

Where Solomon his court of justice then had placed.
His cheeks were blanched, his lips were blue; effects of fright.
Said Solomon to him: "What ails thee? Say aright."
Him answer'd that poor wretch: "The angel, Lord, of death,[9]
Upon me fixed, just now, a look that stopped my breath."
Said Solomon: "What wilt thou I should do for thee?"
He answered: "That the wind may now commanded be[10]
To carry me away forthwith to Hindūstān.
Perchance by fleeing thither, save my life I can."
See how mankind do shun the garb of poverty.
Hence they're a prey to greed and dire necessity.
This fear of poverty is like that man's dismay,
Its Hindūstān, remark, is greed and grasping's sway.
So Solomon the wind commanded, him, forthwith,
To bear to Hindūstān; and land him near some frith.
Another day as Solomon his court did hold,
Death's angel came; the king to him the matter told:
"Thy wrathful look, the other day, upon that man,
Has driven him his home to quit for Hindūstān.
Didst thou in wrath survey the pious man that way,
That he might wander forth a waif, like sheep astray?

Or was thy look's intent, so dreadful to behold,
His soul to separate from its corporeal fold?"
To him replied the angel: "King of sprites and men!
His fancy him misled; he'll ne'er do so again.
'Twas not in anger then that I did look on him;
'Twas wonder him to see here, looking hale and prim.
For God had me commanded: 'Go this very day,
And take his soul in Hindūstān, his debt to pay.'
In wonder, then, I said within myself: 'Had he
A hundred wings, in Hindūstān he could not be.'
But going, still, by God's command, to Hindūstān,
Him there I found, and took his soul with my own hand."
So thou, good reader, understand, the things of earth
'Tis God ordains. Reflect. 'Twas written ere his birth.
From whom to flee? From self? Oh! That's absurd!
From whom to steal? From God? Worse, worse! No word!
The lion now remarked: "The words you speak are true.
But just consider how the prophets, saints, ensue.
What they have wrought hath God blessed, made to prosper still;
Their joys and griefs, their sufferings, pains, were by His will.
Their stratagems dictated by their God were, all.[11]

'Who comes of gentle blood, will gentle words let fall.'[12]
Their traps have taken angels with the baits they placed.
Their seeming slips and faults were all by wisdom traced.
Exert thyself, O man; put shoulder to the wheel,
The prophets and the saints to imitate in zeal.
Exertion's not a struggle against Providence.
'Twas Providence enjoined it,—made it our defence.
Blasphemer may I be, if ever single man
Bestowed in vain one effort to fulfil God's plan.
Thou hast no broken bones; why bind thy limbs in splints?
Have patience yet awhile; then laugh; we're not mere flints.
It is a bad investment to seek worldly gain.[13]
Whose hope is placed in heaven never shall see pain.[14]
The stratagems employed for worldly gain are vile,
But stratagems for gaining heaven are worth our while.
Blest stratagem is that which bursts a prison door.
Curst stratagem is one that spreads a dungeon floor.
The world's a dungeon. We are all in prison here.
Burst, then, thy prison gate, and free thyself from fear.
What is the world? Unmindful of our God to be;
Not gold or silver, wife or children, things we see.

The wealth we hold at service of our God is blest.
'The riches of the just are pure,' Ahmed confess'd.
The water from a leak is danger to a ship;
The sea beneath her keel is just what makes her skip.
Great Solomon despised wealth, sway, with all his heart.
With countless treasures poor he named himself. Best part!
An empty jar will float upon a raging sea,
The air that fills it will not let it sunken be.
Th' afflatus of true poverty man's soul will buoy.
Above the troubles of the world he rides. Ahoy!
Should all earth's boundless riches by him be possessed;
The whole is viewed in his pure sight as naught at best.
Close then the inlet to thy heart; seal it with love;
First filling it with wisdom's spirit from above.
Endeavour is from God; so sickness, and its balm.
He vainly strives who would deny this truthful psalm."
Of this complexion, many proofs the lion brought;
No answer those compulsionists in dispute sought.
The fox, the deer, the hare, and eke the sly jackal,
Were fain to quit compulsion's cause, for good and all.
A treaty they concluded with the forest king,

That he, by this concession, should not lose a thing.
His daily ration ready always should be found;
And he should have no cause to trespass on their ground.
Lots they would cast among themselves from day to day.
On whom the lot should fall, he'd be the lion's prey.
But lo, at length the lot upon the hare did light.
He found it very hard, and wailed his awful plight.
The other beasts remarked: "We each have had our turn;
And none of us refused th' agreement to confirm.
By breach of faith on us fresh infamy bring not.
Begone forthwith; the lion must not be forgot."
The hare replied: "Dear friends, a respite to me grant.
A stratagem I'll plan, and cheat this grim tyrant.
My wily plan shall save the souls of all alive;
And safety heirloom be your children shall derive.
Thus every prophet's promised to his sect, at least,
Salvation from the doom o'erhanging man and beast.
They found a ready way to 'scape beyond the spheres,
So soon as to reflect they turned their minds from fears.
Man sees another's eye is but a wee, wee thing;
He knows how great a service can th' eye's pupil bring."

The beasts in answer: "Jackass! Prate to us no more.
Consider. Thou'rt a hare; a beast of no great store.
What talk is this? Thy betters ne'er have used such speech.
They never would have dared to think as thou dost preach.
It must be thou'rt o'erweening, or our fate's at hand.
For otherwise, pretensions such as thine can't stand."
To them as a rejoinder puss spoke: "My dear friends,
My inspiration's God's; small means effect great ends.
The wisdom God hath taught the little honey-bee,
You do not find possessed by lion, or by me.
We see its cells arranged, with liquid sweetness filled,
The portals of such art to open God hath willed.
Then see the silkworm, how it's taught by God to spin.
Have elephants the power to draw out threads so thin?
The earthy Adam was by God taught all our names.[15]
His knowledge was the admiration of heaven's frames.
Th' angelic choir were silenced; they knew not so much.
The fiend be cursed. He'd not confess the fact was such.
That fasting hermit of six hundred thousand years[16]
Became the new-born babe's dire muzzle,—source of tears.

Lest it should suck the milk religion's teachings give,—

Lest it should soar on high around heaven's towers, and live,—

The learning of external sense a muzzle lies,—

The milk of truth sublime's denied to all its cries.

But God hath planted in man's heart a precious pearl.

Nor seas, nor skies, such gem enclose within their whirl!

How long of form thy talk—form-worshipper—vain man?

Cannot thy senseless soul cast off form's deadening ban?

Did human form alone suffice a man to make,

Ahmed and Abū-Jahl were one in grade, in stake.

A painting on a wall may show the human form.

But look and see what lacks, the figure to inform.

'Tis life it wants, and soul;—the pretty-looking thing!

Ask for its life. No! No! Though portrait of a king.

The heads of all earth's lions bowed down meek and low,

When God the Seven Sleepers'[17] dog applauded. How!

To call it dog, to charge it with defect of race,

No harm can do it; God in heaven hath given it place.

'Twas not the pen prescrib'd the qualities of form;

Th' Omniscient, the Just, 'twas, made it multiform.

Th' Omniscient, the Just, a Spirit is, All-Blest;

Him no place holds; He's not before, behind, east, west.
He influences matter from His high abode;
But heaven of heavens cannot contain the Spirit's mode."
That theme is endless. Let us then just turn away.
Let's ask about the hare; hear what he has to say.
Sell off thy ass' ears; with the price a fresh pair buy.
An ass's ears will never understand this cry.[18]
Go to. Examine well the hare's most foxy wile,—
The subtle stratagem that did the lion foil.
Wisdom's the seal by which great Solomon did rule.
The whole world's but a frame, and wisdom is its soul.
Hence 'tis, by wisdom's spell, as clay on potter's wheel,
The seas, the hills, the plains, are made man's power to feel.
The lion, tiger, leopard, dread him as does mouse;
The shark, the crocodile, he follows to their house.
The demon and the fairy, both constrained to flight,
Have hid themselves from him,—are only seen by night.
The human being has his foes hid every side.
A prudent man by caution may in safety bide.
Those hidden foes,—the hideous, and the fair as well,—
By day and night affect his heart with charm and spell.

Thou enterest a river, just to have a bathe;
A hidden thorn may pierce thy foot, bared of its swathe.
Thou seest it not. 'Tis hid at bottom of the stream.
Thou feel'st it in thy foot; thou knowest it's not a dream.
Plagues, troubles, fears, and cares, of various degree,
All spring from many sides, and fix themselves in thee.
Bear all with patience; slowly thou'lt experience gain.
Thou'lt recognise the truth; the dark will be made plain.
At length thou'lt scout the vagaries of learned men,
And take unto thyself, as patterns, saints of ken.
The beasts on second thoughts resolved to hear puss out.
"Explain," said they, "what 'tis thou'dst have us set about.
Let's hear; 'tis with the lion we shall have to do.
Set forth thy plan; let's see what stratagem's in view.
Deliberation's ever wisdom's truest friend;
Two heads than one are better,—lead to safer end.
The prophet spake: 'O ruling judge, ere thou decide,
Take counsel; for 'tis said: "In councillors confide."'"
The hare objects: "A secret's not for ev'ry clod.
Odd even is at times; and sometimes even's odd.
Too closely with a mirror shouldst thou converse hold,

From prudery it umbrage takes, grows dull; the scold.
On matters three, allow not oft thy lips to speak:
First, going; gold, next; third, the path thou hast to seek.
These all have sundry enemies and deadly foes,
Who'll lie in ambush, each, if he thy purpose knows.
If thou 'Adieu' to only one or two shouldst call,
Remember: 'Two's a secret; three is none at all.'
If fast together thou shouldst bind birds, two or three,
They'll quiet lie on earth, nor strive themselves to free.
Men hold it best to ask for counsel in wide terms.
Beware; and wrangle not with perverse pachyderms.
The Prophet covertly men's counsel used to seek.
His answer he'd obtain; his purpose did not leak.
He'd speak in parables, and so convey his wish,
That foes might hear, but not suspect its purport. Pish!
He'd ferret out in answers all he wished to learn;
And still not give an inkling of his thought's real turn."
Enough we've said of this. Now turn we to our tale.
By puss the lion's held right hungry in the vale.
And so it was; the hare his counsel did conceal;
He would not let his comrades learn how he would deal.
Some hours he now let pass before he took his leave;

Then to the lion went, their honour to retrieve.
He found the brute impatient, chafing at delay,
From hunger's pangs fierce howling, tearing every spray;
And roaring in his rage: "I knew it so would be!
Those vile, time-serving rascals! Thus they worry me!
They're plausible, smooth-speaking, bland, calm, mild; and still
They've cheated me! Alas! Who will be cheated, will!
A too complaisant prince most foully is let in!
Who sees no farther than his nose, none heeds a pin!"
The path is smoothed beneath which lurks a deadly trap.
A missive's filled with compliments; all mere clap-trap.
Bland messages, smooth words, are but a hook or snare.
Civility's a sandbank; life's bark's oft wrecked there,
The sand from which a spring of water's seen to flow
Is rare to find. Go, seek such. Where? I do not know.
Yes, yes! Be sure that sand's a holy man of God,
Unto himself lost, rapt, in union with his Lord.
Religion's crystal waters flow from him apace;
Disciples thence are edified and grow in grace.
A worldling is a sandbank, void of moisture quite,
On which you may make shipwreck, lose all chance of light.

Seek wisdom, then, from wisdom's sons, the pure of mind;
So mayest thou learn the way salvation's port to find.
A seeker after wisdom, is, of wisdom, fount.
"Humanities" he shuns; them, he does trash account.
A memory replete with holy Qur'ān's lore
A "hidden tablet" is;[19] its mind is wisdom's store.
If man begin as pupil to good common sense,
He'll end by being teacher,—mind, his audience.
Man's mind declares, as Gabriel to Ahmed there,[20]
"One step beyond due limit leaves me ashes sere.
Go forward, man of God; leave me; I know my place.
To every one's not given to see God face to face."
Whoever, out of sloth, endeavour's path shall quit,
And patience lose, compulsion's creed must needs admit.
Whoe'er affirms compulsion, brings woe on himself,
Until his troubles to the grave conduct the elf.
The Prophet said: "My mission, 's truth to preach to man.
Much trouble will surround it during my life's span."
Compulsion's but the setting of a broken bone,[21]
Or binding of a muscle, torn, asunder gone.
Thou hast not broke thy leg in travelling God's path.

Why put thy leg in splints? Cast off the idle swath.
He that shall really lose a leg in God's just fight,
To him Burāq shall come, a chariot of light.[22]
Religion's carrier was he; carried then he'll be.
God's precepts he accepted; accepted now is he.
The Great King's orders has he bravely carried out.
Henceforward he's a herald;—shall God's judgments shout.
The planets until now may have affected him;
Above the planets now he rests, and rules their trim.
If forms material find much honour in thy sight,
Thou'lt doubt the truth of writ: "The moon clave," left and right.[23]
Renew thy faith at heart, not merely with mouth's gust,
O hypocrite, who covertly dost worship lust.
While lust is dominant, faith cannot be so strong;
For lust's a bolt to close the door, lest faith should throng.
The virgin text of God explain not thou away;
Reform thyself; deform not what the Lord doth say.
As suits thy lusts thou comments makest on God's Qur'ān.
Vile, as by thee perverted, is its sense, base man.
Thy case resemblance has with one of silly fly,

Who once upon a time himself thought very high.
Intoxicated was he, though he'd sipp'd no wine.
Like sunbeam's mote he saw himself most gaily shine.
He'd heard of noble falcons scorning lure and cage;
And straightway dubbed himself the phœnix of the age.
Our fly on scrap of straw, in pool from ass's ease,
Had poised himself, as though a sailor on the seas.
Then cried: "Lo! I've called forth a sea and ship at will.
Long since I 've had a notion, pleasure's cup to fill.
Behold a sea and ship of which I captain am,
Imbued with naval science, bold as any ram."
Imagination thus had conjured up a sea.
To him it boundless seemed, dwarfing credulity.
Compared with him it was a truly boundless pool.
When people see with their own eyes, call them not fool.
His universe was measured by his power of sight.
To such an eye such pool a sea was. He was right.
A false interpreter of scripture is such fly.
His fancy is the urine pool on which straws ply.
If flies in fancy thus explain the things they see,
By fortune's freaks, in turn, a phœnix each may be.
He's less than fly, of whom this tale example lends;

His soul unworthy is ev'n of the frame it tends.

Just like the hare who'd lion undertake to fight,

How should his soul remain in his poor carcase, slight?

The lion growled in tones of anger and of rage:

"My ear it was bewrayed me; war my foes did wage.

Compulsionists' false wiles placed bandage on my eyes.

Their wooden swords it was that stung my skin, like flies.

Henceforward I'll not list to such cajoleries,—

Of elves and demons, in the wilderness, mere cries.

Tear, rend them; O my heart, pay no regard to them.

Strip off their skins; there's naught beneath; mere stratagem."

When words deceitful are employed as wraps for guile,

They're bubbles on the water, only last a while.

Such words are merely shell; th' intent their kernel is;—

Or coloured portraiture of man; no life is his.

A shell may often cover kernel of foul smell.

A kernel sound can well afford to lose its shell.

If mind be pen; if page be water, in thy hands;

Be not surpris'd when all that's written quick disbands.

On water 'tis to write, t' expect good faith from bail.

Regret must follow. Shrug your shoulders. What avail!

Man with desires is oft puffed up, and wishes vain.
Put out desire; you'll find Jehovah's endless reign.
His messages are peace, and sweet to pious soul;
For He alone's eternal, free from change, and whole.
Men's prayers for kings and princes change full oft in tone.
The prayers of saints and prophets call on God alone.
Th' existence of earth's sovereign's empty pomp and pride,
The glories of a prophet in his God abide.
The names of kings on coins are used a little while;
The name of Ahmed there is ever seen to smile.[24]

That name of Ahmed covers all the prophets still;[25]
As hundred, when 'tis said, ninety includes as well.
Reflections such as these would never have an end.
So turn we through our hare and lion's tale to wend.
The hare but slowly towards the lion took his way.
Wiles in his brain he hatched; weighed what he had to say.
Procrastination served him his design to fill;
He'd secrets, one or two, the royal mind to still.
How many worlds there are that hang on wisdom's worth.

How vast an ocean wisdom! Compasses the earth.

A shoreless ocean is the subtle mind of man

A fearless diver sounds its depths; as who else can?

Our bodies drift about in mind's strong eddies still,

Like basins on the water, at the stream's sole will.

Until they fill, they float like bowls, on ocean's brink;

And, like the bowls, when full, they cannot choose but sink.

The wind's invisible; a world without, we see.

Our bodies are the waves or drops of that vast sea.

Whatever means our bodies seek to grasp, anon,

A billow drives it far; no sooner seen than gone.

Until our hearts perceive the Giver of all good,

The swiftly-flying bolt shot far from o'er the flood,

They hold their coursers to be lost; and out of spite,

They push their roadsters hastily, as thoughts invite.

They hold their coursers to be lost; and all the while

Like noble courser, roadster's borne them many a mile.

They now begin to wail, distress'd, and ask the way.

They knock at ev'ry door they see, they beg, they pray:

"The stealer of our courser was a little child.

What horse is this, my master? Seems it not too wild?"

"O yes, a horse it is; but not the horse you want.
Come to your senses, man; to some one else go chant."
The soul is void of patency and fellowship.
Thou, like a wine-jar, full within, hast parched lip.
How shouldst thou e'er distinguish red from green or brown,
When these are all the colours unto thee well known?
And when thy mind is dazed by colour's magic round,
All colour's lost in one bright light diffused around.
Those colours, too, all vanish from our view by night.
We learn from this, that colour's only seen through light.
The sense of colour-seeing's not from light distinct.
So, too, the sudden rainbow of our mind's instinct.
From sunlight, and the like, all outer colours rise;
The inward tints that mark our minds, from God's sunrise.
The light that lights the eye's the light that's in the heart.
Eye's light is but derived from what illumes that part.
The light that lights the heart's the light that comes of God,
Which lies beyond the reach of sense and reason, clod!
By night we have no light; no colour can we see.
Thus, light we learn by darkness, its converse. Agree!

A seeing of the light, perception is of tints;
And these distinguished are through darkness' gloomy hints.
Our griefs and sorrows were by God first introduced,
That joy to sense apparent thence should be reduced.
Occult things, thus, by converse, grow apparent, all.
Since God has no converse, apparent He can't fall.
Sight first saw light, and then the colours saw.
From converse converse stands forth, as Frank from Negro.
By converse of the light, distinguish we the light;
A converse 'tis that converse shows unto our sight.
The light of God no converse has in being's bound;
By converse, then, man has not its distinction found.
Our eyes cannot distinguish God, decidedly;
Though He distinguish Moses and the Mount from thee.
Form and ideal, gnat and lion, word and sense,
Sound of the voice and thought, learnst thou by dissidence,
The words and sounds take rise from exercise of thought.
The sea of thought is where? Of this thou knowest naught.
Words, as thou seest, rise as waves upon the sea.

The sea of thought thou knowest great, immense to be.

The waves of thought arise, by breath of knowledge raised;

They take the forms of words, of sounds, which ear has seized.

Through words have forms arisen, and passed away again;

As waves still lose themselves beneath the ocean's main.

From realm of formlessness, existence doth take form;

And fades again therein: "To Him we must return."[26]

Each moment, then, for thee death and return await,

As Ahmed hath declared: "Life's transitory."[27] Wait!

Thoughts, bolts are, shot by God into the air like dust.

Whose thoughts can reach to God, through densest air of lust?

The world's renewed each moment, though we still remain

In ignorance that permanence can change sustain.

Life, like a river, ceaselessly, is still renewed;

And apes persistency, in forms by change subdued,

Through fleetness it puts on continuity's shape;

Like squib when 'tis revolved in dark by boy with tape.

A flash of flame, through motion's necessary speed,

Appears unto our eyes a fire of size, indeed.

Its length and its extension, through quickness of fact,
Appear to be effects of God's creative act.

A student of this mystery, a doctor of great skill,
Is our Husāmu-'d-Dīn,[28] whose praises books would fill.
The lion, now enraged with hunger's gnawing pain,
Perceived the hare was coming, bounding o'er the plain.
All carelessly, in confidence, he frisking came,
The lion all the while growled, gnashed his teeth from shame.
No consciousness of fault was visible, no fear;
But confidence, sure sign his conscience he felt clear.
When he'd reached hearing range, the lion him addressed
In tones of wrath: "Thou demon, insolent, possessed!

Know I'm a lion; elephants my prey I make.
The tigers, spotted pards, by me are caused to quake.
A petty hare am not I, slighted thus to be,
Or see my just dominion spurned by likes of thee.
Cast off assumed prim innocence, awake to fact;
Thou hear'st the lion's roar; forget not thus the pact."
The hare replied: "Gramercy! Hear my poor excuse.
Let me explain. Your Majesty will ne'er refuse."
The lion now: "Excuse? Thou basest of the base!

Is this the time to pay thy court? A pretty case!
Unseasonably crowing cock art thou! Reprieved?
Excuse from simpleton can never be received.
A simpleton's excuse is worse than was his fault.
Excuse of ignorance were science to assault.
Excuse from thee, thou hare, were quite devoid of sense.
Take thou me not for hare; with me strive not to fence."
The hare to him: "O prince! Have pity on the weak!
Lend ear unto the tales of them who justice seek.
Thankoffering let it be for thy august estate.
Poor supplicant like me, thou'lt not drive from thy gate.
Great river like, thy boons stream aye through all canals;
Each flower that decks thy hair in price rich pearls excels.
The sea is not dried up by yielding showers of rain.
Thy ease will not decrease by lessening of my pain."
The lion then: "My clemency I show to those
Who've it deserved. 'Tis stature rules the length of clothes."
The hare: "Give ear. Should I of grace unworthy prove,
I'm at thy feet. My life is thine, I cannot move.
At morning's early hour I set out for thy court.
Companion had I with me. True, the way is short.

That second hare I speak of, food was for thy maw;
By lot selected, as the pact lays down the law.
Upon the road, a lion on us onslaught made.
The savage, strange invader, rendered us afraid.
I remonstrated with him; told him our intent;
Said we were coming here; by treaty were we sent.
He answered: 'Prate not to me. Treaty such as this
No value has. I'm king. He a usurper is.
Thy paltry king and thee I'll quickly rend in two,
If thou and thy companion will not with me go.'
I craved of him permission, him to leave awhile,
Till I could come and tell thee of his claim and guile.
He granted leave; but kept my fellow as a pledge;
Saying otherwise he'd kill me, as his privilege.
We strove to coax and pacify the sturdy brute.
'Twas no avail. My mate he'd keep; me he'd depute.
My comrade three times was in bulk more full than I;
More plump, more sleek, more toothful. Dare I tell a lie?
Henceforward, through that lion, who can come this way?
The case is so. I've told thee truly all my say.

From hence, for evermore, thy ration's lost, forsooth.
The truth I speak to thee. Unpleasant oft is truth.
Wouldst thou thy ration have, arise and clear the way.
Come on. I'll guide. Let's see, then, who shall win the day."
The lion now: "In God's name! Come! Where is the beast?
Go thou before, if thou speak truth. Take heed at least.
I'll treat him as he merits, and a hundred such.
But should this prove a lie, thou'lt rue it very much."
The hare set out in front, so acting as a guide,
That he might lead the lion as he should decide.
A well there was not far off, which the hare had seen.
This pit he destined for the lion's last death-scene.
They journeyed thus, the two, towards the well in haste,
The scheming, plotting hare's fell stratagem to taste.
A stream of water freely bears the chaff away;
But how it undermines a mountain's hard to say.
All single-handed, Moses,—Red Sea at command,—
Can drown pursuing Pharaoh's vast ungodly band.
A gnat, by God's behest, a Nimrod may annul;
Its feeble wings may burst the sutures of his skull.[29]
The doom of him who acts on what a foe adjusts,

Is like the end of one his envier who trusts.
The punishment of Pharaoh's listening to Haman,[30]
Resembles Nimrod's, who faith pinned upon Satan.[31]
A foe who talks in friendly guise, a false game plays;
He vaunts the bait; but be thou sure, a trap he lays.
His proffered sugarcandy poison will conceal.
His seeming kindly offices are treachery's veil.
Should God ordain thy fall, thy sight will blinded be;
'Twixt friend and foe the difference thou'lt fail to see.
Since thus it is, betimes betake thyself to prayer;
Fast, supplicate, entreat thee gracious God to spare.
Thus pray: "O Thou, to whom all secrets well are known,
Crush not Thy trusting servant 'neath sore trial's stone.
If doglike acts I've acted, Thou who lions formest,
O let not loose upon me lions Thou informest.
O Lord of mercy, Pardoner of sin, All-just,
Upon me vengeance wreak not, or succumb I must.
Cause not Thy pleasant waters me to burn like fire;
Let not the fiery furnace form of stream acquire.
If Thou me madden with the vials of dismay,
Thou'lt make nonentities the parts of things to play."
What's madness? 'Tis a bandage to the eye of faith.

A stone we see as pearl, an island as a frith.
What's madness? False to judge of every stick and straw.
To seek the violet's perfume in hip and haw.
One day, when Solomon a camp had formed afield,
The birds all flocked around him, homage due to yield.
They found he spake their language, all their secrets knew.
With pleasure, birds of every kind about him flew.
The birds with Solomon all left their *twit-twit-twee,*
And spake a tongue articulate; as one might see.
Synglottism is a link, a very potent spell;[32]
Among mere strangers, man's a captive in a cell.
How many Turks and Hindūs synglottise with us;
How many pairs of each are strange as incubus!
A synglottist is then a man's another self;
But syncardism, than synglottism's much closer, elf.
Besides our words, our signs, our written characters,
From hearts, there rise by hundreds mute interpreters.
The birds about their secrets one by one communed;
About their knowledge, sciences, and voices tuned.
To pay their court to Solomon their notes they raised;
Revealed their capabilities; skill of each praised.

Not out of pride and vanity; excess 'twould seem;
But solely to please Solomon, gain his esteem.
So slaves that seek for favour at a master's hand
Exert themselves to name the talents they command.
But if they feel ashamed of one would them purchase,
Straightway they're sick, halt, deaf, or something still more base.
The turn then came for hoopoe's setting forth his skill,
To say what he could do, what office he could fill.
Said he: "O King, one little talent's all I own.
I'll tell it in few words; succinctness is a crown."
Said Solomon: "Let's hear it. What then is thy skill?"
The hoopoe answered: "This.—I perch where'er I will.
From my seat I look down like plumbline on the ground,
And see if hidden water under it is found;
Where is it; at what depth; what are its qualities;
Whence takes its rise; from rock, sand, clay's varieties.
O Solomon, whene'er thou send'st thy armies forth,
Me call to mind; my skill is surely notice worth."
To him replied then Solomon: "Esteemed good friend,
Thee I will name Purveyor-General on land.
Whene'er my troops go forth, through sandy deserts sent,

With them thou'lt journey; so, ne'er will be water scant."
The crow on hearing this with jealousy was stung.
Addressing Solomon, he said: "This bird a lie has sung.
His insolence is great to boast thus to the king.
Such falsehood's quite disgusting. Who's heard such a thing?
Had he possessed this very wonderful insight,
Would he be caught in springes barely out of sight?
He cannot see those traps beneath a little mound;
So caught he is, and caged. High dudgeon thence is found."
Said Solomon: "O hoopoe, true is this remark.
A gulp of vanity has set thee raving, stark.
How is it thou'rt so tipsy early in the day,
To come and prate of things so far out of the way?"
The hoopoe then replied: "Great King, against poor me,
For love of God, believe not all my foes' false plea.
If untruth I have spoken,—cannot prove my tale,—
I cast myself before thee; kill me without fail.
The crow denies the rule of Providence on earth;
With all his cunning, he's a miscreant from birth."
Of miscreants' defects, if any one in us
Exist, it's sure to spread,—a plague-spot cancerous.

A snare man may detect in every lust of flesh,

If God's decree will not he fall into its mesh.

By God's decree our reason ceases clear to see,

As moon, when darkened all, can hide the sun from me.

Whoever dares deny God's ruling providence,

'Tis Providence decrees his blindness, want of sense.

The Father of Mankind, Lord Nomenclator first,[33]

In every nerve possess'd a vein of knowledge nursed.

He knew the names of all things, right, without default.

From first to last his mind could hold them from revolt.

Whatever name he gave, that name endured unchanged.

If he said: "This thing's active," slothful it ne'er ranged.

He knew at first who was believer in God's word.

He from the first, too, knew the miscreant toward his Lord.

From one who knows them well, of things seek thou the fames,

And mystery of the symbol: "God taught him the names."[34]

The name of everything, with us, is what it seems;

With God, the name of everything, what He it deems.

By Moses was his staff a simple rod proclaimed;

By its Creator, God, a dragon was it named.

'Umer[35] idolater was classed by each array;
God him believer called upon creation's day.
What is by man termed seed upon this transient heath,
Impressed by God was with the seal: "Father of death."[36]
In realm of nullity that seed received a form,
Existent with its God; nor less, nor more; a worm.
Result thereof sprung forth the essence of our name
With the Creator, who will be our final aim.
He each one names according to his last estate,
Not with respect to that which is but passing fate.
So soon as mind of man with light has gained its strength,
It spies the soul, and mysteries of every name, at length.
When man perceives therein the kingdom of truth's rays,
He falls in adoration, worships, spends his days.
That Adam's praise, whose blessed name we're proud to bear,[37]
Should I recite till judgment-day, would not end there.
Decree of Providence so willed, with all his lore,
One single prohibition known, cost him right sore.
He asked: "Was prohibition laid, joy to prevent;
Or can, by gloss, evasion unto it be lent?"
To his mind, explanation having been inferred,

His appetites, perplexed, to taste the wheat preferred.[38]

A thorn the foot of Eden's gardener thus rent.

A thief the chance perceived, the garden robbed, and went.

Amazement o'er, the gardener's himself again.[39]

He saw the thief had carried off th' unguarded train.

He sobbed aloud: "My God, I've deeply sinned;" and sighed:

"A darkness came, and from the road I turn'd aside."

Decree of God was thus a cloud the sun to veil.

A lion, dragon, were a mouse beneath that bale.

When judgment's needed, should I not detect a snare,

Not I alone am blind, my weakness others share.

Blest he, whose steadfast feet have never gone astray!

Who waywardness has shunned, and taught his tongue to pray!

Should God's decree encompass thee with blackest night,

The same decree will readily help set thee right.

Should Providence at times thy life to menace seem,

'Twas Providence that gave it, can prolong its gleam.

Should life's events appear to threaten every way,

God can in heaven prepare a home for thee to stay.

What 'tis thou tremblest at, a special favour count,

Designed to bring thee safe to Zion's holy mount.
And now we turn again from morals,—they've no end,—
To see how fares it with our lion and his friend.
They came to where the well was. Here the lion saw
The hare his pace had slackened, backward 'gan to draw.
At this he remonstrated: "What art thou about!
Come forward still. The enemy we must find out."
The hare replied: "I have no power to move a foot.
From fear I faint. I tremble; courage has ebbed out.
Thou seest how pale my face; like ashes I've become;
An indication sure of fear, most troublesome.
God hath the countenance the mind's true index named.
The adept keeps his eye on countenance enchained.
A face's colour tell-tale is, like tinkling bell.
A horse's neigh of other steeds' approach will tell.
A sound from anything attention brings to pass;
'Tis thus we know the creak of door from bray of ass.
The Prophet said, no point of character t' asperse:
'Enigma is a man until he's heard converse.'
The colour in man's face makes known how stands the heart.
Compassion take on me; thy sympathy impart.

Enjoyments sensual give man a rosy face;
The fame of pale-faced men reports good sense and grace.
I feel within me what makes all my joints seem weak;
It's borne away my colour, strength, and power to speak.
It casts down whomsoe'er it chances to attack;
As tempest uproots trees it meets upon its track.
I'm subjected to that by which both men and beasts
Are turned to stocks and stones;—to say the very least.
They are but parts; that thing a universal is.
It makes men's faces pale; gives ashiness where 'tis;
As long as nature mournful is, or full of glee;—
As long as fields now verdant, naked then we see.
The sun each morning rises, joying in his course;
At eve sinks down again, and goes from bad to worse.
The planets circulating, each within its sphere,
Are subject to *immersion* when the sun they near.
The moon in splendour far excels each tiny star.
But near its change it dwindles almost to a hair.
The very earth, that in firm steadfastness doth sit,
When subject to an earthquake, shakes as in a fit.
How many regions in the world, encroaching sands

Have changed from gardens into bare and sterile lands.
The air, that with its breezes gives new life to all,
When Providence ordains, brings pestilence and thrall.
Sweet water's running stream, a very source of life,
In pond confined, turns fetid, black, and poison-rife.
The fire, so arrogant when fed with breezes long,
With one puff is extinguished by a breath too strong.
The sea, now boisterous with waves and swelling tide,
At times is like a mirror, shrinking from land's side.
The sky, revolving night and day, is never still;
The seven planets like, it works its Maker's will.
Those planets, too, in apogee and perigee,—what not,—
Auspicious, inauspicious are in several lot.
Thyself consider;—little part, of universals mixed;—
And thou'lt divine the state of all extended, fixed.
Since universals are by no means free from toil,
How should a petty part escape from trouble's moil?
A part, too, that's compound of every opposite,—
Of fire, and air, and water; adding earth its mite.
If sheep from wolf should flee, there's really wonder none;
To see them herd together 'd 'stonish every one.

Life springs from concord of th' ingredient opposites.
And death results when discord their pact disunites.
God's mercy hath appointed every lion's mate;
And unto each wild ass a fit associate.
But since the world in trouble prison-like offends,
What wonder that all's transient,—that all suffering ends?"
'Twas thus the hare the lion tricked with specious lies;
And added: "Hence the reason why I cannot rise."
The lion answered: "I see naught to cause thy fear.
Point out to me the object seems to thee so drear."
The hare then: "In this well thy foe takes his repose.
His stronghold is this pit, where he's secure from woes.
A wise man hides himself at bottom of a well;
For 'tis in solitude heart's choicest raptures dwell.
Seclusion's gloom is easier borne than wrongs from men.
Who craves a victor's mercy, saves his life just then."
The lion muttered: "Onward come. My arm is strong.
Go look. At home is he? He'll not live long."
The hare: "Alas! Already I've endured his gaze.
Take me unto thy breast. My mind is all amaze.

From off thy back, most potent lord and prince,
I'll look down in the well. I'll neither blink nor wince."
The lion took him on his back without more fuss.
So, under this protection to the well went puss.
They both looked down; and in the water there
Reflection shadowed forth a lion and a hare.
The lion saw his own shape in the water shine:
"Another lion," thought he, "with fat hare on chine."
His foe he fancied, thus, that in the well he'd spied.
The hare he set down safely; in leapt he with pride.
He thus fell in the pit he had for others dug.
Iniquity will visit those who drink out of her mug.
Iniquity's a pit into which tyrants fall.
Such is the firm conviction of our wise men all.
The wickeder a man, the deeper does he sink.
So justice wills; and so, the wrong'd will doubtless think.
O thou who in thy might injustice dost commit,
For thy own self a pit thou diggest; our tale to wit.
Thou weavest round thyself a web, as does silkworm;
Thou'lt not escape unless to justice thou conform.
Look not upon the weak as quite without a friend.

Reflect; 'tis said: "When God's help comes."[40] Where's then thy end?

If thou'rt an elephant in strength, the weak will flee

To his Protector. Then the Lord's wrath shalt thou see.

Whenever wrong's weak victim on his God doth call,

A clamour rises from the ranks in heaven's hall.

If with his blood, in pride, thou stain thy teeth just now,

The toothache shall avenge him; dentist's victim thou.

The lion saw himself reflected in the well.

Through blindest rage himself from foe he could not tell.

He thought his own reflection was his hated foe,

And slew himself while seeking on him to work woe.

So tyrant, when thou seest injustice in the world,

Thyself behold. Those deeds thy banner have unfurled.

Thine are included with them in God's just decree.

Thy rage, greed, lust's reward most certainly thou'lt see.

They are thy very self; in them thou art condemned.

Thou judgest them; in selfsame manner thou'rt contemned.

In thy own acts thou seest not the sin thou work'st;

Or otherwise thy own self's foe thou'dst be from first.

It is thyself against whom thou mak'st thy attack;

Just as the lion took the hare upon his back.

If thou'd sound deep to bottom of the moral well.
Thyself thou'dst find there; thy own acts would plainly tell.
The lion at the bottom found out who was there.
Let him as likeness serve of many who are here.
Whoe'er beats out the teeth of weaker than himself,
Commits the lion's error;—springs upon himself.
O thou who loath'st a mole upon thy neighbour's cheek,
Reflect. 'Tis but an image. Thy own features seek.
Believers are as mirrors; each sees self in each.
So said the Prophet. His words to us truth may teach.
Thou wearest spectacles, of blue, or red, or green;
And thence thou judgest all is tinged with that sheen.
If thou wilt use a window glazed with coloured glass,
Thou may'st expect the sun will seem of that same class.
If thou'rt not mad, thou'lt know the colour is thy own.
Thyself call evil. Henceforth others leave alone.
Believers see with eye of faith,—the light of God.
How else to them were visible all things' synod?
If thou examine things with hell-fire in thy heart,
How canst thou see distinct the good and bad apart.
Seek by degrees to drown that fire in holy light.

So shalt thou, sinner, soon, thy weakness change for might.

And do Thou, Lord, asperge from mercy's cleansing stream,

To change the fire of sin to light of faith supreme.

The ocean's waters are a mere drop in Thy hand;

The streams of mercy, fire of wrath, at Thy command.

If Thou so will, the fire a pleasant stream may be.

And at Thy word, a lake a fiery pit we'd see.

From Thee spring our devotions, supplications, prayers.

'Tis Thou deliverest the victims from their slayers.

Without our supplication, Thou entreaty gavest.

The stores of Thy great mercy for all men Thou savest.

The hare, for his deliverance, jubilant set out,

To join his fellows, scattered in their homes about.

He saw the lion prone at bottom of the well;

Then rapidly went back his stratagem to tell.

He clapped his hands for joy at his escape from death,

Exuberant as plant sprouts from the earth beneath.

Its stalk and leaf break forth from prison underground.

It rears itself apace, makes friends with th' air around.

The leaves burst from the stem, and spread themselves abroad;

Until by growth a tree, whose grace all men applaud.
It now expands in thanks for favours of the Lord;
Each leaf, flower, fruit intones a hymn of praise, like bard.
"Thou, Giver of all good things, nourishedst my root.
And madest me become a strongly growing shoot."
Our souls, shut up in prison in our frames of clay,
So break forth into raptures when they're called away.
They dance for very joy, from love of God Allwise,
When, like full moon perfected, they in glory rise.
Material beings, thus, their dance perform, and souls.
Ask not of them the subject of their hyperboles.
The hare had lodged the lion in a dungeon safe.
More shame for lion was it, hare should make him chafe.
Just so a shame it is, and subject for surprise,
The state in which he's left, who Fakhru-'d-Dīn would rise.[41]
O, he's a lion, sure, at bottom of a well.
His pride of flesh the hare that cast him down to hell.
His pride, the hare, at large, disporting as it will;
Himself down in the pit. O, what a bitter pill!
The lion-slaying hare now scampered to his friends,
Exclaiming: "Good news bring I; let joy know no ends!

Good news! Good news! Festivities bring into play!
The hell-cat's gone to hell, from which he came our way.
Good news! Good news! That foe to all our lives, and peace.
Has had his teeth extracted, through our Maker's grace.
He who so many crushed with paw of tyranny,
Like rubbish has been swept by death's broom clean away."

A convocation now was held by all the beasts,
Hilarity and joy enlivened all their breasts.
About the hare, as candle, they, moths-like, all flocked.
All their respects presented; none were found who mocked.
They all declared: "Thou art an angel by heaven sent
(Angel of death, however, he to lion went).
Whatever thou may'st be, our souls thy sacrifice!
Thou'st triumphed. For such prowess praise will not suffice.
Our God it was endowed thee with such wondrous skill.
May God be praised! Deliverance is by His will.

Pray, tell us all about it. How was such thing done?
How couldst thou compass to deceive th' experienced drone?
Relate in full. 'Twill comfort give to all our souls.

Detail the facts; balm will they be for bygone doles.
Recount at length; for, ah, how many tyrannies
Did we not suffer from him, who now stark dead lies!"
Quoth he: "Most venerable Sirs! God's grace did all.
What could a hare accomplish without Him at call?
He strength of purpose gave me,—light from heaven above.
That light it was that nerved me in my every move.
God granteth crowning grace, to further cause of truth,
'Tis God also who sends vicissitudes on earth.
He, 'tis, alternately, who parties makes prevail.
Now mere opinionists, now men of light avail.
If then, in turn, thou now thyself find uppermost,
Why let hypocrisy, presumption, make thee boast?"
Joy not o'er great prosperity. It does not last.
Airs give not thou thyself; thou'rt but a passing guest.
They whose eternal kingship lasts beyond all times,[42]
Who sing God's praise beyond the seven spheres and climes,
They more endure than transient reigns of kings' short rolls.
They are the never-failing feeders of men's souls.
If thou the pleasures of the world short time forego,

Eternal bliss may compensate th' imbroglio.

Know that this nether world but for a period lasts.

T' abandon it, eternal rest to man forecasts.

Give ear. Forsake all mundane ease, all earthly rest;

Then will thy soul enjoy heaven's cup with double zest.

Cast thou the carcase vile of earthly pomp to dogs.

The cup of mere surmise reject; the soul it clogs.

---

1. Kalīla and Dimna is the Arabic version of Pīlpāy's fables.
2. This proverb is given in Freytag's "*Proverbia Arabica,*" ii. p. 488, n. 278, as an answer from Muhammed to a foe twice made prisoner.
3. Equivalent to tethering a horse. Cromwell's: "Keep your powder dry."
4. The original says: "*The earner is God's friend.*"
5. The original has: "*Flees the snake, and meets a dragon.*"
6. The words as given in the original, in Arabic, are not in the Qur'ān.
7. A cock that crows out of season, in the night.
8. Qur'ān xiv. 47.
9. 'Azrā'īl, the angel of death, who takes men's souls.
10. Solomon is related in the Qur'ān xxi. 81, and xxxiv. 11, to have possessed power over the wind.
11. In Qur'ān iii. 47, and viii. 30, God is styled "*the best of stratagem-makers.*"
12. I do not find this proverb in Freytag's "*Proverbia.*"
13. Qur'ān ii. 15.
14. See Qur'ān xlviii. 29; lix. 8; and lxxiii. 20.
15. In Qur'ān ii. 29, the account of this is given. Compare Gen. ii. 19.
16. Was Satan this very old hermit? His successful temptation was the muzzle. The original says "*calf,*" where I have said "*babe;*"—meaning Adam, when first created. Instructed by God, he named all things, which the angels were unable to do, and so were silenced.
17. The story of the dog of the Sleepers is told in Qur'ān xviii. 17-21.
18. The Persian name for the hare is "*ass-ear;*"hence the pun.
19. The "hidden tablet" of God's decrees; mentioned in Qur'ān lxxxv. 22.

20. At the "extreme lote-tree" in the highest heaven, on the night of the ascension. Gabriel could go no further. Muhammed went on, to God's presence.
21. The word that signifies "compulsion" also means "reduction" in a surgical sense, and "algebra" mathematically.
22. "Burāq" is the name of the angelic steed on which Muhammed mounted to heaven in his night journey. Not found in the Qur'ān.
23. "The moon clave" in twain as a sign of the near approach of the day of judgment. Qur'ān liv. 1.
24. Muhammed's name is put on most Muslim coins.
25. Muhammed is held to be the supplement of all the prophets.
26. Qur'ān ii. 151.
27. Not in Freytag's "*Proverbia.*"
28. See note in the Author's Preface, and Chapter vi. in the Anecdotes.
29. The commentators on Qur'ān xxi. 69, mention Nimrod's gnat.
30. Qur'ān xxviii. 5, mentions Haman with Pharaoh.
31. He is said to have believed Satan rather than Abraham.
32. The translator has ventured to coin the expressions "*synglottism,*" "*synglottist,*" and "*syncardism*" as specimens of a whole class used in Persian.
33. A title designating Adam,—who named all things.
34. Qur'ān ii. 29.
35. Omar.
36. A very doubtful clause; it may be rendered: "*Thou art with me.*"
37. Adam, in most languages, has come to signify *man.*
38. Qur'ān ii. 33, mentions merely a "*caulescent plant;*""wheat" is one of several glosses by commentators, like our "apple."
39. Qur'ān vii. 22, makes Adam confess sin with contrition, together with Eve, thereby meriting God's eventual pardon.
40. Qur'ān cx. 1.
41. Evidently the name of a rival.
42. These are sainted spiritualists, true and pious dervishes.

VI. THE GREATER (SPIRITUAL) WARFARE.

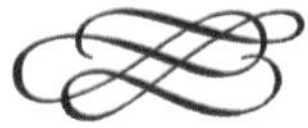

Great Princes all! We've killed our dread external foe.
Within us, still, a worse than he remains, I trow.
To slay this inner foe is not the task of mind;
Our moral lion's not destroyed by tricks refined.
Our flesh, a hell; that hell a fiery dragon is.
Whole oceans can't extinguish those fierce flames of his.
Earth's seven oceans all were lost within his maw;
His raging fires would still burn high, to mankind's awe.
Pitcoal, hard-hearted miscreants; these are its food;[1]
They sink within it, miserable, abject brood.
Withal, its craving hunger ne'er will be appeased,
Until the voice of God cry unto it: "Art eased?"

"Eased?" will it answer; "No; not yet awhile by far;
Behold my flame, my fury,—burning, fiery roar."
It swallows down a universe in its fell mood;
And instantly shrieks out: "More food! More food! More food!"
God, from nubiquity,[2] His foot will stamp on hell.
Then will it cease to burn: "He willed, and it befell!"[3]
Our fleshly lusts in us are but a part of hell;
Parts have the qualities of their universal.
The foot of God alone can stamp out hell's alarms.
Who else but God supreme to bend such bow has arms?
Straight arrows serve alone to be shot from a bow;
But lust's distorted spring shoots crooked arrows too.
Be thou in mind upright as arrow straight for bow.
A bow will not shoot straight, unless the arrow's so.
We've fought our fight and conquered in our outward strife.
Now turn we our attention to the inner life.
We've done with outer warfare, lesser as it is;
And as the Prophet, wage the greater warfare, his.
We put our trust in God; from Him we ask for aid;
With His assistance faith can move a mountain staid.
To rout an armed foe is nothing very fresh;

A lion true is he who conquers his own flesh.
To illustrate this truth, give ear unto a tale,
That thou of these few words the moral mayest inhale.
From Cæsar[4] an ambassador to 'Umer came,[5]
Through deserts far-extending, from Madīna's fame.[6]
He asked: "Where is the palace of the Caliph, men;[7]
That I to it may lead my cavalcade, my train?"
The people answered: "Thou'lt no Caliph's palace find,
Our Caliph's sole pavilion's his enlightened mind.
Through his '*Commandership*' his fame to Rome has come;[8]
But like our other poor, a hut's his ample home.
How shouldst thou see *that* palace, brother, stranger, guest,
When in thy mind's eye thou a beam hast, unconfessed?
Cast out that beam; make clear thy eye from every mote
Then mayst thou entertain the hope to see his cote."
Whoever shall his heart cleanse from all passions' bale,
Will soon perceive therein a court and presence hale.
When Ahmed's heart was cleansed of evil's fire and smoke,[9]
Whichever way he turned, God's countenance bespoke.[10]
So long as man keeps company with evil thought,

How can he understand God's countenance in aught?
He that a window's pierced from heart towards heaven's recess,
Sees in each mote a ray from Sun of Righteousness.[11]
God shines apparent in the midst of other things,
As moon in majesty among the stars' twinklings.
Place thou two finger-tips upon thy two eyeballs.
What seest thou now of all the world? Darkness befalls.
Thou seest it not; but that the world exists, thou'lt trust.
Our vices are the finger-tips of fleshly lust.
Thy finger-tips remove; *instanter,* as before,
Thou lookest around and seest whate'er thou wilt explore.
His people asked of Noah where righteousness might be.
He said: "Lo, there! With muffled heads you cannot see.
You've wrapped your cloaks in folds about your heads and eyes.
Your sense of sight cannot see what before you lies."
The world's eye man is; all the rest's mere skin and shell.
A real eye's he who strives his "Friend" to see right well.[12]
Unless we see our Friend, 'twere better we were blind,
A friend that is not constant's better out of mind.

When Rome's ambassador had heard those words so wise,[13]

His eager curiosity began to rise.

He sought for 'Umer with redoubled zeal and zest;

But in so doing lost his horse, and eke his chest.

He wandered everywhere to seek the Caliph out.

Like one distracted asked each passer-by his route.

"Is't possible," he said, "that such a man there be,

When like the soul to sight invisible is he?"

He sought for him as though he 'd been his truant slave,

But: "He who seeks shall find" 's a very well-known stave.

A desert-Arab woman saw he at the last,

Who told him 'Umer, then, beneath date-palm slept fast.

Beneath a date-palm! Far from mankind's busy plod.

That date-palm's shadow shaded the Shadow of God![14]

He went towards the tree; a station took afar;

He saw 'Umer; a fit of trembling showed his fear.

On that ambassador did awe and dread alight.

While o'er his heart there stole a sense of sweet delight.

Two feelings, love and dread, by nature opposites,

Were mingled in his bosom by some occult rites.

He thought within himself: "I've many princes seen;

In sovereign presence I have ever welcome been.
This fit of awe and trembling's very strange to me;
And yet without dismay this man I cannot see.
I've been in forests where the lions make their lair;
I've met them face to face; yet knew not what was fear.
In battle I've been, oft; in thickest of the fight.
My arm's upheld our cause, when in most desperate plight.
Wounds have I dealt, received, that threatened life to take,
Among the brave, the bravest; my heart knew no quake.
This man is weaponless, supine upon the ground.
Why then this tremor? It my every limb has bound.
A ghostly awe is this; it's not a mortal fear.
Most certainly it's not a dread of this man here.
He who fears God has admonition of the Lord;
Both men and demons stand in awe of his mere word."
Mute he remained in reverential attitude,
Till 'Umer woke from his trance of beatitude.
Profound obeisance and grave salutation made,
As said the Prophet: "First, salute; then, embassade."
The Caliph answered: "And on thee be peace! Draw near;"

Assured him of protection; bade him put off fear.
"Fear not" a word of comfort is to trembling soul;
A generous tribute 'tis, when strong with weak condole.
Men set at ease the object whom they wish to raise,—
Relieve his heart from palpitation; bid fears cease.
But unto one who feels no dread how say: "Fear not"?
What lesson's this thou givest to one whose lesson's got?
So 'Umer put at ease that much perturbed man;
And calmed his wavering mind, as noble hearts best can.
To him he then addressed some subtle words of sense,
Set forth the attributes of God,—man's best defence,
Declared the goodness of the Lord to all who trust
In Him alone; the rank they gain in trance combust.
Saint's ecstasy springs from a glimpse of God, his pride.
His station's that of intimate. He's bridegroom; God is bride.[15]
A bride's veiled graces are not seen by groom alone;
Her unveiled charms solely to him in private shown.
In state she first appears before the people all;
Her veil removed, the groom alone is at her call.
Entranced are many Gnostic worshippers, I ween;
Few gain admission to the presence-chamber scene.

'Umer told all the stations passed through by his soul;—
Its flights, fights, tribulations, ere it was made whole.
He spoke of times when flight of time's of no account;
Of Holiness's station, glorious to recount.
He talked of atmospheres in which his righteous soul
Had soared to seek fresh conquests of devotion's whole.
Its every flight had been beyond th' horizon scant;
Beyond the hope, or e'en desire, of aspirant.
He found a willing list'ner in the stranger guest,
Whose mind was framed t' investigate such mysteries blest.
The teacher was perfection; novice full of zeal;
Like clever jockey on a steed with lightning heel.
He found his scholar apt, of great capacity.
So good seed sowed in fertile soil sagacity.
Th' ambassador now asked: "Of true believers Prince!
How can a soul from heaven come down to earth's province;—
How can so great a bird be cooped up in a cage?"
He answered: "God speaks words of power, most sage.
Those words, addressed to nothings without eyes or ears,
Set them in motion. Like a ferment, fruit it bears.
Those words no sooner spoken, quick those nothings all

In motion put themselves, and reach existence' hall.

Or He commands these beings, creatures of His own;

And they return to nothing, whence He them had drawn.

He speaks unto the flowers; they forthwith burst in bloom.

His voice the flint hears; lo, it's a cornelian stone.

A spell He laid on matter; spirit it became.

By charm from Him the sun sprang forth, a lambent flame.

If He but whisper words of awe, the sun again

Is seized with darkness of eclipse, like night amain.

What is't He says, by which the teeming eye of cloud

Sheds forth its tears, as drops from water-skin unsewed?

What incantation to the earth addresses He,

To make it produce cattle,—whose hides used may be?

The hesitations of each puzzled child of thought

Arise from some enigma by which God's him caught.

On horns of a dilemma is he fixed, poor man.

'Shall I do this,' says he, 'when 'ts opposite I can?'

From God, too, is the power to make selection's choice

Of two solutions. One is taken, through inward voice.

Wouldst thou be always free from hesitation, fool?

Stuff not thy mind's ear tight with doubt's dull cotton-wool;

That thou mayst solve the riddles God may set for thee;—

That thou mayst understand the full of mercy free.

Then shall thy heart receive His inspiration's gift,—

A power of speaking from an inward impulse' drift.

The ear and eye of soul are organs not of sense;

The ears of sense and mind are not like soul's, intense.

The word "*compulsion*" puts me out of humour quite.

Who hath not love of God, compulsion's slave's, by right.

This union's based on truth (compulsion is too proud);

It is a glimpse of sunshine breaking through a cloud.

Be it compulsion. Man's compulsion it is not;—

Not the compulsion of browbeating from a sot.

Compulsion's felt by them, my very worthy friend,

Whose eyes of faith, ope'd in their hearts, on God attend.

The absent and the future patent are to them;

To speak about the past is what they most contemn.

Election and compulsion, theirs, are not the same.

As dewdrops in the oyster-shell rare pearls became.[16]

Outside, they're dewdrops, solely, whether great or small;

Inside they're pearls of price, whose value knows no fall.

Such men by nature are just like the musk-deer's pod;
It's fed with blood of artery, musk it yields, through God.
Ask not how 'tis that outward blood can change like this;
Becoming musk when in the pod secreted 'tis.
Ask not how copper vile, by wise alchemist's art,
Is changed to gold when solved by elixir in part.[17]
Election and compulsion, fancies both, in thee;
But when by saints they're viewed, God's glory may they be.
Upon the table, bread's a lifeless, senseless mass;
When taken in man's mouth, the soul it joins, in class.
On table transubstantiation takes not place;[18]
The soul it is transforms it, nourished by God's grace.
Such is the soul's great power; most perspicacious man,
So long as that soul life and power retain can.
A human being, mass of mingled flesh and blood,
Moved by the Lord, can cleave hill, dale, mine, and sea's flood.
The strength of strongest man can merely split a stone;[19]
The Power that informs man's soul can cleave the moon.[20]
If man's heart but untie the mouth of mystery's sack,
His soul soon soars aloft beyond the starry track.

If heaven's mystery divulged should, 'haps, become,
The whole world 'twould burn up, as fire doth wood consume."
Let's contemplate the acts of God, the deeds of men;
Know, men's deeds do exist. This truth is patent, then.
If men's deeds be not in this nether world of ours,
Say not thou unto others: "Why these deeds of yours?"
God's act it is through which those deeds of ours arise;
Our acts are but the sequels of God's agencies.
The letter, or the spirit, 'tis, our reason weighs.
But both at once it cannot comprehend always.
Examining the spirit, letter we neglect;
At one time forwards, backwards we cannot prospect.
If thou straight forward look at any point of time,
Thou canst not backwards see, whatever be the clime.
Our souls not taking in the letter, spirit too,
How could they e'er create these predicates, one, two?
God comprehendeth all things;—all things doth ensue;
One act's no hindrance, with Him, other acts to do.
The reason Satan gave: "Since Thou hast tempted me,"[21]
The scheming demon strove to hide his sin, we see.
His trespass Adam owned: "Against ourselves we've sinned."[22]

God's act he, like as we, then left not out of mind.
Through shame the act of Satan Adam secret kept.
Self-accusation's fruit, in consequence, he reaped.
Repentance shown by Adam, God in mercy said:
"In thee 'twas I created, sin thou hast displayed.
Was it not My decree and providence that thou,
In asking pardon, shouldst the tempter disavow?"
Said Adam: "Thee I feared; most bitter shame I felt."
God added: "It was I who gave thee shame heartfelt."
Consideration he who shows considered is;
So he who brings the sugar, share of cake is his.
For whom, then, benefits, but practisers of good?[23]
Keep pleased thy friend. Offend him; see what ensue would.
One sole example study,—instance of this law,—
Compulsion and election's difference to draw.
"There is a hand that shakes from palsy or from fear.
Another hand also thou shakest when thou'rt near.
Know: God it is creates the movement in them both;
And yet there's no resemblance in their motions loth.
Thou'rt sorry that thou shakedst that man's hand anon,
When thou seest him annoyed at what thou'st just now done."

A question 'tis of judgment; judgment shrewdness is,
Until some weakness intervene to mar all this.
A question, now, of judgment as to corals, pearls,
Is not the same as one about the soul, you churls.
A question of the soul's another matter quite;
The wine that feeds the soul comes not from grapes, black, white.
When any matter is a question of judgment,
'Umer with Abū-Jahl's in one predicament.
'Umer gave up his judgment; rested on his soul.
'Bū-Jahl received this name through lack of self-control.[24]
In sense and reason Abū-Jahl a master was;
But as to soul, in ignorance he fell, alas!
Of sense and reason questions are cause and effect;
But miracles and wonders show soul is a fact.
Enlightenment of soul, whatever it may see.
By quibbles of school logic cannot silenced be.
We now return again our tale to take in hand,
Though certainly we've never left it out of mind.
In ignorance, our souls are in God's prison chained.
In wisdom, by God's help, their liberty's regained.
In sleep, God's lethargy it is in which we sink.

Awake, we're in God's hands, whatever we may think.
In weeping, we are clouds from which His mercy flows.
In laughter, we're the flash with which His lightning glows.
In anger, we're reflections of the wrath of God.
In amity, the mirrors of His favour's nod.
What are we in this world? All tortuous and bent.
There is not one upright, straightforward, innocent.
Cæsar's ambassador no sooner 'Umer heard,
Than light broke on his heart; at which he stroked his beard.
All questions and all answers from his mind went quite;
All sense of right and wrong had vanished from his sight.
He'd found the source; what need, then, of the streams?
To gather further wisdom, pondering on the means,
He said: "'Umer, pray tell me what's the end and use
Of shutting up that thing of light in darkness' house?
How can clear water be expected from black mud?
Why then is the pure soul combined with flesh and blood?"
He answered: "Most important question hast thou raised.
A sense, a spirit, by the letter paraphrased.
The free, the jocund spirit prisoner thou'st made;

As though the mind, the air, could into letter fade.
Thou hast done this for explanation's sake,—[25]
Thou, who beyond the explanation place wouldst take.
How should the man in whom the explanation's gleamed,
Not yet distinguish what's to me so clearly beamed?
Ten thousand explanations are there, each of which
Is most momentous,—than ten thousand others, rich.
With that, thy speech, now compoundly particular,
A universal explanation were,—no bar.
Thou art a partial,—seekest explanation still;
Why set thyself, then, to deny th' universal?
Unless thy speech contain some use, propound it not;
And if it have, objection quit; give what thou'st got.
Thanks are incumbent upon every mortal's head;
Contention and sour looks are surely no one's bread.
If to put on sour looks, of thankfulness sign be,
Then vinegar the sweetest-spoken thing we'd see.
If vinegar desire to hearts a way to find,
It oxymel becomes, with honey sweet combined.
True, verse is not best vehicle for sense abstract.
It's like a sling; one's never certain how 't will act."

Th' ambassador his senses lost with this one cup
Of wine spiritual. His mission he gave up.
O'erwhelmed with wonder at the power of God, he fell.
He came ambassador; now sovereign was, as well.
A river overflooded constitutes a lake.
Some grains, when sown in earth, a field of corn can make.
When eaten, bread assimilated is by man,
That bread inanimate takes life, and reason can.
When wood or candle is made victim unto fire,
Its substance dark becomes a source of light entire.
Black *stibium*, a stone, when placed in human eye,
Expands the power of vision, objects can descry.
Good luck to him who's saved from his own fleshly self,
And has become a parcel of some living elf.
Alas for him, who, living, sits among the dead.
He's dead himself, his life from out of him has fled.
If thou take refuge in the Qur'ān, God's own book,
With spirit of Muhammed thou'lt soon exchange look.
The Qur'ān is the essence of all prophets right.
They were the whales who swam in ocean of God's might.

If thou canst read or not, the Qur'ān take to heart,

The saints and prophets study; they were as thou art.

Read thou it carefully; read, mark, digest its tales;

Thy soul, like bird in cage, will long to break its rails.

The bird shut up, imprisoned in a little cage,

That seeks not to get out, is ignorant, not sage.

The souls who've freed themselves from cages of the flesh,

Are worthy fellow-travellers with prophets, fresh.

Their voices they lift up, religion to impart:

"The way of sure deliverance is here. Take heart!

175

Religion hath us saved from fleshly cages, sure.

No other way is there, salvation to secure.

You then upon yourselves will chastisements inflict,

That you may be delivered from the world's respect."

Respect of mortal man a heavy fetter is;

Within religion's path the gravest bond is this.

Consider well this tale, ingenuous young friend;

'Twill teach thee many lessons may thy morals mend.

179

---

1. Qur'ān ii. 22, and lxvi. 6, say "mankind and rocks."
2. Another word coined to meet the requirements of the original. "*Ubiquity*" is the converse of "*nubiquity*." *Nulliquity* might be used.
3. Qur'ān ii. 111, and seven other places.

4. "Cæsar" is the Roman Emperor, the Qaysari-Rūm. Other Qaysar there is not.
5. To write this name *Omar* is incorrect.
6. Medina is the usual incorrect spelling of this name.
7. The Arabian title is Khalīfa; of which Caliph is a corruption.
8. "*Commander of the Believers*" is his usual title. "Rome" is the Lower Empire.
9. Muhammed's heart is believed to have been cleansed by an angel.
10. "God's countenance" means also, in Arabic, *God's cause.*
11. God is this "sun;" the "motes" are all created objects.
12. The "Friend" is God, the Gnostic's "*darling.*"
13. "Rome" in Asia means the Lower Empire and Asia Minor; or, for the last few centuries, the Ottoman Empire.
14. "Shadow of God on earth" is an Eastern title of royalty.
15. These two propositions give the pith of the doctrine held and inculcated by the mystics and spiritualists of Islām: "*He's bridegroom; God is bride.*"
16. This First Book of the Mesnevī was written before the Būstān of Sa'dī. The myth of the dewdrop and pearl is much more ancient.
17. The date of the poem will be recollected; who disbelieved alchemy then?
18. Here is a beautiful and true application of the idea of "*transubstantiation.*"
19. The original mentions Ferhād, a kind of Persian Dædalus, by his title of "*Mountain-Excavator.*"(See Tale vii. dist. 365.)
20. Qur'ān liv. 1.
21. Qur'ān vii. 15, and xv. 39. At the fall, Satan accused God of tempting him; whereas Adam confessed his sin, and did not accuse Satan.
22. Qur'ān vii. 22.
23. Qur'ān xxiv. 26.
24. 'Bū is often used as a contraction for Abū. Abū-Jahl (*Father of Ignorance*) was a nickname (see Tale iv. dist. 48, note) given by Muhammed to 'Amr, son of Hishām, a chief of the Quraysh, his bitter enemy, formerly entitled Abū-'l-Hakem (*Father of the Arbitrator*). He was killed, a pagan, in the battle of Badr, in the second year of the Hijra, a.d. 624.
25. The word rendered by "explanation" here, means also *information,* and *use, advantage, profit, benefit,* &c.

VII. THE MERCHANT AND THE PARROT.

A merchant there was, who a parrot did own;
Confined in a cage, wisest bird in the town.
This merchant to journeying made up his mind
To fair Hindūstān, there some rich wares to find.
From generous motives, to each of his slaves,
To male, and to female, some gift to bring craves.
He made them all tell him what best they would like;
And promised to bring it, most gentlemanlike.
He said to the parrot: "Poll! Poll! With the rest,
From Hind I must bring thee what thou mayst like best."
The parrot replied: "Sure, thou'lt see parrots there,
To them pray impart how it is that I fare.

Inform them, a parrot who loves them all well,
By thee's kept confined, close shut up in a cell.
He sends you his love, and his very best wish;
Desiring from you wise advice, parrotish.
He fears he may pine, through longing to see
His dear absent friends,—die in foreign countree.
He asks if it is altogether thing fit,
That he should be caged, while you on the trees sit.
If this is the way in which true friends should act;
Leave him in his cage, while you forests affect.
He wishes you'd call to your mind your lost friend,
When drinking your bumpers, ere fieldward you wend.[1]
'Tis sweet to be thought of by far-away dame,
One's sweetheart, whose love's set one's heart in a flame.
While you are disporting with those you love best,
He's eating his heart out; grief gives him no rest.
One bumper you'll drink for the love of poor Poll,[2]
If only you wish him your love to extol.
Or, thinking of him who's in slavery kept,
Your bowl's whole contents dash to earth, as though wept.
O where is the promise, and where is the oath,

Th' engagements sworn to him by sugarsome tooth?[3]
If absence of his came from truancy's pranks,
You've set your forgetfulness 'gainst his sin's ranks.
The ills you inflict out of spite and disdain
Are sweet to your lover, he does not complain.
Your petulance prized is beyond fairy gifts;
Your vengeance most dear is; his hope it uplifts.
No soul can imagine what pleasure is felt,
Or grace seen, in all the fell blows you have dealt.
Your wrath is thus sweet; how much more so your grace!
If mourning so grieve, what from feast would take place?
He weeps; but he hopes you'll believe not his tears;
And, out of affection, not lessen his fears.
He loves your great kindness, your anger as well.
He equally dotes on those opposites fell.
The thorn escape should he, and visit the rose,
He'd warble as nightingale, moved by love's throes.
Most wondrous this bird's strangest use of his bill;
With thorns, as with roseleaves, he would his mouth fill.
Not nightingale this; fiery dragon it is;
All wrongs seem to him, through his love, purest bliss.
He loveth a rose, and himself is a rose.

He loveth himself; and seeks love for its woes."
Just so is the soul. Its tale, just parrot's tale.
O where is the One to whom all souls make wail?
Where is the man, feeble, who's yet innocent?
His heart, Solomon and his whole armament.
When he, with tears bitter, is heard to complain,
The seven vaults of heaven re-echo the strain.
In anguish he groans; God, in mercy, him hears.
His cry is: "O Lord!" And God wipes off his tears.
Abasement in him, is by God highly prized.
His blasphemies, o'er other men's faith are raised.[4]
Each instant, in soul, he ascends to heaven's gate;
His mitre's with crowns capped, of infinite state.[5]
His frame's here on earth; his pure soul with the Lord
In heaven's highest sphere, above man's thought or word.
A heaven such as this thou contemplatest not;
Thou every moment imaginest—what?
With him "*where*" and "*nowhere*" are quite equal felt.
To angels the "*four rivers*" seem a mere belt.[6]
Break off we this theme. Let's discuss other things.
Cease trifling. "'Tis God who knows best" sense's rings.[7]

Let's seek to inquire how it fares with our friends,—
The merchant, his parrot. Who is't understands?
The former had promised, at latter's request,
To give to the birds of far Hind his bequest.
So when he had reached that land, greatly renowned
In wooded retreat, flock of parrots he found.
He stopped his beast, cried out, at top of his voice,
That message his Polly had made, as his choice.
One bird of the flock, he saw, then took to quake,
Fell prone to the earth; no more breath seemed to take.
The merchant regret felt for what he had done,
Exclaiming: "Alas! The poor bird I've slain, lone!
That creature was surely related to Poll;
Two bodies; one soul; just as is magic doll.
Why did I deliver that fatal message?
I've killed a collateral of Poll's lineage!"
The tongue, by itself, acts just like flint and steel.
A word from it, fire-like, we scathing can feel.
Strike not, then, so rashly, fire's sparks from thy tongue,
In message or talk, feeble hearers among.
The night is pitch dark; strewn around, cotton beds.
Amongst beds of cotton, 'tis, sparks one most dreads.

He sins who, unmindful of dire consequence,
Lets fall spoken spark,—fires a whole world, immense.
One rash word may set an assembly ablaze.
Molehills into mountains, and higher, it can raise.
In basis, our souls would appear Jesus-like.
To kill, to resuscitate, words are godlike.
If lifted could be from our souls the dark veil,
Each word of each soul would with miracles trail.
Dost wish to speak always to men with sweet words?
Have patience. Impatience must not fret the cords.
'Tis patience beloved is by all men of sense.
Impatience a fault is, of children, intense.
Who patience exhibits shall mount to heaven's dome.
Impatience who showeth, tastes wrath that's to come.
A saint is not hurt, whate'er else may betide,[8]
To swallow fell poison should he once decide.
He's whole, and he's sound; strict diet's his rule.
Poor students are healthy in fever's dread school.
The Prophet has cautioned: "Brave though you may be,
Commit not mad rashness, howe'er the foe flee."
Within thee's a Nimrod. Approach not the fire.
Approach it thou must? To be Abr'am aspire.

A swimmer thou art not;—nor seaman by trade;
From headstrongness strive not the deep sea to wade.
From fire Abr'am brought forth a fresh-plucked red rose.
A diver, from sea-bottom, pearls' store can choose.
A saint handles earth, turns it straightway to gold.
A sinner, by touch, to earth turns this;—behold.
A just man's accepted of God, the Most High.
His deeds are the works of God's hand, still. Eigh! Eigh!
Th' imperfect one's hand is aye Satan's foul limb;
Responsible rests he, howe'er he may climb.[9]
To him wisdom's self's but a mere misguidance.
Th' imperfect man's science is crass ignorance.
Whatever as cause acts, as cause counted is;
A perfect man's blasphemy's pure faith, my quiz.[10]
Rash combatant, fight'st thou on foot 'gainst horseman!
Thy point thou'lt not carry;—as sure as thou'rt man.
So, Egypt's magicians, in old Pharaoh's days,
Contended 'gainst Moses; and rashly, always.
At length they owned Moses superior was;
Men honour, revere him, who most of power has.
They said to him, then: "Command 's thine! See! Purely!

Thy heart thou'lt find filled with deep love for Godhead.
Thy infant soul wean from the gross milk of greed,
Then teach it to join, next, in angel's pure creed.
So long thou remainest in darkness and thrall,
A bantling of Satan thou art, out at call.
The morsel that brings a pure light to the soul
Is earned by endeavour; not begged with a bowl.
Should oil, upon trimming, extinguish a lamp,
Not oil may we name it; 'tis water; 'tis damp.
The honestly-earned morsel, wisdom imparts;
Gives softness to souls, and a warmness to hearts.
If thou be aware that from thy morsel spring
Heartburnings and hate, know it's not a blest thing.
Hast wheat ever sown, and reaped barley instead?
Hast known colt of ass from a mare in birth bred?
A morsel, when eaten, 's a seed; its fruit, thought.
A morsel, when swallowed, 's a sea pearls has brought.
From good, honest morsels come, taken in mouth,
Good works, and firm strivings to shun the soul's drought.
Reflections, though true, we'll now bring to an end.
To merchant and parrot's tale ear we will lend.

Our merchant his trading had quickly despatched,
Then homeward he turned; with joy housedoor unlatched.
To ev'ry male slave a rare present he brought;
For each of his handmaids some gift he had bought.
The parrot him questioned: "What news bringest thou me?
And whom hast thou seen? What's been said? Tell. Let's see."
The merchant him answered: "I'm sorry for that.
I'd rather my hand eat, than tell it thee;—flat.
In thoughtlessness, folly, ah! why did I prate
About thy fool's message, until 'twas too late?"
The parrot then asked: "What's this fuss all about?
What's caused tribulation? Let's hear it right out."
The merchant now said: "I told all thy sad grief
To flock of green parrots;—so like thee, their chief.
Of them, one, affected with thy tale of woe,
Heart-broken, a gasp gave, expired, and fell low.
I conscience-struck was for the words I had said.
But what is the use? A word breathed can't be stayed."
A spoken word's arrow swift shot from a bow,
It can't be recalled, whate'er we may do.

An arrow once shot off will never come back.
At source, inundation alone can have check.
An outlet once found, there's no stoppage for it.
A world is then ruined, through lack of quick wit.
Act, consequence little dreamt of may produce.
The progeny's far 'yond our power to reduce.
The work of one Maker 's this universe all.
Our acts' consequences to our accounts fall.
Jack shoots off an arrow;—directs it to Jill.
The arrow poor Jill hits;—straightway does her kill.
If only it wound her, for great length of time
It tortures. Pain's God's work; wherever the clime.
Should Jack, at that moment, expire from his fright,
To plague her Jill's wound would not cease, day or night.
If from the effect of great pain, then, she die,
Remote cause is Jack, still, of her misery.
Account he must render for those pangs of hers.
Although they're God's acts, man to man them refers.
And so propagation, seed-sowing, and all;
Effects of them operate. God's sole, the call.
A saint acquires powers, most astounding, from God.[14]
The flying bolt he can avert with a nod.

The door can be shut between cause, consequence,
On saint's reclamation, by God's prescience.
He makes said unsaid, from beginning to end.
Hence, neither does skewer burn, roast to coal trend.[15]
From every mind that has knowledge of fact,
Remembrance effaced is, though brains may be racked.
Of this, dost thou proof require, most worthy friend,
The text read: "What verse We annul, or We mend."[16]
Again: "They my warning made you to forget."[17]
By these is oblivion's great power 'fore us set.
To make us remember, forget, they power have.
They've hearts subjugated o'er creation's wave.
Whene'er dull forgetfulness blinds eye of man,
No act can he do, howe'er wide his scan.
Dost dare, thou, great saints to make laughingstock?[18]
To words of the Prophet give heed, silly block.
Earth's lords have dominion o'er bodies of clay.
Enlightened saints rule hold o'er hearts;—their own sway.
All acts are fruits, doubtless, of experience.
Man, then, is but pupil. All's, else, mere pretence.[19]
I'll close now this subject; much more I might say;

Prevented I am by the rules I obey.

Remembrance, forgetfulness, both are of God.
Support and aid, too, must depend on His nod.
Of thoughts, God, men's good and bad souls voids, each night,
By millions. Since this has seemed good in His sight.
By day, their hearts fill with their thoughts all, again,
Those oystershells He fills with rich pearls amain.
He knows all the thoughts that here trouble our frames.
'Tis He that gives guidance to souls in their games.
Thy talent, thy judgment, unto thee are given,
That means thou may'st have to redeem thy fallen leaven.

The goldsmith's rich art's not by weaver possessed,
By jocund vein here, there another's distressed.
Though mind's frame and talents endowments are, all,
They seem to a foe mere machines for his thrall.
When sleep is departed, thoughts, talents return,
One's foe so comes back, has of war one more turn.
With dawn, all our thoughts, all our talents, awake,
As erst, good or bad; ere repose we could take.
So carrier pigeons, wherever they've been,
Return to their homes, quit the woodlands all green.

We see, thus, that all things revert to their source.
Parts ever must go shares in whole's intercourse.
So soon as our bird heard that parrot's sad state,
A shudder he gave, fainted, grew stiff as slate.
The merchant, on seeing this, seized with dismay,
Himself dashed to earth; wished he'd been far away.
His clothes rent in sorrow; his beard he plucked out;
And moaned, in distress wildly sobbing, throughout:
"My parrot, why, dearest, thus broken of heart?
Dead art thou, now, really? So fain to depart?
Poor pet! Darling bird! With thee, hours I could talk.
My sweetheart! My second self! Loved was thy walk.
Alas for poor Polly! Where's now his sly chat?
Alas, my companion! How shall I bear that?
Had Solomon seen a green parrot like mine,
What pleasure had he felt in other birds' line?
Dear prattler, in whose words I took such delight!
And then, thus to leave me, with naught in my sight!
Thy tongue to me dearer than gold's wealth untold;
At sound of thy sweet voice my joy was tenfold."
O tongue! Thou'rt a fire, and also a cornstack![20]

My patience, the cornstack! Hark! How its flames crack!
My soul doth, in secret, of thee complain sore;
But whate'er thou wishest, it does evermore.
O tongue: Thou'rt a treasure, beyond all earth's price!
And yet thou'rt a plague, that's not always too nice!
A whistle art thou, birds decoying afield.
A solace to love's wayward, fitful, spoilt child.
To men thou'rt all darkness, and blasphemy's bale;
To saints, guide, companion too, through this dark vale.
Thou'rt pitiless! Pity on me take, awhile.
Thy bow thou hast strung, on poor me to work guile.
Thou hast taken my bird; thou hast flustered my soul.
So cruel why be? Why delight take so foul?
An answer pray give; or else, deal out justice;
Or hope let me have to taste joy's chalice.
My dawn! Thou dispellest my deep'ning darkness.
My light! Day with thee is all sunshine brightness.
Alas! That swift bird, boldly soaring, of mine,
My lowest fall plumbed, traced my lineage divine.
The ignorant, wooers of trouble are, all.
"I swear," down to "misery" read, thou poor thrall.[21]
From misery free made me thy countenance.

From spume, so the clear stream of thy assistance.
Regret is a nursing of phantoms by day.
Neglect, stern realities drives not away.
A zeal for the truth is in God, there's no doubt.
The heart, with God's will, is constrained to burst out.
He's zeal, Who is "other," far, than all things else,[22]
Beyond all praise, laud, blessing, thanks, in heart's pulse.
Alas! my hot tears have become briny lake,—
An offering worthy my lost idol's sake.
My parrot! My wise bird! My starling art thou!
Interpreter, reader of thoughts, secrets, thou.
All daily events, results, just or unjust,
By Him ordained were, as I know, from the first.
The Parrot, inspired, who by voice of man spoke,
Existed ere dawn of existence first broke.
That Parrot is plainly within thyself felt;
Around thee His motto is ev'rywhere spelt.
Art joyful? From Him, know, all joys here do spring.
Art wronged? Thou submittest. Thou'rt under His wing.
O thou, who for body dost injure thy soul,
Thy proud flesh to pamper, dost wrong to thy whole.
I, too, am in flames. Who, then, seeks burning brand,

The trash to consume of conceit from the land?
That which is once burnt cannot blaze out again.
Select flaming brand, living fire choose, amain.
Alas! Lackaday! What has thus come to me?
My full moon in clouds why thus hidden to be?
I scarcely can breathe; with deep sorrow heart burns;
Male-lion-like, grief all kind condolence spurns.
He who in his senses has thus become drunk,
How fierce would he rage, if in cups he were sunk.
A lion in heat, he, despising all bounds;
No forest would hold him, nor dense jungle-grounds.
Of rhymes do I dream? 'Tis my love orders me[23]
Of love still to dream;—swain devoted to be:
"Thyself make thou happy. Rhymes leave, now, alone.
The rhyme I seek, thou art. I love thee, my own.
What's rhyme, that thou turnest thy thoughts thitherward?
Mere bramble on wall, hedging round our vineyard.
I care not for words, for asseverations;
My time if I pass in these sweet delusions.
Suggestion there is, one, kept secret from men.
To thee I'll impart. Thou keep'st secrets, like pen.

Suggestion occult, Abr'am knew not one jot.
One secret, that Gabriel as yet conceives not.
One mystery, to Jesus that never was known,
In jealousy God spake to me all alone."[24]
What do we with tongue? We affirm; we deny.
I'm no affirmation; denial am I.
In impersonality, person I find.
In ungenerosity, goodness of mind.
Earth's potentates slaves are of their own slaves' will.
All mortals, mere corpses of dead corpses, still.
Kings, subject are here to their own subjects' whim.
Man's drunk with those intoxicated of him.
The hunter of birds them entraps in his toils,
Himself is then pounced on, despite of his foils.
A beauty makes prey of the men soft of heart.
Sweethearts fall the victims of false lover's dart.
If lover thou see, know, a sweetheart he's, too,
'Tis but a relation. Each one's one of two.
If thirst seeks for water in this wide domain,
The water, on its side, the thirst courts again.
Should any one love thee, do thou silent be.
Thy ear claims he then, thou attentive should'st be.

The torrent bank up that threats dire overflow;
Or ravage 'twill make of the lands down below.
What care I if cities in ruins should fall,
In ruins we treasures find dear to us all.
Man merged in God, most entirely is drowned
As wave of a sea, soul but goes a set round.
Is bottom of that sea preferred more, or top?
Is God's shaft desired more, or shield, it to stop?
By doubts and by fears thou'lt piecemeal be torn, heart.
If thou well distinguish from joy, sorrow's smart.
Desir'st thou to taste, then, true happiness, joy?
'Tis not thine to choose. Beauty ever's most coy.
Each spangle of beauty's star outshines the moon.
To wreck a whole world's naught to beauty's full moon.
What is it we're good for? To sacrifice self.
Then hasten, my good friend, to offer thyself.
A lover's whole life is but self-sacrifice;
He wins not a heart, save his own heart's the price.
A heart I once courted with soft blandishment;
With pretexts was put off, most magniloquent.
I said my heart brimful was quite with her love;

Said she: "Hold thy tongue, now; that theme let's not move."

What have you been doing, you two eyes of mine?

Why saw you that cruel one? Left me to pine?

Presumptuous man! Didst thou hold her so cheap,

Because, by her kindness, made easy thy sleep?

What's easily got in this world, 's easy spent.

A child will give jewels at cake's allurement.

With love I'm o'erwhelm'd, now, of such a sad sort,

That ancients and moderns to it are all sport.

I've made short my story; details are not given.

'Twould otherwise scorch heart and tongue's whole joint leaven.

When I may say "lip," I mean "margin of sea;"

When "No!" you may take its true sense "Yes!" to be.

My sourness of looks by much sweetness is caused.

By words' multitude, silence strict I've imposed.

My sweetness I'll hide, in this world, in the next.

As veil, austere features I've firmly annexed.

My secrets to shield from the ken of all ears,

One out of a hundred, alone, here appears.

The world is right jealous, for reason that best:

God first jealous was, long before all the rest.[25]

He's soul. The two worlds His august body form.[26]
The body, through soul must receive good or harm.
Whoso in his worship turns truly to God,
Foul shame 'twould be for him to bow to faith's rod.
Whoever's a keeper of wardrobe to king,
Brings loss to his sovereign by petty trading.
With potentate, whoso, by grade, council holds,
If placed as a guard at a gate, roundly scolds.
Admitted to honour by kissing of hands,
To stoop, kiss the foot, degradation now stands.
To kiss foot of sovereign's a great honour, sure.
Compared with hands-kissing, ignominy pure.
A king would be jealous of servant so base
His foot who should kiss, when his hand was the place.
God's jealousy wheat is on full threshing-floor;
Man's jealousy, chaff blown away out of door.
Know: Jealousy rise doth take, still, in our God;
Man's jealousy budded from that noble rod.
Let's quit that deep subject; take up plaint and wail,
Against the great hardship of love's chastening flail.[27]
I cry, for that He loves to hear all my cries.

My moans, lamentations, are what He enjoys.
How should I cease wailing at His fell caprice?
I'm not of His darlings, nor in His service.
How should I not be, in my soul, black as night?
Deprived of His look, sweetness, warmth, and mild light.
All his disagreements are pleasant to me.
My life I'd give up, sacrifice I would be.
I love all my anguish; I dote on my pain,
So long as it pleases my heart's treasured swain.
My sorrow's my eyes' choicest collyrium;
My tears are as pearls from deep-sea tedium.
Tears poured forth by lovers at His adored feet,
Are pearls; though we're used them as tears to misgreet.
My soul's Soul's the tyrant of whom I complain.
Complaint I make not. I describe but my pain.
My heart but pretends it has been too much hurt;
Excuse is this merely. I smile at such blurt.
Do justice now, God, of all justice the fount!
Thou sittest in justice' seat; threshold I count.
From chief seat to threshold! How far raised above!
Where stand "*we*" and "*I*" in the sight of our love?[28]
O Thou who art free, quite from "*I*" and from "*we*,"

Thou heart's-joy of all men and women that be;
Where men and where women join, One art Thou, Sole!
Where units appear, Thou'rt the sum of the whole!
This "*I*" and this "*we*" Thou'st ordained for Thy state;
That psalms, hymns, and lauds may still rise to Thy gate.
When "I" and when "we" shall unite both in One,
Absorbed they'll be in Thy essence alone.
Existencies, potencies, all rise from Thee.
Denial and potency, Thou'rt from these free.
Can eye now behold Thee as truly Thou art?
Can heart Thy love picture, and smiles, e'en in part?
The heart that's a slave to a love or a smile
Can never be worthy to see Thee awhile.
Engrossed he that's now with pleasure and pain,
Can he, by these accidents, live o'er again?
Green pastures of love, in their infinitude,
More fruits yield than care, and than beatitude.
Love's far above these evanescent two states;
Without spring and autumn, its verdant estates.
Pay beauty's high toll, Beauty, on Thy sweet face;
Set forth lover's torments with all due preface.

That archness of look of my coquettish Swain
Anew has my heart fired with love's brand of pain.
I gave Him permission to pour out my blood.
I spoke of permission. He fled me for good.
Why fleest thus, always, the groans of complaint?
Why pourest Thou suffering's floods on the faint?
O Thou, whom each morn, as it dawns in the East,
Has found, like the sun, full prepared for a feast,
What cause have I furnished for all this sad pain,
O Thou, whose lips sweeter than sugar remain?
Thou ever new life givest to this old world;
The prayer hear of one whom from life Thou hast hurled!
For heaven's sake, quit talking of spring's roses red,
And think of the nightingale banished their bed.
My eagerness grows not from joy, or from grief;
My senses cajoled will not be by whim's thief.
My state is just one very often not seen;
Contest not; truth's ever victorious been.
Think not my state that of all these common men;
Be not benefactor, to tyrannise then.
If kindness and tyranny, joy, grief, are new;
All new things must die. God inherits.[29] That's true.

'Tis dawn. O of dawn Thou who art the sole cause!
Excuse for me make to Husāmu-'d-Dīn's laws.[30]
Excuses for angels and souls Thou canst see;
Thou art the soul's life; coral's shine is from Thee.[31]
From Thy light have sprung men and brightness of dawn.[32]
We're all aided by Thee, Thou cup of wine drawn.
Why does Thy gift keep me in constant suspense;—
Thy spiritual wine, that still charms ev'ry sense.
A beggar from me's wine in fermentation!
Spheres lessons take from me in revolution!
With me wine gets drunk; I get not drunk with it.
From me body grows; I spring thence not one bit.
We're bees, all of us; and our bodies, the wax;
With it we build cells to conceal our dark tracks.
These considerations would grow longer still.
We'll turn to our merchant. We left him so ill.
He thus, lamentations, sad groans, sadder moans,
Shot forth, with sighs, burning;—grieved hearts' crater-stones.
Complaints, contradictions, petitions, like words,
Now literal, then keen metaphors, sharp as swords.
The drowning, 'tis known to each one who breath draws,

To save threatened life, will, though vain, grasp at straws;
In hopes that some aid to his rescue will come,
He struggles, he flounders, he thinks of his home.
His sweetheart takes pleasure his struggles to see;
An effort's more noble than despondency.
A bridegroom is, surely, not quite free from cares.
His moans we expect not. Pain's not what he fears.
The reason this, why the Lord's blest scripture says:
"Each day He's engaged in some one of His ways."[33]
Therefore thou, my dear son, thyself still exert
Until thy last breath. Seek not toil to avert.
Then, at the last moment, the time may have come,
When favor 'll be shown thee for all thou hast done.
How much, and how long, strives the soul of each man,
The king's at the window;—hear, see all, he can.
Our merchant the parrot cast out from his cage.
The parrot flew up; on a tree took high stage.
The bird that was thought dead, now swift flew away.
His course like the sun's from the morn to midday.
The merchant sore marvelled at his flying bird;
Could not understand it; thought: "What has occurred?"
Then cried, looking upwards: "Come, pretty Poll mine!

Relate all about this freak strangest of thine.

What was that bird's game, there, of whom then thou spokest?

What trick was 't he played? Grief in me thou awokest."

The parrot him answered: "He taught me the trick.

He came and said: 'Free thyself now. Up! Be quick!'

No sooner had sounded thy voice in his ears,

He, as was agreed on, fell dead, it appears.

As much as to say, here, to me in my cage:

'Thou death counterfeit; so thou savest thy old age.'"

Become thou but grain; thou'lt be pecked up by birds.

A flower make thyself; all the children go thirds.

Thy grain hidest thou? Thou'rt naught else but brick-trap.

Thy flower shuttest up? Thou'rt a weed on house-top.

His beauty whoever may offer for sale,

Invites many troubles his heart to assail.

Hopes, fears, wraths, and jealousies strike him at once;

As rain on his head pours in winter;—the nonce.

All sorts of opponents, by jealousy moved;

With them, even friends joy to see him so proved.

Whoever may put off to sow seed in spring,

Ignores the true value of time's swiftest wing.

Let each one take refuge in mercy of God,
Who grace manifold on our souls has bestowed.
Then shalt thou find shelter, when shelter thou needest.
Fire's, water's protection thou'lt have, as thou heedest.
It was not the sea alone Noah, Moses, saved.
Nor sea alone was it, their foes that ingraved.
It was not the fire that stood Abr'am in stead,
Till God conquered Nimrod by gnat in his head.
It was not the mountain that called John to it,
And drove back pursuers with huge rocks that hit.
It cried: "Hither, John; refuge come take with me.
Thy life I will save from foe's sharp sword. Come; see."
"Adieu, master dear; I'm now off to my home.
May'st thou, too, be free, when the judgment shall come.
Good-bye, my kind master; compassion thou'st shown.
From tyranny's chains, now, through thee, have I flown."
He gave to our merchant some words of advice.
Then flew away, shouting: "Good-bye! Very nice!"
The merchant a "Safe journey" augured to him.
Then thought: "Useful lesson I've learned, and trim.
His doings may serve as a pattern for me.

I'll imitate him. Better teacher can't be.
My soul is not, sure, inferior to his.
See how souls should act, to gain heavenly bliss."
The body's a cage and a thorn to the soul.
Hence, seldom are body and soul wholly whole.
The body says: "I'll follow where thou mayest lead."
The soul answers: "Nay! Thy desire's all I heed."
The body then argues: "There's none like to thee,
Thou'rt perfect, kind, beautiful, good as needs be."
The soul now demurs: "This and next worlds are thine.
All hearts to the feast hasten, where thou'rt to shine."
The body then says: "'Tis a time for delight."
And soul responds quick: "Season, sure, to bedight."
When body sees crowds, throngs, profess love for it,
Control of self loses, in teeth takes the bit,
It does not reflect how the thousands and more,
Itself like, has sin brought to ruin's grim shore.
The bait of gross flattery is always found sweet.
Therewith be not caught. Lurid fire's 'neath its greet.
Its sweetness is present; its flame's not forecast;
Its smoke of destruction will burst forth at last.
Say not: "I'll ne'er listen to flatterer's tale;

They're sordid, its motives;—like 'sprat to catch whale.'"
A lampoon should thy panegyrist indite
Against thee in public, thy rest's disturbed quite.
Thou knowest it was spoken in sheer angry spleen,
When he in some wish unsuccessful had been.
The barb of it rankles, still, in thy heart's core,
The price paid for flattery, 'tis, makes thee feel sore.
Long, long shalt thou feel the deep wound it inflicts.
It stimulates pride; all the soul it infects.
Man shows not how sweet flattery is to his soul.
The instant he's lampooned, he's lost self-control.
Thus, pill or draught taken to combat disease,
A long time, indeed, you're thence robbed of all ease.
And if you eat sweetmeats, their tastes are soon lost.
Nor one, nor the other, is worth half the cost.
Duration they have not; effects they produce.
By contraries, contraries all we deduce.
As hidden effect of a diet of sweets,
By long incubation, boils break out, or gleets.
The flesh, with praise pampered, a Pharaoh becomes.
The flesh, mortified, due submission assumes.
A servant to all be; princely power be forgot.

Submit to cuffs, ball-like; like bat, batter not.
So soon, otherwise, as thee fortune forsakes,
Thy flatterers will turn. 'Tis greed only, them makes.
The throngs of gross flatterers, who sang loud thy praise.
Will shake their heads, shout out: "Poor de'il! What a craze!"
On seeing thee, then, as thou wanderest about,
They cry: "Cursed hobgoblin! From grave he's come out!"
Like beardless, vain boy they've addressed as "My Lord,"
To work on his vanity, fair fame defraud,
In vice when he's nurtured, his beard thickly grown,
E'en Satan would blush a pact with him to own.
'Tis men Satan seeks out, to work them mischief.
Thee he'll never seek; worse than him, thou, a thief.
So long as thou'rt man, Satan follows thy track.
He tempts thee to drain manhood's lees, still, and wrack.
When thou'rt become devil, just like to himself,
He flees thee in fright; leaves thee quite to thyself.
All they who before refuge took in thy power,
With horror fly from thee, in this thy fallen hour.
Our words are mere lies, all tergiversations.[34]
Without the divine grace, they're sheer delusions.

Without grace of God, holy aid from His saints,
Best "record" of man must be blots and complaints.[35]
O God! Thy grace, sole, 'tis sustains us as men.
Another to name with Thee suits not a pen.
To servants, sound judgment Thou'st kindly vouchsafed.
This gift made the means, we've from error escaped.
One drop from the sea of Thy knowledge, does us
With omniscience, surely, make confluous.
That drop have I gathered up in my soul's trust.
Do Thou save it, Lord, from lust's soil and sin's gust.
Sin's soil, oh! permit not that drop to absorb!
Those gusts forbid Thou more to lessen its orb!
True, Thou art All-Powerful, and Thy gracious will
Could force them to yield it back, grace to fulfil.
A drop, lost in air, dispersed in the soil,
Is still, through Thy providence, safe from despoil.
Become it, or others, a nonentity,
Thy beck can them summon to new entity.
How many diverse still combine to form one.
Thou givest the word, they part, each to its zone.
Each moment, from naught fresh creations still come,
In flocks and in crowds. 'Tis Thou makest them a home.

Each night, in profound sleep our consciousness sinks;
Becomes non-existent;—waves on seashore's brinks.
When morning afresh dawns, they wake up anew,
Like fish in the sea, plashing drops, falling dew.
In autumn, the leaves see. They quit, then, the trees;
Like scattered battalions, they fly with the breeze.
The rook, in robes sable, as mourner acts, chief;
In wood and field croaks for his much-deplored leaf.
Command from Thee goes forth;—Thou, true Forest-King;
Nonentity gives back each late stolen thing.
O Death! Thou restorest, now, the whole prey of thine;
The leaves, flowers, and fruits, in their due season shine.
Consider, my friend, in thyself; now, awhile,
The spring and the autumn thou in thee seest smile.
Look thou that thy heart be green, yield its good fruits
Of righteousness, purity,—heaven's best recruits.
Through garlands of verdure thy rough branches hid;
With bloom in profusion, hills, plains, all tumid.
These words of mine come from the Spirit supreme,
To call to mind heaven's everlasting grand scheme.
Thou smellest a perfume of flowers. Flowers are not yet;

Thou dreamest fermentation, though wine is not set.
That odour will draw thee to where the flowers grow,[36]
The joys of sweet paradise, "where rivers flow."[37]
Of hope it perfume is that leads our souls on;
As hope led forth Jacob in quest of his son.[38]
Bad tidings and fearful cost Jacob his sight.
Reunion, in hope, to him brought back the light.
If thou'rt not a Joseph, a Jacob be yet.
As he did, weep, mourn; joy, like him, thou shalt get.
If thou art not Shīrīn, thou may'st Ferhād be;[39]
And if not Laylà dear, Majnūn's ravings see.[40]
Accept the advice of old Gazna's sage, wise.[41]
To thee, ever, new life from old life may rise:
"To give one's self airs, requires, first, a fair face;
If beauty thou hast not, run not thou that race."
An ugly face ugly is, all the world round.
A blind eye's affliction, where'er it be found.
In presence of Joseph, no coquetries use.[42]
But humble thyself; soft entreaties infuse.
The parrot had death simulated, as prayer.
Do thou to pride die; thou mayest so live for e'er.

From Jesus a breath may, then, blow upon thee;
Transform thee to what he was, what thou mayest be.
A stone will not blossom because it is spring.
As earth make thyself; flowers around thee may cling.
For years thou a stone 'st been; lay this well to heart.
Try patience a short time; 'twill give a fresh start.
373

---

1. Literally, "your morning cup," drunk at dawn ere leaving a house.
2. Asiatics drink "to the love" of a friend; not "to his health."
3. The parrot is known by the title "Sugar-eating."
4. A shade of an explanation to this very hazardous saying of the Sūfī Gnostics is found in Qur'ān xvi. 108: "Whoever denieth God after he hath believed, except him who shall be compelled against his will, and whose heart continueth steadfast in the faith, shall be severely chastised."
5. The dervish orders call their peculiar cap a "mitre" or "crown" (*tāj*).
6. The "four rivers" of Paradise, of water, milk, wine, and honey. Qur'ān xlvii. 16.
7. Qur'ān iii. 31; and numerous other places.
8. This section purports to have been suggested by the following couplet from 'Attār:—
   "O heedless child of lust, weep thou tears of blood.
   If a saint eat poison, honey-like 'tis food."
   The original expression for "saint," here, is: "a man of heart."
9. Canonical "responsibility" falls on all of sane mind and adult age.
10. See note to dist. No. 33 of the present poem.
11. Qur'ān vii. 112, &c.
12. By a *"perfect man"* a saint is intended; as by "imperfect," here and before, an ordinary mortal is depicted.
13. Qur'ān vii. 203; xlvi. 28. By "ear" and "tongue" a learner and a teacher are symbolised.
14. A hazardous assertion. See Anecdotes, Chap, iii., Nos. 2, 5, 7, &c.
15. A proverbial expression, like: "All's well that ends well."
16. Qur'ān ii. 100.
17. Qur'ān xxiii. 112.
18. Also Qur'ān xxiii. 112.

19. The *"pupil"* of the eye; in Persian called *"the manikin;"* in Arabic, *"the man."*These both allude to the small image of ourselves seen reflected in the pupil.
20. This rhapsody is mystical, like the Song of Solomon. A "tongue" is a teacher, informant; a prophet; and, apparently, even God himself.
21. Qur'ān xc. 1-4.
22. "Other," as opposed to self; also opposed to "we two" in the case of lovers; it is a term much used in Eastern poetry and philosophy.
23. The poet's *"beloved"* appears, here, to be God.
24. Allusion appears to be made to Qur'ān xxi. 107.
25. This section is stated to be a gloss upon the following apostolic tradition: "Verily, Sa'd is really jealous; but I am more jealous than he, and God than I. Out of His jealousy hath He made all excesses sinful; whether of outer or of the inner man." This Sa'd, son of 'Ubāda, was a disciple of Muhammed, and the most munificent man in Madīna. He embraced the faith before the Hijra. See An-Nawāwī, p. 274, l. 5.
26. The "two worlds," spiritual and material, future and present.
27. The poet's "love," is still God. This section purports to be an excursus on the following distich of the poet Sanā'ī, who died a.h. 576 (a.d. 1180):—

    "Why leavest thou thy guild, its rules or faith or sin?
    Why quittest thou thy mistress, be she plump or thin?"
28. Reflections on God's unity, and the plurality of created being.
29. Qur'ān xix. 41, &c.
30. Anecdotes, Chap. vi.
31. "Life" and "coral," in Persian "jān" and "merjān."
32. Men from moral, dawn from material light.
33. Qur'ān lv. 29.
34. This section purports to be a dissertation on the dictum: "What God wills, is."
35. Man's "record" is the register of his thoughts, words, and deeds, kept by angels, to be produced in the last judgment.
36. The same word in Persian, *bū*, signifies "odour" and "hope." The thing hoped for becomes a distant, odoriferous flower.
37. Qur'ān ii. 23, and forty places in all.
38. Jacob is said to have wept himself blind on losing Joseph; the smell of his son's coat, when refound, later, restored him.
39. Ferhād was Shīrīn's lover. (See Tale 6, distich 107, note.)
40. Majnūn, in story, went mad for love of Laylà.
41. The "Sage of Gazna" is the poet Sanā'ī, already mentioned in the notes to the present tale, distich 230.
42. Joseph is held to have been most superlatively beautiful.

VIII. THE HARPER.

Hast heard, perchance, there was in days of good ‘Umer
A minstrel talented, whose harpings moved the sphere?
The nightingales all wept in transports at his voice,
One pleasure made men’s hearts a hundredfold rejoice.
His song enchanted every gathering where he went,
Applause as thunder broke forth, to his heart’s content.
Like voice of Isrāfīl, whose trump on judgment day,[1]
Will wake the dead to life, his made the saddest gay.
Dear friend to Isrāfīl he was, and mendicant;
His notes made plumes to sprout on hide of elephant.
Some day will Isrāfīl attention pay to moans.

Their souls he will recall to old and putrid bones.
The prophets, likewise, all, musicians are on hearts.
Disciples hence expire with joy by fits and starts.
Our outward ears the strains hear not which thence proceed;
Those ears, in many ways, degraded are indeed.
Mankind the songs of fairies never hear at all,
They are not versed in fairies' ways, their voices small.
'Tis true, the chants of fairies' sounds are of this world;[2]
But songs sung by men's hearts are far above them hurled.
Both men and fairies pris'ners are in earthly cage.
Both, too, are thralls of sinful ignorance's rage.
Read thou the text: "O fairy troop," in book of God.[3]
Consider, too: "Can ye pass out?" Who holds the rod?
The inward hymn that's sung by all the hearts of saints
Commences: "O component parts of that thing not."[4]
Now since they take their rise in this not, negative,
They put aside the hollow phantom where we live.
Ye putrid corpses, wrapt in rank corruption's cloth,
Our everlasting souls are free from birth and growth.
Were I but to recite one stave from their blest song,
All living souls would rise out from their tombs among.

Lend ear attentively; that may not distant be;

As yet, however, leave's not given to tell it thee.

The saints are Isrāfīls of this our passing time.

The spiritually dead through them live life sublime.

Our souls mere corpses are; their graves, our bodies' crowds.

At voice of saint do they arise, clothed in their shrouds.

They say: "This voice has in it something to be feared.

To raise the dead, God's voice alone has power, we've heard.

We were all dead, and unto earth had we returned.

The voice of God we've heard; our prisons we have spurned."

The voice of God without, also within the vail,

Can give the gift to all, it gave to Mary: "Hail!"

O ye whose death was not that which attacks the flesh,

At sound of the Beloved's voice ye've risen afresh.

That voice the Bridegroom's voice most truly was, 'tis said,

Although 'twas from the lips of His servant, Ahmed.

God said to him: "Thy tongue, thy eye, thy ear, I am;

All thy contentment, anger, thoughts, 'tis I undam.

Go on; 'By Me he hears, by Me he sees;' that's thee;

Thou art the head; thou holdest the place of Head's trustee.

In ecstasy, since thou art 'He the Lord's who is,'[5]

I will be thine; for see, 'tis said: 'The Lord is his.'

Now will I say to thee: 'Thou art;' and now; 'I am.'

What I may say's as clear as is the sun in heaven.

Wherever I may shine an instant in a lamp,

A world of doubts I solve; on all My seal I stamp.

The darkness which the sun could never yet illume,

By magic of My breath grows bright as peacock's plume.

Wherever gloom may reign as undisturbed night,

When shone upon by Me, like noonday's forthwith bright."

'Twas He who taught to Adam ev'ry thing's true name,

Through Adam to mankind imparted He the same.

Take thou enlightenment from Adam or the Lord.

Draw wine as thou mayest list from jar or from the gourd.[6]

The distance is not great between the gourd and jar.

The gourd is not, like thee, made drunk by grape's nectar.

Draw water from the brook, or from a pitcher's mouth;

The brook is still the source whence pitcher's filled; forsooth.

Seek light as listest; whether from the moon or sun.
The moon derives her sheen from daystar's golden tun.
Imbibe what light thou canst from any twinkling star.
The Prophet said: "Stars are all my disciples." Hear![7]
He further said: "How happy they who see my face,[8]
And happy they who look on them in their own place."
He said: "Good luck to all who have the happy chance[9]
To look on my disciples,—mirrors of my glance."
If thou by taper's aid proceed to light a lamp,
The eye that sees its light, perceives the taper's stamp.
If one lamp from another should be lighted; well!
The light received from this, has come from that one's cell.
And so, if through a thousand wicks the light should pass,
Who sees the last enjoys the gift of all the mass.
The light of this last lamp's as pure as is the whole;
No difference is there. And thus 'tis with the soul.
The light diffused by teachers in these latter days,
No other is than what was shown by earlier rays.
Our Prophet said: "The breathings of the Lord your God,[10]
In these your days of pilgrimage, on all sides prod.

Your ears and minds lend ye to all signs of the times;

Perchance ye may inhale those breathings in these climes."

One breathing came and found you. Straightway it was gone.

To all who sought, new life it gave. It then had done.

Another breathing's come. Be ye not unprepared.

Ye may not let it go by. Something must be shared.

It found your souls on fire. 'Tis thence they cease to burn.

Your souls it found all corpses. Life it made return.

Your fiery souls by it all quickly were puffed out.

Dead souls of yours by it began aloud to shout.

Their present calm, and this vivacity's from heaven;

Resembling not the turbulence by which man's driven.

One breathing from the Lord, when blown on earth and air,

Ill qualities converts straight into all that's fair.

For fear lest any breathing such as this thee shake,

Read thou the text: "They shunned the task to undertake."[11]

Had not "they shrunk from it," where now would'st thou have been?

Had they not feared, would'st thou this grade have ever seen?

But yesterday an opening gleamed for better things;

Till greed for fleshly morsels stopped the way of kings.

For sake of some such morsel Luqmān was made bail.[12]

The time's now that for Luqmān morsel'd not avail.

The troubles we endure are all for morsel's sake.

Be Luqmān. Thou'lt extract the thorn that makes thee ache.

A thorn or chafing hurt not Luqmān's horny hand.

Through greed thou lackest the discipline made him so bland.

The thing thou thoughtest a date-palm, know, is but a thorn.

Ungrateful, uninformed thou art, now, as when born.

The soul of Luqmān was a vineyard of the Lord.

Why then into his soul did thorn pierce like a sword?

Thorn-eating camel, truly, is this world of ours,

Ahmed, then, came and mounted;—him that camel bears.

O camel, on thy back thou bearest a vase of rose.

On thee from thence have sprouted rosebuds, as God knows.

Thy tastes thee lead to camel-thorn and wastes of sand.

To thee the thorn's a rose; the wilderness, rich land.

O thou who in such quest hast wandered up and down,

How long wilt thou contend rose-garden's sandy down?

Thou canst not now extract the thorn from thy sore foot.
With that blind eye of thine, how wilt thou see its root?
A man whose vast desires the world could not contain,
Is sometimes by one thorn's point sent to death's domain.
Now Ahmed came; a tender, kind companion, he.
"Speak to me, O Humayrā," said he, "speak to me."[13]
Put thou thy shoe, Humayrā, quick into the fire.[14]
The rocks will rubies turn, from his feet's blood in mire.
This Humayrā's a woman's name, the poet's love.
Such is the Arab custom. Soul is meant. Now move.
That Soul's no need to fear from being named as girl.[15]
Of sex, as male or female, that Soul has no twirl.
That Soul is far above sex, accident, and mood.
That Soul is not man's darling, made of flesh and blood.
That Soul is not the life that grows from cakes of bread;
That's sometimes of one mind, and other then instead.
Of good is He the worker, good He is also.
From goodness separate, no goodness e'er will flow.
If thou'rt made sweet through sugar, it may happen still,
That sugar none thou find, to sweeten thee at will.
But if thou sweet become, like sugar, through good heart,
This sweetness from thy sugar never will depart.

How can a lover find love's nectar in himself?
That question passes comprehension, my good elf.
Man's finite reason disbelieves love's potent sway.
Himself he yet esteems endowed with head to-day.
He's clever, and he's knowing, *nil* he's not; anon.
Until an angel's nothing,[16] he's a sheer demon.
In word and act a man may be a friend of ours;
But when it comes to heart and mind, he huffs and lours.
If he from *esse*, reach not *posse's* state, he's *nil;*
And willingly;—unwillingly, we may worlds fill.
The Soul, our God, 's perfection. Perfect is His "call."[17]
His Ahmed used to say: "Ensoul us, O Bilāl![18]
Lift up thy voice, O Bilāl,—thy harmonious voice.
Put forth the breath that I infused at thy heart's choice.
The breath that 'twas made Adam lose all consciousness;
While all the hosts of heaven, too, felt their helplessness."
That Ahmed, Mustafà, at one blest sight stood lost.[19]
His wedding-night it was. Dawn-worship it him cost.[20]
He woke not from the sleep his blessed vision shed.
Dawn-worship he o'erslept; the sun shone overhead.
On that, his wedding-night, in presence of his bride,

His sainted soul kissed hands, high honour's fullest tide.
Both love and soul are occult, hidden and concealed.
If God I have "bride" named, let it stand fault repealed.
I silence would have kept, from fear of love's caprice,
If for a moment only, I'd been granted grace.
But He still said: "Say on. The word is not a fault.
It's naught but the decree there should appear default.
It's shame to him who only sees another's faults.
What fault is noticed by the Soul safe from assaults?"
A fault it is to eyes of creatures ignorant.
But not with God the Lord, our Maker benignant.
E'en blasphemy is wisdom with th' Omnipotent;[21]
Attributed to mortals, mortal sin patent.
If one sole fault be found amidst a hundred truths,
'Tis like a stick that's used to prop sweet flowers' growths.
Both will be surely weighed in justice' equal scales;
For, like the soul and body, both are pleasant tales.
The saints have therefore said, for sweet instruction's sake:
"The bodies of the pure with souls just balance make."
Their words, their selves, their figures, whate'er these may be,

Are all Soul Absolute, without a trace to see.
Sworn enemy is Body to their spiritual life,
Just as one game of backgammon, with names full rife.[22]
The body goes to earth; is soon reduced to clay;
The soul endures like salt, and suffers no decay.
The salt, than which Muhammed far more sapid is;
From "Attic salt" that's found in each *dictum* of his.
That Attic salt's an heirloom, heritage from him;
His heirs are here with thee. Seek unto them *passim*.
They're sitting in thy presence. What's in front of thee?
Thy soul demands thy care. Where can thy forethought be?
If thou still be in doubt, and not sure of thyself,
Thou'rt slave unto thy body; soul thou hast not, elf.
Behind, before, above, below, stands body's shade.
The soul has no "dimensions;" clearly it's displayed.
Lift thy eyes, dear Sir, in glorious light of God;
That thou be not accounted most shortsighted clod.
Thou nothing knowest or carest about, save grief and joy;
Thou nothing, by mere nothings hemmed in, man or boy.
To-day's a day of rain. Yet journey thou till night;
Not on account of downpour, but because it's light.

One day did Mustafà go to the burial-ground.
The Prophet at a funeral, his friend's, was found.
At filling in the grave he lent a helping hand;
A living seed he planted in that holy land.
The trees thereof are emblems,—cypress, fir, or yew;
Their boughs are hands in prayer uplifted,—if men knew.
They many lessons inculcate to men of sense,
He who hath ears to hear may thence draw inference.
A contemplative mind from them new secrets culls.
The heedless are amused with what men's reason dulls.
With tongue-shaped leaves and finger-twigs they us address;
From inmost heart of earth they publish mysteries.
As ducks dive into water, they plunge into earth.
Like rooks they were, now peacocks, gay in their new birth.
The winter shuts them up, as prisoners, in its ice.
Black rooks then, bare; as peacocks spring bids them arise.
God makes them look like dead in winter's frozen reign,
But with returning spring wakes them to life again.
Dull atheists contend this is a story old,
And ask why we to God attribute it, so bold.

They say these alternations ever thus were seen.
The world of old, they think, as 'tis, has ever been.
In spite of their contention, in breasts of His saints
Has God at all times reared rich gardens free from feints.
Each flower that yields to sense agreeable perfume,
Speaks volumes to saint's heart with its mysterious tongue.
Each perfume from a flower rubs atheist's nose in dirt;
Although he rush about, and boundless nonsense spirt.
An atheist's like a chafer clinging to rosebud,
Or like a nervous patient tortured by drum's thud.
He makes himself as fussy as each touting wight;
But shuts his eyes to flashes of conviction's light.
He shuts his eyes perversely, with them will not see.
The saint, on other hand, 's clear-sighted certainly.
The Prophet, when returned home from the funeral,
Found 'Ā'isha was waiting, him to welcome all.
So when her eyes fell on him, just as in he came,
She him approached, and on him hand placed; gentle dame.
She touched his turban, cloak and coat, his sleeves and shoes,
His hair and beard, his face and hands, peering for news.

He asked her what she sought with so much eager zeal.
She answered him: "To-day of rain there's fallen a deal.
I'm lost in wonderment to feel thou art not wet;
No dampness is there here. I marvel still more yet."
He asked: "What veil worest thou God's service to fulfil?"[23]
She answered: "I a plaid of thine threw o'er my frill."
He said: "That plaid it was for which the Lord, to thee,
My lady pure, a shower caused visible to be.
That shower was not of raindrops from the clouds that fall;
A shower of mercy 'twas; its cloud and sky, His call."
["In regions of the soul so many skies are there![24]
They issue their commands to spheres of earth and air.
The ups and downs in spirit's path form quite a class;
So many hills to climb; so many seas to pass."]—*Sanā'ī.*
The unseen world has other clouds, and other skies;[25]
Its sun is different; its water God supplies.
Its rain proceeds from other clouds than does our own.
God's mercy 'tis that forms that rain when it pours down.
Those rains are never seen, save by the eyes of saints.
Mere men "by new creation puzzled,"[26] judge them feints.

One rain there is that nourishment brings in its track;

Another rain also that works a whole world's wreck.

The rain of spring does wonders in the garden's fold;

The rain of autumn chills like ague's shivers cold.

The spring rain nourishes whate'er it falls upon.

Autumnal showers but bleach and shrivel; all turns wan.

Thus is it with the cold, the wind, and eke the sun;

They're means from which such different phases seem to run.

In things invisible the same rule still holds good;

Advantage, loss, annoyance, fraud, affliction's flood.

The words of saints are like the vernal breeze in power;

They cause sweet flowers to open in man's bosom bower.

And like the rains of spring on herbage of the field,

They raise in pious hearts a harvest of rich yield.

If thou shouldst see a trunk that's blighted, dead, and dry,

Attribute not this state to quickening air's supply.

The air still quickens, though dead stumps feel not its power.

'Tis only what's alive, that freshens by a shower.

The Prophet gave advice: "From breezes cool, in spring,[27]

Your bodies cover not; they're invigorating.

Allow them, then, full play; they'll give your sinews strength.

See how, with them, the trees are clothed with leaves, at length.

Beware, however; autumn's chills ye must not court.

They're fatal to men's lives; the trees they strip, in short."

Traditionists report the Prophet's blessed words;

But there they have stopped short; they add naught afterwards.

The whole class, ignorant of application's call,

The mountain have discerned; its mines they have missed, all.

The autumn chill, with God, is fleshly lust and pride;

The vernal breeze, the spirit, wisdom, sense to guide.

Of wisdom, in thy head, a glimmering thou hast;

Seek then for perfect wisdom; be to it steadfast.

Thy partial stock from thence completed thou wilt bring.

On neck of flesh completed wisdom put, as ring.[28]

Thou seest now, applied, the breeze of spring is he,

Who, perfect in himself, men perfect helps to be.

From words of his take care thou close not up thy ear.

Thy faith they will confirm; religion fruit will bear.

Reproachful, or in praise, hear all he has to say;

From thee the fires of hell they'll help to turn away.

Reproaches, admonitions, life will bring at last

If faith they but confirm, flesh in subjection cast.

By admonition is the heart encouraged to good deeds;

And by reproaches is the soul kept back from evil's meeds.

Upon the heart of teacher clings dark sorrow's pall,

If one twig from heart's garden's seen away to fall.

Good 'Ā'isha, the gem of honour's casket wide,

Then asked the Prophet (who's of both the worlds the Pride):

"O thou who of all creatures every essence art,

What was the reason rain this day has played its part?

Was it a rain of mercy, such as sometimes falls;

Or was it as a menace justice fitly calls?

Was it a vernal rain, dispensing benefits;

Or was it an autumnal shower, to dig grave pits?"

He answered: "'Twas a sprinkle, sent to soothe our care, —

That fruit inherited by all who Adam share.

Should man remain exposed for long to care's fierce flame,

'Twould work him wrack and ruin, crush his mortal frame."

The world would go to ruin in a little while;
Man's greed would get the upper hand, did he not smile.
The prop of this wide world is heedlessness, my son;
And thoughtfulness on earth below's a curse, when won.
For thoughtfulness belongs unto the upper world;
Triumphant here below, all's soon to ruin hurled.
This thoughtfulness a sun is; greed's a mass of ice.
This thoughtfulness is water; greed, the filth of vice.
So from the upper world scant tricklings are sent down,
That greed and envy may not ruin every town.
If those scant tricklings were to prove a copious rill,
Defects and talents both would cease our soil to till.
Let's leave these moralisings; they would have no end.
So go we back to seek the minstrel, our old friend.
That minstrel's talent had been rare; the world he'd charmed.
At sound of his sweet voice, imagination 'd swarmed.
Each heart, birdlike, began to flutter in its cage;
Surprise enchained men's minds when his notes threw the gage.
But now he was grown old; long years he'd passed on earth.
Like falcon chasing gnats, he'd little cause for mirth.

His back was double bent, like belly of wine-jar;
His brows above his eyes with crupper-straps on par.
His voice, the former joy of all who might it hear,
Was now cracked, out of tune, uncouth, none could it bear.
His tones, that might have made dame Venus mad with rage,[29]
Were now like donkey's brayings in his sinking age.
What is there beautiful that goes not to decay?
Where is the roof that will not ruin be one day?
Unless it be the words of saint[30] from God; they'll last
'Till echoes of his voice shall sound in judgment blast.

He is the inner joy that glads our inner man;
The source from whom our beings rose when time began.
He is the amber draws the motes of thought and speech;
He gave the means to measure revelation's reach.
Our minstrel in old age felt poverty's sure pinch.
No money could he earn; bread, not enough for finch.
He prayed: "O God, long life and full to me Thou'st given,
To worthless sinner Thou hast shown foretaste of heaven.
I've slighted Thy commandments seventy years and more,
Not one day hast Thou let me pangs of want feel sore.

No longer can I earn; I'm now Thy household guest;
I'll harp for love of Thee, Thou giver of my feast."
His harp on shoulder slung, he went, in quest of God,
To burial-ground of Yathrab;[31] sat down on the sod.
Said he: "I'll ask of God the hire of my harpstrings;
For He accepts the heart's most humble outpourings."
He harped awhile, and then he laid him down and wept.
His harp his pillow was; upon a grave he slept.
With sleep his soul was freed from prison and from pain,
The harp and harper both were now made young again.
His soul, free, wandered forth, exempt from all dull care,
In spacious fields of heaven, the soul's park, light as air.
There he began to warble, merry as a lark:
"O that I here might dwell without a care to cark!
How joyous I should be in such a paradise;
These sweet ethereal fields breathe balm, and myrrh, and spice.
I'd wander all about; no need of feet or wings.
All sweets I'd feast on; lips and teeth were useless things.
My mind at rest, from all care free, I'd ever roam.
The angels I'd not envy in their heavenly home.

With bandaged eyes I'd survey realms without an end;

All sorts of flowers I'd gather, yet not soil my hand.

Like duck in pond, down deep I'd plunge in honey lake.[32]

In Job's own fount I'd bathe, in wine I'd revel make.

For Job with wine from heaven was cleansed in every pore;

From head to foot he came forth healed, without a sore."

If these poor rhyming verses covered heaven's vast vault,

They'd not tell half a tithe, they still would be at fault.

The sum of heavenly joys I find an endless theme;

My heart is far too narrow to embrace its scheme.

The world I would enclose in my poor poem's fold,

Has lent my thoughts the wings that make their flight so bold.

Were but that world in sight; its road, were it but known;

Few souls would here remain, were but its glories shown.

Commandment has been given: "Thou shalt not covetous be."

The thorn from out thy foot is drawn; thy thanks let's see.

"My Lord! My God!" loud cried our minstrel in that place,

Those glorious realms of mercy, boundless shores of grace.

About that time the Lord on 'Umer slumber sent.

He could not keep awake; beneath sleep's burden bent.

With wonder thought he 'twas unprecedented: "See!

This sleep's divinely ordered; purpose there must be."

His head he bowed; sleep bound him fast; a dream he saw,

A voice from God he heard,—for him a sacred law.

God's voice the real source is of every cry and sound;

The only voice, in fact; all other's echo found.

Turks, Kurds, and Persians, Arabs, all have understood

That voice most wonderful,—of lip and ear no mood.

What say I? No! Not merely Turks and Persians all,

The very rocks and trees have answered to that call.

Each moment's clearly heard: "Am I not, then, your Lord?"[33]

Ideas and essences became "things" at His word.

Had they not answered: "Yes, Thou art our God, O Lord,"

From out of nothing straight that answer 'd come, in word!

About what's here been said respecting stocks and stones,

Let's hear what tell tradition's most veracious tones.

We'll find related there how various rocks and trees,

Both understood and spoke, as human being sees.

A post in his own house, at Mustafà's retreat,

Sent forth a sob of grief, like heart in sorrow's heat,
As he his sermon preached, surrounded by his flock,
So that the moan was heard by old and young; no mock.
Disciples one and all were petrified, perplexed,
And marvelled what might make its wooden heart so vexed.
The Prophet put the question: "What may be thy need?"
The column answered: "Prophet, grief my heart makes bleed.[34]
Against me, in thy sermon, thou'st been used to lean;
A pulpit now thou'st mounted; far from me thou'rt seen."
The Prophet said: "Thou most affectionate of posts!
Good fortune thee attend, sent by the Lord of Hosts!
If thou so wish, thou mayst become a fruitful palm;
And men from east and west sing of thy dates in psalm.
Or God may thee transplant to realms of paradise;
Where as a cedar thou eternally mayst rise."
It answered: "I elect what ne'er will know decay."
Lend ear, O heedless man! Hast thou less sense than they?
That post was forthwith buried, like a corpse of clay,
In hopes of resurrection at the judgment day.

Thou hence mayst learn that any whom the Lord doth call,

Breaks straightway with the things of this our earthly ball.

Whoe'er receives a mission from the Lord his God,

Forsakes the world, himself prepares the path to plod.

Who's not received the gift of knowledge from above,

Will ne'er believe a stock could sigh and moan for love.

He may pretend to acquiesce; not from belief;

He says: "'Tis so," to 'scape a name much worse than thief.

All they who're not convinced that God's "Be" is enough,

Will turn away their face; this tale they'll treat as "stuff."

By thousands are confessing Muslims, men of mark,

By doubt most sadly haunted; faith they've not, one spark.

Conformity with them is founded on surmise,

And all their heart and conscience quieted with lies.

'Tis Satan sows the seed of doubting in their breast,

Like blind men they will fall into the pit at last.

Mere reasoners are cripples, propped on wooden leg;

And, like such cripple, often falling as they beg.

How different's a pillar of our holy creed!

As mountain he is steadfast; faith his living meed.
A blind man's leg's his staff; upon it he must lean,
Or he will risk to fall at full length on the green.
A knight is he who sole has routed hosts of foes;
Wise leader then becomes of liegemen's ranks through woes.
Those blind men find their way by trusting to a staff.
They lean upon a creature; their sight is in a gaff.
For, otherwise, they'd be far-seeing; they'd be kings;
As 'tis, they're blind, they're corpses,—lifeless, senseless things.
The blind can never sow, and surely never reap;
They cannot edify; their talent they must keep.
If 'twere not for God's mercy, favour, and free grace,
Their staff of reason 'd snap; they 'd fall prone on their face.
That staff's a weapon made for quarrelling and fight;
Then break it up in pieces, man of feeble sight!
That staff was given thee, to help thee on thy way;
With it men's faces strikest thou, angry, ev'ry day.
What's this you're doing, blind ones? What are you about?
Some constables call in, to calm this frightful rout.

Fall down, and Him entreat, who furnished you with staff.
Look well, and see what signs your weapon may engraff.
Consider Moses' miracle; reflect on Ahmed's too.
One's staff became a serpent; one's post chose what is true.
From that staff came a serpent; from this post, loud moan.
Five times a day for praise we hear the crier's tone.
This trouble otherwise had been a senseless suit;
So many miracles, so very little fruit.
What's reas'nable the mind can easily allow,
No need's there then for miracle, for tide to ebb and flow.
The plan of miracles unreasonable count;
But know it is accepted; faith it does not daunt.
Just like as demons, and as wild beasts, out of dread
Of man, fled to the wilds, when envy reared its head,
So, out of dread of miracles by prophets wrought,
Do cavillers take refuge in sophisms of thought.
In name, they're Muslims; and, by virtue of their wiles,
We can't know what they are; their faces are all smiles.
Precisely as false-coiners on their metal base
A coat of silver put, the sovereign's name then trace,
In word, God's unity confessed, and holy law,

Their hearts are like the poison-grain in sweet kickshaw.
Not Venus will convince a sophist in debate;
But true religion speaks, confutes his postulate.
His body's like a stock, his spirit's but a stone.
Howe'er he contradict, them God directs alone.
In words, mayhap, he may detect a hitch or two;
But his own soul and body witness God is true.
Some stones were held in hand by Abū-Jahl one day.[35]
Said he to Muhammed: "What hold I here? Now say.
Since thou'rt a prophet, tell: What hold I in my hand?
The secrets of high heaven thou claimest to command."
Said Muhammed: "How can'st suppose I should not tell?
The things themselves shall speak. I'm truthful; they know well."
Said Abū-Jahl: "This last pretension's harder still."
To him replied the Prophet: "They'll obey God's will."
From out of his closed hand a chorus now burst forth;
Confession of God's unity; His Prophet's worth:
"There is no god but God," the stones distinctly sang;
"Muhammed is God's prophet," also clearly rang.
When Abū-Jahl this heard, he cast the stones away,
In anger from his hand, as then he dared to say:

"Most surely no magician ever was like thee.
Magicians' chief art thou; crown on their heads thou'lt be."
May dust alight upon his head, blind miscreant!
'Twas Satan closed his inward sight;—cursed recusant.
Now turn we once again to hear the minstrel's tale,
For all this time he's waiting; anxious, wan, and pale.
The heavenly voice the Caliph called: "Ho! 'Umer! Ho!
Our servant's want relieve; set thou him free from woe.
A servant whom we hold in very high esteem,
In public burial-ground, go, visit; him redeem.
From out the public treasury do thou extract
Seven hundred golden sequins, with due care and tact.
To him deliver them; and say: 'O man of good,
For present needs let this suffice; 'twill give thee food.
Thy harpstrings' hire it is. Go hence; and when 'tis done,
Do thou again come hither; look for me alone.'"
At sound of that dread voice did 'Umer now awake,
And straight himself disposed that task to undertake.
Towards the burial-ground he turned his steps amain,
The money in his breast, to seek the stranger, fain.
He walked about the ground, right, left, and everywhere.

No second soul was seen; the minstrel only there.
Thought he: "This cannot be my quest." So, off again
He wandered; still no other offered; this was plain.
He said within himself: "The Lord of servant spake,
Devout, approved, accepted, loved for God's own sake.
An ancient minstrel this. Of God can he be loved?
Some mystery is here. Hail, riddle, by God moved!
Once more he wandered o'er the spacious burial-ground,
As lion seeking for his prey goes round and round.
Convinced at length no other was there choice to make,
He thought: "When I'm in doubt, light from above I take."
Respectfully he then approached the sleeping guest.
A sneezing seized him. Straight the harper woke from rest.
When 'Umer he espied, he marvelled, sore amazed;
And rose to go away. Fear's tremor held him dazed.
He thought: "O Lord, have mercy Thou on me!
This magistrate austere no harper 'll kindly see."
Now 'Umer him considered; saw he was afraid;
His cheeks all pale and wan; looks, modest as a maid;
Then said: "Fear not! From me seek not to go away;
Good tidings from on high to thee I bring this day.

Of thee the Lord hath spoken in terms of highest praise.
The heart of 'Umer's moved to love thee and thy lays.
Be seated, then, by me, as friend by side of friend;
While I to thee impart the message God doth send.
The Lord doth thee salute; thy welfare doth inquire;
Trusts thou'st supported well all thy afflictions dire.
This trifle sends for present needs, as harpstrings' worth.
When it is spent, come here again, and fear not dearth."
The old man trembled as he heard those words so kind;
His finger in astonishment he bit;—near lost his mind.
Then cried aloud: "O God! Thou all-unequalled One!
In my old age I sink for shame; this mercy I've not won."
A torrent, now, of tears, he shed, in anguish deep;
His harp then dashed to pieces. Why it longer keep?
He thus apostrophised it: "O thou source of ill!
Thou'st barred me from heaven's path, as highwaymen who kill.
My blood thou'st sucked these seventy years, thou thing of shame!
Through thee I'm rendered vile in eyes of men of fame.
O Lord, Most Merciful! Thou giver of all good!
My past life pardon, squandered ill, in heedless mood!"

Man's life's a gift of God. Alas! How few will think!
The value of each moment's great, so near death's brink.
I've spent my life, not thinking how the moments fly.
I've sung and harped as though a man should never die.
Alas! that I in singing songs of mirth and glee,
Entirely had forgot that death would visit me.
Alas! that shrillest notes have set my ears in flames,
And scorched my heart to shamelessness! Sad names!
Alas! the gamut's intervals were heard all night.
The day has dawned; the caravan passed with the light.
My God! Help, help! Me save from him who cries for help!
Protection I implore from self;—I, who thus yelp!
I never shall obtain my right, except through craft.
For craft is german more to me than self ingraft.
By craft this self itself doth rear across my way.
Beyond my craft myself I see, when craft's at bay.
Just like as when a man is telling gold with thee.
Alone it thou considerest,—self thou dost not see.
So did the harper weep, and loudly did complain.
His sins he numbered up, committed in life's train.
To him then 'Umer: "This contrition deep of thine

Is proof thou sober art, though grief thy heart entwine.
Thy worldly journey's over, other path now take;
For this sobriety's a sin thou must forsake.
Sobriety's a virtue in the road thou'st trod.
The past and future both are curtains hiding God.
Set fire to both of them! How long wilt thou remain
Partitioned up by diaphragms like a reed cane?
So long as reed has diaphragms, it's not our friend;
With lips and voice of ours its notes it cannot blend.
So long as thou goest round the house, thou waverer art;[36]
But when thou'st entered, then full ease reigns in thy heart.
O thou, whose knowledge of full knowledge is not half,
Contrition is, with thee, worse than thy fault, mooncalf.
Thou'rt contrite for the past. On what occasion
Wilt thou contrition feel for this contrition?
At one time worshipper thou wert of notes of harp;
And now, like lover, thou'dst kiss sighs and moans so sharp."
Like mirror, 'Umer having thus reflected truth,
The harper's heart received enlightenment, forsooth.
He, spirit-like, became relieved of moan and smile.

His old mind took its leave, his new heart was docile.
Amazement fell upon him, stupor bathed each sense,
Ecstatic trance then followed, earth and sky flew hence.
A yearning and a longing past description.
As I cannot explain; try thy perception.
Such ecstasy, such words, beyond all mood and tense;
Immersion total in God's glorious effulgence.
Immersion such, escape therefrom impossible;
That sea henceforth to him became impassable.
Our partial wisdom's not part of omniscience,
Until God's promptings come its promptings to enhance.
But when our souls are made those impulses to feel,
That sea in waves straight rises, under which we reel.
The story of the harper and his state now ends;
Both harper and that state have grown to be our friends.
The harper sealed his mouth from any further song.
We, too, will leave his tale half told; it is too long.
In order to attain to his high state of bliss,
Had one a hundred lives, they might be staked for this.
Be thou, then, like a falcon, ever on the wing,
To catch that gnat, thy soul; sunlike, for ever sing.
He casts himself, for love, from highest heaven's height;

If flagons empty, he with wine fills them, so bright.
O spiritual Sun, transfuse Thou life to all.
A new life give, O God, to this our earthly ball.
Into the frames of men both life and soul infuse
From out Thy hidden world, as water dost diffuse.
The Prophet has informed us that, for warning's sake,
Two angels evermore sweet invocation make:
"O God, dispensers bless! Do Thou them feed and tend!
Give them ten thousandfold for every mite they spend!
But hoarders, O our Lord God, in this lower scene,
Do Thou afflict with loss,—no profit intervene!"
How many hoardings better than dispensings are!
Save in God's service, wealth of God spend not. Take care!
So mayst thou get in recompense a hundredfold.
So mayst thou 'scape the punishment of sins untold.
Men offered up their camels as a sacrifice;
In hopes their swords 'gainst Mustafà would do service.
Seek thou the will of God from him who has it learnt;
Not into every soul has God's will been inburnt.
The Prophet's words forewarned those sons of heedlessness,
That all such offerings are a heap of worthlessness.

In war with God's apostle, chiefs of Mekka all
Such sacrifices offered, ghostly aid to call.
Just like the unjust steward, who, as justice due,
The treasure of his lord bestowed on rebel crew.
He falsely pictured to himself he'd justice wrought,
With public money spent, the poor to terms he'd brought.
Such justice from such culprit, what could it effect?
His lord, to anger moved, excuses did reject.
Hence is it, every Muslim, fearing he may stray,
In his devotions begs: "Lead Thou us in right way."[37]
Their substance to dispense suits men of generous mood.
A lover's ready gift's his life for his love's good.
Dispense thou food for God's sake; food thou'lt surely have.
Lay down thy life for love of God; thy life thou'lt save.
We see the trees here shed their leaves at God's command.
Without their toil or trouble, other leaves He'll send.
Shouldst thou, dispensing much, one day be found in want,
The Lord will not forsake thee; His supply's not scant.
Whoever sows, must empty storehouses of grain;
His fields will yield him richly tenfold heaps of gain.

But he who's left his corn in garners, to be used,
Mules, horses, mice, and accidents have it reduced.
This world's a negative; the positive seek thou.
All outward forms are cyphers; search, the sense to know.
Lay down thy wretched life before th' uplifted sword;
New life thou'lt purchase, never-ending, of the Lord.
But if thou do not know, well, how to quit this scene,
To me, then, lend thy ear; this tale for thee I mean.
In days of old there was a Caliph, as is said,
Whose generosity Hātim Tāyī 'd dismayed.[38]
His fame for liberality went through the land;
All poverty, all want, relieved was at his hand.
The very sea went dry through his dispensing zest;
And rumours of his benefits spread east and west.
A fruitful cloud of rain was he to this our race;
In turn, the object he of God's surpassing grace.
So large his gifts, that seas and mines were out of date.
Still fame brought caravans of suitors to his gate,
His courts and halls the temples of the indigent.
The noise had gone abroad how largely he had spent.
The Persian, Roman, Turk, and Arab, all were there,
And all admired his liberalities so rare.

A Fount of Life was he, a very sea of gift.

All nations profited,—in praise their voice did lift.

359

---

1. Isrāfīl is the angel who will blow the last trump, twice. At the first, all living will die; at the second, all the dead will rise to be judged. His voice is the most musical among all those of the angels.
2. Our word "fairy" is connected with the Persian *"perī,"* used here by the poet instead of the Arabic *"jinn,"* whence our "genie."
3. Qur'ān lv. 33.
4. That is, it would appear: *Individuals created out of nothing.*
5. That is: *The Lord is with him who strives on the Lord's side.*
6. A dried gourd, a calabash, is commonly used as a wine-decanter.
7. An apostolic tradition.
8. Also an apostolic tradition.
9. Another apostolic tradition.
10. The traditionary saying of Muhammed, of which this section is an amplification, is the following:—"Verily your Lord hath, in your time, sundry breathings; lo, then, turn ye towards them."
11. Qur'ān xxxiii. 72. When all things had declined responsibility, Adam voluntarily accepted it; was tempted; and fell. Had they not shrunk, man would not have been the sinner or the saint that he is.
12. Luqmān's story may be read in D'Herbelot, *voce* "Locman."
13. Arabian poets sing of women; often imaginary. In Persia, this is considered very immodest. In Persian poetry, a boy, imaginary also, is always assumed to be the beloved object. Muhammed so addressed his youthful wife, 'Ā'isha. Humayrā means Rosina, *—little rosy-cheeks*. See also No. 9, distich 184.
14. A horseshoe, as a charm, with an absent one's name on it, placed in the fire, is supposed to exercise a magical influence over him, and make him come there in all speed, even though his feet bleed from his haste.
15. That "Soul" is God, the *"animus mundi."*
16. Through humility.
17. The "call" of God is the call to divine service, the *'Adhān* (*ezān*).
18. Bilāl, a negro, was the first caller to divine service. He was an early convert, a slave, then 'Abū-Bekr's freedman; then Mu'edhdhin.
19. Mustafà, *Chosen, Elect,* is one of Muhammed's titles.
20. The night of his marriage with Safiyya, after the capture of Khaybar, in the seventh year of the Hijra, as he was returning to Medīna. That night has a special name, based on this circumstance: *the night of the early morning halt* (laylatu 't-ta'rīs).
21. An explanation of this wild expression were much to be desired. Doubtless there is one.

22. There are seven different Persian games of backgammon. The second of the seven, the one mentioned by the poet, is called "Plus" (*Ziyād*). At each throw of the dice, one is added, arbitrarily, to each number shown on the two, ace becoming deuce, &c. The poet likens the body to this supposititious number, the soul alone being real.
23. In performing her devotions, a Muslimess has to veil herself, even at home, as though she were abroad in public.
24. These four lines are quoted from Sanā'ī, for comment.
25. This section and the next two form a comment on Sanā'ī.
26. Qur'ān l. 14. The "new creation" is the resurrection.
27. The tradition, in prose, is as follows, quoted by the poet: "Take ye advantage of the coolness of spring; it invigorates your bodies, as it acts on plants. Avoid ye also the cold of autumn; it acts on your frames as it acts on vegetation."
28. Prisoners and fugitive slaves have iron rings or a kind of wooden pillory fastened round their necks to prevent flight or insubordination.
29. Venus, the musician, who inhabits the planet. See Tale iii., dist. 223.
30. Muhammed.
31. The original name of Medīna,—*Jatrippa.*
32. Qur'ān xlvii. 17.
33. Qur'ān vii. 171.
34. Tradition relates that at first, Muhammed used to pronounce his sermon seated on the floor in the midst of his congregation, with his back against a certain wooden pillar. The congregation increasing, he was obliged to adopt the use of a raised platform, a kind of pulpit, so as to be seen and heard of all. The deserted pillar is the one spoken of.
35. This is a traditionary legend.
36. The circumambulation of the "House of God" at Mekka, is one of the ceremonies of a pilgrimage, &c.
37. Qur'ān i. 5.
38. Hātim Tāyī is the proverbial prince of Arabian generosity. Many anecdotes are current respecting him. His full name was Hātim, son of 'Abdu-'llāh, son of Sa'd, of the tribe of Tayyi'. For instances of his generosity, as handed down by tradition from a time shortly prior to the promulgation of Islām, see Mr. Clouston's "*Arabian Poetry for English Readers,*" p. 406; London, 1881; Trübner & Co., Ludgate Hill. But Hātim lived and died before the Caliphs ruled. He, too, was a poet.

IX. THE POOR SCENITE ARAB AND HIS WIFE.

An Arab woman once thus to her husband spake,
Insisting strongly he'd of these words notice take:
"How very poor we are! What hardships have we borne!
The whole world lives in pleasures; we're the butt of scorn!
We have no bread; for condiment we've grief and cares.
Jug, pitcher we possess not; drink we naught but tears.
By day, our only raiment's scorching solar heat;
Our bedclothes in the night, the moon's rays pale and sweet.
The disk of Luna we may well imagine bread.
Our hands we lift to heaven; keen hunger's pangs we dread.

E'en mendicants feel shame at our dire poverty.

Our days are dark as night, through drear adversity.

Our kindred, as all strangers, sight of us now shun.

Just like the wandering Jew, for fear we should them dun.[1]

When I would borrow half a handful of lentils,

The neighbours wish me dead; their wrath on me distils.

Amongst us Arabs pride is felt in war and gifts,

Among those very Arabs thou'rt devoid of shifts.

What need of war have we? We're wounded; we are slain;

The dart of want has pierced us through and through with pain.

What need of faults, O sinless one? We're in hell-fire!

What solace have we? Overwhelmed with deep desire!

What gifts have we to give? We silent beggars sit!

Could we but seize a gnat, its throat we'd straightway slit!

If guest should come to us, as sure as I'm alive,

When he was sunk in sleep, to strip him we would strive."

Such grumblings, and as follows, going on all day,

She made her husband wish her fifty miles away:

"Unbroken destitution's brought us both to straits.

My heart burns for our sorrows; hope's gleam ne'er awaits.

How long are we to suffer torture such as this?
With hunger's agony, like coals of fire we hiss.
Should any stranger guest come unexpectedly,
What shame we'd feel him to receive dejectedly.
If any visitor should pass our way this eve,
Unless we eat his sandals, what food can we give?"
"Hence 'tis the wise have said in proverb, rendered free
'A guest should never go where he'll not welcome be.'
Who'd wish to be the guest confiding of a man,
Who'll strip thee to the skin, bare, gladly, if he can?
Unhappy in himself, can he thee happy make?
He can impart no light; deep gloom's his only stake.
Not feeling gladsome in himself, with others met,
He cannot yield to them what he has not as yet.
Suppose a man ophthalmic start as oculist;
Of granite-dust alone will his eye-salves consist.
So 'tis with all in times of misery and need;
Let no one, then, come blindly to our house to feed."
Hast never seen reality of famine near?
Look well at us; thou'lt see effects of food too dear.
Our outward look is black, like dark pretender's heart.

This lacks enlightenment, though his exterior's smart.
He has no hope of God, nor any good to show,
Though more than Seth or Adam he pretend to know.
Ev'n Satan unto him no trace of self has shown,
And yet he claims to be a Vicar of God's own.[2]
Some Gnostic terms he uses as a plagiarist,
That he may lead the people as though secretist.
A critic, 'sooth, is he; complains of Bāyezīd;[3]
Whereas Yezīd himself would blush at his bald creed.[4]
Of heavenly bread and table, nothing has he known;
The barest bone to him, vile dog, God has not thrown.
He pompously proclaims: "My table have I spread;
Vicegerent's son, God's Vicar, here am I indeed!
Then welcome, all ye simpletons! Come in; Come in!
From table of my bounty fill yourselves within."
For years he dupes them with "To-morrow's" promise still.
The arrant arch-deceiver, whose "To-morrow's" *nil*.
A long time is required to sound a human mind,
To find out what defects may lurk the mask behind.
A buried treasure is there under body's wall?
Or is it hole of serpent, toad, or scorpion, all?

At length when 'tis discovered, impostor is he,
His pupil's life is wasted; what use then to see?
But on some rare occasion, pupil of great parts
Will come to the impostor, profit by his arts.
He comes with good intention to the lecture-hall,
Expects a guiding soul; he finds a carcase; all.
As when, in dead of night, one does not know the east,[5]
To offer one's devotion's licit, turning west.
Pretenders carry famine in their heart of hearts.
We suffer only want of bread for our repasts.
Why, then, pretender-like, should we our want disguise?
Why, for appearance' sake, our soul, too, bastardise?
The woman's husband answered: "Pray now, silence keep!
Our life is most part o'er. What's left us but to weep?"
"The wise man cares not for a little more or less.
These both will pass away, like torrent's waywardness.
A torrent may be clear, or muddy, black as ink.
It will not last. Why then should we about it think?"
"Within this world what millions, living creatures all,
A life of joy still lead, quite free from let or fall.
A dove is always cooing praises to the Lord,

Upon a tree, so long as day may light afford.
A nightingale sings hymns, God's name to bless alway.
For unto Thee he trusts, Who hearest us when we pray.
A falcon, when he sits upon a royal fist,
No longer stoops to carrion, wherewith to subsist.
And so from gnat to elephant like state we find,
They all depend on God, the best of feeders' kind."
"All those anxieties that fall on us like darts,
Are but the vapours, tempests, of our human hearts.
Those cares are like a sickle, made to cut us down.
This is a fact, though we are slow the truth to own.
Our ev'ry suffering, here, a portion is of death.
This part of death, then, drive away whilst thou hast breath.
If from this part of death thou findst thou canst not run;
Thou'rt sure whole death will follow, as the light the sun.
If thou canst learn to think this part of death is sweet,
Thou knowest that God will make its whole thy tastes to meet.
Our troubles are the heralds of our death to come.
Turn not thy face away from herald, as do some."
"Whoever leads a joyous life finds death severe.
And he who's slave to body, mars his soul's career.

When sheep come home from pasture in the meadows green,
The fattest ones are slaughtered, soon as they are seen.
The night is spent, the morn is come, my bosom friend,
When wilt thou bring thy grumbling gossip to an end?
Once thou wert young, and more content a hundredfold;
Then covetous becamest, though thyself art gold.

A fruitful vine thou wert; a blight's come over thee;
Thy fruit will never ripe, 'twill shrivel on the tree.
Sweet fruit, with flavour, give, thy inward worth to prove.
Thou backwards shouldst not walk, as ropemakers all move.
Thou art my helpmate fond; and fellow-workers all,
Of one mind still should be, or their joint work must fall.
A pair should ever be conformable in aim.
A pair of shoes examine; pair of boots, the same.
If one boot of a pair be too small for the foot,
The pair is useless; vain, the other's size to moot.

One boot is small; the other, 'haps, too large is found.
Hast ever known a lion consort with a hound?
Two packs upon a camel equipoise require;
The one must not be half, the other bale entire.

I choose the road that leads straight to contentment's door,
Why takest thou the path to sin and misery's floor?"
The woman's husband, suffering, but resigned still,
Thus spake unto his wife, to calm her restive will.
The woman raised a shout: "O man of simple mind!
I will no longer listen to thy words, though kind.
Talk not to me of claims, pretensions, and such stuff.
I care not one pin's point for pride and flimsy fluff.
Why preach so loud of sentiment and honour's call?
Just look at our condition. Shame upon thee fall!
Pride certainly is wrong; much worse in beggars' camp.
The day is cold and snowy; all our clothing's damp.
What nonsense and frivolity thy weak pate doles!
And all the while thy tent, like cobweb, 's full of holes.
Where didst thou learn contentment's rule to make thy pride?
Has thy contentment taught thee shame from men to hide?
The Prophet has declared: 'Content a treasure is.'
But what knowest thou of treasure? Suffering's all thy bliss.
Contentment's but a water-reservoir that leaks.

Do hold thy tongue, thou plague; and cease these foolish freaks.

Thou namest me thy helpmate; lower, pray, thy tone.

I'm fellow unto justice; mate to knavery, none.

Since thou equality with lords and princes claimest,

Why suck the blood of locusts that by chance thou maimest?

Thou fightest for a bone with dogs in this debate.

How shall I not complain, with hunger at our gate?

Don't look at me contemptuously, and all askance.

Lest I tell all my mind, thy baseness to enhance.

Thou holdest thyself much wiser than poor soul like me.

Hast ever found me wanting sense to make thee see?

Think not to fall upon me, wolf-like, unawares,

O thou at whose great wisdom woman's folly stares!

The wisdom thou so holdest superior to all,

Not wisdom is; but serpent's, scorpion's, deadly gall.

A foe may God prove ever to thy drivelling guile!

So mayst thou turn out weaker than weak woman's wile!

Thou art both snake and snake-catcher, in one combined.

A serpent-charming serpent! Arab's pride enshrined!

Did crows but realise their ugliness supreme,

As white as snow they'd change, through rage and arrant shame.
A charmer sings a charm against a snake, his foe;
The snake charms him in turn; hence follows boundless woe.
Were not his trap a charm prepared by the snake,
Would he become the victim of some small mistake?
The charmer first is caught in toils of greed and lust.
And sees not 'tis the snake has charmed him, bound him fast.
The snake addresses him: 'O charmer! See now! Look!
Thy own work thou perceivest, my wiles hast mistook.
Thou charmest in God's name to make me thy bond-slave,
And lead me captive, make me sport for fool and knave.
The name of God it is that holds me fast enchained;
That name thou usest as my trap. Art not soft-brained?
That name will one day vengeance on thee for me take.
In fear of that dread name, I, soul and body, quake.
He'll either take thy life with poison-fang of mine;
Or, like me, unto prison He will thee consign!'"
Thus spake the woman bitterly unto her spouse,
Whole volumes would not hold the words that she let loose.

He answered her: "My wife! Art woman? Art thou mad?
'My poverty's my pride.'[6] Reproach me not when sad.
Possessions, wealth, are but a cap the scalp to hide.
The scaldheads or baldpates alone in caps confide.
Whoever's hair has grown in curls or tresses full.
Is always proud when he his cap away can pull.
A man of God resembles precious sense of sight.
Our eyes should not be bandaged, or we can't see right.
The dealer who exposes slaves free from defects,
Strips off the useless cloak that hides all ill effects.
Were they not sound, would he the sheltering mantle strip?
Nay! Contrary! With clothing he'd their vices clip,
And say as an excuse: 'He's timid; she's shamefaced,
And shrinks from being here bare of vestments placed.'"
"A man of wealth may full of sundry vices be.
His riches are his mantle; none his failings see.
Men all are covetous; their greed 'tis blinds them all,
One touch of fellow-feeling binds them as one ball.
But should a poor man say what's precious more than gold
His saying is not heeded by the world so cold."
"The functions of a dervish far transcend thy ken.

The aim of mendicancy's folly to most men.
True dervishes retire away from wealth and power.
Their bread the Lord, majestic, furnishes each hour.
Our God is just. When had it happened that the just
Have acted with injustice towards the poor who trust?
To one, all blessings God gives, favours, luxuries;
Another one, at will, with coals of fire He tries.
Who doubts that God thus acts with uncontrolled will,
His portion be the fire of tribulation still."
"'My poverty's my pride' is not an empty word,
Therein are hid a thousand blessings well assured.
In anger, imprecations thou hast cast on me.
I am a humble suitor; snake-catcher thou'dst see.
If e'er a snake I catch, I still extract its fangs,
That harm may never follow, when its head one bangs.
Those fangs are enemies to every serpent's life,
When I extract them, then, I make him free from strife."
"I never will submit to spell of lust and greed.
For cov'tousness I've conquered. Its maw I'll not feed.
Thank God that greed is not among my sins, at least.
Contentment fills my heart;—a true, perpetual feast.
Thou lookest at the crown of pear-tree full of fruit,

Come down from that idea; no good will it boot.
In raising up thyself, thou giddy hast become;
'Tis not the house that reels; thy brain's grown troublesome."
"Once Abū-Jahl saw Ahmed; spitefully he said:
'Thou ugly portraiture from Banū-Hāshim bred!'
Said Ahmed: 'True thou'st spoken, most veracious man;
Thy words are worthy credit, let who cavil can!'
Then Abū-Bekr saw him, said he was a sun
Of perfect beauty; east, west, everywhere he'd run.
To him, too, Ahmed answered: 'Thou hast spoken true,
O upright man, set free from all the nine spheres' clew.'
The company assembled marvelled at these words,
And asked: 'How can two contraries be what accords?'
Said Ahmed then: 'A mirror am I, polished bright.
Both Turk and Hindū see in me reflection's light.'"
"O wife! If ever thou hast thought me covetous,
Come forth from such idea,—too preposterous.
That which thou takest for greed is heaven's mercy, sure.
And how can greed and mercy both at once allure?
Make trial of true poverty, but for one day, or two.
Thou'lt find therein true riches, with contentment, too.

Be patient with our poverty, and banish grief;
For poverty's a crown bestowed by our great Chief.
Put off sour looks and see, how many thousand souls,
Through sweet contentment are as happy as the fowls.
See other thousands, also, drinking dregs of grief:
It permeates their being, as sugar scents roseleaf."
"Alas! Thou wast a treasure valued by my heart!
I loved to pour my soul forth in thy ears apart!
A kind of milk is speech; its teat the soul,—or gland.
To make it freely flow requires a loving hand.
If but the hearer listen, hang upon his lips,
The speaker, though a corpse, grows eloquent, ne'er trips.
Attentive audiences still confer the powers,
To stutterers and stammerers, to speak for hours.
If strangers should break in upon my privacy,
My womenkind retire, from mere delicacy.
But if my visitor be confidant and kin,
They come forth freely, play about with gladsome din.
Whatever best they know, of work, or play, or jest,
They do and say, for show, before a welcome guest.
What use of sound of harp, of bass or treble notes,
For deaf or senseless ear, that on no music dotes?"

"Our God has made the earth, the sky, and all between;
His light, and eke His fire, upon that stage is seen.
The Lord without a purpose gave not musk its scent.
For odour 'twas, not for diseased nostrils, meant.
The earth He stretched forth, and fixed as man's abode.
The heavens He upreared to be by angels rode.
Th' inferior creature, man, 's at strife with all on high;
He bids for every place he sees, for all he'll sigh."
"Dear wife! Chaste, modest matron! Art thou well prepared
Into the tomb to sink, ere thy doomed hour's declared?
Were I to fill the earth with pearls of countless price,
Thy daily bread thee failing, could they thee entice?
Then cease from all contention, strive not 'gainst the Lord,
Or separation from thee will be my last word.
What taste have I for strife, contention, or annoy,
When even in peacemakings I've no longer joy?
Be quiet! Hold thy peace! Or, by the Lord of life,
I'll quit this tent for ever; thou'lt not be my wife!
Much better to walk barefoot than with shoe too small!
The toil of travel's sweeter than strife in one's wall!"
She knew, thence, he was angered;—will had of his own;

She burst in tears. Was ever woman tearless known?
Quoth she: "I'd never thought from thee such words to hear;
Far different had I hoped; knew not I'd aught to fear."
She made herself most servile, thing of small amount;
Remarked: "Thy humble servant am I; so me count.
My soul and body, all I have, 's at thy command;
Sole arbiter art thou; dispose; I'll not withstand,
If I of poverty impatiently complained,
Not for myself, for thee, was our sad lot disdained.
In all afflictions thou our remedy hast been;
I grieve to see thee want; my anguish thence grows keen.
Dear, darling spouse! For thee was all my deep dismay;
My sighs and moans for thee came into bitter play.
I call my God to witness, in my heart and mind,
I'm ready life to lay down, if thou'rt so inclined.
O that thy heart,—the life with which my soul's endued,—
Could trace aright the channel by my thoughts pursued!
If merely through suspicion thou art vexed with me,
My life I value not; breath,—body's naught! Just see.
I scorn all gold and silver, count them less than dirt,
If they to thee bring anguish. No! I'm no such flirt.

Thine is the only picture painted on my heart;
And canst thou talk of leaving me, from home depart?
Discard me, if thou wilt. Thou hast the right and power,
O thou for whose divorce excuse I make each hour!
Recall to mind the time when I thy idol was,
And thou, priest-like, didst worship me! Alas! Alas!
My heart I cultivated just as thou desiredst.
Thou thoughtest 'twas fond. I knew thou it with love inspiredst.
Like potherbs o'er the fire, thou addedst what thou wouldst,
Sharp vinegar, or honey. What thou wishedst, thou couldst.
If blasphemy I've uttered, lo, I faith profess!
My life is in thy hands; but, be not pitiless!
I wot not thou wouldst prove imperious, like a king;
So, like an ass turned loose, before thee took my fling.
Thy pardon now I crave. Let me know joy again!
Contention I forswear, repentance I maintain.
With sword and winding-sheet I fall at my lord's feet;
Should he decapitate me, death to me'll be sweet.
Thou'st talked of separation;—bitter, worse than gall;
Do what thou will with me, that hideous word recall.

In thee, for me, a pleader ever will be found;
If I be mute, thou'lt still hear intercession's sound.
My potent advocate is, in thyself, thy heart;
Relying upon that, I dared to sin, with art.
Have mercy slily,—see thy grace thyself not, Lord!
To me far sweeter than a honeycomb full stored!"
Thus pleaded she; in coaxing, wheedling terms, with skill.
Her tears rolled down in streams, fast coursing at her will.
Her weeping and her sighs were past endurance felt,
Whose features, tearless, e'en his heart of steel could melt.
That shower precursor was of lightning's vivid gleam,
Whose flash lit in his breast a fire, with pity's beam.
She, of whose beauty was a slave her husband still,
A double spell exerted through entreaty's thrill.
One, whose least coolness sets man's heart in flames,
By turning supplicant a twofold witchery claims.
If he, whose pride at times pain causes to thy mind,
To supplication stoop, thou'lt small resistance find.
He, whose fierce tyranny our bleeding hearts most grieves,

By tendering excuses, us excuseless leaves.
"Is goodly made to man"[7] 's a text from God's own word;
As truth made manifest, is by man ever heard.
God, too, therein decreed: "that he with her may dwell;"[8]
Whence Adam's love for Eve survived lost Eden's dell.
A hero man may be, a Hercules to grieve,
But slave to woman's will is he, without reprieve.
He, to whose words the universe has all bowed down,[9]
Was he who sang: "Humayrā, speak to me!" Life's crown![10]
Of fire and water, fire is quelled through water's wet;
Still, water boils through fire, when in a cauldron set.
The cauldron, like a veil, those lovers keeps apart;
And water's influence no longer cools fire's heart.
To outward show, as water, thou mayst rule thy wife;
In stern reality, thou cleavest to her,—thy life.
This attribute, humanity must own its force:
"Man quails to sensual love," which springs from failing's source.
The Prophet hath declared that woman, over sage,
Despotic power e'er wields, and over men of age;
That fools the upper-hand o'er women still maintain,

Because they're harsh, gross, senseless, careless to cause pain.

No gentleness, no pity, faith, or ruth have they;

In that a bestial nature o'er them holds its sway.

Humanity 'tis claims, for self, love, charity;

While lusts and rage are marks of bestiality.

Fair woman is a ray from out the sun of Truth;

Not loved? A creator; not created, forsooth.[11]

The husband, now, contrition felt for what he'd said,

As sinner, at death's door, repents of evil deed.

Thought he: "I have assailed the life of my life's life;

I've plagued and broke the heart of my dear darling wife!"

When God decrees an ill, man's judgment falls asleep.

And perspicacity knows not which way to leap.

The doom of ill struck home, man straight feels deep regret;

Propriety outraged, he turns to mourn and fret.

Addressing, then, his wife, he said: "My shame is great!

I've acted as a heathen, ah! I'm ready to entreat!

'Gainst thee I've trespassed, prithee, pardon to me grant;

Upon me vengeance wreak not, root not up the plant!

An infidel, however old, if he confess his sin,

And make amends, God's sheepfold opes and takes him in.

Thy heart is full of pity, goodness, kindness, grace;

All being, eke nonentity, 's in love with thy sweet face.

True faith, e'en blasphemy, adores thy majesty;

With that elixir all to gold turns instantly."

In Moses and in Pharaoh parables we see.

'Twould seem that Moses' faith was right; Pharaoh's sin's fee.

By day would Moses pray unto the Lord of Hosts;

At midnight Pharaoh, too, bewailed his impious boasts,

And said: "Thou, Lord, this yoke upon my neck didst lay;

Were't not for yoke imposed, the egotist who'd play?

'Tis Thou'st enlightened Moses' mind, of Thy free grace;

And hence hast left me blindly groping on my face.

The countenance of Moses Thou'st lit up, like day;

My heart, like moon eclipsed, Thou'st darkened with dismay.

My star was never brighter than the full-faced moon;

When darkened with eclipse, it surely sets too soon.

True, kings and princes sound my praises in their routs;

My star eclipsed, the rabble raise their clamorous shouts:

With cleavers, marrowbones, tongs, pokers, hideous 'larm,

They seek to fright some monster; really, shame all charm.

Alas for Pharaoh, with those fearful yells and noise!

Alas his 'Lord Supreme,'[12] drowned in that discord's voice!

Both I and Moses servants are of Thee, our King;

Like woodman's axe on tree, Thy wrath on me takes swing.

Some boughs Thou loppest, to plant. They quickly grow again.

Some others but as firewood burn, or moulder on the plain.

What can the bough, to cope with axe's severing edge?

Can bough resist, return the blow, as blacksmith's sledge?

I call on Thy omnipotence! Thy axe withhold!

Thy mercy manifest! These wrongs set right! Behold!"

Then to himself did Pharaoh think: "O wondrous thing!

All night I've prayed 'Good Lord' to heaven's Almighty King!

In secret I'm humility, a very worm!

But when I Moses meet, how greatly changed my form!

Base coin, if tenfold gilded o'er with finest gold,

Upon the fire when cast, its baseness all behold!
Are not my heart and body wholly in his hand?
Why brain me, flay me, thus? So cunning, soft, and bland!
Commandest Thou me to flourish? As cornfield I'm green.
Decreest Thou me to wither? Straight I'm sallow seen.
One day I'm bright as full moon; next, as eclipse dark.
But is not this of all God's works the constant mark?
'Be, and it is!'[13] A bat that drives man on, His laws!
Of entity, nonentity, that course is cause!
Th' uncoloured being stained with colour's various tinge,
One Moses 'gainst another's certain to impinge.
If th' unconditioned state, that was, should e'er return,
With Moses Pharaoh, then, may live in peace; not burn."
Does doubt invade thy bosom from this subtle theme?
Think! When was colouredness exempt from doubt extreme?
The wonder is how colour rose from hueless source;
How colour, huelessness, in ceaseless warfare course!
The origin of oil is water. This is known.
Then why are oil and water foes, as may be shown?
From water oil's created by mysterious power;
'Gainst water why does oil rise up, and war, each hour?

The rose springs from a thorn; thorns, from the rose.

In open warfare are these two. Why? What suppose?

Or is this seeming warfare all a cunning sham,

Like donkey-dealers' wordy strife, some dupe to flam?

'Tis neither this nor that. 'Tis puzzle for the wise.

The treasure's to be sought; the ruin's 'fore our eyes.[14]

That which thou deemest the treasure's naught but vanity.

By deeming it a treasure, makest thou it to flee.

Thy deemings and thy thoughts build up a pile too fair;

For treasure never lurks where buildings crown the air.

"To edify" means: *"Being, warfare eke, to sow."*

Nonentity is shamed with entity's false show!

Not entity 'tis calls for aid. It is the void

For restitution asks,—encroachments would avoid!

Think not 'tis thou wouldst flee non-entity's fell grip;

Nonentity encroachment dreads from thy short trip.

Apparently, it thee invites unto its breast;

But really, it repels; club-like is its protest.

Know then, dear friend, that Pharaoh's shrink from Moses' call

Was, really, like a wrong shoe on one's foot. That's all.

Opinions are agreed 'mongst philosophic folk:

"The sky's an eggshell; in it lies this globe, as yolk."
A questioner once asked: "How rests this little ball
Within the circumambient spheres, without a fall?
'Tis like a lamp hung up to vault of high-pitched dome;
It never sinks below, nor soars above its home."
To him one wise man answered: "By attraction's force,
On all sides equal poised, it's kept from all divorce.
Just as an iron ball would centrally be hung,
If loadstone vault there were to hold it freely swung."
A caviller objected: "How should heaven's pure vault,
Attracting to itself, this vile black ball exalt?
Say rather it repels with equal force all round.
The earth thus rests amidst air's tides that hold it bound."
Thus is it by repulsion from the souls of saints,
The Pharaohs of each age are fixed in error's taints.
Repelled, then, they are from this world and the next;
In neither have they portion;[15] shunned are they, and vexed.
From God's anointed ones dost thou draw back in heart?
Know, thy existence grieves them, frets them, makes them smart.
They're like the amber, then. When chafed, it shows its power.

The mote of thy existence quick they'll force to cower.
If they conceal that power,—exert it not for thee,
All thy docility will turn to pride. Thou'lt see.
E'en as the bestial quality, in man aye found,
Unto its human yokemate[16] slave and serf is bound.
This human element, too, in saints' hands, my friend,
Is pliant, like the bestial; to their wish they't bend.
By true faith, Ahmed called the world, his docile sons,
To table spread: "Say: 'Servants mine!'" Thus God's text runs.[17]
Thy mind's a camel-driver; thou, the camel, still,
Urged by decree: "Command!"[18] it drives thee as it will.
God's saints are minds of minds. Men's minds, beneath their sway,
Are camels, too. And thus the lengthening series play.
Look unto them, then, if the truth thou'dst fully know;
A pilot is the life of thousands, here below.
But what are pilots? Camel-drivers what? Still seek
Thou one whose eye looks on the sun, and feels not weak.
The world's plunged, nailed, in thickest pitchy dark of night;
For day to break, it wants the rise of God's sunlight.
Behold a sun for thee, in mote contained and hid;

A rampant lion, clad in pelt of gentlest kid.
Behold a hidden sea, beneath a blade of grass.
Beware! Tread not thereon in doubt. Thou sink'st, alas!

Doubt and incertitude, when felt in pious breast,
Are mercies from on high; a leader gives them rest.
A prophet 's sole and solitary in the world.
Sole; but within him bears a thousand systems furled.
As though by magic, the vast universe he makes
Around himself revolve, who smallest compass takes.
The fools saw him alone; thence judged him some weak thing!
Weak can he ever be who's upheld by the King?
Those fools thought: "He's a man. He's really nothing more."[19]
Alas, for fools! They're void of common sense in store.

The prophet Sālih's camel was, in form, a beast;[20]
His people her hamstrung; 'twas ignorance, at least.
They cut her off from water; drink they her refused.
Ungrateful such return for meat and drink they'd used!
"God's camel" drank the water brought as dew by mists.
God's water they held back from God. Monopolists!
Thus Sālih's camel, as of saint the fleshly form,
Became an ambush;—sinners' ruin thence would storm!

Upon that sinning race what dreadful judgment fell!
"God's camel and her drink"[21] the text is, us to tell.
God's vengeance, as pursuer, sought from that vile crew
The price of her shed blood, a country's whole space through.
The soul to Sālih's like; his camel is the flesh;
The soul communes with God; the flesh pines in want's mesh.
Good Sālih's soul was safe from effort of their whim;
His camel felt the blow they dared not aim at him.
No hurt could fall on Sālih's soul,—that priceless gem,—
Such holy emanation was not sport for them.
The soul unto the flesh is joined, by God's decree,
That it may be afflicted,—trials made to see.
Who hurts a body hurts also its soul, no doubt;
The life-blood in that vase from being's fount was brought.
God enters in relation with material form,
That He may be asylum to each earthborn worm.
No man can inlet find to injure soul of saint;
An oyster-shell is crushed; its pearl escapes attaint.
Then serve the camel; that is, list to saint in flesh;
And with his righteous soul thou'lt serve one Lord afresh.

When Sālih saw the evil deed they'd foully wrought,
In three days' time a judgment from his God he sought.
"Three days from hence," said he, "affliction will befall;
Of which, three signs precursors shall be. You'll see, all.
The colour of your faces shall be changed to view;
Complexions various shall be seen in each of you.
Upon the first day, saffron's hue shall be their tinge;
The second, scarlet red each countenance shall fringe;
And on the third, as black as coal shall be each face;
Upon which ensuing, God's wrath shall then take place.
If sign of me you ask for truth of what I say,
Observe the path that camel's foal shall take to-day;
Then strive to catch it. If you can, by chance, succeed;
Good. If not, hope is gone;—from bow the arrow's freed!"
No one of them the camel's foal could overtake.
It fled among the hills,—was lost to sight. Heartache!
E'en so the soul, when once its prison bars are burst,
Unto the Lord of Grace its winged flight takes first.
The prophet then: "The threatened judgment now must storm;
All hope's gone by;—dead as that camel's lifeless form.
Still, if, by coaxing, you her foal can win back here,

In calm tranquillity, from whence it's fled through fear,
With its return of confidence you may be saved;
But otherwise, despair and gnash your teeth, depraved!"
His threat they heard; dejected were at its import.
Their looks sank downcast;—sad anxiety's resort.
The first day came; they saw each visage jaundiced o'er;
And thence, in fell dismay, they laments uttered, sore.
Their scarlet skins, the second day, told plainer still,
Time for repentance was but short, and hope was *nil*.
The blackened faces, on the third day, clearly told
The prophet's threat was strictly true. Their blood ran cold.
Thus being brought to quit their menaces and scowls;
Upon their knees, hams, breasts, they crouched like roosting fowls.
This cringing posture has that abject, trembling crew,
In holy writ, inspired, dubbed "crouching;"[22] and 'tis true.
(Kneel, thou, at times when by instructors thou art taught,
And when thou'rt warned that "crouching" 's with abjection fraught.)
In hopeless expectation God's blow to ensue,
The countryside entire within their homes withdrew.

The prophet Sālih left his cell to view the town.
Enveloped in a smoke and blaze he saw it drown!
Low, moaning noise he heard proceed from its remain;—
Sighs, as it were, and sobs;—he sighers sought in vain!
Those sighs were fitful cracklings of their burning bones;
Those sobs, the hissings of their blood, in clots, on stones!
On hearing these sad sounds the prophet burst in tears;
Responsive to those moans, he groaned.—No listening ears!
The dead he then addressed: "O people, chid in vain!
How often 'gainst you to the Lord I've wept, with pain!
The Lord me answered: 'Patience have with their misdeeds;
To them give counsel still; not long will last those needs!'
Remark I made: 'With such misdeeds will counsel count?
As milk, kind counsel flows from love's unsullied fount!'
The untold wrongs you'd heaped upon my patient head
Had curdled milk of counsel in my bosom's stead.
The Lord replied: 'A grace I'll now on thee bestow;
I'll soothe the wounds inflicted by their rancour's bow.'
With that, God made my heart as tranquil as of yore;
Swept clean away the cobwebs of your paltry score."
"Again I proffered counsel to you, sage and safe;

In parables soft couched, with words that might not chafe.

Once more that milk flowed, mixed with honey, from my lips;

The dulcet tones were tempting, not like stinging whips.

Alas! Within your ears they all to venom turned;

Because, like poisonous plants, your nature goodness spurned.

Why do I weep? You've burnt the substance of all grief;

Like bone in throat, ye obstinate, you've choked relief!

Ought any to lament when grief is laid in bier?

Man justly tears his hair, his head if broke by spear!"

With that, reproachfully upon himself he turned,

And cried: "Those fellows were not worth the tears they spurned.

Recite not wrongfully, O master of address,

The text: 'How will I grieve[23] o'er crew that none should bless!'"

Still, in his eyes and heart more briny tears he found,

A pity, really motiveless, in him 'd ta'en ground.

As summer-rain he wept, through feeling ill at ease;

A summer-rain, quite cloudless, from compassion's seas.

His conscience smote him sore: "Why weepest thou, man of sense?

Are they of tears fit objects,—men of violence?

What motive for thy tears? Say. Grievest thou for their acts?

Mournest thou th' extinction of their merciless, vile pacts?

Or is't, perchance, their hearts, corrupt, gangrened, thou'dst weep?

On their empoisoned tongues, so adderlike, thou'dst keep?

Those tails and fangs is't, are the objects of thy grief?

Their scorpion claws and sting that thou regrettest in chief?

Contentiousness, foul mockery, rude violence?

Thank God, instead, who's checked their boastful insolence!

Their hands were evil; evil were their feet, their eyes;

Their peace, their friendship, as their wrath, were all unwise.

From rule of meek obedience, customs handed down,

They'd swerved;—to follow mere devices of their own.

They wished not for a teacher, asses obstinate;

Their own ideas alone they'd stoop to cultivate.

God therefore sent His servants, smoke and fire to wit,

From heaven, the miscreants to chase to dire hell-pit."

Behold the damned and blessed, thus, in one scene conjoined;

Between them is "a great gulf fixed by none o'erclimbed."[24]

Those "sons of fire" and "light" together seemed immixed;

But barrier impassable 'tween them was fixed.

The mine's rich golden ore in soil imbedded lies;

But really separated, far as eagle flies.

Like pearls and jet beads in one row of necklace ranged;

A motley company, like inn's chance guests, oft changed.

Or like an estuary, half soft, sweet to drink,

Most palatable water, clear, bright as moon's twink;

The other half salsuginous, wormwood and gall,

Foul, black as ink, and fetid, shocks the senses all.

These dash together; now this, now that, uppermost;

Their waves a turmoil make, as though by tempest tost.

That show of fierce collision's made by matter's form;

In truth, the spirits 'tis that compacts make, or storm.

When gentle waves, in friendship's reign, roll gracefully,

Contention quits each breast, all goes on merrily.

With rough war's hideous billows, (mark the altered scene!)

All love is straight renounced; dire hate's to supervene.
Affection coaxes rancour to subside, appeased;
Because its origin's in reason fixed, soon pleased;
While raging anger stirs up thoughts of bitter strife.
For how can man be tranquil, when the stake's his life?
Our outward eye discerns not pure from tainted hearts;
Futurity's small lattice oped, the curtain parts.
The eye of true sagacity distinct can see;
This other eye, 'tis, fails;—is ne'er from error free.
How many seeming pleasures, fair, as sugar sweet,
Have poison lurking in them, death to all they meet!
Men of discernment know them surely by mere smell;
And others find them out, though late, when tasted, fell.
That taste's enough; ejected are they; swallowed, not;
Although the fiend may urge, with: "Eat, while hot!"
Again some others find in throat they firmly stick;
And others yet are vexed with intestinal prick.
Still others by sharp purgings find they've done amiss;
Indulgence of the palate's changed to pangs their bliss.
Again there are some suffer after months or years;
And others pay the penalty within the tomb, with tears.
E'en should there chance a respite, granted in the grave,

At resurrection's trump, disclosure naught will save.
Each plant, each honied morsel, in this lower sphere,
A term has, fixed, him to affect who tastes the cheer.
What ages of submission to sun's influence,
E'er ruby can acquire ripe tinge, bright effulgence!
The salad cress is ready in a month or two;
The rose requires some years before it shows its hue.
To this end has the Lord, whose name be ever blessed,
In holy writ declared: "Appointed term."[25] We've cessed.
Hast thou this heard? Read, mark, and learn with diligence!
Life's water is it. Hast thou drunk? Health spring from thence!
Those *words* thou mayst consider life's fount, if thou list;
Their *sense* it is important thou shouldst not have missed.
One other theme, my friend, fix firmly in thy mind.
'Tis patent as thy soul; as subtle thou'lt it find.
At times as venomous as adder's fatal fang;
At times as healthful as the food from heaven that sprang.
Now lethal; now again remedial, by God's will.
At one time blasphemy; then, holy rapture's thrill.
Thus will it, now, be fatal to a human soul;

And then, again, a remedy for all that's foul:
"The juice of unripe grapes is sour, as is well known;
But when the fruit has ripened, sweet and fragrant grown,
In wine-jar when fermented, nauseous and unclean;
When vinegar, again, most wholesome is it seen."
If saint a poison swallow, wholesome it will prove;
But if disciple taste it, death will him remove.
"Lord, grant unto me," was the prayer of Solomon,
"The power and kingdom solely (not to Abaddon);
This favour grant not unto other after me!"[26]
Which reads like envy. Such, however, it can't be.
Put not, in heart, construction that must disagree
Upon those words so read: "to other after me."
He saw a thousand dangers in the sway conferred;
Saw that earth's empire is a snare to be abhorred;
A danger to one's life, one's faith, one's inner self;
Such trial has no equal on the whole world's shelf.
E'en Solomon sagacity did much require,
To shield him from mistakes in all his vast empire.
The wondrous power he wielded could alone suffice,
To quell rebellion's perils, rising in a trice.

So when he rested from due ordering his wide realm,
He felt that other kings misrule might overwhelm.
Then interceded he: "This rule, this much-prized flower,
Vouchsafe to none, save with the selfsame power.
To whom Thou mayest it grant upon these very terms,
He's Solomon, he is myself, my sway confirms.
He'll not come after me, he'll reign with me indeed;
With me and in me, free from rival's dreaded meed."
This to expound appeared a duty paramount;
Return we, and our tale of man and wife recount.
A sequel to that incident 'tween man and wife
Is looked for by the mind of him who's watched their life.
The incident of man and wife recounted here
Of each man's soul and flesh the parable is, clear.
The wife the flesh is; man's the soul; he's wisdom, too;
They're emblems also of all good and evil, true.
The two, of need, existing in this earthly home,
By day and night at war are;—always quarrelsome.
The wife requires her various household garniture,
Her bed and board, her comfort, and her furniture.
The flesh, like woman, to be gratified still seeks;
Submissive sometimes; oft would play ambitious freaks.

The soul has no idea, itself, of such instinct;
But seeks to muse upon its love for God, distinct.
Existence is the secret of their constant war;
The form in which 'tis waged thou'rt now about to hear.
Had psychic indication proved sufficient sign,
Material creation 'd been a useless coin.
Is love for God thy thought, aim, wish, design, intent?
To forms of worship, fasting, thou wilt yield assent.
The gifts and little presents interchanged by friends,
Are not their love's pure essence. Signs they are, not ends.
Mere outward witnesses, that simply testify
Th' affection's feelings. These the heart, 'tis, sanctify.
For all men know that kindnesses bestowed by hand
Are proofs of sympathy. Mind can this comprehend.
A witness may speak falsely; also, may speak truth;
Is sometimes drunk, with wine; sometimes, is urged by ruth.
When wine is drunk, intoxications supervene;
Its vapours rise into the head, erst so serene.
Behold yon hypocrite! He fasts; he worships, prays;
That he a man of God may seem. He's not. Mere ways!
Results of outward actions are of outward kind,—

The signs of what is inward, working on the mind.
Grant unto us, O Lord, discernment to perceive
What sign is true, which meant fond mortals to deceive!
Suppose not that the senses with discernment plod;
Discernment is the inner, gracious gift of God!
Effect not being visible, we look to cause.
We know that kindred moves to friendship, by fixed laws.
But him, who judges by the light of God's own truth,
Effect and cause no longer hold a slave, forsooth.
When love for God is lighted in the human heart,
It fiercely burns; it suffers not effect's dull smart.
No sign of love does it require to seek for, there;
For love is love's own sign, giv'n from the highest sphere.
Details there are, far more, to make this theme complete.
If wished for, each can find them. They're not obsolete.
Sense must be gathered from material, outward form;
Some sense is patent; some is hard to find, difform.
The indication's feeble;—tree and water see;—
How different, apparently, their natures be!
Let's leave now all these words,—cause, nature, sign;—
And turn we to our Arab and his wife benign.

The husband said: "I've now abandoned all dispute.
All rule is in thy hands; thy power is absolute.
Whatever thou ordain, submissive thou'lt me find;
Its good or bad results shall not weigh on my mind.
I'm non-existent; save, that by thee I must move;
A lover; therefore am I deaf and blind, through love."
His wife him answered: "Is this all in kindness meant?
Or dost thou seek by craft my plans to circumvent?"
He swore: "By God; who knows the secrets of each heart;
Who hath created Adam free from treacherous art;
Who, in three cubits' stature unto him dispensed,
The mysteries of all decrees, all souls, condensed:
Whatever is to be, to all eternity,
To Adam taught, with every name of Deity,
So that the very angels wearied under him,
As he them taught, but ever gained by each maxim!"
The revelations Adam made to them were vast;
Had never been disclosed before, from first to last.
The compass, spacious, of his all-inclosing mind
Far wider was than heaven of heavens a grasp could find.
The Prophet hath declared God made him clearly know:

"I'm not contained, not held; by aught above, below,
On earth, in heaven, above the heavens, I am not held.
This know, then, thou also, My friend, as though beheld.
But, wonderful! Believer's heart can Me contain!
If Me thou'dst seek, there look for Me, with might and main!"[27]
His words were: "Seek within My servants. There thou'lt meet
The paradise of My aspect. Thou most discreet!"[28]
The heaven of heavens, with all its wondrous wide extent,
At sight of Adam's glory into tremors went.
The marvellous expanse of heaven's a stretch extreme.
But what is matter, all, when spirit is the theme!
Each angel made remark: "Until this very hour
I had a certain knowledge of the wide earth's bower.
Much duty I've performed upon its soil, down there.
Surprise I've felt, not small, attachment so to bear.
For what was my attachment to that ball of clay;—
I, that am moulded from the glorious light of day?
What was my strong affection? I'm light; darkness, earth!
Can light and darkness mingle;—live in jocund mirth?
O Adam! Now it's clear! My love was mere instinct;

In that the earth material gave for thee, succinct!
Thy earthly body here was wove out of its clay;
Thy spirit, pure, created was beyond the realm of day!
The honour which we, spirits, have received through thee,
Before all worlds had sparkled, by divine decree!
When we were on the earth, we inattentive were;
And little recked the treasure trusted to its care!
When orders were received to quit the earth, and mount,
We felt regret to change; knew not on what account.
We thought of reasons for the shift, and question made:
'O Lord! Who then shall take our place when we're thus bade?
Wilt Thou exchange our praise and service here below,
For mere lip-homage from a worm Thee will not know?'
An answer from the Lord, benign, did we receive:
'What you allege is somewhat many might deceive.
Each word upon your tongues is surely out of place,
As lisping talk of son to sire, without preface.
Your rash objections would deserve to be chastised,
But that I have decreed that mercy's higher prized.
Behold, O angels! Since you've made confusion strange,

In you henceforth I've placed a sense of doubt and change!
Since you demur, and I refrain from chastisement,
None can gainsay my mercy; none may raise comment.
A hundred mothers, fathers, meet not My decree!
Each soul that's born a zero is compared to Me!
Their love is but the froth; My love, the sea of love!
Froth comes and goes; the ocean none remove.
More I may say. For, in this earthly oyster-shell
There's naught but froth of froth, of froth of froth to tell!'"
The Lord thus spake;—the Lord, that sea of purity!—
He spake not by conjecture;—truth's own entity!
What I here state is said in love's humility.
The Lord is He to whom I fly,—sole Deity!
If thou wouldst put to test what I have here set forth,
First prove thy test. Make truly sure it's trouble's worth.
Cloak not thy secret thoughts. So may my thoughts be known.
Propose whate'er thou list; within my power, 'tis shown.
Thy heart conceal not. I'll lay bare my heart of hearts;
Accept all, of acceptance worthy, thy mind starts.
That I may do whatever lies within my power,
Do thou observe my heart's condition in its bower.

The wife observed: "A very sun of good is risen;

Through whom a gladsome world's enlarged from want's sad prison.

Vicegerent of th' All-Merciful, Caliph of God,

Fair Bagdād's city prides itself to kiss his rod.

If unto him thou have recourse, a prince thou'lt be.

Why, then, to misery cleave, such as we hourly see?

Companionship with fortune's minions brings good luck;

Where's an elixir like their power, my dearest duck?

Ahmed's esteem raised Abū-Bekr such a height;

For once confirming Ahmed's word, 'Faithful' he's hight!"

The man demurred: "How can I gain access at court?

Without an introduction, how find sure passport?

Connection we must seek; or else invent excuse.

No artizan can work without his tools. The deuce!

Thus Mejnūn, when he'd heard by chance from passing wight,

His Laylā was an invalid (which caused him fright),

Exclaimed: 'Alas! Without excuse I cannot go!

And if I visit not the sick one, I'm all woe!

Would that I were physician, with his healing art;

Then could I see my Laylā; none would dare me thwart!'

And now he cries: 'I have it! I've a right to go!
No bashfulness shall keep me from her portico!'
Had bats but eyes, with which to see and find their way,
They'd fly about, disport themselves, jocund, by day."
The wife replied: "The Caliph's public pageant is
For all who introduction lack; their griefs are his.
To be, and have a grief, is introduction sure.
Thus poverty and lowliness work their own cure."
He still objected: "Shall I fall in love with want,
That I may urge my need as matter for some grant?
E'en then, a witness credible I should require
T' attest my indigence, when almoners inquire.
Point out for me a witness; not mere words and wiles;
That so the sovereign's favour may be won, and smiles.
For, otherwise, a mere pretext, without a proof,
In justice' court would fail, and bring reproof.
A witness credible is, then, *sine quâ non*.
For suitor's plea to stand, proof it must rest upon."
His wife rejoined: "The witness thou requir'st to bring,
Must, by some shrewd contrivance, from thy prospects spring.
Rain-water's all we have in store within our hut,

Estate, possessions, wealth, lie in our water-butt.
A little pot of water shalt thou bear with thee,
As offering to the Caliph. This present from me;
And say: 'No other wealth on earth do I possess.
To Arabs of the desert, water's happiness!
The Caliph's treasury is full of gems and gold;
A pot of water such as this, its coffers do not hold!
What is this pot? It is an emblem of our lives!
The water in it, matchless virtue of our wives!
Accept, then, gracious prince, this little pot from me;
And out of all God's gifts repay its value, free!'
That pot's five lips are emblems of our senses. Sure!
Keep them all clean; so may thy honour, too, be pure!
The pot will then relation keep with ocean's wave;
And I, perchance, advantage from that ocean have.
If clean thou carry it before the sovereign's eyes,
He may be pleased therewith;—buy it from mere surprise.
The pot will, then, of water never lacking be;
My little water-pot shall suffice thee and me.
Close tight its lips, and bear it full from our supply.
A holy text 'tis says: 'From lust close every eye.'[29]

His beard, his moustache, both, will swell with joy at this.

For prince supreme like him, my offering's not amiss."

Thou, woman, didst not know that there, in Bagdād's midst,

A Tigris flowed with water, sweet as honey.—Didst?

A very ocean is it, rapid in its course;

With boats and ships, with fishers' hooks, both fine and coarse.

Go then, good man! The Caliph thee his state shall show!

Thou'lt comprehend the text: "Beneath which rivers flow."[30]

Thus, likewise, are our intellects, our thoughts, our sense;

A drop compared with God's boundless omniscience!

The husband now chimed in: "Yes! Plug the pot's mouth tight.

Thou'st hit the very offering;—useful, good, and right!

Sew it up carefully in case of felt, threefold.

Our Caliph's breakfast-water[31] shall it be;—so cold!

No other water's like it in this world of ours;—

It's heaven's pure ambrosia, 'still'd from vernal showers!

Poor cits know none but waters hard and bitter all;—

Whence various maladies, with blindness, them befall!"

The bird that lives where salt-marsh noisome airs exhales,

Knows naught of joys pure water gives, and spicy gales!

So thou, good man, who dwelledst 'midst the desert's waste,

Hadst never seen a Tigris, known Euphrates' taste!

As he, again, not yet from worldly cares set free,

Is ignorant of ecstasy, of rapture's glee;

Or, having heard thereof as tales from men of old,

Knows them as names alone, in storybooks oft told;

Child's A, B, C; as taught to every lisping elf;

But whose real meaning's hidden from the teacher's self.

Our Arab man now takes that water-pot in charge.

By day and night he travels;—load not over large!

Anxiety fast holds him, lest the pot should break;

Most watchfully he guards it from misfortune's freak.

His wife spends all her days in prayers on his behalf;

Her worship o'er, she adds: "Lord! shield my better half!

Secure our pot of water from all thievish hands!

Send it may prove a pearl in sea of Bagdād's lands!

My husband, true, is shrewd; and know's what he's about;

But pearls have enemies, we trow, in every rout!

What is a pearl? A drop from fount of life sent down;[32]

A drop from non-existence,—whence all substance known!"
Those prayers' reward,—as guerdon of her sighs and tears;—
His care's requital, watchfulness, and constant fears;—
Their pot reached Bagdād safe from robbers' grip;
Secure from shock of stone, from chance of fall or slip.
A city, there, he sees, with every blessing filled;
Where craving mortals ply each art, as they are skilled.
Each moment, here or there, some extra-lucky wight,
His object gains, receives from court what glads his sight!
To Muslims, Unbelievers, equal grace is doled,
Like rain and sunshine. Not so paradise, we're told!
One set of men he sees arrayed in honour's robes;
Another set endure, through hope and fear, sharp probes.
As gentle, or as simple, prince or worm, pismire,
All are alive, as though last trump's notes them inspire!
The worldly, in apparel sumptuous to behold;
The godly, all immersed in transports clearly told!
The hopeless have become as though their hopes were fair;
The hopeful show enjoyment of fruition's share!
A voice proclaimed: "Come forward, all ye sons of want!"

Beneficence seeks beggars, as for gifts they pant.
Beneficence hunts up for beggars and for need,
As beauty seeks her mirror, with a special greed.
A pretty face is charming in its mirror seen;
Beneficence gleams lovely through want's chilly sheen.
God hath enjoined in holy writ: "By forenoon's glare!"[33]
"Muhammed, chide not thou too much at beggar's prayer!"[34]
A beggar is a mirror wherein bounty shines.
Dull not that mirror, then, with breath of anger's whines!
The beggar 'tis shows forth what charity achieves;
A charitable man for this those wants relieves.
A beggar, then, 's a mirror of th' Almighty's grace;
And whoso's with the Lord, therein sees his Lord's face.
He that hath love for other than the Lord of all,
Is dead at heart,—not living;—shadow on a wall!
Whoe'er adopts God's poverty, without false show,
Secures the prize of God's rich pleasure here below!
Who puts on sham of poverty deserves no bread.
(Bones are not given to effigies of dogs. They're dead!)
His want craves pelf; 'tis not the love of God he'd seek.
Lay not thy bounty at the feet of one too sleek.

A landshark is a mendicant for mere pelf's sake.
He's fish in form; but will not to the water take.
Domestic fowl is he; not eagle of free air.
With Lot he sips of wine; God's water's his despair.
He loves his God, if but his God will grant him wealth;
But nothing cares for God's mere grace;—for spirit's health.
Should he conceive th' idea of love for God alone,
God's essence he'd deny, God's attributes disown.
Man's fancy is a creature;—born with mortal lot.
God was not born. His scripture says: "Nor was begot."[35]
The man in love with self, and with his fancy's freak,
Can never be a lover who to God will seek.
Were fancy's lover true, and free from crafty guile,
His fancy's tropes had led him to the truth erewhile.
That *dictum* would require a commentary, full,
But fear withholds me. Prejudice will have its pull!
Old prejudice, quite purblind to the truth, I see,
A hundred phantoms conjures up to frighten me.
Not every man has heard aright the still small voice;
Not every bird's a fig-pecker, that sweets rejoice;
How then a bird that's dead,—turned putrid long ago;—

A man of prejudice, all sightless, eyeless, so!
A painted fish cares not for water, or for land.
Soap to a blackamoor is one, or tar, in hand.
Shouldst thou depict a portrait overwhelmed with grief,
Would grief or joy be felt, though shown in strong relief?
The picture would look sorrowful;—no sorrow feel;
Or smiling happiness;—without gay laughter's peal.
The joy or grief depicted by a pencil's art,
Is naught but simulated;—knows nor thrill, nor smart.
Lugubrious countenances are for our behoof;
That we may be reminded not to court reproof.
And beaming visages are not without their use,
If they recall us from mere form to sense occluse.
The various effigies we see in this bath-house,[36]
Disguised in draperies, are dolls;—blind fools to chouse.
So long as thou'rt outside, naught else but clothes thou'lt see.
Undress thyself. Come in; and see the nude, the free.
There's no admission granted to a bath, while dressed.
But clothes, the body, this, the soul, leave all unguessed.
Our Arab man, from far in desert's sandy waste,
Has reached at length the walls of Bagdād,—home of taste.

The guards, the officers, on duty at the gate,
Received him with politeness, kindness delicate.
Without a question asked, his case they'd understood.
Their charge was to show kindness first, ere asked for food.
So they addressed him thus: "Ho, thou, good Arab prince!
Whence comest thou? How fares it? Straight thy wish evince!"
He answered: "Prince I am, if you to me be kind;
But if you me contemn, I'm naught in my own mind.
Your aspects indicate you're men of wealth and rank;
Your speech and smiles betoken breeding, noble, frank.
Mere sight of your kind features salve is to the eyes;
Your looks alone enrich;—gold in your voices lies.
Each one of you expression is of God's own grace;
In Caliph's bosom nurtured, favoured with high place;
That you, in turn, dispense th' elixir of support,
And brighten longing eyes by words of kind import.
I am a stranger, poor, come from the desert's sands,
In hopes some favour to obtain from sovereign hands.
The rumour of his goodness fills the wilderness;
Each atom in its wastes blooms thence in joyfulness.

In search of wealth have I approached his capital;
Now I'm arrived, I burn with pleasures optical.
E'en as the lass in search of bread at baker's shop,
Struck with his 'prentice' beauty, swooned;—a lifeless drop!
Or like the saunterer for air in royal park,
Who lost his heart to one he met, gay as a lark!
Or like the desert merchant drawing from a well
What he thought water, was entranced by Joseph's spell!
Again, as Moses hasted for a coal of fire,
And found the burning bush, that led him to empire!
Or Jesus, who escaped his foes with one fleet bound,
And found himself then landed where the sun goes round![37]
An ear of corn it was that baited Adam's trap.[38]
But thence himself became the source of mankind's sap!
The falcon stoops to earth enticed by luring fate;
He there meets man's good teaching, soars to princely state.
A child is sent to school to teach him learning's prize,
In hope of toys and treats he studies till he's wise.
On leaving school he sits in seat of law or power;

He paid his schoolpence then;—he's now lord of the hour!

So Abbās[39] sallied forth to war, with fierce intent,

To put Muhammed down,—Islām to circumvent.

Defender of the Faith, till death, he then became;

The Caliphate was destined, in his line, to fame!

So am I come, in hopes at this court to advance;

Though at its gate as yet, I feel I've every chance.

In quest of bread am I; as offering, water bring.

The hope of bread sets wide heaven's portals at one swing.

'Twas bread that drove out Adam from his paradise;

'Tis bread will gain me entrance where my hopes take rise.

From bread, from water, both, as angels, far I stroll;

And, following the spheres, around this centre roll!

Without an object none will toil on earth, you see,

Save true and godly lovers. They're from motives free!"

Th' Infinite's lovers finite's worshippers are not.

Who seek the finite lose th' Infinite, as we wot.

When finite with the finite falls in love, perforce,

His loved one soon returns to her infinite source.

A beard that puts itself into another's grasp,

In lather's smothered; emblem of a weak mind's gasp.

He's not his own lord; cannot guide his own affairs;

He does but what he's told; where'er he's bid, repairs.

Would'st sin with woman? Choose, at least, one that is free.

Would'st rob and steal? Let pearls and jewels be thy fee.

A slave obeys a master; has himself no will;

The scent is all the rose's; thorns show no such skill.

A slave may not attain to wish that he may form;

His toil is vain, his trouble profitless;—poor worm!

Shall hunter snare a shadow? Where were then his food?

A shadow's not a substance;—can do no one good.

A foolish hunter seized the shadow of a bird!

The fowl, on tree securely perched, not one foot stirred;

But, wondering, thought: "What is the stupid fool about?

Demented, sure; his little wit he's let ooze out!"

But if thou thinkest finite's of th' Infinite born;

And sayest: "For love of rose, do honour to the thorn;"

Consider: finite unto Infinite's not joined.

Or what need of the prophets? They've not scripture coined.

The prophets have been sent to link the two in one.

If they're not two, but one, what have the prophets done?

But let that be. Th' inquiry has no useful end.
The day is waning; let us to our tale attend.
The Arab now his little pot of water showed.
As seed to earth, he it on Caliph's court bestowed;
And said: "Present my offering at the sovereign's feet,
If beggar save his king from want, it's surely meet.
The water's fresh; the little jar green-glazed and new;
Filled from a pool replenished by the rain and dew."
On hearing this the guards were laughing in their sleeves;
But still, as precious, took the jar;—polite court-reeves!
The Caliph's kindly nature, active, well-informed,
To kindness had each member of his court reformed.
For as the sovereign is, so will his subjects be.
The azure vault of heaven makes green the earth;—you see.
A king's a reservoir; his servants are his mains,
Through whom his bounty flows, to swell his subjects' veins.
The stream, if flowing from a tank all sweet and pure,
Each main distributes bounty, courtesy;—be sure.
But should the reservoir prove foul and nauseous, then,
The mains can flow with naught but venom, like a fen.
The mains can only what they get convey around.

Remember this. We're treading now on solid ground.
A sovereign's goodness is an unembodied soul,
That permeates the clay of human frame, its goal.
It is the mind, the all-informing, well-derived,
That brings the body into discipline, where hived.
Love is a wanton, restless, reckless of control,
That drives the man to madness; passion does extol;
But goodness is a stream as sweet as Fount of Life;
Its pebbles are all pearls, all jewels, beauteous, rife.
Whichever be the science makes a teacher famed,
His scholars' minds with that will surely be inflamed.
A jurist's pupils study principles of law,
If but their mental principles be free from flaw.
A lawyer's prentice over subtle cases pores;
The principles, with him, are most unwelcome bores.
A syntax-teacher rears a host of grammar's sons,
With whom his syntax passes for the sun of suns.
A teacher who inculcates abnegation's creed,
Surrounds himself with pupils free from lust and greed.
But at the hour of death, of science's long roll,
The art of poverty's what most behoves man's soul.
A syntax-teacher, once, was mounted in a boat,

Who to the skipper turned, as soon as e'er afloat,
And asked: "Hast studied syntax?" "No indeed," quoth he.
The teacher then: "Thy life's half-wasted! Dost thou see?"
The skipper felt heart-broken at this pert remark;
But, for the moment, held his peace;—wise man's bulwark.
The wind arose; the bark was sorely tempest-tossed;
The skipper then addressed the teacher, sickness-crossed:
"Knowest thou the swimmer's art, good friend? With speed reply."
"Nay," said the teacher, "that's an art the schools decry."
The skipper now remarked: "Thy whole life's gone to waste.
The ship must go to pieces. Water salt thou'lt taste.
With syncope, not syntax, now we'll have to deal.
With syncope, from water comes nor hurt, nor weal,
The sea bears on its surface bodies of the dead;
But living men it drowns; them sinks, as though of lead.
So soon as thou'lt be dead to every human art
To thee eternity its secrets will impart.
Thou hitherto hast deemed us mortals asses all;
Now thou thyself, as ass on ice, must have a fall.

Although thou be the very Plato of the age,
Thou'st still to learn that time, the world, is but a page."
This tale about the syntax-teacher we've tacked on,
To show the grammar dissolution turns upon.
All syntax, grammar, jurisprudence, law, and art,
Thou'lt find, my friend, of knowledge is but a small part.
Our little learning is the Arab's water-pot.
In Caliph, of God's wisdom we've an emblem got.
We bring our pot of water to great Tigris' stream.
If we ourselves not asses call, us asses deem.
The Arab of our tale excusable was,—troth;
He knew not of a Tigris. Where's the Arab doth?
Had he, as we, known Tigris' stream, and all its store,
His water-pot had never travelled to its shore;
Had he become aware of what a Tigris meant,
Arrived at Bagdād, he'd his pot to fragments sent.
The Caliph, when he saw that pot, and heard that tale,
The vase had filled with golden sequins, like a bale,
Our Arab thus to free from poverty's rude grasp;—
A robe of honour, too; and presents for his clasp,
He ordered. Then the whole unto the guards were sent,
With kindliest injunctions, fruit of good intent:

"That all unto that Arab man be safely given,
Whose journey home by Tigris' arrowy stream be driven.
By land he came; he'd travelled all the way on foot;
But Tigris' stream may bear him back a shorter route."
Our Arab in a boat was placed at river's side;
The stream he saw, admired, bowed low, lost all his pride;
Exclaiming: "Wondrous goodness of the sovereign will!
Th' acceptance of my water-pot more wondrous still!
How could that sea of wealth my drop deign to accept,
And largely thus to recompense the trifle kept?"

Know now, my friend, this world's one mighty water-pot,
With wisdom and with beauty teeming; as all wot.
One drop, however, 'tis, from ocean of His grace,
Whose fulness cannot be confined in any place.
That treasure latent was. Through fulness it burst forth,
More glorious than the heavens became thenceforth the earth.
The latent treasure, pouring out its riches great,
The earth made kinglike, clothed with more than regal state.
One little branch canal from th' ocean of God's grace,
Thus overwhelms this mighty water-pot of space.

They who see God are ever rapt in ecstasy;
And raptured, hold that water-pot mere fallacy.
O thou! envy of whom is to that pot a stone!
Though fractured by the shock, the pot yields sounder tone.
The pot is cracked; but, still, its water is not spilt;
The crack's the very source through which it's sounder built.
The jar's each single particle's in dance and revery,
Though unto man's poor wisdom this seems foolery.
The pot, the world, all it contains, are lost to view.
Consider well this fact! God knows it's simply true.
If thou canst grasp this meaning, thou'rt like falcon strong.
Beat, then, the pinions of thy thoughts. Be hawk, ere long.
Thought's pinions are bemired in thee, and heavy move;
Because thou feedest on clay; clay's bread to thee, I'll prove.
As flesh, bread is but clay. Trust not thereon for strength;
Or thou'lt remain, claylike, within the earth at length.
Dost hunger? What art thou, then, but a dog?
Fierce, ill-affected, raging; lusts thy vitals clog!
And when with food thou'rt filled, polluted straight becomest.

Thou losest strength and sense; mere stock, thou sleep welcomest.

So, being doglike or a stock, senseless, impure,
How canst thou progress make in path of virtue, sure?
Whatever 'tis thou huntest, dog thou art, in sooth.
Feed not, then, thus, the dog of lust's voracious tooth.
When dogs are satisfied, obedience they forswear;
To follow up the game they one and all forbear.
His want it was disposed the Arab of our tale,
To travel till he'd reached the Caliph's courtly vale.
We've shown the bounty of that sovereign merciful,
Shed on the Arab's wretchedness, most plentiful.

Whate'er a lover says, the sentiment of love
Shines through his words, if but thoughts towards his mistress rove.
Discourses he on law, love furnishes the theme;
Throughout his labouring periods, love's the enthymeme.
Should blasphemy rise to his lips, of faith it smacks.
Doubt, when by him expressed, shows confidence's knacks.
The spume that rises from the sea of his pure heart
Partakes the nature of its source, truth's counterpart.
We must esteem such spume as foam of mountain-rill;—

Upbraiding from a lip beloved is worshipped still.
Attention we pay not to harsh words issuing thence;—
The features we adore divest them of offence.
However strange such utterances, they all seem true;
The stranger they appear, to sense they lend more cue.
If sugar we should cast in mould to look like bread,
Then eat it, we the sugar taste. Form's of no stead.
Should true believer golden idol light upon,
Will he for worship set it up, anon, anon?
Nay! To the fire he'll quickly it in wrath consign,
And strip it of the form that makes it sin's foul sign.
The gold, abstracted from the idol's form, is pure.
That form it is corrupts,—can men to sin allure.
The gold's an essence fixed, produced by nature's God;
The idol stamp is transitory;—soon downtrod.
Thou for one flea to flames thy bed wouldst never give;
For one musquito's hum, not wish to cease to live.
If form-entrapped thou be, idolater thou art!
Eschew mere form; attend to essence, as thy part.
Art bound on pilgrimage? Seek other pilgrims out;—
Be they from Hind, from Tatary, or Hadramout.

Peer not into their features; look not at their skins.

Inquire their thoughts, their hearts;—if these be free of sins.

A negro findest thou one with thee in faith and creed?

Him deem a white;—thy brother is he in thy need.

Our tale is told. Its ups and downs are manifold.

Like lovers' thoughts, it's wandering, unconnected, bold.

Commencement it has none;—eternity's its sign;—

Still less conclusion;—so, eternity's design.

Or, rather, it's like water;—every drop, so rich,

Commencement is, and end;—yet shows not which is which.

But, God forbid! Our story's not a fable. See!

Its narrative's a point concerns both me and thee!

A gnostic, in possession of his wits and sense,

Repeats not what is past;—he bides the present tense.

The Arab, his poor pitcher, Caliph, all, observe,

Ourselves are. "He shall swerve whom God shall cause to swerve!"[40]

Our Arab, know, 's the mind; his wife, our lusts and greed.

These two are tenebrous; the mind's the torch they need.

Now hear whence has arisen the ground of their dispute:

Th' infinite finites holds, of various attribute;—

Parts finite;—not parts infinite of th' infinite,
Like scent of rose,—part infinite of definite.
The verdure's beauty infinite is, as a part;
The cooing of the dove's as infinite, in logic art.
But go we not too far afield for sorts and kinds;
Or poor disciples ne'er will slake their thirsting minds.
Dost doubt? Art racked with difficulties? To excess?
Have patience. "Patience is the key of all success!"[41]
Be abstinent. Let not thy crowding thoughts run wild.
Thoughts lions are, and antelopes. Mind's forest; child!
The prime of remedies is abstinence, we know.
And scratching irritates the itch;—as leeches show.
Of treatment medical the base is abstinence.
Therefore be abstinent. Show strength of mind and sense.
Accept my counsel. Lend an ear as I advise;
In golden earrings, counsel's pearls shall be thy prize.
Be thou as slave to this, my cunning goldsmith-art;
I'll teach thee how to soar beyond the stars' bright chart.
Know, first of all, creation's minds are manifold,
As are its forms;—from Alpha to Omega told.
From this variety, disorder seems to rise;

Though, in true sense, to unity the series hies.
In one sense, they're discordant; other, in accord;
They now as folly, now as wisdom, pass a word.
The day of judgment will to each assign its place;
All men of wisdom yearn to see that day of grace.
He who, as blackamoor, is steeped in sin's dark dye,
In that dread day shall gulp dishonour's foulest lye.
The wretch whose countenance beams not bright as the sun,
Shall strive in vain behind the densest veil to run.
If, like some thorns, his stem display no single rose,
That springtide will prove fatal to his safe repose.
But he that blooms from head to foot with righteous deeds,
With joy shall welcome spring's awakening of those meads.
The useless thorn desires the nipping wintry blast,
To lay all low and simplify the flowery vast;
That so, all beauty cloaked, all squalor hid, the same,
All glorious hues, all hideous sights, be rendered tame.
The leaf's fall to such thorn more grateful is than spring;
The ruby and the flint are one in tithesman's ring.
True, that the gardener's eye in winter knows the thorn;

But what is one eye's scrutiny to general scorn!

The vulgar public is, as 'twere, one witless wight;

Each star's a clipping of the moon, in its fond sight.

Not so great men of wisdom, radiant with troth,

They shout with joy: "Good tidings! Spring breaks into growth!"

Unless the flowers blossom on the fertile trees,

How can the fruit be gathered, honey store the bees?

The flowers blow and fade; the fruit begins to swell.

So, when our bodies die, our souls in glory dwell.

690

The fruit's reality; the flower is but a sign;

The flower's the harbinger; the fruit, the true design.

The flower blown and past, the fruit then comes in sight;

The first must perish ere the other can see light.

Unless a loaf be broke, no nutriment it yields;

Until the grapes are crushed, no cup of wine man wields.

So drugs, to prove a solace to the sufferer's ache,

Together must be blended, rolled in one smooth cake.

694

---

1. Qur'ān xx. 97, makes the wandering Jew, Sāmirī, who produced the golden calf, to shun every one, saying, "Touch me not!"
2. Vicar of God is one of the Caliph's titles. This "pretender" must have been some particular adversary of the poet's. The satire is bitter.
3. Bāyezīd of Bestām, in Persia, an early Gnostic saint; died a.d. 874 (a.h. 261).

4. Yezīd, second Caliph of Damascus, persecutor of Husayn, son of the fourth Caliph 'Ali.
5. The original naturally mentions the "qibla" of Islām; not the "east," as used in Christian churches.
6. "My poverty's my pride" is a saying traditionally attributed to Muhammed.
7. Qur'ān iii. 12, mentions several things "made goodly to man."
8. Qur'ān vii. 189, relates the creation of a helpmate for Adam.
9. Muhammed.
10. For Humayrā, see a note in No. 8, dist. 69.
11. Yet Europe still pretends to believe that Islām has denied the possession of a soul by woman!
12. Qur'ān lxxix. 24. So Pharaoh is there said to have styled himself.
13. Qur'ān ii. 3, &c.
14. Not Easterns only have a superstition about treasures hid in ruins.
15. Qur'ān xxii. 11.
16. Man has a triple nature, vegetative, bestial, and human.
17. Qur'ān xxxix. 54.
18. Qur'ān vii. 142, &c.
19. Qur'ān xxxiv. 42.
20. Qur'ān vii. 75; xi. 65-70; xxvi. 142-158. Sālih was sent to the tribe of Thamūd, troglodytes who dwelt in the valleys about half-way between Medīna and the Gulf of Akaba.
21. Qur'ān xci. 13.
22. Qur'ān vii. 76, 89; xi. 70, 97; xxix. 36.
23. Qur'ān vii. 91.
24. Qur'ān lv. 20.
25. Qur'ān vi. 2, 60.
26. Qur'ān xxxviii. 34.
27. Not textually from the Qur'ān.
28. Not textually from the Qur'ān.
29. Qur'ān xxiv. 30.
30. Qur'ān ii. 23, &c.
31. Rich Muslims everywhere break their fast in Ramazān with water from the well of Zemzem, in Mekka, if possible.
32. A pearl is believed to be a special dewdrop, caught by a special oyster, and thence brought to perfection by a special providence. (See Sa'dī's ode at the end of translator's preface.)
33. Qur'ān xciii. 1.
34. Qur'ān xciii. 10.
35. Qur'ān cxii. 3.
36. The world.
37. The belief is that Jesus was not crucified, but was caught up to the fourth heaven, that of the sun, where he will live until he comes again in glory.
38. The belief is that Adam plucked an ear of corn, the forbidden fruit, in paradise.
39. Abbās, Muhammed's uncle, ancestor of the Abbāsī Caliphs.

40. Qur'ān li. 9.
41. Von Hammer, in his History of the Ottoman Empire, so entirely misunderstood this beautiful Arabian proverb, *"Es sabru miftāhu 'l faraj,"* as to read *"farj"* (pudendum), for *"faraj"* (success); and cloaked his blunder by the remark: "Too pungent for literal translation."

X. PATIENCE AND PERSEVERANCE UNDER A TEACHER.

Husāmu-'d-Dīn, Light of the Truth, take up, my friend,
A sheet, that thou a Teacher's virtues mayst append.
True, thou'rt not strong; thy frame is delicate, at best;
But thou'rt the sun that lights my thoughts to their safe nest.
Thou art both lamp and lantern, all in one. Dost see?
Guide to my heart's behests, clue to my wish, —thou'rt he.
Their thread is in thy hand; thy guidance can it shift;
The pearls upon it strung are gems, thy soul's free gift.
Write down the qualities by which a Teacher's known.
Select thy Teacher first; then, follow all he's shown.

A Teacher's summer's glow; cold winter, crowd terrene;
The rabble's darkness self; the Teacher, moon serene.
Young Fortune have I named my Teacher, for the nonce;—
Young Fortune, truth's real Teacher; vigorous at once.
An ancient Teacher he; commencement he ne'er had;
A solitary pearl;—all peerless, never sad.
Increase of age gives wine fresh strength, as well is known;
Especially truth's wine, that flows from God's high throne.
Select a Teacher, then. Without such, travel's vain;
The way is dangerous,—beset with evil's train.
By well-known road, though travelled many times before,
Without a guide to venture, opens peril's door.
How then an unknown path thou ne'er hast followed yet?
Go not alone, without a guide;—act not in fret.
Unless thy Teacher be at hand to lead thee right,
The clamours of the demons surely thee'll affright.
Those demons will mislead thee, into danger cast;
More clever ones than thou have lost their wits at last.
Learn from the Prophet's words the error of their ways;
How Satan led them far astray in bygone days.

From off the track to all that's good he them misled;
Them carried off; them rendered blind, by vain thoughts fed.
Behold their bones, their skeletons, along the road!
Take warning thence. Drive not thy beast with maddening goad!
Dismount; and to the rightful path safe lead him back,
Where guides abound,—experienced travellers dot the track.
Leave not thy beast; his rein loose not thou from thy hand.
His inclination is to wander o'er the land.
One moment only leave him carelessly to roam;
Towards the pastures he at once will rush, all foam.
Thy beast is not a friend to travelling by the road.
How many muleteers through this have lost a load!
Know'st not the way? Observe which path thy beast would take,
And follow the reverse. Secure this will thee make.
"Consult thou them;"[1] but then, do not what they advise;
For he who them opposes not, to ruin hies.
Lend not thyself to lust and fancy's every wind;
For these are what lead men astray; to God's truth blind.
There's nothing in the world that better curbs the lusts,

Than holy company. Protected, he who trusts.

The Prophet said to 'Ali: "Cousin, list to me.
The 'Lion of the Truth'[2] art thou; a hero. See!
Trust not too much, however, to thy courage, sole;
Confide, much rather, on God's arm to keep thee whole.
Put faith in aid from His divine, omniscient mind,
That never can be baffled by disputant blind.
His shadow on the earth is what keeps it in place;
His spirit, sunbird-like, soars in supernal space.
Were I to speak His praises until judgment day,
No end, no interruption, would admit my say.

Himself He's veiled in man, as sun behind a cloud.
This seek to comprehend. God knows what mysteries shroud.
The sun He is;—the sun of spirit, not of sky;
By light from Him man lives;—and angels eke, forby.
Then, 'Ali, of all service man can offer here,
Do thou choose trust in God, dependence firm, sincere.
Each man betakes himself some special worship to;
And each some special friend selects, without ado.
Do thou take refuge in God's wisdom, full, divine;
He'll foil the secret foe that would thee undermine.

Of all the modes of worship, this choose thou, the best;
Thou'lt distance all competitors, the prize thou'lt wrest.
Thy Teacher having chosen thus, obedience yield,
Implicit; even as Moses journeying o'er that field.[3]
Whate'er events betide, beware, and question not;
For fear thy guide should turn, and drive thee from the spot.[4]
Should He destroy a ship,[5]—no murmur from thy mouth;
Should He an infant choke,[6]—let slip no word uncouth.
God hath declared his hand is like the hand of God,
By saying: 'God's right hand above all hands doth plod.'[7]
God's hand it is that kills him; makes him living, too.
But what is living? The everlasting spirit. Lo!
Whoever journeys, now and then, this road alone,
The prayers of saints it is leads him to safety's zone.
A saint's protection is not less than angel's aid;
His help is God's right hand, when all is truly said.
Now, if an absent saint have such portentous power,
A present Teacher's honour sure must higher tower.
If for the absent tempting viands are prepared,
For present guests what may not largely be outshared?

The varlet who to serve his lord is present there,
Must rank before the absentee, for goodly fare.
Thus, having Teacher chosen, be not too thin-skinned,
Nor wishy-washy, to a muddy puddle kinned.
For every buffet, see thou do not umbrage take:
How can a mirror polished be, unless it bear a shake?"
Hear now this pregnant tale narrators have preserved;
A practice it relates in Qazwīn much observed:
Upon the breast, the arms, the bladebones, and the like,
With needle's point and indigo, tattooed designs they strike.
A certain Qazwīn bully to an artist hied,
To have a brave design imprinted on his hide.
The artist first inquired what pattern he'd select.
The man a lion rampant thought he must elect;
And said: "My luck resides in Leo,—lion-sign;
Depict thou then a lion, deep-blue stained, benign."
The artist then demanded where he'd wish it done;
Our man replied: "Between my bladebones it enthrone."
The artist then began to ply his needles' train;
The Qazwīn bully bellowed, smarting with the pain.
The artist he addressed: "Most clever man of skill,

Thou'lt drive me mad. What picture works me so much ill?"
Said he: "A lion's form is what thou didst enjoin."
"O yes!" replied the bully. "What part dost thou coin?"
The artist: "At the tail have I commenced this time."
Our man: "O never mind the tail, designer prime!
Your lion's tail has whacked me on my rump so hard,
That I've no power to breathe, nor such pain disregard.
Allow thy lion to remain without a tail;
Thy needles have unnerved me with their sharp assail."
The artist then began upon another part,
And worked his instruments. They soon induced new smart.
The patient screamed again: "What member limnest thou now?"
Our artist answered: "'Tis the lion's ear, I trow."
His man replied: "O leave him without ears this time;
An earless lion's not so bad. Cut short the rhyme."
Anew the artist on a part assayed his hand.
Afresh the bully interfered, by pain unmanned.
"What part art now at work on? Say, my worthy friend!"
"O," said the artist, "now his body I append."
"Leave out his body!" gasped the suffering Qazwīn man;

"The pain's unbearable. Make short work, as thou can."
The artist now quite lost his wits, as well he might;
He scratched his head; sought how to mend his plight;
Dashed all his needles, indigo, design, to earth;
In anger saying: "What the plague's come now to birth?
A lion tailless, headless, bodiless, who's seen?
God such a lion ne'er created, sure, I ween!"
Have patience, thou too, brother, with thy needle's smart.
So shalt thou 'scape the sting of conscience in thy heart.
They who have conquered,—freed themselves from body's thrall,
Are worshipped in the spheres, the sun, the moon, stars, all.
Whoever's killed pride's demon in his earthly frame,
The sun and clouds are slaves, to do his bidding, tame.
His heart can lessons give of flaming to the lamp;
The very sun not equals him in ardent vamp.
For God hath said, in speaking of the scorching sun,
These words: "It swerved from them."[8] It had new course to run.
The sharpest thorns are welcome, as the roseleaf soft,
To finite who to th' Infinite can soar aloft.
What signifies to glorify the Lord of heaven;

To humble self to dust; with meekness, pride to leaven?
What use to learn to formulate God's unity;
What use to bow one's self before the Deity?
Wouldst shine as brilliantly in sight of all?
Annihilate thy darksome self,—thy being's pall.
Let thy existence in God's essence be enrolled,
As copper in alchemist's bath is turned to gold.
Quit "I" and "We," which o'er thy heart exert control.
'Tis egotism, estranged from God, that clogs thy soul.

---

1. Qur'ān iii. 153.
2. 'Ali's title is "The victorious Lion of God."
3. This journey is recounted in Qur'ān xviii. 64-81.
4. Qur'ān xviii. 69.
5. Qur'ān xviii. 70.
6. Qur'ān xviii. 73.
7. Qur'ān xlviii. 10.
8. Qur'ān xviii. 16.

XI. THE LION'S HUNT, IN COMPANY.

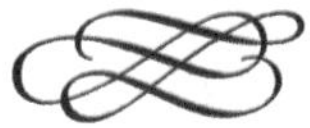

A lion, wolf, and fox together went to hunt;
Among the hills, in quest of game, they turned their brunt.
By mutual help and aid, they hoped to make the field
Too hot for other animals not under union's shield.
Co-operating with each other, they surmised,
A heavy bag they each would make of what each prized.
'Tis true, the noble lion felt of this ashamed.
Still, he politely showed towards them his spirit tamed.
A king feels inconvenienced by throngs of troops;
But out of kindness makes them share his warlike swoops.
The sun would feel ashamed, did stars with him appear;

'Tis generous in the sun to grace the starry sphere.
'Twas God's command to Ahmed still: "With them consult."[1]
True, they gave no advice; no counsel did result.
Upon the balance barley's weighed, as well as gold;
But barley, thence, has not acquired gold's value told.
The spirit with the flesh is fellow-traveller now;
A dog has sometimes charge of palace-yard below.
The company, then, set out for the woods amain,
As followers of the lion's majesty, and train.
A mountain-ox, an ibex, next a hare, they took;
Since fortune smiled on them in each succeeding nook.
A lion's followers on the plain of strife and war,
Of food, by day or night, shall know no want, no bar.
Their prey they carried from the hills into the plain;
Or dead, or sorely wounded;—bleeding, or clean slain.
The wolf and fox were moved to pitch of keen desire,
To see the prey shared out with justice by their sire.
The shade of their cupidity caught Leo's eye,
He understood their confidence, their longing's dye.
Whoe'er has insight to the hearts and minds of men,
Knows at a glance what's passing under his sharp ken.

Beware, O heart, thou ever-fond one, in his sight,
Thy secret to betray,—thy wish to bring to light!
He knows it all, though ignorance he may pretend;—
His smile is but a veil thy aim to comprehend.
The lion, having measured all their secret thought,
Made no remark; he knew how they could both be bought;
Within his breast revolved their fitting punishment:
"I'll show you, my fine fellows, what's by *lion* meant.
My pleasure's, for you both, what you should seek to know;
Not calculate beforehand what I may bestow.
Your every thought should but reflect my sovereign will,
And thankfully await what I may give you still.
Have pictures aught to say to guide the artist's hand?
His cunning 'tis decides what portrait shall expand.
So all your paltry surmise of my royal mind
An insult is,—an arrogance,—that must be fined.
'They who conceive an evil thing of God'[2] are cursed;
And if I spare you, justice will be clean reversed.
To rid the world of scandal, I must end your lives;
Your story shall a moral point; whoe'er contrives."
With this he smiled again most grimly on the pair.

Trust not a lion's smile, all ye to live who care.
The riches of the world are smiles of Providence;
They make men proud, and lead them to their fate prepense.
Through poverty and suffering we may escape
The trap that riches bait; and so avoid the scrape.
The lion now addressed the wolf: "Share out the spoil.
Do justice to us all. Thou'rt versed in cunning's foil.
Be thou my factor. Carve the game as may be fit.
So shalt thou honour win from all who see thy wit."
The wolf then: "Royal Sir, the mountain-ox is thine.
Thou'rt great; the ox is large and fat; let none repine.
The ibex is my share. As I, so it's the mean.
And thou, O fox, shalt have the hare. 'Tis not too lean."
The lion interposed: "Wolf! What is this thou'st said?
I present; and to talk of 'thou' and 'I,' so staid!
What rubbish is a wolf, to deem himself a judge
In presence of a lion, who'll soon make him budge?
Come hither, ass! Thyself alone it is thou'st sold!"
With this he tears the wolf to pieces, all too bold.
He saw the wolf had not one grain of common sense;
So stripped him of his hide, his life, his brain so dense.

Then said: "Since sight of me chased not all thought of self
From thee, death by my paw was due, thou wretched elf!
Thyself thou shouldst have vanquished in my presence dread.
Not having done so, thou'rt now numbered with the dead."
"All perisheth, except His counsel" 's holy writ.[3]
If we're not of "His counsel," life cannot us fit.
He that will lose his life for God's sake, hath it still;
"All perisheth" hath then no power his soul to kill.
He's of th' excepted; not of those to perish doomed.
For, who's excepted, saved is he. His spring hath bloomed.
But he that, in God's court, of "me" and "thee" shall prate,
Will be cut off;—far banished from the heavenly gate.
A man once came and gaily knocked at a friend's door.
The other asked: "Who's there? Is this a threshing-floor?"
"'Tis I," said he. "O then thou straight mayest go away.
'Tis dinner-time. Mature, not crude, must be who'd stay.
Thou'rt thou? Most crude thou art; by rawness' self estranged.
By fire of trial those crude humours must be changed.

'Tis fire matures the crude. Let absence be the fire,
Shall purge thee of thyself, burn out all selfish mire."
Away he went in anguish; travelled a whole year;
Saw not his friend; so pined with yearning, anxious fear;
Matured his soul with suffering's searching throes and pains.
Then sought the door from whence he'd been repulsed, again.
He knocked anew,—his heart with many fears oppressed,
Lest from his lip some word unwelcome drop confessed.
Within, the question's heard: "Who knocks at my street door?"
He answered: "Thy own second self;—though all too poor."
The invitation followed: "Let myself walk in.
My cot's too small for two selves to find room therein.
The thread's not double in a needle's single eye.
As thou'rt now single, enter. Room thou'lt find. Pray, try!"
The thread and needle have relation, each to each;
For needle's eye a camel's far beyond all reach.
How shall a camel ever be so fine and slim
Unless long fasting his redundant flesh should skim?
The hand of God is wanted, then, to make it pass;—

The God who by His word creates both man and grass.

Impossibilities are possibles to Him;

The stubbornest is docile when His will curbs whim.

The blind from birth, the leper, e'en the dead, arise,

Whole, sound, whene'er th' Omnipotent "Come forth" but cries.

E'en non-existence, death of death, at His command,

Starts into life, compelled by His supreme demand.

Recite, my friend: "Each day He's busied with a work:"[4]

And know, He's never idle, unemployed to lurk.

His smallest daily toil,—a work like pleasure still,—

Is to send forth three armies, bound to work His will.

One, from the loins of spheres the elements to stir;

So that all plants may vegetate, from moss to fir.

One, from the wombs of mothers to earth's surface prone,

That male and female may increase, not lie like stone.

The third hence wends its way to sepulchre's dread bourn,

There to receive, at length, reward; and joy, or mourn.

Leave we this theme;—'tis endless,—never would have done.

Let's see, now, how the friends enjoyed themselves alone.

Our host invites his guest to enter, free from scorn:

"Thou'rt welcome, self of mine! We're not like rose and thorn.
Our thread is single,—free from knots and tangle; done,
As 'Be,' though duplex as to form, in sense is one."
That "Be" 's a rope, of power collective, to the end
That nullity may be united to a friend.
Thus duplex means are wanted, for appearances;
Though, in effect, one means there be of all that is.
The biped, as the quadruped, goes but one road.
The one-edged knife, the two-edged shears, make one inroad.
Observe yon pair of bleachers at their daily toil.
Apparently, they differ, combat, as they moil.
The one's for ever wetting cloths in their stream's tide,
The other dries them just as fast in hot noontide.
The first, again to soak the scarce-dried cloths makes haste;
As though in opposition to his partner's waste.
But, in reality, the two have but one aim:
Co-operation's what they jointly, both proclaim.
Each prophet, every saint, has his especial rite;
But, as all tend to God, they're one, multipartite.
Sleep overcomes alike the followers of all creeds;

As water makes all mills to turn and grind, at needs.
The water flows from upwards, down upon the mill;
Its flowing through the trough is but man's wants to fill.
No sooner has man's need been fully satisfied,
He turns the water off;—straight in its bed it's tied.
To teach men wisdom, stream of speech flows through the mouth;
But spirit hath another course, far less uncouth.
Without a voice or repetition it rolls on,
As through elysium, streams;—flowers springing aye, anon.
O Lord! Do Thou vouchsafe to my weak, erring soul
To see the realm where, voiceless, spirit thoughts may stroll,
That so my mind, in glee, on foot or head, may wing
Its flight to the far bourn that parts from nothing, thing,
Careering o'er the boundless fields of ecstasy,
Where fancy joins reality in entity.
Far-reaching more's nonentity than fancy's stretch;
And thus, his fancy is a source of woe to wretch.
Then, being's narrower far than fancy's power of wing;
E'en as the full moon wanes, till it becomes a string.
The world of matter and its forms is narrower still;

A prison all too strait for mind to have its will.
Plurality and composition are the cause;
Our senses these alone can comprehend, and pause.
Beyond our senses lies the world of unity.
Desirest thou unity? Beyond thy senses fly!
Divine command, "Be!" was one act; two-lettered word;
Of grave import, though short, sprung from all being's Lord.
But leave we this, and turn to see how fares it now,
With our acquaintances, wolf, fox, and lion;—trow.
The lordly lion 'd torn poor wolf's head from his tail,
That so two heads there might not be for one avail.
"On them We vengeance took"[5] 's a well-known sacred text;
Wherefore, poor wolf, not quash thyself, when lion's next?
The lion turned, then, to the fox, and bade him share
The prey they'd seized; that they might make a meal, not spare.
The wily fox, low bowing with a reverence meet,
Said: "Sire, the ox your share is, for your breakfast treat.
The ibex, then, will suffice for your midday lunch,
To serve as stop-gap in the interval of munch.

The hare a light repast will furnish ere you sleep;
The royal paunch from indigestion's pains 'twill keep."
The lion answered: "Well said, fox. Thou'rt justice' self.
Who taught thee with such judgment rare to portion pelf?
Where didst thou learn to do full justice with great art?"
Said he: "My Lord, to teach me was that dead wolf's part."
The lion thus replied: "For us much love thou'st shown.
Take thou all three unto thyself, as very own.
Good fox! Thou'st given up thyself entire, for us.
Why should I injure thee? Thou'rt I myself. No fuss!
Myself am thine; the prey is thine; all,—every bit.
Exalt thy head above the spheres. For that thou'rt fit.
Thou'st taken warning from that wretched, selfish wolf.
No longer fox art thou, my lion, my own self!
A wise head ever lessons learns from others' ills,—
Who sees his neighbours victims fall, knows what them kills."
The fox now thanked his stars a hundred, thousandfold,
For that the lion first the wolf to share had told;
And reasoned: "Had he given me first his high command
To share the prey, my life I had not kept in hand.

Then praise to Him who 'th placed me low in this world's scale,
To follow after mightier ones when they regale."
So have we heard God's judgments wrought in ages past
On people of the eld;—set forth as mountains fast,
That we may learn from them,—the wolves of early days.
Then let us, as the fox, glean wisdom from those lays.
"God's people sanctified" 's the title on us cast,
By God's own Prophet, truthful witness, and the last.
The bones, the skeletons of all those old-world wolves,
Consider well, ye readers;—think upon yourselves.
Who's wise will from his heart cast out all fond conceits
Of greatness, when he hears of 'Ād's[6] and Pharaoh's feats.
Unless he warning take from what on others fell,
Men shall a moral draw from his case, sad to tell.
Cried Noah: "Ye stiff-necked race! I am not I, indeed.
My self I've sacrificed; of God's love have I need.
From every fleshly sense and wish I'm severed, quite.
God is my light, my mind, my visual organ's site.
I am not I. The breath I breathe is God's own breath.
Whoe'er gainsays this word, blasphemes, courts his own death.

Within my form of fox there lurks the lion's power;
Against this feeble fox 'tis useless now to lower.
Unless you lay aside scorn for my fox's form,
You'll hear the lion growl more fierce than raging storm."
If Noah had not possessed the mighty aid of God,
Could he a world have upside down turned with a nod?
Within his form whole herds of lions, as one paw,
Lay hid. A fire was he; the world a stack of straw.
That misled straw refused to pay its tithe to him.
Fire flashed. Forthwith the straw in smoke and flames sank grim.
Whoe'er 'gainst the hidden lion in saint's form
Upraise the voice of pride, like to our wolf, base worm,
Shall, like that wolf, be torn by lion piecemeal quite;
The text: "On them we vengeance took" he shall recite.[7]
A stroke shall lay him low, as wolf by lion's paw.
A madman must he be who'd rush in lion's maw.
O that the stroke had fallen upon the body frail;
And that the heart and faith had 'scaped! 'Twere vast avail!
Upon this point I feel my strength must all give way.
How shall I tell the secrets of this mystic play?
Just like the fox, do you yourselves deny in all.

In lion's presence raise no cavil, or you'll fall.
Relinquish thoughts of "I" and "We" when "He" 's afield.
The kingdom is the Lord's; to God the kingdom yield.
The straight way enter all, like paupers as you are.
The lion and the prey will both fall to your share.
God is a spirit pure. All-Glorious is His name!
He hath no need of praise, of honour, glory, fame!
All these, and all besides, whatever may befall,
Upon His servants He bestows. He's Lord of all!
God hath no envy, wish, desire for creatures' ruths;
And blessed is he who takes to heart this truth of truths.
'Twas He created both worlds;—all their pomp and pride.
Shall He desire what He hath made in His own tide?
Keep, then, your hearts pure in the sight of God the Lord,
That you may never be ashamed of thought or word.
He knows the secrets, aims, desires of all your hearts;
They're patent to Him, as a hair in milk at marts.
Whoever hath a breast cleansed from all thoughts of guile,
His breast a mirror is, where heavenly truths will smile.
Its secrets are all known to God;—its every part;
"Believer's heart's the mirror of believer's heart."

He tries our metal on the touchstone of His law.

The fine, the base, He will distinguish, without flaw.

Our talents being tried by His omniscient skill,

What's good, what's bad, will sure appear, plain, by His will.

139

---

1. Qur'ān iii. 153.
2. Qur'ān xlviii. 6.
3. Qur'ān xxviii. 88.
4. Qur'ān lv. 29.
5. Qur'ān vii. 132.
6. See Tale iv., dist. 121.
7. Qur'ān vii. 132. See note, p. 224.

XII. JOSEPH AND THE MIRROR.

The kings of yore a custom had, so I've been told,
Of course thou'st heard it;—must remember it, of old,
On their left hand their champions took their usual place;
Because the heart is on the left of body's space.
Their chancellor and scribes stood on their right hand all;
In that the writer's art to the right hand doth fall.
Before their face the holy teachers stood erect,—
The mirrors of the soul;—than mirror more correct.
Their breasts they've polished with the acts of thought and praise,
That, mirror-like, they catch each image facts may raise.
Each object born in nature with a lovely mien

Should always have a mirror set to catch its sheen.
A beauteous face enamoured is with mirror's glance;
Heart's piety's the polish best the soul can chance.
A friend of tried sincerity came from afar,
And guest became with trusty Joseph;—free from bar.
They had been friends before, in childhood's artless days;
Had leant their elbows on one cushion, in their ways.
His brethren's envy and wrong-dealing touched upon,
Said Joseph: "'Twas a chain. It bound a lion. 'Non!
Disgrace affects not lions, if with chains they're bound.
With God's decree I quarrel not;—it's always sound.
A lion with a chain around his lordly neck,
Is still the lord of them who forged the chain as check."
The friend asked: "How wert, in the well, the prison, cast?"
Said Joseph: "As the moon in wane and change at last."
At change, the new moon's bent in two, a poor weak thing,
But ripens to the full apace, night's matchless king.[1]
Pearls in a mortar pounded are, by chance, sometimes;
Still, they're esteemed a joy to glad eyes in all climes.
Then, grains of wheat are cast into the lowly earth;
But golden ears thence spring, a source of glee and mirth.

These, too, are ground to dust in mill;—vile as to show;

Increased in value, thence, bread it becomes, we know.

Again 'tis crushed between the teeth; to chyme it turns,

And feeds the mind, the thoughts, the soul;—in wisdom burns.

The soul, in turn, is subject to the stress of love;

New miracles, as seen, "the sowers marvel"[2] prove.

But truce to these reflections; let us follow now

The words of Joseph's friend. 'Tis worth while these to know.

That conversation closed, said Joseph to his guest:

"What gift, my friend, hast brought in token of thy zest?"

To go with empty hands and visit friends long missed,

Is like a man who goes to mill without his grist.

E'en God will ask His creatures in the judgment day:

"What offerings have you brought to meet your Maker? Say!

'Alone, and empty-handed? Is it thus you come?

E'en as We first created you? Gifts left at home?'[3]

What have you brought as timely offerings in your hands?

What are the gifts with which you'd grace your new life's lands?

Or, was it that you'd no belief in this return?

Our promise of this day by you was laughed to scorn?
If you denied thus the hope to be My guest,
Then dust and ashes wait you in My realm, at best.
If you did not deny it, whence your empty hands?
How come you to a friend's gate, scorning just demands?"
Put by a little from thy daily meat and drink,
So shalt thou have a store for offerings' binding link.
"Sleep little" when thou art of those "who lay them down."[4]
"Of mornings," be of them who "ask for pardon's crown."[5]
Give signs of life, though slight;—as babes do in the womb;
So may God grant thee inward light to cheer thy tomb.
And when thou 'scapest from dark and narrow prison there,
Then mayst thou soar from earth beyond the realms of air.
"The spacious land of God" 'tis named in holy writ,[6]
The land to which the prophets all have gladly flit.
The heart is never lonesome in that vast abode;
Its green trees never wither, frosts no leaves corrode.
If now thou load thyself with sensual burden's weight,

Fatigued and jaded, faint thou'lt prove beneath their freight.

In sleep thou bearest no burden; borne thou art, instead.

Fatigue is thence recruited;—strength regains its head.

Know then, thy sleep's a foretaste of what is to come,

From the rapt state of saints arriving at their home.

The saints were well prefigured by the "Sleepers Seven."[7]

"Their sleep," "their stretchings," "their awaking," lead to heaven.

Without the least exertion on their parts by acts,

The "right and left-hand registers" draw them by facts.

The "right-hand register" 's the record of good deeds;[8]

The "left-hand register" 's the list of fleshly greeds.[9]

But both of these abolished are in case of saints.

To them such things are but as echo dies and faints.

Though good and evil may their echoes round thee peal,

The echoing mountain hears them not in the ordeal.

Now Joseph once again inquired: "What offering bringest?"

His friend, ashamed of urgent pressing, sighed. Thou singest?

Said he: "Full many offerings have I sought and seen;

But none was worthy of thee; or I much misween.

How could I bring a diamond to its native mine;
Or add a drop of water to a sea of brine?
Shall I to Kāshān cummin bring, whence it is drawn,[10]
By offering up my life and soul to beauty's fawn?
I know no rarity that's not surpassed by thee;
Thy loveliness the rarity men nowhere see.
The fittest present, then, I've found, a mirror is.
And this I've brought; unsullied, bright, refulgent 'tis.[11]
Therein thou'lt contemplate thy beauteous, matchless face,
As beaming as the sun that decorates sky's space.
A mirror have I brought, thou charming, witching one;
In it admire thyself; and think of me, when gone."
The mirror now he drew from underneath his skirt.
A mirror is, to beauty, with attractions girt.
In non-existence' mirror if existence gleams,
Present this mirror to it, thou, as best beseems.
In non-existence mirrored, being we may see;
As wealthy men their wealth may show by beggars' glee.
The hungry man's the mirror best shows what is bread.
And tinder mirrors flint and steel's gleam, quickly spread.
Wherever want, defect, is seen, beauty's most prized.

The mirror of perfection's then best realised.

If clothes grew, ready cut and sewn, to meet our needs,
Where'd be the use of tailor's art, to fashion weeds?
The unhewn trunk is needed, for the carver's skill,
And carpenter, to cut out thence his frames, his thill.
The surgeon hastens to the couch where suffering lies;
Where limbs are broken, there his bandages he ties.
Were there no patient, malady, no fever, ache,
Could art sublime, the medical, its marvels make?
If humble brass and copper were not to be found,
Th' alchemist's stone could not to gold transmute them round.

Defect is thus the mirror whence perfection's seen;
And vileness is the foil to show off grandeur's sheen.
By contrast does each opposite its fellow show,
Sweet honey by sharp vinegar we best can know.
The man who sees and feels his imperfections sore,
Exerts himself to cure them quickly all the more.
And he'll ne'er take his flight towards heaven's eternal King,
Who holds at heart the thought that he's a perfect thing.
No worse disease exists, to taint the human mind,
Than self-conceit, that paints its owner gold refined.

How many bitter tears has not the vain to shed,
Ere arrogance can be expelled, and pride be dead!
The malady of Satan,—self-conceit:—"I'm best,"[12]
Exists in germ in every panting human breast.
These fancy they have mortified themselves throughout.
Take them to be pure streams; their filth seek in the grout.
Just stir them up a little, for a trial's sake;
Thou'lt see their mud discolour all the water's lake.
There's ooze at bottom of the pond,—be sure of that,—
However clear the surface of the dull dead flat.

Our greatest teacher is endowed with fair device.
He digs a conduit in the very soil of vice.
How can he make the water of that conduit pure?
All human wisdom's but one spark from God's vast store.
Does sword inflict a wound in its own handle,—blade?
Find me a surgeon who shall cure a gash so made.
Where wound exists, the flies will ever flock amain,
To hide its hideousness from sight, and lull the pain,
Those flies the symbols are of man's vain, baseless thoughts;
The wound they cover over's ignorance high-wrought.

'Tis only when the teacher salve applies with skill,

The throes are quieted that shoot across man's will.

He then imagines that his wound is healing fast.

Effect this is of cunning used, that salve to cast.

O man, whose back is galled, accept his salve with thanks.

Thy solace thence arises; not from thy own pranks.

78

---

1. In Semitic and Muslim lore the moon is "he," the sun "she."
2. Qur'ān xlviii. 29.
3. Qur'ān vi. 94.
4. Qur'ān li. 17.
5. Qur'ān li. 18.
6. Qur'ān iv. 99.
7. Qur'ān xviii. 8-21.
8. Qur'ān lxix. 19.
9. Qur'ān lxix. 25.
10. The Persian equivalent of our "*carrying coals to Newcastle.*"
11. A metallic mirror, formerly much used.
12. Qur'ān vii. 11.

XIII. THE PROPHET'S FIRST AMANUENSIS.

There was a scribe,[1] before 'Uthmān[2] had filled that post,
Most diligent in noting revelation's host.
Whatever text the Prophet had to promulgate
On parchment did this scribe trace all its terms of fate.
The splendour of those inspirations filled his soul.
His mind became enlightened, as a glowing coal.
The substance of that wisdom from the Prophet came.
The silly scribe imagined 'twas his genius' flame:
"The texts the Prophet promulgates with rare effect,
Appear *verbatim* in my mind, without defect."
The Prophet was aware of this egregious sin.
The wrath of God descended from high heaven's welkin.

The scribe renounced his office, and his faith at once.
Religion's fiercest foe he stood now, for the nonce.
The Prophet questioned him: "Benighted, wretched man!
If light there be in thee, whence this thy darkest plan?
Hadst thou a fountain of God's truth been, verily,
This turbid stream had never flowed thence, heavily."
Not caring to expose his scribe to all his friends,
The Prophet held his peace, to watch th' adventure's ends.
The scribe's heart hardened more and more as time rolled on.
Repentance he felt not; his pride grew thereupon.
He sighed. His sighs were not the signs of contrite heart;
But tokens sure that justice made him feel its smart.
God caused his pride to weigh more heavy than a chain.
How many thus are fettered; none can heal their pain.
His blasphemy and pride held him in iron grip;
His very sighs he felt constrained to stifle on his lip.
He cried: "'The iron collars they're compelled to wear;'[3]
There's naught but iron collars; these are all we bear!
'Behind them is a barrier; but We've bound their eyes.'[4]
So that they see not what's before, behind those ties."
The barrier so upreared appears a level plain;

He knows not 'tis a bourn that checks him like a chain.
Thy witness is a barrier, bars sight of the Lord;
Thy teacher is a veil, shuts out God's holy word.
How many infidels, oh! long faith to possess!
Their pride, their honour, stands between them and success.
That barrier, unseen, 's than iron firmer still.
An axe can hew through iron; not through stubborn will.
A bond of iron may be broken by due means;
A moral bond is what holds firmest, where it leans.
A bee, a wasp, may sting one to the very quick;
Yet may the same be warded by precaution's trick.
But what's to do when sting is in our very selves?
The pain is then most biting, deeper far it delves.
Unwillingly has leaped this subject from my mind.
I fear 'twill leave despair in many, deep behind.
Despair thou not; take consolation to thy soul;
And cry to that Deliverer who can make thee whole:
"Thou Lover of forgiveness! Pardon to me grant!
Physician of the soul! Relieve my direful want!"
Such counsel wise drove mad that erring sinner, quite.
Think not of him. 'Twill tire thy mind beyond respite.

My friend! This counsel tells with equal force on thee.

It flows through all the saints, though transient thou it see.

Within the house a gleam of light has been espied.

This light comes from a neighbour's lamp, with oil supplied.

Give thanks for it. Be not puffed up. Snort not, good man!

To me lend ear. Presumption chase to utmost span.

Alas! that this most transient ray of dubious light,

The nations has seduced from God's sole path of right.

I'll be the very slave of him, who, at each stage,

Will not suppose the goal 'tis of his pilgrimage.

How many stages are there must be left behind,

Before the traveller reach the home he bears in mind.

Although the iron may glow red, the colour's not

Its own; 'tis but reflection of the fire that's hot.

A window or a house with light may be suffused;

But still, the source of light is in the sun, diffused.

Each wall, each gate, may cry amain: "I shine! I shine!

I have no need of other's light. 'Tis mine! 'Tis mine!"

But then the sun demurs: "O thing of little sense!

So soon as I shall set, thy darkness will be dense!"

The plants may think their verdure's all their very own.

So fresh, so green; so pleasant every flower full-blown.
But then again the summer season makes comment:
"When I am past, your present charms will soon be spent."
A beauty's lovely body prides itself as fair.
Her spirit, having hid itself within its lair,
Remarks: "Thou dunghill! Wherefore all this silly pride?
Thou bloomest but a day or two, while I preside.
Thy affectation, vanity, 's too vast for me.
But stay till I depart: then straightway thou shalt see.
Thy lovers then shall loathe thy charms, adored before.
To worms, and toads, and snakes they'll fling thee, as cheap store.
Thy stench shall make him hold his nose in deep disgust,
Who lately in thy presence would have licked the dust."
Reflections from the spirit are the tongue, the eye, the ear.
Accessions from the fire steam's bubbles 'tis upbear.
E'en as the soul's reflection on the body acts,
Reflection from th' inspiring saints my soul impacts.
When my soul's life shall quit my soul, alack-a-day!
My soul shall lifeless be, like mortal soulless clay.
'Tis therefore that I cast myself down in the dust,
That earth may witness bear for me before th' All-Just.

In day of judgment, "when the earth shall quake with fear,"[5]

Earth shall itself bear witness to my prayerful tear.

Command shall issue: "Loud proclaim the acts thou'st seen."

The earth, the rocks, a tongue shall find, to tell what's been.

Philosophers deny this, in their pride of mind;

But tell them: "Dash your heads against a wall, ye blind!"

The speech of earth, of water, and of plastic clay,

Is audible unto the ears of saints that pray.

Philosophers who will deny God's saving grace,

Are strangers to the powers of saints' inspired race.

He holds that inclination, working on man's brain,

Gives rise to heated phantasy's legerdemain.

True, his own blasphemy and lack of firm belief

Have raised in him denial's phantom, reason's thief.

Philosophers deny the devil does exist;

While they themselves his sport are, in his cursed fist.

Hast never seen the devil? Look at thy own self!

Who'd paint his forehead blue, unless deceived by elf?[6]

Whoever hath a doubt or trouble in his mind,

In secret's a philosopher, as you may find.

He wears the outward semblance of belief; but then,
Anon and ever his philosophy claims pen.
Beware, all ye believers! In you lurks this germ;
Within yourselves lies latent vile deception's sperm.
The two and seventy sects are all within your hearts,[7]
And only wait a chance to play their fatal parts.
Whoever hath the bud of faith grown in his breast,
As aspen-leaf must tremble, lest it be supprest.
Thou laughest at the devil in thy foolish pride;
Thyself thou hast imagined sin's stern deicide.
But when thy soul shall manifested be to all,
Sad sighs and moans shall rise from those who're seen to fall.
Exhibitors of base coin in this world below
Smile now; the touchstone yet is hidden in form's glow.
O Veiler of men's sins! Lift not Thy veil from us![8]
In day of trial be our Helper, gracious!
Adulteration now contends with purest coin;
The gold awaits the day of trial to rejoin.
It slily thinks in its mute way, without ado:
"Await a little, false ones! Trial comes! Soho!
For was not Satan's self, in ages long gone by,

Of light an angel, Prince of Powers, a galaxy,
Until he envied Adam in his froward heart?
And then he fell, an outcast from heaven's high rampart.
The son of Beor, Balaam, in the world's esteem,
Was equal unto Moses. So all men did deem.
To him alone was homage paid by high and low;
His prayers were reckoned medicine for every woe.
To Moses he opposed himself, in foolish pride.
The Scripture tells us how most miserably he died.[9]
Of Balaams, and of Satans, in this world of ours,
Some manifest, some secret, troops come at all hours.
God granteth them celebrity within their spheres,
That they may witness bear against their own compeers.
Then, both are elevated on a gallows high,
As warning unto others who for honours sigh.
They both were covetous of homage and applause;
And both received due punishment through God's just laws.
Thou, man, perchance, the idol of some crowd mayst be.
For God's sake, then, beware thou transgress not as he.
And setting up thyself against a better man,
Thou come to grief, and bring to wreck thy every plan.

The tales of 'Ād[10] and Thamūd[11] have the moral clear,
That saints of God, and righteous men, are held more dear.

Those signs, and swift destruction overwhelming them,
Proclaim aloud the power that saints around does hem.
As brutes are slain that man may live a life of ease,
So men are slaughtered when they sin 'gainst God's decrees.
For, what is wisdom? 'Tis th' omniscience divine.
Man's wisdom is but folly, set against that mine.
The brutes are timid, shun man's presence everywhere;
Though man, in numbers, yields to them within this sphere.
Their blood may lawfully be shed for needs of man;
Because they lack th' ennobling spark of reason's scan.

The brute is held of low degree on this our earth;
As being weighed against great man's superior worth.
What value will attach to thee, thou arrant fool,
If, like an ass, thou spite the lords of reason's school?
The ass, that renders service meet unto his lord,
Men slay not. 'Tis the wild ass does them chase afford.
The ass reaps naught of recompense for merit due;
Yet, when he errs, fell punishment awaits him, true.

If man, then, go astray, much more he's worthy blame;
Most justly shall chastisement visit him with shame.
The blood of misbelievers righteously is shed,
With sword and arrow, like wild ass on mountain fed.
Their wives and children fall a prey to victor's hand;
In that they lack true wisdom, cursed of God they stand.
The reasonable creature fleeing reason's Lord,
Renounces reason, brute becomes, calls for the sword.
Hārūt, Mārūt,[12] two angels famed throughout the earth,
Through pride and insolence lost paradise for dearth.
They trusted in the wondrous power they held of old;
As though a buffalo 'gainst lion should wax bold.
His horns are mighty weapons, fearful to the foe;
The lion tears him piecemeal; horns but work him woe.
Had he as many horns as hedgehog quills, all o'er,
They'd help him not; the lion still would him o'erpow'r.
The hurricane roots up the forest trees amain;
While pliant reeds from it no injury sustain.
The fury of the blast hurts not their supple ease.
Of strength, then, boast thee not, man. Seek wrath to appease.
The axe is nothing daunted, seeing boughs of trees;

But, one by one, hews through them all; their end foresees.

The axe sets not its trenchant edge to lop off leaves;

'Tis not the silky down of thistles that it cleaves.

A flame is not abashed, though many thorns collect;

Whole herds of sheep can never butcher's knife deflect.

To inward idea's power the outward sign must yield.

That power, 'tis, makes revolve the heavens' vast starry field.

The sphere, the circling firmament, consider now.

What makes it turn? A force that rest will not allow.

The movements of our bodies have no other source;—

The soul it is originates all vital force.

The circulation of the air's from an idea;

The millstone turns by water from the fields' area.

The ebb and flow of tides, breath drawn, again expired,

Whence all? 'Tis life compels, diffused through all, respired.

The spirit 'tis decides what words our pen shall write;

Or peace, or war, or anything our minds indite.

To right, to left we go, e'en as the spirit wills;

A rose, a thorn,—the spirit says which place it fills.

Our God it was who sent this vital air in blasts,

Like breath of dragons, to destroy old 'Ād's[13] outcasts.

While to the faithful it gave peace, and health, and strength;

In gentle zephyrs softly breathing whole days' length.

The Prophet hath assured us God's the soul of all.

The Lord's the ocean whence the rills of spirit fall.

The strata of the heavens and earth, with all therein,

Are merely straws afloat on waves where powers begin.

They dance about, are carried here and there by turns;

Their movement's from the waves that power divine still churns.

Decrees this they shall be at rest? At once they're flung

Aside upon the shore, there to decay like dung.

Wills it that they be tossed about on waves high-flown?

They're but the leaves of autumn by the wild winds blown.

Now turn we from this subject, most engaging still,

To learn about those angels, victims of self-will.

The sins of all mankind were known to them as sure;

No wickedness escapes the glance of spirits pure.

In anger at such baseness they were moved to scorn;

Their own defect was hidden from their sight, heaven-born.

An ugly man once saw his face in looking-glass.
He turned away enraged with that reflecting mass.
So, when one self-conceited sees another's fault,
A flame from hell is lighted in his bad heart's vault.
'Tis pride inflames him;—holy zeal he dubs it straight;
Not conscious of the vanity that makes his freight.
A zeal for holiness by other tokens shines;
And lights a fire by which to ashes earth declines.
God said to them: "If you both shine with virtue's ray,
No notice take of man's backslidings from its way.
Give thanks and praises, rather, you're not made like them.
Lusts of the flesh, concupiscence, soil not your stem.
Had I imposed upon you that great burden, sore;
The heavens would not have been your home for evermore.
The chastity that decks your spirit-nature now,
Reflection is of purity that lights My brow.
Know, this is but a quality you hold from Me.
So shall th' accursed one not make you slaves to be!"
E'en as the Prophet's scribe, with self-importance puffed,
Imagined holy wisdom's light shone as he'd stuffed.
Himself he fancied equal of prophetic quire;

His raven croak as their sweet song he dared admire.

He who sets up to write the notes of every bird,

Knows not th' inspiring springs within their bosom stirred.

Could man acquire the note of nightingale so sweet,

Would he have learnt as well its love the rose to meet?

Should he achieve a notion of that love's intent;

'Twould be mere surmise, like deaf man's from lips' consent.

Such deaf man once was made aware by some kind friend,

That next door dwelt an invalid near to his end.

The poor man thought within himself: "I'm deaf as stone,

How can I hope to comprehend this neighbour's tone?

More 'specially as sick men speak so very low.

Still, go I must; mere decency demands my bow.

When I advance, he'll me address,—his lips will move.

From thence I'll glean a notion, may not quite false prove.

I'll ask him how he feels to-day, 'mid so much pain.

He'll answer surely: 'Thank you; better in the main.'

Reply I will: 'Most happy! How's the appetite?'

He'll answer: 'Pretty good, if chicken-broth invite.'

I'll say: 'Good! Good! And what are you allowed to drink?
Who is your doctor?' He'll respond, as one may think.
Then I'll remark: 'With so much talent at command,
You can't do better. Soon I hope to see you stand.
I've had experience of his skill; I know his worth;
With him as guide, you'll not go wrong.' So forth."
Thus having got his fancied answers all by heart,
He goes to see the sick man; deftly plays his part.
On asking: "How are you?" the patient says: "Near dead."
The deaf man straight rejoins: "Of that I'm very glad."
The sufferer felt insulted by this joy expressed.
The deaf one had surmised,—had failed in what he'd guessed.
He now inquired the diet: "Oh! It's poison all!"
Complained the sick man. "Glad to hear it," he let fall.
Still more the patient wondered. "Who attends you, pray?"
Asked Deafy; "whose advice is't leads you on your way?"
"Death tracks my hours!" said he; "pray leave me now to rest."
The other answered: "Better can't be found; he's best."

The visitor retired, quite pleased with his rich art;
And offered thanks for having played so kind a part.
The sick man, on the contrary, was all on fire:
"Whence comes this malice? Who has roused his soul to ire?"
So, turning in his mind the matter o'er and o'er,
A message he determines that shall pay the score.
Just so, a man who's eaten ill-digesting food,
Can have no rest till it's ejected, well and good.
Long-suffering is thy better part, reject it not;
With patience, thou shalt find soft words best heal a plot.
But our sick man found no such solace for his mind;
He called the deaf one "Ass," and "Fool," and "Sot," and "Blind."
Said he: "I'll serve him out; I'll pay him what's his due!
Till then, my spirit will his hateful visit rue!
A visit to the sick's for consolation's sake;
His visit I abhor, his insults I'll not take.
He's wished to gloat on foe laid prostrate at his feet;
Some joy to gather thence his secret hate to greet."
How many pious men there are, to outward view,
Reward of joy in heaven, as object, who pursue.
At heart they're sinners still, despite the show they make.

Alas! Hypocrisy for righteousness they take!
Just as our deaf man thought he'd done a friendly act;
And yet, withal, had vexed his neighbour, as a fact.
He soothed his soul by thinking: "Kindly part I've played!
I've acted as a neighbour! Sorrow I've allayed!"
Whereas, in truth, a fire he'd lighted for himself;
And his sick neighbour's heart inspired with vengeful elf.
Beware the fires you kindle by such acts as this!
Beware offence to give, while proffering a kiss!
The Prophet said one was a hypocrite, he knew:
"Go, worship, friend; thy act's no worship, as I trew!"
For fear lest we should trespass, even as we pray,
Our worship has the prayer: "Lord, guide us in Thy way!"[14]
"Permit not Thou, O God, that my devotion's act
Be counted erring hypocrite's unwelcome pact!"
The surmise of our deaf man wide was of the mark.
A ten years' friendship 'twould have wrecked! Beware such spark!
Man's judgment, friend, that's based on sense's treacherous sand,
Can never be compared with revelation's wand.

Hast ear to hear? Hast mind to recognise the truth?
Know, then, thy moral ear is deaf to godly sooth!
The first who followed sense, and reason—as he thought—
Instead of God's true light, the devil was, we're taught.
He judged: "The fire more noble is than sordid earth;
From fire was I created; clay gave Adam birth.
The stock from whence it springs decides each kind of fruit;
From darkness Adam's sprung; light at my birth did suit."
The Lord replied: "'Tis not a question of descent.
Pre-eminence is here the prize of righteous bent.
'Tis not a heritage of worldly wealth to share.
Why talk of ancestry? Heart's qualities declare.
The heritage we've now to give is prophecy;
The heirs thereto are they whose spirits hate a lie.
The son of Abū-Jahl believed, and saved his soul;[15]
A son of Noah rebelled; became perdition's goal.[16]
The son of earth was made resplendent as the moon;
Thou, son of fire, begone, disgraced, cursed, none too soon!"
Investigations, reasonings, on days of cloud,

By night, in darkness, guide the doubting crowd;
But, when the sun shines,—when God's temple's clearly seen,
No doubt remains which way to turn one's face, I ween.
The temple hidden, its direction quite unknown,—
Then use thy judgment. God this method's kindly shown.[17]
Whene'er you hear a note of God's truth-warbling bird,[18]
You straightway seize its literal sense, just as 'tis heard.
You then use suppositions of your darksome mind,
And form, through wrong conclusions, guesses worse than blind.
The saints use terms of technical significance,
Unknown to worldly reasoners' crass ignorance.
The language of the bird you learn, as to its notes;
But clean destroy its sense; as sure as fancy dotes.
E'en as the sick man of our tale, saints' hearts are grieved;
Though, like the deaf man, you suppose you've good achieved.
The scribe of writ inspired had all its text by heart;
Then thought himself inspired;—would play a prophet's part.
The Prophet, warbler-like, smote him with powerful wing;

He forthwith sank to blind despair, through conscience' sting.
So 'tis with you. Perversely, or with vain surmise,
You would interpret words descended from the skies.
Like Hārūt, and like Mārūt, well you've learnt the tune
They sang of old in pride: "We're God's elect," jejune.
You pray for grace on all the sins of wicked men;
You curse your own foul egotism, greed's hungry ken.
Beware lest God's just jealousy break forth amain,
And smite you to the earth, ne'er more to rise again.
Those angels owned, in words: "To rule is Thine, O God.
Without Thy strong protection, safety's soon downtrod."
Such were their lip-words. But their hearts' rebellious pride,
With foolish boasting, thought: "No harm can us betide."
They never ceased to brood on vanities thus framed,
Till fire of arrogance burst forth from breasts inflamed;
Then proclamation made: "O elemental men!
How little have ye known the range of angel's ken.
We'll weave dense curtains o'er the sky's revolving face;
Descending then to earth, we'll there our temple place.
We'll justice distribute, and worship we'll commend,
Returning every night to heaven, whence we descend.

So shall we be admired by all who dwell on earth,

And fill the world with gladness, safety, peace, and mirth."

Alas! Such fancy's false! Earth cannot heaven be;

Their difference is radical, as all may see!

199

---

1. I have failed to discover the name and history of the individual here used to point a moral by our great poet. Ibnu-Hishām and Nawawī do not mention him.—*Translator.*
2. Osmān.
3. Qur'ān xxxvi. 7.
4. Qur'ān xxxvi. 8.
5. Qur'ān xcix. 1.
6. In allusion to the Brahminical marks used in India.
7. The heterodox sects of Islām are commonly said to be seventy-two.
8. *"The Veiler," i.e.,* of sin, is one of "the most comely names" of God, but is not found in the Qur'ān. *"Yā Sattār!"*
9. Some of the commentators hold that Qur'ān vii. 174, alludes to the opposition of Balaam to Moses and the Israelites.
10. See Tale iv. dist. 121; and xi. 112.
11. See Tale ix. 266.
12. Qur'ān ii. 96.
13. See Tale iv. dist. 121.
14. Qur'ān i. 5.
15. 'Ikrima, son of Abū-Jahl, embraced Islām at sea, as he fled from Mekka at its capture by Muhammed. He returned and was pardoned.
16. Qur'ān xi. 44, 45.
17. This is a canon of Islām. If a worshipper has no means of knowing the direction of "God's House" at Mekka, he may face in any direction he judges most probable, and so perform his worship.
18. The Prophet.

XIV. THE CHINESE AND ROMAN ARTISTS.

Give ear to this advice from one who's well informed:
"Lay down your head where'er by wine you've been transformed."
Whene'er a drunken man reels forth from tavern door,
A laughingstock he's made by urchin and by boor.
Now here, now there, he lurches, stumbling on his road;
Falls in the mire; is mocked and jeered, scorned as a toad.
The children of the neighbourhood his steps surround,
Unconscious what is wine's hilarity profound.
So are all people children, round the saints of God;
None adults are, save they who've cast off passion's clod.
'Twas said: "The world's a toy, a plaything; and men all

Are infants."[1] These are God's words. True in sense they fall.

No child but loves his toys, his playthings, games, and sports;

By cultivation of the mind man sense imports.

Man's love for worldly things is like child's love for toys;

The child and man, in these, repeat each other's joys.

The child, in play, performs the very selfsame part,

He'll act when grown a hero, learnt debating art.

Men's quarrels are the same as those fought out by boys;

They're senseless, reasonless; they squabble for mere toys.

Their weapons are but wooden swords, as used in play;

Their objects are not worth a thought, by night or day.

They mount their hobby-horses, ride about on sticks;

Declaring 'tis Bucephalus, Eclipse, that kicks.

'Tis they who bear a burden, pack-horse-like, or ass;

Their vanity converts them into horsemen's mass.

So let it be till that day when God's riders shall,

On steeds of fire, transcend the seventh heaven's rolling ball.

"The spirit and the angels mount unto their God."[2]

The spheres shall shake, when under saintly footsteps trod.

Whereas the raff of mankind mount their own coat-tails;
Imagining they're horsemen, prancing as ship sails.
The Lord hath said: "Imagining's of no avail."[3]
Imagination's steed to scale heaven's heights must fail.
Imagination's best is but a choice of doubts;
Man ne'er disputes about the sun, whate'er the whim he flouts.
The time will come, he'll see what wretched screw he rides;
That which he deemed a courser's but his own shanks' sides.
His senses, thoughts, and reasonings, he then will find,
Are but the infant's hobby,—pa's cane, more refined.
The wisdom of the saints is what bears them aloft.
The science of the worldly is their load;—how oft!
The wisdom of the heart sustains and elevates;
But knowledge sensuously acquired as burden rates.
'Tis God hath said: "An ass with volumes for his load."[4]
So knowledge is a burden, when not of God's code.
All science not received from word of God direct,
Hath no endurance; paint it is; our eyes detect.
Still, if man bear his burden well, he's recompensed;
His burden is removed; ease to him is dispensed.

See, then, you bear not science' load from fleshly lust;
Lest you should suffer inwardly fatigue,—disgust;
But mount the agile steed of sacred lore divine;
So shall the burden on your back at once decline.
Unless you drink His cup, how 'scape from fleshly lust?
O you, who, in His name, content are with the Just!
When from His name and attributes some inkling's born,
This inkling points the road to union one fair morn.
Thou'st never known a guide, but some one must be led;
And when no road is travelled, gnome can't dog man's tread.
Thou'st never heard a name, but indicates a thing;
A flower thou'st never plucked from verbal *rosa*'s ding.
Hast thou pronounced a name? Straightway the thing ensue.
The moon seek in the sky;—not in lake-waters, blue.
But wouldst thou cast aside all names and words, as vain,
Thyself, then, purge of self. Abstraction thou shalt gain.
Wouldst be a sword? Cast off soft iron's yield refined;
By discipline the mirror burnish of thy mind.
Discharge thyself of every particle of self;
So shalt thou see thyself pure, free from soil of pelf.
Within thy heart thou'lt see the wisdom of the saints,

Without a book, a teacher, or professor's plaints.
The Prophet said: "That man is one of my true flock,
Whose heart and mind are hewn from my own calling's rock.
His soul perceives me through the selfsame holy light
That unto me reveals his soul serenely bright.
Reports, traditions, chains of evidence, are lost;
When soul communes with soul, minds freely can accost."
This riddle solve: "A Kurd I last night was, by birth;
And then, this morning, Arab am, by afterbirth."[5]
If one, sincere, a Kurdish boor was overnight,
Sincerity an Arab made him by daylight.
Example seekest of science springing in the heart?
This contest heed of Chinaman and Roman's art.[6]
The Chinese urged they had the greater painter's skill.
The Romans pleaded they of art the throne did fill.
The sovereign heard them both; decreed a contest fair;
Results the palm should give the worthiest of the pair.
The parties twain a wordy war waged in debate;
The Romans' show of science did predominate.
The Chinamen then asked to have a house assigned
For their especial use; and one for Rome designed,

Th' allotted houses stood on either side one street;
In one the Chinese, one the Roman, artists meet.
The Chinese asked a hundred paints for their art's use;
The sovereign his resources would not them refuse.
Each morning from the treasury rich colours' store
Was served out to the Chinese till they asked no more.
The Romans argued: "Colour or design is vain;
We simply have to banish soil and filth amain."
They closed their gate. To burnish then they set themselves;
As heaven's vault, simplicity filled all their shelves.
Vast difference there is 'twixt colours and not one.
The colours are as clouds; simplicity's the moon.
Whatever tinge you see embellishing the clouds,
You know comes from the sun, the moon, or stars in crowds.
At length the Chinamen their task had quite fulfilled.
With joy intense their hearts did beat, their bosoms thrilled.
The sovereign came, inspected all their rich designs,
And lost his heart with wonder at their talents' signs.
He then passed to the Romans, that his eyes might see.

The curtains were withdrawn, to show whate'er might be.

The Chinese paintings all, their whole designs in full,

Reflected truly were on that high-burnished wall.

Whatever was depicted by the Chinese art

Was reproduced by mirrors, perfect every part.

Those Romans are our mystics;—know, my worthy friend;

No art, no learning; study, none;—but gain their end.

They polish well their bosoms, burnish bright their hearts,

Remove all stain of lust, of self, pride, hate's deep smarts.

That mirror's purity prefigures their hearts' trust;

With endless images reflections it incrust.

The formless Form the thousand thousand hidden forms

Flashed in his breast on Moses' heart, like mirrored storms.

That Form, 'tis true, the heaven of heavens cannot contain;

Nor all the space between the zenith and the main.

These numbered are, and limited within their bounds;

The mirror of the heart is boundless in its rounds.

Here, reason stands aghast, O erring child of sense;

The heart's with God,—the heart is God,—boundless, immense!

From all eternity, the figures of all things,
Unnumbered, multitudinous, gleam in heart's wings.
To all eternity each new-created form
In heart of saint reflected is, most multiform.
His polished heart is cleansed from being's soiling stain;
And at each moment contemplates fresh beauty's train.
The outward gilt, the shell, of science they despise;
The banner of real certitude floats where they rise.
They've thought abandoned; light and life they've truly found;
Their breasts and hearts are filled with love's inspiring sound.
Death, that dread thing of which all mankind stand in fear,
Is laughed and mocked at by the saints, when it draws near.
No man has power to dominate their tranquil minds.
The shell may injured be; the pearl harm never finds.
The rhetor's art, the jurist's skill, they set at naught;
But poverty, abasement, to themselves they've taught.
The scenes of all eight paradises[7] are consumed
In that full blaze with which their holy heart's illumed.
They're more exalted than the heavens and what's beyond;

Their place is in the court of love divine, all-fond.

---

1. Qur'ān vi. 32; xxix. 64; xxx. 6; xlvii. 38; lvii. 19.
2. Qur'ān lxx. 4.
3. Qur'ān x. 37.
4. Qur'ān lxii. 5.
5. See, in the author's own preface, his eulogistic mention of Sheykh Husāmu-'d-Dīn, p. iii., where this saying is also given.
6. By "Roman," in the East, is meant what Europeans incorrectly name "Greek." Since Alexander of Macedon's time, no "Greeks" have existed. Their very memory is lost in Asia, and Alexander himself is styled there "*the Roman*."
7. Commonly, in Islām, eight paradises, or, properly, eight mansions of Paradise, are reported, mentioned, and believed. Baydhāvī, in Qur'ān ii. 23, gives only seven, and one of those is wrong. Guided by him, however, I have corrected this, and verified the others, besides finding the eighth. Their names, then, are as follows:—1. *Jennatu-'l-Khuld*, the Paradise (garden) of Eternal Duration; 2. *Jennatu 'Aden*, the Garden of Eden; 3. *Jennatu-'l-Firdaws*, the Garden of Paradise; 4. *Jennatu-'l-Me'và*, the Garden of the Abode; 5. *Jennatu-'n-Na'īm*, the Paradise of the Pleasantness; 6. *Dāru-'s-Selām*, the Home of Security; 7. *Dāru-'l-Maqāma*, the House of Sojourn; 8. *'Illiyūn*, the Sublime Heights. Baydhāvī has *Dāru-'l-Khuld* for *Jennatu-'l-Khuld*; but that is one of the names of Hell, as occurring in Qur'ān xli. 28. There is also a *Dāru-l-Qarār*, Home of Permanence, mentioned in Qur'ān xl. 42; but it applies to Hell and Heaven, as does the *Dāru-'l-Baqā*, Home of Duration, commonly used, but not found in the Qur'ān.

XV. ZEYD'S INSPIRATION.

The Prophet asked one morn of Zeyd, in tender tone,[1]

"How art thou, dear disciple, faithful to the bone?"

"I'm pious;—a believer," Zeyd replied; and he

Inquired again: "What proof of faith resides in thee?"

He said: "Whole days I've burnt with parching fever's thirst;

By night I've watched; with love's sweet pangs my heart's nigh burst.

Thus have I traversed days' and nights' enduring space,

As point of spear through shield makes way in war's embrace.

For, in love's view, the church of faith one body is;

Ten million years, one instant, are alike, when His.

The past eternity and future join in one;
Though reason cannot compass how the marvel's done."
The Prophet then: "Bring forth some souvenir from thence,
Shall satisfy all men of judgment and of sense."
Said Zeyd: "As men behold the sky above their heads,
So I survey the heavens, and all their flowery meads.
Eight paradises,[2] seven deep hells,[3] are in my view,
As patent as the idol to its silly crew.
Apart, and one by one, I can discern all men,
As wheat and barley well are known to miller's ken.
I see who's heavenward bound, who takes the other road;
As men distinguish fish from snake in walks abroad."
'Tis thus that saints, within the bounds of present life,
See who'll be blessed, who cursed, when tried in judgment's strife;
Before each soul contracts the sins will cause its shame;
While yet in mother's womb,—while yet without a name.
The wretch is he conceived for wretchedness' sad thirst.
Each soul is marked for future bliss or woe, at first.[4]
The body, as a mother, bears within a soul.
Death's but the throes that launch the spirit to its goal.

Departed souls are all agog at each fresh birth,
To see what class the new-born enters in its mirth.
The blacks presume 'twill prove to be of their dark gang;
The pale-faced Romans hope they'll profit by the pang.
But when the little stranger shows itself at last,
No room remains for doubt; the question's judged and cast.
The new-born black is borne in triumph by its kind;
The rosy-cheeked fair bantling's claimed by Roman mind.
Until its birth the child's a riddle to all men.
Who knows an unborn infant's rare sage in this glen.
Unless, mayhap, he see with light divine's blest aid;
For this can penetrate through densest shell e'er made.
The life-conveying fluid's colourless and clear;
But living men their various shades of colour bear.
The soul sustains complexions in our mortal frames,
Until our halves material find rest from their games.
But turn we now away to other subjects, high;
For fear events should leave us to regret and sigh.
"When settling-day 'brings forth the colour of each face,'[5]
Mankind are separated sharply, race from race.
Within the womb nor Turk, nor Hindū, yet is seen;[6]

So soon as born, all, high and low, know what to ween.
As in the day of judgment all men all will know,
So now to me each man and woman forms a show.
Say: Shall I all declare; or shall I hold my peace?"
To this the Prophet in reply made motion: "Cease."
"Ha! Prophet of the Lord! I'll tell that secret, all!
To men I will declare the deeds of that dread hall!
Permit me to tear off the veil that hides it now;
My heart shall light the world as sun in midday glow.
I will eclipse that lamp, by giving out more light.
I will set plainly forth the thorn and fig-tree right.
Th' events of judgment day I'll lay before all men.
I'll separate the gold from spurious coin, as then.
They of the left hand shall be maimed to public view,[7]
And all shall then the fruits of misbelief eschew.
I will expose the seven pits of wrath divine,[8]
By aid of light from truth's great luminary's shine.
I'll rend away the rags that veil the wicked's shame.
I'll sound the trump, that all may hear the Prophet's name.
Hell, heaven, the gulf between, I'll set before men's eyes,
That misbelievers may be warned of error's dyes.

The fountain of 'Kawthar' shall throw its highest jet;[9]
Its rush shall greet their ears, its spray their faces wet.
They who will flock around it, burning with fierce thirst,
I'll make apparent unto all, from last to first.
Their shoulders jostle 'gainst my shoulders in the crowd;
Their shrieks are sounding in my ears, as thunder loud.
While heaven's citizens, rejoicing with delight,
Hug one another lovingly, to glad my sight.
They visit one another's thrones, high rapture's seats;
They kiss each other fondly; each all others greets.
My ears grow deaf through listening to those cries of grief,
And sorrow's anguish from the lips where sin sat chief.
These are slight indications; much more could I say;
I pause; the Prophet's wearied; cease from speech I may."
Thus spake the Prophet's servant, in delirious guise.
The Prophet shook his collar,—sign of deep surprise.
Then spake: "Rein in thy steed! He risks to run away!
Reflected Truth declares: 'God blushes not.'[10] Heyday!
The mirror's fallen out from its protecting case!
A mirror and a balance never truth debase!
A mirror and a balance never facts conceal,

Although some one be hurt by what they do reveal!
The mirror and the balance tests are of my rule;
Though for a thousand years thou serve it's strict formule.
Hide not the truth from thought of deep respect for me.
Show forth the whole, in full. Deficiency mayn't be.
What is't that tells thee: 'Play not, joke not with the truth?'[11]
The mirror, balance, God,—who smites falsehood with truth!
Sure, God hath raised me up for that one sole intent,
That through me truth be preached unto its full extent.
Were this not so, what value's in me, valued friend?
Did I become instructor, only good to mend?
But shut thy mirror tight within its felten sack,
If Sion's miracle's repeated in thy track."
Said Zeyd: "Can man e'er grasp beneath his feeble arm
The sun of truth, eternal luminary, warm?
'Twould burst his grasp asunder; all his wiles were vain,
Though madness he should add to reason in his brain!"
Replied the Prophet: "On thy eye thy finger place;
The world is straight deprived of all the sun's bright face!
A finger-tip suffices to blot out the moon;

A symbol, this, of God's great sin-effacing boon.
A point can cover up a whole world with its shade;
The sun can be eclipsed by what's a mere monade.
Shut close thy lips. Consider now the mighty sea.
By God's command the ocean man's meek slave must be.[12]
Ev'n as the fountains Selsabīl and Zenjabīl[13]
Are given for use of angels, Michael, Isrāfīl.[14]
The rivers four of paradise are at our beck;
Not by our merit, but by God's constraining check.
Where'er we will, they flow, obedient to our call;
Like magical effect, magician's docile thrall.
So also are our eyes, those founts of sentient beams,
Subservient to our will, whichever way it streams.
As we direct, they look; see what's like adder's sting;
Or notice facts that to our minds their warnings bring.
If so we will, they scrutinise objectiveness;
As we desire, they lend themselves to study dress.
By our direction, universals are their bound;
If so we wish, they prisoners are in partials' ground.
Each of the senses five acts thus but as a spout,
To bring unto the mind that which it cares about.

Whichever way the heart directs them forth to stroll,
They turn, and glean a harvest for its pleasure sole.
The hands and feet are servants to the heart's request,
As Moses' rod obedient was to his behest.
At heart's desire, the feet begin the nimble dance,
Or seek advantage, or avoid some sore mischance.
The heart commands, the hands to calculations fall;
Should it prefer, they write a book or treatise small.
A hand there is, 'twould seem, within these hands of ours;
A hidden hand, that moves the body's wondrous powers.
If that incites, this wages battle with the foe;
Should that induce, this aids a friend to stand tiptoe.
It pushes; straightway spoon's plunged into soup;
It wills; a ponderous club forthwith attacks some group.
What is it that the heart says to them all by turns?
Most wonderful accord! Most marvellous alterns!
The ancient seal of Solomon the heart has found!
With that alone it guides the senses o'er their ground.
Externally, five senses serve its high command;
Internally, five faculties obey its hand.
Ten senses, thus, seven organs, wait upon its wants;

Besides a host of minor servants, confidants.
As Solomon thou sittest, O heart! Thou reignest supreme!
On fairy and on demon, set thy seal, thy scheme.
In this thy realm be upright; practise thou no fraud;
No demon, then, shall rob thee of thy seal, thy gaud.[15]
The world shall learn thy name, shall practise all thy rites;
Time and eternity remain thy perquisites.
But should a demon carry off thy seal, perchance,
Thy reign is o'er; thy fortune loses all advance.
Thenceforward vain regret shall canker in thy breast,
Until the day thou'rt called to thy account at last.
Unless thy heart renounce all selfish use of wit,
By mirror and by balance canst thou be held quit?"
Luqmān the sage, in presence of his noble lord,[16]
Among the slaves and servants was a mere byword.
The lord one day commanded; straight some slaves were sent
To gather fruit from orchard for his throat's content.
With them did Luqmān go, as parasite to feast,
Brimful of wisdom, black as night, a negro beast.
Their labour o'er, the slaves lay down to rest awhile;
The fruit they tasted, tasted still, consumed the pile.

Returning home, on Luqmān the whole blame they laid;
His lord was angered mightily at what they said.
Luqmān inquired the cause of this estrangement keen.
The lord gave vent in loud abuse to his roused spleen.
Said Luqmān: "Lord, I swear by God's most holy name,
Dishonest servant ne'er can hope for aught but blame.
Make proof of us. 'Tis easy. Lord thou art of all.
Command. We'll drink our fill of water hot as gall.
Then make us run about within the meadow's bound.
On horseback thou, on foot we, 'll all trudge quickly round.
Thou soon shalt witness sights to show 'the milk who spilt.'
Hearts' secrets' Great Revealer will disclose the guilt."
Their lord so ordered. Scalding water soon was sought.
Each had to drink his fill, as hot as could be brought.
Then all were made to run as fast as they could tear,
All up and down the meadow, as their legs could bear.
Now lo! What happens? Sickness on them, each, soon falls;
To vomit they're constrained, with starting of eyeballs.
The stolen fruit contained within their stomach's sack,
The water's stimulus compelled them to give back.

When Luqmān's turn was come to cast up his accounts,
Clear water was the only issue from his founts.
Luqmān's philosophy this trial could evolve;
God's wisdom far abstruser riddles will resolve.
"The day when our hearts' secrets shall be all revealed,"
Man's secret foe in ambush shall not lie concealed.
Hell's victims, then, shall taste of scalding water's pang;
And all veils be torn off from sins they overhang.
Hell-fire's decreed to be the lot of misbelief;
Since fire the ordeal is by which stones come to grief.
How often have we spoken to those hearts of stone,
In softest accents of advice! They would hear none!
To foulest ulcer, sharpest remedy's applied.
The teeth of dogs alone are fit for ass's hide.
"Filth to the filthy" is philosophy right sound.
"Birds of a feather flock together" goes its round.
What mates soever for thyself thou choose at last,
Their habits and their qualities acquire thou fast.
Wouldst glory have? To glory must thou raise pretence.
Wouldst it reject? Think well; and take thy road from thence.
Wouldst find a way out of this dismal dungeon vile?

Submit to God; bow down in worship with a smile.
Again we'll turn. Again we'll hear what Zeyd may say;
What road he'll follow, on his steed, in reason's way.
When reason sets itself t' expose the faults of men,
It pulls aside the veils that hide them from our ken.
God sometimes wills that actions should concealed remain,
Drives reason's drum away, forbids its noisy strain.
Loose not thy tongue alone; it bridle; hidden's best.
Let each be happy in his own opinion's zest.
God wills that they who might despair to win His grace,
Shall persevere, not slacken, in their worship's pace
That they may seek a hopeful one, and him ensue;—
In his society may follow worship's clue.
God wishes that His peace should light upon us all;
That His salvation should embrace good, bad, great, small.
That princes and that captives all should turn their face,
In hope and fear, up heavenward, looking for His grace.
That hope and fear are nourished by a curtain's shade.
'Tis through uncertainty that hope and fear invade.
But tear away that veil; where then are hope and fear?
'Tis veiledness lends interest to landscapes drear.

Upon a river's bank a youth, who chanced to spy
A fisherman at work, guessed: "Solomon, surely![17]
If he it be, why here, in secret and alone?
If not, whence come those features, fit to grace a throne?"
So he remained in doubt, 'twixt two opinions tossed,
Till Solomon recovered all the power he'd lost.
The foul usurping demon fled the royal state;
The king's avenging sword pursued and sealed his fate.
The signet-ring of power once more on royal hand,
The demons and the fairies flocked to his command.
Mankind came crowding to his court, by levee swelled;
Among them came the youth who'd that opinion held.
He saw the signet-ring. This sufficed. Doubt was past.
No room was left for surmise. All was clear at last.
Opinion may be formed of what's behind a veil.
Conjecture lends its aid where knowledge 'gins to fail.
Conjecture's potent when the subject's hid from view.
Let it be visible; no surmise can we brew.
Although the sky of light is not without its rain,
The earth of darkness, too, produces plants and grain.
I love that text: "They who believe what is not seen."[18]
Thence have I closed my eyes, the body's windows keen.

But should I cleave the firmament with my swift glance,
Could I exclaim: "Perceivest thou a flaw, perchance?"[19]
To scrutinise what's hid behind the darkness' screen,
Each man his method chooses; guesses what's between.
A certain space of time confusion reigns supreme.
The robbers hang the magistrates by their own scheme,
Until at length a chief, blessed with a genius rare,
Springs up to serve his servants; all their troubles share.[20]
To render secret service is a thing beloved.
To hide a service rendered adds to what's approved.
What's he, commends his king with lies before his face,
And in his absence needs lament his lack of grace?
The warden of a castle on the marches laid,
Far from his sovereign, distant from much-needed aid,
Defends his post with valour from beleaguering foe,
Disdains to be bought over, scorns the tempter's moe.
His station's on a frontier, no eye sees him act;
To duty true, he honestly fulfils his pact.
Then in his monarch's presence honours due he gains,
Above the brave men fighting in the royal trains.
More merit's in a little secret service given,

Than in much more performed when by an eye it's driven.
Man's faith and piety on earth are prized of God.
But after death professed, less value have than clod.
The absent and the hidden being thus the best,
The silent mouth and sealed lip surpass the rest.
Then boast not, brother; whatsoever thou hast done,
God knows thy merits; will requite them every one.
The sun requires no other witness but his face.
Man has a greater. God's his witness. Vast the grace!
If I proclaim it not, how many are prepared
To witness to each fact! God, angels, men, full wared.
"God will bear witness, angels, and all they who've known,"[21]
That: "Lord there is no other, save th' Eternal One."[22]
When God himself our witness is, who'll angels need,
That they should share, participate, in His sole deed?
Unless it be that, as the fervent, blazing sun,
Pours forth such beams no mortal eye can look upon.
Just like the bat, man cannot bear full light of day;
So, in despair, he seeks the darkness, shuns noon's ray.
Thus, like us, know, the angels are a loving crew,
Who bask in beams of heaven's Sun, beyond our view.

They say: "Our light we have received from a sun;
As substitutes we shine upon the weak, outrun."
As new-born moon, or five days old, or at the full,
Each angel has his rank, degree, place, wonderful.
His glorious wings in pairs, two, three, and even, four;[23]
So that his beams are doubled, trebled, fourfold, more.
Just like the grades that mark the various human minds,
Do differences vast exist in angels' kinds.
Thus every man's companion-angel's like himself,
Or good, or bad, or high, or low, as china, delf.
When weak-eyed mortals cannot look upon the sun,
They have to seek for taper's aid, ere they may run.
The Prophet hath declared: "Stars, my disciples are;
They're lights to them who seek; though devils they may scare."
If every man had strength, and faculty of sight,
To look straight at the sun, trust him alone for light,
What need were for the stars, or lamps, of feeble ray,
To help them on their path, in quest of source of day?
The moon declares to man, as do the clouds, the shade,
"I, too, 'd been human, but for revelation made.[24]
Like you, I had been darksome, as within, without.

But revelation gave me sunlight, shade to rout.
Compared with the sun, I'm darksome as a cloud;
Compared with men's dark bosoms, I may well be proud.
I shed a feeble light, that men may bear my beams,
He cannot look upon the sun's too ardent streams.
I've mixed with honey vinegar; made oxymel;
A remedy to bring to man's diseases fell."

Art rid of thy disease, my friend? Then set aside
The vinegar. Rejoice thy soul with honey's tide.
When freed from lusts, the heart of man in full health shines.
God said: "The Merciful on heaven's high throne reclines."[25]
God rules the heart direct, free from all means to aid,
So soon as it is purged from dross that low it laid.
We'll now go back to Zeyd, and proffer him advice;
We'll warn him not to risk dishonour, paltering's price.
Thou shalt not Zeyd now find; he's surely run away,
He's clean absconded by the door; had naught to say.

Had'st thou been Zeyd, like him thou'dst lost been in a maze;
As stars die out when sunlight sets the skies ablaze.
E'en as no track points out where was galaxy's place;

Thou'lt find no signs of Zeyd, no footstep, sign, or trace.
Our senses falter, all our reasoning is lost,
In splendour of the wisdom of th' All-Ruling Ghost.
Men's senses, and their reasons, must be shut within,
"In waves when all before us to appear begin."[26]
When night returns, the sky again a court appears,
The hidden stars shine forth, and mark the rolling years.
The senseless dead unto, will God their wits restore;
In circles, like attendants, Him they'll stand before.
They'll foot the dance, they'll spread their hands, they'll shout His praise;
They'll sing their song: "Thou, Lord, us from the dead didst raise."
Their mortal skins and bones they'll shake off in the earth;
On angel-wings they'll ride, and whirlwind-dust call forth.
Their course they'll take from nullity to entity,
In judgment day, ungrateful, grateful laity.
Why turn away thy head, pretend not to have seen?
Hast thou not, first, in nullity, a truant been?
In nullity, so firm thou settedst down thy foot,
And ask'dst: "Who shall remove me when I've taken root?"

Dost thou not see the wondrous works of God's high will?
How He it is who "leads thee by thy forelock" still?[27]
He draws thee into states, conditions, turns of weal,
That never entered in thy mind to seek with zeal.
Nonentity obedient is to His command.
Of demon, and of Solomon, He rules the hand.
A demon can contrive "the trays of fishpond size."[28]
He dares not make refusal these to organise.
Contemplate now thyself in agony of fear;
And know, nonentity, too, quakes His wrath to hear.
Thou stretchest forth thy hand to seize preferment's place;
From fear of thee, some soul itself must quick efface.
All else but love of God, the Truest and the Best,
Though sweet to thought, is but a snare to break thy rest.
What's all thy effort worth? Thou hast to die at last;
Put out thy hand and grasp the cup of life right fast.
Men fix their eyes on what is dust and ashes, death;
Refuse belief in what is life and healthful breath.
Exert thyself. Reduce thy doubts from ten to nine.
Employ the night. Thou sleepest. Night's not so supine.
Employ the night to seek the everlasting day,

Increase in knowledge. Wisdom 'tis shall light thy way.
Though night be dark, and darkness be of woe the doom,
Much good is in it. Fount of Life's in land of gloom.[29]
How can a mortal hope to raise his head from sleep,
When seeds of slothfulness are all he cares to reap?
The dead man's sleep's the body-snatcher's open door.
Householders slumber, robbers rifle every floor.
Thou knowest not who are thy foes around thee placed.
The imps of hell are enemies to man high graced.
The fire's the foe of water and of water's brood;
As water's foe to fire, and drowns it in a flood.
To water, and its cousins all, the fire swears death;
To fire shall water never quarter give, or breath.
'Tis water puts the fire out; and the reason's plain;
The fire has mission to destroy the water's strain.
And then, the fire's the heat of passion's baneful lusts.
And lust, the root of frailty, sin, misdeeds, mistrusts.
Material, outer fire, 's by water soon put out;
The fire of lust may carry man to hell, no doubt.
No water can avail to quench the flames of lust;
For lust is hell-born. Torments end not; last they must.
Religion's light, alone, can quench lust's fiercest flame,—

The light that can put out the Syntheist's wicked game.[30]
What can extinguish fire of sin, save light of God?
My master, see that Abr'am's light be ne'er downtrod;
That from the fire of lust, by inner Nimrod fanned,[31]
Thy body may escape; not be, as firewood, banned.
The lust of man's desires cannot be driven forth;
But may resisted be, reduced to what it's worth.
So long as thou shalt fuel pile upon that flame,
Canst thou expect the fire will die away and tame?
So soon as fuel is withheld, a fire goes out;
Through piety is lust brought down, and put to rout.
Shall that sweet face e'er blacken through sin's dismal smoke,
That's brightened by such sheen as virtue must invoke?
A conflagration raged in days of great 'Umer,
Stones were devoured therein, as firewood in the air.[32]
The buildings it consumed, and left whole households waste;
The nests and nestlings were destroyed;—last trump's foretaste.
One half Medīna fell a prey to ruthless flame,
Whereat th' aqueous element might well feel shame.
Whole cisterns were exhausted in the combat wild;

And vinegar was added. Hope was thus beguiled.
The fire grew fiercer under stimulus of strife;
Extension gave it wings, success infused new life.
The people now came flocking to the Caliph's gate,
In marvel, that, through water, fire would not abate.
He told them that the fire burnt by divine command;
That all those flames arose from their too frugal hand:
"What use are water, vinegar? Distribute bread;
Eschew cold avarice, if by me you'll be led."
They answered: "Wide our doors stand open every day,
We've ever lavish been; almsgiving is our play."
'Umer replied: "In form and custom, bread you've given.
But not from love of God. You're hands to dole were driven.
'Twas pride and ostentation led to your display;
Not charity, not pity, sense of duty, say.
Your riches are your seed. Cast not such seed to waste.
Place not a sword in robber's hand with senseless haste.
Distinction make 'twixt friend and foe to truth divine;
Seek out God's saints, and leave them not to starve, to pine.
You've spent your stuff upon your cherished kindred sole,

And fancied stupidly you'd followed God's law whole."

223

---

1. Zeyd, son of Hāritha and father of Usāma, the freedman and adopted son of Muhammed, one of his most devoted disciples.
2. For the eight paradises, see Tale xiv. dist. 74, p. 253.
3. The seven hells are:—1. Jahannam; 2. Latzā; 3. Hutama; 4. Sa'īr; 5. Jahīm; 6. Hāwiya; 7. Saqar. All these names for Hell occur in the Qur'ān.
4. This is predestination indeed. But does not our "vessels of wrath" come to about the same thing, at least in some opinions?
5. Qur'ān iii. 102.
6. "Turk and Hindū" is synonymous with *"fair and dark."*
7. "They of the left hand," Qur'ān lix. 8; xc. 18.
8. "The seven pits of hell" are named respectively: Jahannam, Latzā, Hutama, Sa'īr, Jahīm, Hāwiya, and Saqar, as above mentioned, p. 254, note 3.
9. "Al-Kawthar," Qur'ān cviii. 1, is variously explained, but probably means: *the great multitude*, scil., *of mankind*; not "a fountain."
10. Qur'ān ii. 24.
11. Qur'ān ii. 231; and, indirectly, in many texts.
12. Qur'ān xvi. 4; xl. 23.
13. Qur'ān lxxvi. 17, 18.
14. Michael is mentioned in Qur'ān ii. 92; Gabriel is also there mentioned, and in two other places; but no other angels by name.
15. Solomon was robbed of his seal by a genie, and temporarily deprived of his kingdom.
16. Qur'ān xxxi. 12. *Lokman*, the commonly received orthography, is doubly erroneous; the first vowel of the name is *u*, the Italian *u*, the French *ou*, the *oo* of our words *foot, good, wood*; not of *coot, moot, root*. Our *q* is, historically, the only true representative of the Phoenician letter that equally gave rise to the Hebrew ק, to the old Greek Q, to the Latin Q, and to the Arabic ق; as may be seen by comparing the letters in the last element of the Arabian numeral alphabet, قرشت, with the Hebrew *Koph, Resh, Schin, Tau*; with the Greek Q = 90, P = 100, Σ = 200, T = 300; and with the Latin Q, R, S, T. The proof is still more conclusive by comparing, in order, the whole alphabets, as to positions, names, shapes, values in sound, and numeral values.
17. Solomon, when deprived of his kingdom, became a fisherman.
18. Qur'ān ii. 2. Our: *"Credo, quia impossibile."*
19. Qur'ān lxvii. 3.
20. Muhammed is reported to have said: "The prince of a people is their servant." This may be compared with Matt. xx. 26 and 27.
21. Qur'ān iii. 16.

22. Qur'ān ii. 256.
23. Qur'ān xxxv. 4.
24. Qur'ān xxi. 108.
25. Qur'ān xx. 4.
26. Qur'ān xxxvi. 53.
27. Qur'ān xi. 59.
28. Qur'ān xxxiv. 12.
29. See the Translator's "Turkish Poetry" (p. 32 or 45), 1879; published by Trübner & Co., Ludgate Hill, London, E.C.
30. Qur'ān ix. 32; lxi. 8. The expression "polytheist," generally used by translators to render the meaning of the Arabic "*mushrik*," is not correct; to attribute one "partner" to God is as much "*shirk*" as to attribute many. See note in p. 36, Tale iii.
31. Qur'ān xxi. 68, 69, alludes to this.
32. Qur'ān ii. 22; lxvi. 6.

XVI. ALI'S FORBEARANCE.

From 'Alī may we learn sincerity of meeds.
"God's Lion" we may hold free from all gross misdeeds.
In fight he'd conquered one who'd earned a hero's crown.
His sword he'd swiftly raised, his victim to hew down.
That champion spat in 'Alī's face, to mark disdain;
The face of one, the Prophet's pride, all saints' chieftain.
He spat upon a face to which the moon bowed low,
And offered adoration in the temple's show.
That instant 'Alī dropped his sword, high poised in air,
And left the spitter harmless;—action debonnair.
This raised the foe's astonishment; called forth his awe.
That pardon, that forgiveness, grew not from war's law.

He said to 'Alī: "Thou thy sword hadst raised to slay.
Why hast thou dropt it now,—prolonged my forfeit day?
What hast thou seen, surpassing prowess of my arm,
That thus thou hast repented,—left me free from harm?
What may it be has calmed the fury of thy breast,
Which as the lightning gleamed, and straightway sank to rest?
What didst thou see, that, by reflection on me cast,
A spark has leapt to life in my despairing breast?
What was thy vision, far above the world of fact,
Than life far sweeter, whence my life receives new pact?
For bravery, 'God's Lion' art thou justly named.
For kindness, I now know, thou art too little famed.
For generosity, thou'rt Moses' cloud divine,
From which poured forth the quails and manna, as from mine!"
The clouds rain wheat. Man, then, by labour and by skill,
Reduces this to food, when finely ground in mill.
But Moses' cloud, more generous far, with open hand,
Sent down in plenty food prepared, by God's command.
For them who ate at Providence's table, free,
God's mercy was displayed;—a banner all could see.
For forty years that daily bread—abounding grace—

Failed not. Fond expectation's utmost stretch took place.
But satisfaction followed not. The thankless crew
Demanded "leeks and onions;" as of old they knew.[1]
Ye who are Ahmed's people, graced beyond compare,
Are promised spiritual blessings till last judgment's blare.
Whoever says, at heart: "My trust is in the Lord,"[2]
God's promise: "Him I'll feed," will find a faithful word.[3]
Without a twist accept this promise, as is meet;
You'll find it in your mouth as milk and honey sweet.
To twist a term, and so deny gift's incidence,
Is to invent a cloak to change the word's true sense.
To think th' expression's wrong sad weakness shows of mind;
Wisdom divine's a kernel; human reason, rind.
Twist then thyself; change not the sense of words divine;
Conceive thy nose at fault; chide not the sweet woodbine.
O 'Alī! Thou who mind and eye entirely art!
Relate a little of the knowledge in thy heart.
Thy calmness is a sword that cleaves our minds in twain;
The fountain of thy wisdom makes us whole again.
Speak out! I know these mysteries are Jehovah's own;
To kill without a sword's a power of God well known.

He is Creator, without limbs and without tools;
The Giver of all blessings, copious as sea's pools.
How many kinds of wine are savoured by our souls,
While eye and ear perceive not whence the wave that rolls!
Pray tell us, 'Alī,—falcon, soaring in heaven's heights,—
What didst thou see that instant, to forego thy rights?
Thy eyes have learnt to catch seraphic visions' gleam;
Around thee, all unconscious are, as in a dream.
Thou seest the moon, all brightly shining in the sky;
We see but darkness, clouds above us seem to fly.
Thou seest three moons together, shining bright, outspread;
While three of us are scarcely sure one's overhead.
All three have eyes and ears fixed on thee, in suspense,
In keenest expectation. I'm stone of offence.
"Is this a spell to witch the eyes? Is it the truth?
To me thou art a wolf; I'm Joseph to thee, sooth.
Though worlds there may be, eighteen thousand globes, and more;
Not every eye has power to witness all their store.
Disclose thy secret, 'Alī,—God's own 'Chosen One!'[4]
How many 'judges' errors' work God's will alone!

Pray tell me what, just now, has been revealed to thee;
Or I'll disclose the vision I've been made to see.
If thou the secret keep, I will declare its sense,
Moon-like, on me thy knowledge shines, with light intense.
But if the moon's bright disk break forth from 'neath the cloud,
Poor midnight travellers safely, then, pursue their road.
They then are safe from error, risk no wandering vain;
Protection of the moonlight shields from terror's chain.
The mutely-teaching promptings of the silvery moon,
If couched in words, would homewards guide us doubly soon."
Thou art "the Gate;" the Prophet, "Science' City" is,[5]
Thou art the ray that beams from lustrous sun of his.
Then open, Gate! Unfold thyself to those who seek!
Let rind of science overgrow their minds, all meek.
Stand open, Gate! Thou portal of God's mercy sure!
Thy court's the court of Him "who hath no peer," secure![6]
True, every breath and atom's watching to get in.
But if kept closed, who'd say there is a gate to win?
Unless the Keeper open wide the portal's wing,
No soul would dream an entry were an easy thing.

E'en when the gate is opened, lo! surprise is felt.
Hope and desire are scared; each suitor's heart must melt.
As one who finds a treasure in a ruined maze,
Seeks evermore for ruins;—treasures are his craze.
Unless a man receive a pearl from beggar's hand,
He'll never venture pearls from beggars to demand.
For years, should mere opinion wander up and down,
It never will outpass the rents of its torn gown.
Until a fragrance strike thy nostrils from above,
Thou'lt follow thy own nose, but never meet thy love.
Thus spake that new-converted warrior in surprise;
Expressing wonder, such as words may symbolise.
Then added: "O! Command, of Faithful Church thou Prince.[7]
That as a babe a spirit new I may evince."
The planets seven o'er every unborn babe keep watch,
Each for a stated period, ere its birth's despatch.
When life's infused into the nascent atom's form,
The sun takes charge, as watcher o'er the feeble worm.
The babe its life derives from Sol's all-quickening rays.
That radiant orb's the fount of life's all-wondrous ways.
The other planets help to modify its limbs;

Each, when the sun has life infused, then onward climbs.
What is the channel of connection with the sun,
Discovered in the womb by fœtus ere't can run?
Deep-hidden from our senses, many an occult road
Leads to the sun in heaven, and needs nor whip, nor goad.
One road, by which gold draws its nutriment from thence;
Another, whence the ruby's colour grows intense.
A road, by which the garnet gathers igneous glow;
A path, pursued by lightning to the horseshoe low.
A channel, through which fruits their ripeness draw, select;
A track, for wit to flow, and senseless form inject.
"Declare, thou falcon, with thy glistening plumage, bright,—
Our chief's companion, on his gauntlet sitting, light;—
Make known, thou phœnix-hunting bird of prey,—
Thou conqueror of foes,—sole,—clear of troops' array.
A nation in its millions, one sole man art thou.
Speak! Speak! I cast myself upon thy mercy now!
Instead of anger, what has moved thee to relent,—
To proffer to a foe forgiveness transcendent?"

To him made 'Alī answer: "For the truth I fight.
God's servant am I. Slave I'm not to fleshly might.
'God's lion' I've been named; not 'Ravening Wolf of Lust;'
My actions are the proof my faith is in the Just.
God is the Archer. I'm His bow;—and arrow, too.
He is the Smiter. I'm the weapon;—sword, bamboo.
'Thou castedst not, when stones thou castedst in the fight.'[8]
God is the Warrior mighty. I'm dust in His sight.
Thought of myself I've banished, wholly, from my path.
Save God, all else as naught I hold;—a mower's swath.
I'm but a shadow;—shadow cast by Sun of Truth.
Door-keeper am I;—veil, I'm not, to hide His sooth.
I'm a sword. My trenchancy's union with God.
In battle, life I give. I slay not whom's downtrod.
Blood does not soil the blade I wield in righteous cause;
Nor gusts of passion raise a craving for applause.
A straw I'm not. A mountain am I;—firm, staid, fast.
No whirlwind can remove me with its tearing blast.
'Tis sticks and straws, alone, are driven by the storm.
Their nature is to move;—to every breath conform.
The gust of anger, breath of lust, and blast of greed,—

Each agitates the man not anchored in Truth's creed.
Firm mountain am I. God it is that firmness gives.
Were I a straw, His whirlwind is the force that drives.
A breath from God alone has power to move my soul.
My love for God's the motive o'er me has control.
Their anger rules e'en kings. My anger is my slave.
My wrath I've bridled;—bitted;—leave, it aye must crave.
My anger's stifled by reflection's strong embrace.
God's wrath to me's a message of His pardoning grace.
My roof's a ruin, true; but light pours through the rent.
I'm dust. But from my soil flowers blow, and yield sweet scent.
"Just cause if I perceive, with foes when waging war,
I make no scruple, but my sword from blood debar.
For God's sake do I love. Such is my fame with men.
My hate's in Truth's sole cause. I'm raging lion then.
My generosity springs all from love of God.
For God's sake, too, I'm parsimonious as clod.
I'm avarice, munificence, to one sole end.
I'm God's in all things. To myself I ne'er attend.
That which I do, for God's sake flows; not from schedule.
'Tis not a guess, an inference;—'tis sight's safe rule.

I've no occasion to investigate, to seek.
God's prompting's what I follow, docile, meek.
"Is soaring my vocation? Heaven's my pinions' goal.
Do I revolve? My centre's fixed in highest shoal.
If load I carry, I well know where this is due.
I'm but a moon; a Sun before me gives the cue.
I've no desire for converse with material things.
An ocean flows not from a meadow brook's scant springs.
I frame discourse to suit the feeble minds of men.
This system has no fault; it met our Prophet's ken.
"I'm free from prejudice; accept a free man's oath.
Against one free man, crowds of slaves possess no truth.
By law, in canon of Islām, the word of slaves
No value has, as evidence;—the chain depraves.
Ten thousand slaves may witness bear in court of law;
Their testimony weighs not in the scales one straw.
The slave to passion bondsman is, in sight of God.
He's lower than the captive 'neath taskmaster's rod.
A slave may be enfranchised by his owner's word;
Lust's victim, though freeborn, dies bound with strongest cord.
The slave to passion cannot loose his heavy chain.

God's mercy, special grace, can set him free again.
He's fallen into a pit, unfathomed, bottomless.
His own sin this. Compulsion 'tis not, fate, nor cess.
Into a pit he's cast himself, for which my mind
Cannot imagine sounding-line, its depth to find.
"It's useless to continue further in this strain.
Not hearts alone, but rocks, may weep at folly's train.
If men's hearts break not, 'tis that they are harder still,
Through carelessness, preoccupation, sloth, ill-will.
They'll break and bleed one day, when tears will not avail.
Be contrite, then, before repentance' sighs must fail.
Since slavish testimony's not accepted there,
His word alone is valid who from lust is clear.
The Lord's Commissioned One's a valid witness. See!
Because, from all eternity, from slavery's stain he's free.
I, too, am free. Wrath cannot bind my soul with chains.
God's attributes, alone, have power to rule my brains.
"Come in, thou. Grace of God hath set thy spirit free.
A flint thou wert. Rich pearl henceforward shalt thou be.
Thou'rt plucked from blasphemy's vast thorny desert sands.
A flowering shrub henceforth in faith's rich garden lands.

Thou art become myself; I, thee; beloved friend!
Thou'rt Alī. Can I 'Alī slay? May heaven forfend!
Thy past transgression rank's as highest virtue's deed.
In twinkling of an eye heaven's bounds thou mayest outspeed.
"How blest is the transgression pardoned of the Lord!
The rose, from thorny stem, He calls forth at a word!
Remember 'Umer's guilt,—his murderous design[9]
Against the Prophet! This brought him to faith benign.
Was't not to practise magic Pharaoh called his priests?
The grace of God converted them to saints from beasts.
Had they not been magicians, he not obstinate,
They'd ne'er been made assemble, truth excogitate.
How would they e'er have seen the staff, the miracles?
Your sin proved your conversion, reprehensibles!
"The Lord can far remove our state of deep despair,
Our sin can change to righteousness; foulness to fair.
God can our worst offences purge away, make clean;
Imputing virtue to us, spite of vice's mien.
For this is Satan chased away with igneous bolts;[10]
His proud inflation bursts in twain, from envy's jolts.
He strives to multiply the direful load of sin,

That, under its dead weight, he man in hell may pin.
And when he finds unrighteousness as service told,
His torment is redoubled, heartache twenty-fold.
"Come in! A door I've opened for thy entrance, wide.
Thou spattest on me. I reply with favour's tide.
On him who injured me I benefits bestow;[11]
My head I lay before the feet of friends, below;
Thou mayest conceive what gifts I hold in store for them,
My faithful servants;—treasures, thrones, and diadem.
I'm such a man that whoso strives to shed my blood
Forgiven is, and overwhelmed with favour's flood.
The Prophet quiet notice whispered to my slave,
The day would come when he to take my life would crave.
Me, also, he informed, through revelation's voice,
That I should die, smote by a hand of my own choice.
That servant begged and prayed for instant death's release,
So he'd be spared from sin so heinous,—love's decease.
But I replied: 'Since 'tis decreed that by thy hand
My life be ta'en, why should I seek a countermand?'
Before me prone he fell, this prayer he warmly made:
'Hew me in twain! For love of God, let me persuade!

Pray save me from so vile, so villainous, a fate.
Remorse for ever as its prey will hold my hate.'
"Again I firmly answered him,—decidedly:
'No counsel will avail. Pen's mark must needs apply.
I bear no grudge against thee in my inmost soul;
I hold thee not responsible for deed so foul.
Thou'rt but the instrument, 'tis God that strikes the blow!
How can I chide His instrument,—His arrow's bow?'
"He asked: 'Why, then, this sentence sternly passed on me?'
My answer was: 'God knows the germ of His decree!
Should He find fault with what results from His resolve,
From reprehension's self He can a heaven evolve.
He hath a right to take exception to His deed.
He's Lord of grace. But Lord of wrath, also! Take heed!
He's Prince of all within this sphere of new events.
He's Arbiter of all;—of kingdoms, as of tents.
If He see fit to break the weapon of His will,
The broken tool still hastens His word to fulfil.
"The mystery of His word: 'We abrogate, annul,'[12]
Remember, straight is followed by: 'We better cull.'[13]

Whatever law the Lord hath abrogated yet,
Is but a weed plucked up;—a rose blooms where 'twas set.
The night He promulgates; day's work refrains from act.
Consider! Mind becomes like inorganic fact.
Again, night disappears; the light of day is spread;
And nature shows its marvels; reason wakes from dead.
With darkness comes the sleep that locks our reason fast,
But spirits know not darkness; life's stream still goes past.
Is't not that mind's refreshed in darkest hours of night?
Its silence 'tis gives birth to every voice of light."

By contraries are contraries brought forth to view,
From out of darkness was the light created new.
The Prophet's wars have brought about the peace that reigns;
These tranquil latter days the fruits are of his pains.
How many heads lay low beneath that hero's blows,
That peace might be enjoyed by faith's true yoke-fellows!
'Tis thus the gardener prunes away the surplus twigs,
That fruitful boughs may prosper, yield their loads of figs.
Sagacity roots out all weeds from cultured space.
The orchard, thence, new vigour finds, and blooms apace.

A wise physician will extract a tooth decayed,
To give relief from pain to his beloved maid.
How much increase grows out of decrease here below.
The martyr gains eternal life by death in show.
Man, fed by bread, cuts down the harvest corn when ripe;
"Partakes the blessing joyfully,"[14] with drum and pipe.
When brutes are slaughtered with due sense of wisdom's law,
Man's life is nurtured;—learning, science, vigour draw.
If man be slaughtered, see what woes from thence arise.
Compare the two;—their difference you'll recognise.
The vegetable world lives by God's sun and rain,
God's care takes charge of it. His care is not in vain.
The slaughtered beasts have food and drink as well as those.
They die, because they've throats. Those have no life to lose.
Withhold thy hand in season, man of little sense!
That so thy food suffice. Thy life's thy recompense.
Thou art as fruitless as the barren willow-branch,
Because thy honour's sacrificed mere bread to scranch.
If thy brute nature will not practise abstinence,
Administer the remedy. Bring it to sense.

If thou wouldst cleanse thy garments—free them from all soil,—
Despise not thou the bleacher, nor his useful toil.
If greed of food have fractured abstinence in thee;
Lay hold on Him who fractures heals. From self get free.
No sooner shall the fracture be by Him fast bound,
New union will take place,—the broken part grow sound.
If thou hadst made the fracture, it would thee invite
To make it whole again,—the sundered bones unite.
Thou canst not? Thence we see, the right is His to break
Who can unite the fractured limb—make strong whatever's weak.
Who knows to mend hath privilege a cloth to tear.
Who knows to sell, to buy hath also learnt, 'tis clear.
He may disturb a house, and turn it upside down,
Who can arrange it better than the whole wide town.
If God destroy one creature in His boundless might,
By thousands He creates, and brings again to light.
Had He not set a punishment for each offence,
Or had not said: "*Lex talionis* is life's fence,"[15]
Who'd had audacity, of his own will,
To put to death a man who should another kill?
He knows each creature by His power endued with sight.

And He's aware a slayer does but work His might.
If His command be set on mortal's head to slay,—
Albeit his own child,—he must the word obey.
Go! Stand in fear! Blame not, too much, the bad!
Know, thou art equally a slave with him who's mad!
The eye of Adam fell upon a demon foul,
Him viewed with proud disdain, with haughty scowl.
His self-esteem, his egotistic pride him drove,
With smile sarcastical, the cursed imp to reprove.
God's wrath was roused. He him addressed: "Ho! Adam! Ho!
Hast thou no insight into mysteries of woe?
If I tear fiercely off a hide from heels to head,
A mountain I can also wrench from its firm stead.
A hundred Adams of their fig-leaves I can strip;
A thousand demons into true believers whip."
In terms contrite and meek was Adam's answer couched:
"Forgive, Lord God! I stand reproved! My fault's avouched!
Henceforth, I vow, I never will repeat such fault.
Repentance I profess. Do Thou forego assault."
O Answerer of prayer! In mercy guide us right!
Our knowledge, as our riches, null is in Thy sight!

Lead not astray a heart enlightened by Thy grace![16]
Turn from us every evil threatening to take place![17]
Reprieve our souls from judgment merited, severe!
Repel us not from out the fold of saints, sincere!
More bitter is there naught than severance from Thee.
Without Thy shelter, naught but anguish can we see.
Our minds' accomplishments impede our hearts' advance.
Our flesh the deadly enemy that wrecks our souls' best chance.
Our hands, like robbers, seize on all our feet may earn.
Unless Thou prove our refuge, life's not worth concern.
If we perchance escape with life from danger's snares.
Our fears and anguish make it prey to carking cares.
Should not our souls in union be with Thee, O Lord,
Eternal tears our eyes will blind, and mad discord.
A way shouldst Thou not open, lost must be our souls.
Without Thy presence, life is death;—all smiles are scowls.
Shouldst Thou find fault with service rendered unto Thee,
Thy chiding's merited, no doubt; as all may see.
If Thou be discontented with the sun and moon,

Or if Thou call the cypress "hunchback," "macaroon,"
Or if Thou say the skies and spheres are all too low,
Or find the mines, the seas, a paltry puppet-show,
All this, compared with Thy perfections, is the truth.
Thine is the kingdom; Thine the power to mend all ruth.
Thou art removed from danger, as from nullity.
To non-existences Thou givest being. Why?
He who makes all things grow, can make them wither, too.
For He can all repair, as He can ruin woo.
Each autumn, vegetation dwindles by His will;
Again 'tis He calls forth the flowers in dale, on hill.
His voice is heard: "Come forth, ye withered ones, anew;
Once more put on your beauty,—charm each mortal's view."
Narcissus' eye was blinded; lo! its twinkle's seen.
The reed, that down was mowed, becomes sweet music's queen.
We are but creatures. To create we have no power.
Our weakness we confess. Contentment's our best dower.
We're things of flesh. The flesh to vanity unites.
Unless Thou call us, we become rebellious sprites.
From Satan we escape, because Thou'st paid a price;

And bought our souls, to set us free from vice.
Thou art the Guide of all who live upon the earth.
Without his staff and guide, what is a blind man worth?
Besides Thee, all that's goodly, all that shocks our sense,
Is fatal unto man,—consuming fire intense.
If any seek the fire, to make thereof a shield,
A Magian he becomes, of Zoroaster's yield.
All else besides the Lord is vain, and of no worth.
The mercies of our God, a bounteous rain, poured forth.
Now turn again to 'Alī and his destined foe.
His great forbearance contemplate; this wretch's woe.
He made remark: "My murderer's before my eyes,
All day and night. No anger towards him in me lies.
Death is to me as sweet as life;—as my own self;
My death and resurrection, two sides of one shelf.
A deathless death's a welcome change to loving heart;
A lifeless life has been its present counterpart."
Death to appearance, life is,—in the main;
Externally a loss;—intrinsically, gain.
Within its mother's womb a child's lot is to roam.
It has to blossom in the world, as ocean's foam.
I have a wish, a longing, towards the world of doom;

But God forbids: "Cast not your lives away," in gloom.[18]
All prohibition's but a bar from what is loved;
No prohibition's needed from a thing reproved.
A grain with bitter kernel, still more bitter rind,
Full prohibition carries in itself, we find.
The fruit of death is savoury, in my esteem.
Nay more. "The slain do live" a blessed text must seem.[19]
Then slay me, O my trusty friends, without reproach.
My death is life eternal. Let it, then, approach.
In death I'll find my love. My dearest friends, adieu!
How long shall I be barred from darling interview?
Unless our separation be from one we mourn,
Why should we say: "Forsooth, to Him we shall return?"[20]
'Tis only he returns, who comes back to his home.
Our true return's from severance to union's dome.
That servant once again appealed and begged: "'Alī!
Put me to death, that sin so heinous I may flee!
My life's at thy behest; forthwith pour out my blood!
So shall my soul escape the burden of crime's brood."
Then 'Alī answered: "Should each sun-mote take a knife,
Or sword draw, with design to sacrifice thy life,

One single hair's-breadth could they not, yet, take effect,
Since Providence decrees 'tis thou must work that act.
But sorrow not! Thy intercessor I will be!
Lord of my soul am I;—not slave to fleshly fee.
My body frail no value has now in my sight;
From flesh when liberated shall my soul feel light.
The dagger and the sword may take root in my limbs.
Death's but a banquet; wounds, a flower that graceful climbs."[21]
Now, who can thus despise his body in his heart,
And yet feel greed for empire, or for pontiffs part?
He strove, 'tis evident, upon the judgment seat,
To set a good example to all future great;
To breathe a righteous spirit into monarchs' breasts;
Make sure that goodly fruit come from their deeds and gests.
The Prophet's high endeavour, Mekka to subdue,
Had no foundation in a lust for revenue.
He had refused the treasures of the lofty spheres;
On day of trial shut his heart to hopes and fears.
To catch a glimpse of him the blest angelic train
Had crowded heaven's bounds full as they could contain;
In dainty guise, to honour him themselves arrayed;

He took no note. On God alone his thoughts were stayed.
His heart was filled with sense of his great Maker's grace.
The angels, or the prophets, there could find no place.
He said: "I'm he whose eyes swerved not;" no crow, I! See![22]
"The Limner is my love; from juice of vine I'm free."[23]
The treasures of "the spheres," their "animating souls,"
As rubbish were accounted, driven by breeze that rolls.
What, then, would Mekka weigh,—the Persian, Syrian lands,—
That he should covet them, spoil make them for his bands?
Suspicion such as this springs from a jaundiced mind.
It judges by itself;—all, tinged as self must find.
Green spectacles who sets upon his foolish nose,
To view the sun, will find him green, we must suppose.
Take off the spectacles, the source of colour's tinge,
He straightway sees aright. Now, nature's hues impinge.
A horseman had stirred up the dust in clouds, not faint.
A distant looker-on supposed the dust a saint.
Thus Satan saw a dust; and cried: "This son of earth
Excites in me much envy, hatred, malice, wrath."
If thou, too, so observe God's saints with envy's eyes,

Be sure thy vision's tainted. Satan's hatching lies.
Thou obstinate! Art not one of that hell-hound's sons?
Then, whence this heritage of hate's foul orisons?
"I am no hound, God's Lion am I. God I love.
I'm 'Lion of the Truth.' Mere form I aye reprove."
A lion of the world may hunt for prey and spoil.
A lion of eternity, death's freedom from turmoil.
In death he sees a hundred thousand modes of life.
So, mothlike, death he courts; his candle, murderer's knife.
To court grim death's a collar round the true man's neck.
This was the text proposed, that wrought recusant's wreck.
God's word revealed hath said: "O men of human race!
Death to the faithful is a blessing, and a grace."[24]
A love of gain is innate in the human breast.
To court death's doubtless profit, is to wish the best.
Then, O ye stiff-necked people, do, for honour's sake,
The wish for speedy death upon your tongues' ends take.
No recusant was found who dared to lisp that prayer,
When thus Muhammed put it as the truth's assayer.
He knew that should they venture that ordeal to prove,
In all the world no recusant would thenceforth move.

They all preferred to pay their tribute for their lives,
And begged: "O lamp of truth, destroy us not, our wives!"[25]
How many more examples could be pointed out!
But, if thou seest the truth, give me thy hand. Quit doubt.
Forsake thy dunghill. Enter our abode of bliss.
From darkness thee to guide, a light shines o'er th' abyss.
Shake off all hesitation. Enter heaven's gate.
Avoid the pit that's bottomless! Be not too late!
The Prince of all Believers thus addressed that chief,
In tones serenest: "Know, that in our contest brief,
When thou didst spit upon me, giving scorn its vent,
My choler was aroused;—to wreck my patience went.
Half warmed with zeal for God, half stirred with anger's fire,
Unholy partnership was formed 'twixt truth and ire.
Thou wast designed and fashioned by a hand divine.
To God dost thou belong;—no creature art of mine.
Defacement of God's work should be by God's decree;
To break God's pitcher, man a stone of God should see."
The Magian heard. The light flashed on his heart and soul.
The clouds of misbelief, as fog, away did roll.

He spake: "The seed of wrongfulness is what I've sown.
Thou'rt altogether different from what I've known.
Thou art a balance, with an equitable soul;
Or rather, index art thou, of just balance-bowl.
Thou art become my kith and kin,—my brother true;
Thou art a ray to light the path I shall pursue.
The slave I have become of that fair Source of light,
From whence thou hast derived the beam that charms my sight.
The slave of every billow of that glorious Sea,
That casts such pearls ashore, as I admire in thee.
Teach me to formulate the motto of thy creed;
For, henceforth thou'rt my guide, of whom I stand in need."
Full fifty of his household,—of his stock and race,
With zealous love the noble law of Islām did embrace.
Thus 'twas, the hero, by decisive wisdom's stroke,
Averted death from many, slavery's fetters broke.
The sword of wisdom's sharper than the finest steel;
Its words more efficacious than an army's wheel.

---

1. Qur'ān ii. 58.
2. Qur'ān ix. 130, &c.
3. Qur'ān lxv. 2.

4. 'Aliyyu-'l-Murtadzā—"*in whom* (God) *is well pleased*"—is the chiefest of the titles of 'Alī, Prince of Princes, Captain-General of Saints.
5. Muhammed is reported to have declared: "I am the City of Science, and 'Alī is the Portal thereof;" alluding to the heavenly secrets he had intrusted to the latter, for communication to the worthy. See Anecdotes, chap, iii., No. 79.
6. Qur'ān cxii. 4.
7. "Commander of the Faithful;" but "Commander of *the Believers*" would be more correct.
8. Qur'ān viii. 17.
9. 'Umer swore he would kill Muhammed, and went to execute his design. Arrived at the house of his own sister, who was already a secret Muslim, he heard chanted the twentieth chapter of the Qur'ān, and was immediately converted. He then went to Muhammed, and publicly professed the faith.
10. The shooting stars.
11. Shanfarà says: "The most excellent is he who confers a favour."
12. Qur'ān ii. 100.
13. Idem.
14. Qur'ān iii. 163, 164.
15. Qur'ān ii. 175.
16. Qur'ān iii. 6.
17. Qur'ān xxv. 66.
18. Qur'ān ii. 191.
19. Qur'ān ii. 149.
20. Qur'ān ii. 151.
21. All Muslim poets speak of wounds as "flowers."
22. Qur'ān liii. 17. There is a pun here. The Arabic for "swerved" and the Persian for "a crow," are identical in orthography,—*zāg*. Muhammed has been called by other Persian poets: "The nightingale of the garden of *mà zāg*;" which really means "swerved not," but may be rendered: "we, the crows."
23. The "Limner" is, here, God, of course. He was intoxicated with love, not wine.
24. Qur'ān ii. 88.
25. These were the Christian Arabs of Nejrān. They sent an embassy to Muhammed at Medina. He proposed to them a trial by invocation of God's curse on the liars, their wives, and children. He uttered it; they shrank, and accepted submission to him, on condition of paying tribute.

XVII. CONCLUSION.

Alas! By one poor morsel, tasted through a sin,
The fount of thought's congealed; heart's blood diluted thin.

One grain of wheat has cast eclipse o'er sun of mind,
As "dragon's tail" doth dull the full moon, when inclined.[1]

Behold! How delicate is thought! One mite of clay,
From full-moon glory, it reduced to disarray.

The bread of life, received, digested, gives man power.
Material bread excites distrusts, contentions, sour.

The thorn, while green, cropped by the camel, far from fords,
Not only pleasure gives, but nutriment affords.

That selfsame thorn, grown dry and void of juicy sap,
If ventured on by starving beast in desert gap,
His palate and his lips will puncture, blood make flow;
As if conserve of roses should with daggers glow.
The word of life's the green, the tender, juicy thorn.
Material become, it's dry, as hard as horn.
And thou, poor flesh, expectant of the living word,
Bitest at the word material, dreaming not of sword;—
Snappest at the hard, unyielding *dictum,* with fond zest;
And findest it horny, flinty, irksome to digest.
10
It has become a stone. It wounds; it draws forth blood.
Then shun it, human camel. Seek it not for food.
Words are most foully mixed with troubling thoughts of earth.
The water's muddy. Close the spring whence it comes forth.
Until the Lord, again, shall make it clear and sweet;—
Shall purify the inky stream, as He deems meet,—
Shall patience add to wish,—not haste and oversight,—
Wait thou contentedly. God best knows what is right.
14

THE END.

---

1. The "*canda draconis*" was the "descending node," one of the ecliptical points. The "forbidden fruit," in Islām, is held to have been *wheat*.

Credit Images: Canva, by Hanafi-maturidi - Own work, CC BY 3.0,
https://commons.wikimedia.org/w/index.php?curid=14844683

www.ingramcontent.com/pod-product-compliance
Lightning Source LLC
LaVergne TN
LVHW092012090526
838202LV00002B/111
* 9 7 8 2 3 5 7 2 8 7 0 9 9 *